Richness in Writing

EMPOWERING ESL STUDENTS

edited by

DONNA M. JOHNSON
University of Arizona

DUANE H. ROEN
University of Arizona

Longman
New York & London

Richness in Writing: Empowering ESL Students

Longman, 95 Church Street, White Plains, N.Y. 10601

Associated companies:
Longman Group Ltd., London
Longman Cheshire Pty., Melbourne
Longman Paul Pty., Auckland
Copp Clark Pitman, Toronto
Pitman Publishing Inc., New York

To Our Grandparents

Executive editor: Naomi Silverman
Production editor: Ann P. Kearns
Cover design: Joseph DePinho
Text art: Charlene Felker
Production supervisor: Kathleen Ryan

Library of Congress Cataloging-in-Publication Data

Richness in writing.

  Bibliography: p.
  Includes index.
  1. English language—study and teaching—Foreign
speakers. I. Johnson, Donna M.   II. Roen, Duane H.
PE1128.A2R493   1989   428°.007   88-8423

ISBN 0-8013-0176-9

2 3 4 5 6 7 8 9 10-MA-9594939291

Contents

Contributors

Diane Clymer (M.A., University of Arizona) is a member of the Composition Board, which coordinates the University of Arizona's writing across the curriculum program. She has trained English as a second language (ESL) teachers in the United States and Mexico, has collaboratively developed ESL composition curricula and programs, and has taught composition for eight years.

Jim Cummins (Ph.D., University of Alberta) is Associate Professor in the Modern Language Centre of the Ontario Institute for Studies in Education, Toronto, Canada. His major research interests include bilingualism and bilingual education, language pedagogy, and computer networking. He is the recipient (with J. P. Das) of the 1979 International Reading Association's award for the best paper in the detection and prevention of reading disability.

Carole Edelsky (Ph.D., University of New Mexico) is an Associate Professor of Elementary Education at Arizona State University, where she teaches classes in language arts methods, language in education, language acquisition, and qualitative research. Her research interests include gender and language, literacy, and conversational analysis. She is author of *Writing in a Bilingual Program: Había una Vez,* published by Ablex.

David E. Freeman (Ph.D., University of Arizona) is Director of Secondary Education and Codirector of the Language Development Program at Fresno Pacific College. He teaches ESL education methods, cross-cultural awareness, language acquisition, miscue analysis, and reading. His research interests include whole language approaches to second language (L2) teaching. He has lived and taught abroad and has coauthored and authored articles and book chapters dealing with literacy.

Yvonne S. Freeman (Ph.D., University of Arizona) is Director of Bilingual Education and Codirector of the Language Development Program at Fresno Pacific College. She teaches bilingual/ESL education curriculum and methods, language acquisition, and reading. Her research interests include a whole language approach to bilingual and ESL literacy. She has lived and taught abroad and has coauthored and authored articles and book chapters dealing with literacy.

William Grabe (Ph.D., University of Southern California) is Assistant Professor in the Department of English at Northern Arizona University. He has taught ESL and writing in China, Morocco, and the United States. His research interests include L2 reading and writing. He coedited (with Fraida Dubin and David E. Eskey) *Teaching Second Language Reading for Academic Purposes* (Addison-Wesley) and is writing (with Robert Kaplan) a book titled *Theory and Practice in Writing*.

Bruce W. Gungle (M.F.A., University of Arizona) has taught freshman composition at the University of New Hampshire, Durham, reading and study skills to nonnative speakers of English in Puerto Rico, and writing at the University of Arizona. He is a Ph.D. candidate in English Education with an ESL minor and serves as a Graduate Assistant to the director of composition at the University of Arizona. He also edits the University of Arizona's text *A Student's Guide to Freshman Composition* (Bellwether).

Sarah Hudelson (Ph.D., University of Texas, Austin) has been involved in bilingual/second language teacher education at Arizona State University, Florida International University, and the University of Miami. Her research and publications have focused on bilingual children's language and literacy development. She is editor of *Learning to Read in Different Languages*, published by the Center for Applied Linguistics, and author of *Hopscotch*, an elementary content-based ESL series published by Prentice-Hall/Regents.

Donna M. Johnson (Ph.D., Stanford University) is Assistant Professor in the Department of English, University of Arizona, where she teaches graduate courses in theory, research, and practice in L2 acquisition and teaching. She was formerly Senior Research Associate at RMC Research Corporation. Her research and publications have focused on social and contextual factors in L2 acquisition, program evaluation, and teacher preparation. She has taught in Brazil, Guatemala, and the United States.

Robert B. Kaplan (Ph.D., University of Southern California) is Professor of Applied Linguistics in the Linguistics Department and Director of the American Language Institute at the University of Southern California. He has taught and consulted in many countries. He is editor of the *Annual Review of Applied Linguistics* (Cambridge University) and co-editor (with Ulla Connor) of *Writing Across Languages: Analysis of L2 Text* (Addison-Wesley). He is currently coediting (with Henry Widdowson) the Applied Linguistics volume of the *Oxford Linguistics Encyclopedia*.

Mary M. Kitagawa (M.A., University of Arizona) teaches sixth grade at Richey Elementary School in the Tucson Unified School District, Tucson, Arizona. She is coauthor (with Chisato Kitagawa) of *Making

Connections with Writing (Heinemann). The book is based on eight months of research in Japan on a writing education movement. She participated in the English Coalition, sponsored by the National Council of Teachers of English and the Modern Language Association, and serves as cochair of the Tucson chapter of Teachers Applying Whole Language.

Robert E. Land, Jr., (Ph.D., University of Pittsburgh) is a lecturer at the University of California at Irvine, where he teaches and supervises courses in rhetoric and composition. His main research interests are in contrastive rhetoric, responding to student writing, and effective teaching. He has published articles in *Written Communication* and *English Journal*.

JoAnn Mackinson-Smyth (M.A., Gallaudet University) has taught hearing-impaired students for seven years at Kendall Demonstration Elementary School on the campus of Gallaudet University. She initiated a pilot project to encourage young students' involvement in interactive writing using computer networking, which she has directed for two years. She was awarded a University Presidential Award to develop and expand this project. She is also actively involved with teacher training in the areas of reading and writing.

Kate Mangelsdorf (M.A., University of Arizona) is a Ph.D. candidate in English Education with a minor in ESL and a graduate teaching associate at the University of Arizona. She has taught L1 and L2 composition and has trained and supervised teachers in the English Department's ESL Composition Program. Her research interests include audience awareness and response techniques in ESL writing. She has presented papers at the Conference on College Composition and Communication as well as numerous regional Teachers of English to Speakers of Other Languages (TESOL) conferences and coedited *The Student's Guide to ESL Composition* (University of Arizona).

Luis C. Moll (Ph.D., University of California, Los Angeles) is Associate Professor in the Division of Language, Reading, and Culture in the College of Education, University of Arizona. His research interests include child development and education, bilingualism, literacy, and telecommunications. His forthcoming book, *Vygotsky and Education,* will be published by Cambridge University Press.

Sandra Lee McKay (Ph.D., University of Minnesota) teaches graduate ESL methods and materials courses and undergraduate composition at San Francisco State University. She has trained teachers in Latin America and in Hong Kong, where she spent 1985–86 as a Fulbright scholar. She has published several composition textbooks and reference books, as well as articles on the use of literature in the ESL classroom.

Robert Mittan (M.A., University of Arizona) is a Ph.D. candidate in English Education with a minor in ESL at the University of Arizona. He has taught composition to both native and nonnative English speakers and worked as a writing consultant for the College of Architecture. In addition to peer interaction in the composition classroom, his research interests include writing across the curriculum and the use of computers in composition.

Joy Kreeft Peyton (Ph.D., Georgetown University) is a Research Associate at the Center for Applied Linguistics in Washington, D.C. Her interest in interactive writing and literacy development was sparked in 1980, when she began studying the dialogue journal writing of native English speakers and students learning ESL. She has written numerous articles about dialogue journal writing and coauthored a book (with Jana Staton, Roger W. Shuy, and Leslee Reed), *Dialogue Journal Communication: Classroom, Linguistic, Social, and Cognitive Views* (Ablex). She is involved in a project funded by Annenberg/CPB to study classroom networks with hearing and hearing-impaired populations across the United States.

Joy M. Reid (M.A., University of Missouri, Columbia) is the Academic Administrator of the Intensive English Program at Colorado State University. She has published articles on ESL learning styles and on the use of computer text-analysis programs with ESL students, as well as three ESL composition textbooks. She chaired the international TESOL conference in Chicago in 1988.

Duane H. Roen (Ph.D., University of Minnesota) is an Associate Professor of English and Associate Director for Freshman Composition at the University of Arizona. He teaches undergraduate composition courses as well as graduate courses in discourse analysis, linguistics, and composition theory, research, and methodology. He has published more than thirty chapters and articles on text structure, composing processes, and writing across the curriculum.

Dennis Sayers (M.A., School for International Training, University of North Carolina) is Coordinator of the Connecticut Satellite of the New England Multifunctional Resource Center, University of Hartford, and Director of the Bilingual Teachers Writing Project. He is pursuing a doctorate at Harvard. His work focuses on innovative writing pedagogy that promotes bilingualism. He is coauthor (with Jim Cummins) of *Micro-Trends: Computer Writing Networks and Empowerment* (forthcoming).

Ann Schlumberger (M.A., University of Arizona) has taught high school, community college, and university composition classes, as well as ESL classes abroad and in the United States. From 1984 to 1987, she served on the University of Arizona Composition Board as Coordinator of Curriculum and Instruction for the ESL Composition Program. She is completing work on a doctorate in reading.

Victoria Taylor (M.A., University of Arizona) is a Ph.D. candidate in English Education with a minor in ESL. She has taught ESL composition at the University of Arizona for three years and has taught both L1 and L2 learners at the secondary, community college, and university levels and in Adult Basic Education. She has presented her work in ESL composition at local, regional, and national conferences and provided in-service teacher training. She coedited *The Student's Guide to ESL Composition* (University of Arizona).

Catherine Whitley (M.A., University of California at Irvine) teaches composition courses at UCI. For the past three years she has conducted research that centers on ESL and contrastive rhetoric. She has presented papers at the Conference on College Composition and Communication. Her other scholarly interests include modernism, post-modernism, feminism, and critical theory.

Foreword

It was little more than a decade ago that a "writing crisis" was dramatized for the American public in a *Newsweek* cover article entitled "Why Johnny Can't Write." Evidence that large numbers of students were leaving school without having achieved even minimal writing ability generated a great deal of discussion and numerous calls for reform. How effectively our public schools and institutions of higher learning have responded to this challenge is a matter of debate. What is undeniable is that the last ten years have witnessed a remarkable surge of inquiry into the development of writing ability, the nature of writing processes, and the ways in which insights can be translated into effective instructional practices.

Now, even as a widely hailed paradigm shift in the teaching of writing is beginning to be more widely disseminated, a new challenge has emerged: to fulfill the needs of the increasing number of students who must become effective writers in a second language. The changing demographics of school enrollment, from elementary school to graduate school, has further required that we rethink traditional methods of writing instruction and raised questions about the values implicit in these methods.

The title of this informative and thought-provoking volume is well chosen, for it reflects the means and ends of the kind of writing programs recommended by recent research, critical thought, and experience. A common theme unifying the chapters—and perhaps the key question for writing instructors and writing programs—concerns the degree of control that students are to have in learning how to write. Another way of putting this is that we must decide whether writing is to be viewed as fundamentally a set of skills and practices largely, if not altogether, external to students—that is, as competencies and conventions to be imparted *by* a teacher *to* students—or whether the point of departure for writing instruction is the students themselves.

Many of the contributors to this volume argue explicitly or implicitly for the latter view. They thus see the notion of empowerment as involving two phases. First, composing processes used by effective writers are powerful means by which students (if they are allowed to learn and adopt those processes) can develop intellectually as they use language to discover and then express meaning. Writing is a mode of learning, facility in which gives students the power to create meaning and to affect those with whom they share their writing. Writing, then, is far more than merely the act of transferring thought to paper; the act of writing helps to shape and refine our thinking.

In the second phase, students who have had authentic experiences with the communicative potential of their writing can then be invited to develop proficiency in the conventions of writing for a range of particular purposes and in different discourse communities. This second focus is of course crucial for the broader form of sociopolitical empowerment that educational policy and practices must inevitably nurture or discourage.

If the goal of writing instruction is empowerment—both personal and social—then appropriate environments in which to learn the writing craft and in which to write must be created. To do this, argue many of the contributors, we must acknowledge who our students are; we must understand and value their experiences and interests; we must offer tasks and challenges that create a genuine sense of urgency to communicate; and we must foster forms of interaction and collaboration within the writing class that stimulate thinking, writing, and responding to writing. In short, we must change writing from a school subject into an activity with rich potential for the creation and expression of meaning.

As becomes clear in reading this volume, however, the distinction between means and ends is artificial. For writing instruction to be truly effective, teachers must be willing—and they must be allowed—to empower students-as-writers. The classroom writing environments in which this can take place will involve a radically different relationship between teacher and students, and among students themselves, than is to be found in the traditional classroom. Students who are offered the opportunity to pose and solve problems in the writing classroom are thus likely to discover not only the uses of writing and the nature of the writing craft, but a great deal about themselves as individuals and as participants in social units, both small and large.

Collectively, the contributors to this volume explore the nature of writing instruction for language-minority students. However, to suggest that they speak with a single voice would misrepresent the diversity of concerns, perspectives, and approaches contained in this collection. Nonetheless, the volume makes a forceful and coherent statement about the need for educators to respond throughtfully and creatively to the needs of diverse students learning to write in a second language in a variety of contexts. The discussions of the issues are reasoned and reasonable, and it is to be hoped that the insights offered will lead to productive initiatives on behalf of language-minority students.

STEPHEN J. GAIES

UNIVERSITY OF NORTHERN IOWA

Acknowledgments

This volume is the result of coequal collaboration across the overlapping fields of second language learning and teaching and composition studies. The roots of our emphases on richness in writing and empowerment, and the choices we made about the content for the book, were influenced by a great many people and experiences.

The excitement and satisfaction of participating in highly interactive and collaborative writing at RMC Research Corporation and the Center for Educational Evaluation and Measurement at the University of Arizona taught me (DMJ) how much could be accomplished by a small community of writers with common goals. A grant from the Carnegie Corporation of New York to study the roles of computers in second language teaching, and conversations with many second language scholars about these topics, strengthened my conviction that technology can and should be put to good use to enrich second language learning and to connect people. Both of those experiences contributed to my strong social view of the writing process.

For me (DHR), many experiences have helped to shape this collection. My former students at New Richmond High School in Wisconsin, at the University of Minnesota, at the University of Nebraska-Lincoln, and my students at the University of Arizona all have guided me to teach with energy and compassion. My mentors and close friends Nicholas Karolides, Gene L. Piché, and Les Whipp have taught me that teaching and research are equally important endeavors.

Both of us owe much to our students—especially our graduate students who, with their intense interests in both the practical and theoretical aspects of second language teaching and the teaching of writing, inspired us to assemble this collection. We are grateful to them for conversations in hallways, for sharing resources, and for their enthusiastic support of the project.

Naomi Silverman, who saw potential in this project when we first mentioned it to her early in 1987, offered us guidance and support throughout the project. We value her in many ways.

We are grateful to Charles E. Davis, Director of Composition at the

University of Arizona, who gave his time, encouragement, and financial support to the project. We also appreciate the computer hardware support provided by Gerald Monsman, head of the Department of English.

Bob Mittan's assistance with copy editing and word processing was invaluable, as was the assistance of Penelope Gates and Rachel Beck with word processing.

To our families, to David, Maureen, and Nicholas, we owe special thanks for patience, support, and encouragement. Above all, we wish to thank the chapter authors for their interest in collaborating with us in this project. It was a pleasure working with these conscientious and professional writers.

DONNA M. JOHNSON
DUANE H. ROEN

Introduction

Donna M. Johnson and Duane H. Roen

SOCIOPOLITICAL CONTEXTS

In the last decade, theoreticians, researchers, and practitioners have joined to examine English as a second language (ESL) writing and writing instruction at all levels. Their investigations have suggested that many trends, movements, and sets of societal conditions impinge upon our views of ESL students and their writing. Demographic changes in schools, colleges, and universities have caused scholars, teachers, and administrators to revise their views of the nature of student populations. In public schools, for example, the number of students coming to school from varied cultural backgrounds and using languages other than English has increased dramatically. In some large urban school districts, in fact, so-called minority students comprise over half of the student body. The second language (L2) learner is no longer a rarity. Similarly, in colleges and universities, foreign students and other second language learners constitute a significant proportion of the student population. Educators and professional organizations are making increased efforts to meet the needs of these students.

Because of the surge of recent studies in first language composition and literacy in general, writing instruction has been rejuvenated in the schools and improved in colleges and universities. Meanwhile, assessments of students' writing performance have gained a firm foothold. The assessment of writing is now a legitimate part of such major testing projects as the California Assessment Project, the National Assessment of Educational Progress, and the Test of English as a Foreign Language (TOEFL). Writing is also assessed for L1 and L2 freshman composition placement, for university upper-division writing proficiency assessments, and as a part of entrance and exit examinations in colleges and univer-

1

sities. Graduate academic programs such as the Harvard Business School, for example, now require writing samples for admission. It has become increasingly important for all students to gain adequate control of written English for advancement.

Assessments of writing in the schools, however, have indicated that some groups of minority students do not fare well in comparison with other groups, and drop-out rates for some minority groups remain too high. For example, many migrant students, who are learning English as a second language and who move frequently, find it difficult to keep up in school and perform poorly on required tests (Johnson, 1987). Much effort in the mid-1980s has gone into assessing the reasons for school failure of students who are viewed as "at risk" of not achieving their full potential. Work in this area has focused, for example, on how students' language uses, which often differ from those expected in educational settings, can cause problems and misunderstandings (Cook-Gumperz, 1986; Heath, 1986). In universities, work along these lines has focused on the various reasons that professors denigrate foreign students' compositions. Much has been written about the so-called language crisis (see Ruiz, 1987 for a critique), the lack of a common "cultural literacy" promoted through schooling (Hirsch, 1987), and the low literacy rates among adults. Hirsch (1987), for instance, while stating that he supports foreign language learning, also asserts that in the United States, "encouragement of multi-lingualism is contrary to our traditions, . . . and could . . . create serious barriers to universal literacy . . ." (p. 93). He and others overlook the fact that many students are already multilingual, that abilities in various languages are interconnected, and that there are many benefits of expanded language abilities for human creativity and productivity. The bilingual and multilingual competencies of students are best viewed as personal, social, and national resources (Jernudd & Jo, 1986; Ruiz, 1984; Troike, 1983).

Teachers of English, teachers of composition, and teachers of history, math, and science often do not know how to promote second language development, nor do they see it as part of their role to do so (Penfield, 1987). Conversely, L2 teachers have not viewed many of the issues in teaching composition as within their realm of expertise or responsibility. Yet, as demographic conditions blur simplistic distinctions between mainstream and nonmainstream students and between monolingual and multilingual students, more educators are coming to view their roles as contributing to the total and rich educational experiences of all their students. Therefore, in teacher preparation in universities there has been an increasing recognition of the common threads that link the preparation of teachers of bilingual education, of foreign languages, of English as a second language, of English, and of language arts at all levels (Saville-Troike, 1984; Tucker, 1985).

In school contexts, other work has focused on the relationship between ESL professionals and other educators and on the relationships among ESL teaching, the teaching of other courses, and the ways writing might bridge those disciplines. Current theory, research, and practice are moving toward more global and more positive views of second language learners (Langer, 1987; Penfield, 1987).

The movements toward content-based L2 learning and English for special purposes in ESL are consistent with the writing-across-the-curriculum movement in the teaching of English and language arts. Both reflect more functional views of language use and the need to allow students to learn as they engage in writing for real and important purposes related to their success in other academic and nonacademic endeavors.

TOWARD INTERDISCIPLINARY APPROACHES

A look at the major influences on current approaches to studying and teaching writing in L2 reveals an increasingly broad, multidisciplinary theoretical base. Linguistics has been for many years the major contributing discipline to L2 scholarship and teaching, with psychology running a close second (Brown, 1987; McLaughlin, 1987; O'Malley, Chamot, & Walker, in press). However, scholars have recognized the importance of investigating second language acquisition, use, and teaching from the perspectives of other related disciplines such as sociolinguistics (Wolfson & Judd, 1983), social psychology (Gardner, 1986; Genesee, 1987; Giles & Byrne, 1982), anthropology (Heath, 1986), sociology and educational theory (Stern, 1983). First language (L1) composition researchers have drawn extensively on theories of cognitive development such as those of Piaget (1926/1955), Moffett (1968, 1981), and Vygotsky (1934/1962), as well as on literature in cognitive problem-solving in writing (Flower, 1979; Flower & Hayes, 1980, 1981; Hayes & Flower, 1980). Both L1 and L2 writing work draws on theories of child language acquisition (Edelsky, 1986; Freedman, 1985), such as work by Wells (1981, 1986) and others. Studies of text linguistics (Conner & Kaplan, 1987; Halliday & Hasan, 1976) and discourse analysis (Bach & Harnish, 1980; de Beaugrande, 1980; Duran, 1981; Freedle, 1977) have contributed many insights about the nature of the texts students read and write. This broader, multidisciplinary base is important in examining issues in L2 writing, for no single theory from a single discipline can account for the complex and interacting social, cultural, cognitive, and linguistic processes involved. A broader theoretical base is also important for teachers, as L2 teaching has become more integrated with content teaching and the development of intellectual abilities. In fact, most L2 curriculum theorists (Breen, 1987; Raimes, 1983;

Widdowson, 1983; Yalden, 1987) now emphasize the need to go beyond a strictly linguistic base in making decisions about L2 course content. Therefore, we feel that it is not productive for L2 writing theory or practice to value the contributions of those working in certain disciplines and research traditions while dismissing the contributions of those working in very different areas. Research on process, on text, on context, and re-search on the complex interactions among social, cultural, cognitive, lin-guisitic, and contextual factors impinging on L2 writing are all important for increasing our understanding of L2 writing development and teaching.

ISSUES SPECIFIC TO L2 WRITING

One theme running through research in L2 acquisition in both oral and written modes has been: In what ways is the process of learning a second (or third, or fourth) language similar to or different from learning an L1 (Brown, 1987; Ellis, 1984, 1985)? Work in L2 writing reveals that here, too, some researchers and teachers focus on similarities between L1 and L2 writing while others focus on differences. Both are important. Authors in this book focus both on the similarities between writing development in the various languages a student uses and on issues that define L2 composi-tion as a distinct area of study and teaching. The authors view the L2/L3/L4 writer as a traveler through discourse communities. They present some of the issues L2 writing scholars have been addressing, some definitional problems in research, and some cautions regarding the direct application of L1 composition research to the teaching of L2 writing.

The L2 Writer: Traveling through Discourse Communities

Writing is not only a cognitive and linguistic activity, but also a social and cultural activity. Learning to write is part of a process of enculturation into the social life of one's community, school, and workplace (Freedman, Dyson, Flower, & Chafe, 1987, pp. 3–4). As students move from homes and preschools to elementary and secondary schools, and on to universities in their own or different cultures, they must learn to function adequately in a continuing series of discourse communities (Fish, 1980; Lees, 1987; Pur-ves, 1986). "As students progress through school, classrooms exist not only as literacy communities in their own right, but also as avenues to the intellectual and social conventions of disciplinary communities" (Freed-man et al., 1987, p. 5). The students that the authors in this volume describe, from young elementary children to university students, are on a journey, often back and forth, through an array of discourse communities in which they must function. To each new encounter they bring with them a rich repertoire of ways of using language.

The Linguistic Repertoire of the Multilingual

Many of the students learning to write in English are already users of more than one other language. They are often multilingual students who come to English writing situations with a rich repertoire of ways of using written and oral language based on their experiences in various cultural and educational settings. To help them become better writers in English, it is useful to know as much as possible about their backgrounds and interests so that we can build on these to expand their options for making meaning and having an impact through writing.

One way to do this is to become aware of the languages and language varieties that coexist in students' linguistic repertoires and the ways those languages are used in different domains. Kaplan (1986), in the introduction to a volume on multilingualism, writes of a Malaysian citizen studying in a U.S. university who spoke Bahasa Malaysia, Bazaar Malay, English, French, Straits Chinese, and Tamil. All of these languages coexisted in his repertoire, and he used them in somewhat different domains. Clearly, concepts of L1 versus L2 are sorely inadequate for looking at this student's repertoire. Kaplan points out that "it is virtually impossible to ascribe mother-tongue status to any one of the several languages in his repertoire except in a purely chronological sense; that is, he learned some of the languages in his repertoire before he learned others" (1986, p. viii). In fact, Ferguson has suggested that "the whole mystique of native speaker and mother tongue should probably be quietly dropped from the linguists' set of professional myths about language" (1982, cited in Kaplan, 1986, p. viii). Many of the students referred to in this volume use a number of languages and are learning not a second but a third, fourth, or n-th language. Throughout this volume, then, the term *L2* is used as a cover term to include, if applicable, L3, L4, and so on. Similarly the term *English as a second language* is used in a broad sense to refer to English as an additional language.

Another way to appreciate students' background knowledge is to become aware of how ways of using language grow out of students' cultural experiences, both as members of groups and as individuals. Heath (1986) points out that there is a universe of possible ways of using language but that each cultural group transmits and reinforces only a few. The information that researchers are gathering about the ways of using written language across different cultural groups helps provide a knowledge base for assisting educators to expand the abilities of all groups to both create and learn new information and to adapt to new circumstances (Heath, 1986).

We need increased understanding of how we can build on what students know and can do with language in order to help them increase their control over what they need to do with written English.

While researchers have found differences in the ways cultural groups approach second language use and learning (Heath, 1986; Wong Fillmore, 1986), individual differences also exist among students (Hudelson, this volume; Kitagawa, this volume). Information about a cultural group cannot necessarily be applied to individual members of that cultural group. Moreover, each student's experience with English writing differs. A student who is adept at writing one kind of text may not be able to write another kind, not necessarily because one kind is inherently more difficult or demanding than the other, but because the student lacks experience reading and writing that kind of text (Halliday & Hasan, 1985, p. 68; Rose, 1983). Thus, students' cultural experiences, background knowledge, linguistic repertoires, and personalities all shape their engagement in L2 writing. Their status as an experienced or inexperienced writer for a defined writing task in a specified situation comes from both personal and social experience. Recognizing this, we need to set goals that expand the range of ways of using written language and that are consistent with students' needs and purposes. We must at the same time not devalue students' other abilities; further, we must always be mindful of all they may want to accomplish through writing in the future in any of their several languages.

Labels for L2 Writers

Numerous terms used to describe students acquiring a second language appear to imply certain assumptions about L2 users and L2 teaching. We wish to clarify these terms. The first issue is the labeling of ESL writers in university English courses as *basic* and *inexperienced,* in community colleges as *developmental,* and in elementary and high schools as *limited.* One problem with these terms is that they imply a unidimensional view of students' abilities to use written language that represents neither the reality of students' repertoires nor their capacity to use languages. We believe such terms ignore students' abilities to accomplish tasks not only through the many functions of writing in one language but also through the additional languages and language varieties they can use. A person's ability to produce an effective text clearly depends on the functional purpose of the writing, the language and language variety in use, experience with the discourse type at hand, and the most important features of the situational context. Every writer is more skilled in certain types of writing and less skilled in others. To categorically label any ESL student as an unskilled writer because he or she is not fluent in English is inappropriate, disempowering, and can have negative consequences for curriculum design.

These terms are in wide use because there is much research comparing relatively expert and novice writers. Two groups are compared on several tasks to determine what skills, processes, or strategies the more group uses. The less expert group is seen as lacking these skills, processes, or strategies and needing to learn them. The assumption is sometimes made that students are cognitively incapable of using them (Witte, 1985, p. 253). Consumers of research often overgeneralize results to other aspects of writing ability in English, to writing ability in general and, more important, to writing ability in any language. Clearly, we have gained many insights from this type of research. A serious problem arises, however, from lumping students into categories and from making subsequent, unsupported assumptions about what students cannot do. If teachers directly and rigidly apply such research results to practice, an unintended consequence can be to discount the full range of abilities of the less expert group on tasks and in situations other than those few that were examined and in languages and varieties other than those that were examined. The more teachers inappropriately overgeneralize such results, the more they discount abilities of certain students. We end up hearing that ESL students are basic, unskilled writers; that ESL students can't attend to audience; that ESL students are egocentric; that ESL students can only revise at the surface level.

These kinds of studies are parallel in design and exhibit some of the same problems of interpretation and implication as the early psychological research on bilingualism (for a recent summary and analysis, see Hakuta, 1986). More recent work in both writing and L2 acquisition addresses the very complex nature of L2 use in varying social contexts. Teachers, too, need to take a more global look at what L2 learners can do, particularly in the context of more supportive and linguistically rich settings. We hope that this volume will contribute to a valuation of diverse approaches to examining the communicative competencies of ESL students and to teaching that enriches L2 writing experiences.

RATIONALE FOR THIS BOOK

While English composition has become an established field with several dozen journals and hundreds of scholarly books, the field of L2 writing has only recently begun to gain scholarly impetus. Most research in L2 acquisition has focused on the spoken language (Brown, 1987; Celce-Murcia, 1985; Day, 1986; Ellis, 1984, 1985; Gass & Madden, 1985; McLaughlin, 1987; Perdue, 1984; Widdowson, 1987). Recently, however, there has been a wave of scholarly inquiry into the composing processes of L2 learners. Researchers and theoreticians like Vivian Zamel (1982), Ann Raimes (1983), Ruth Spack (1984), Stephen Krashen (1982; 1984), Carole Edelsky (1986), Sarah Hudelson (1984) and Sandra McKay (1984) have clearly demonstrated some of the issues involved in enhancing the development of L2 writers. But there are still relatively few resources available to those who wish to enrich their ESL students' writing experiences.

Given the relative dearth of publications in ESL composition, this collection offers resources to theoreticians, researchers, and practitioners interested in writing in a second language. We designed this collection to meet the needs of a wide audience of teachers, instructors, and professors working in a variety of settings. It is designed for teachers in the schools working within various types of programs, including ESL and bilingual programs, "mainstream" English programs, and various immersion programs. It is also designed for those working with college, university, or adult ESL/EFL students. Some of the chapters are aimed at teachers working at a specific level: elementary, secondary, college. Others, however, speak to audiences at all levels. Although the focus is on learning English as a second language, this book also offers strategies that can be readily adapted and adopted by second or foreign language educators, such as high school Spanish teachers, elementary French immersion teachers, and university foreign language professors. Further, the book is suited for second language methods courses in universities because it blends theory, research, and practice. Many of the chapters present scholarly research conducted by the authors, yet each chapter proposes specific suggestions for instruction that are directly applicable to the classroom. For this reason it is also suited for composition methods courses partially devoted to ESL composition instruction.

Because we believe that it is helpful to look at issues from many different perspectives, we invited teacher–scholars with diverse backgrounds to contribute to this book. Some of them have taught or studied writing at the elementary level, some at the secondary level, and some at the college level. Many of the authors in this volume have taught, conducted research, and trained teachers at the college level in addition to one of the other levels. While most have worked in classes enrolling only ESL students, some have worked in classes with mixed L1/L2 enrollments. The authors have drawn on their teaching and scholarship in many fields: composition, rhetoric, bilingual education, second language acquisition, linguistics, discourse analysis, congnitive psychology, reading, contrastive rhetoric, sociolinguistics, psycholinguistics, and educational technology. We intentionally designed this volume to explore a relatively wide range of ESL composition topics. We think that a wide focus is necessary at this point in the development of the field.

As the title of this volume indicates, the authors collected here have all written chapters that address what we consider to be an important theme: empowering ESL students through richness in writing. In our view, the interdisciplinary theory underpinning all of the chapters is brought to bear upon three goals for students: writing development, L2 development, and the empowerment of language minority students through nondeficit models of schooling. To help teachers pursue these goals, many of the authors in this volume address the social contexts of schooling as they relate to establishing the kinds of interactive contexts for writing that promote intellectual growth, collaboration among learners, authentic communication, and the input and interaction needed for continued L2 acquisition.

We hope that this book helps to equip students with the kinds of control that Elbow (1981) has advocated: " . . . power over words and readers; . . . power over yourself and over the writing process; knowing what you are doing as you write; being in charge; having control; not feeling stuck or helpless or intimidated" (p. vii). To this end, contributing authors focus on approaches and techniques that help students use writing for communication.

We also hope that this volume offers resources that will help students become empowered in Ashcroft's (1987) sense:

> An empowered person . . . would be someone who believed in his or her ability/capability to act, and this belief would be accompanied by able/capable action. Since power has both capability and action components, the belief and resulting action are inseparable. (p. 143)

ORGANIZATIONAL PLAN

Part I, titled "Settings, Networks, Connections," presents the empowerment framework for the book. Drawing on interdisciplinary theory and research in L2 learning, the schooling of language minority students, and composition, the authors in this section define important aspects of the contexts in which ESL students engage in composing. These contexts involve the local community, communities across cultures, organizational structures in schools, the sociolinguistic and sociocultural contexts in classrooms, and contexts for collaboration among teachers in both their training and their teaching. The eleven authors suggest ways that these contexts can influence the kinds of composing experiences that ESL students have in classrooms. They propose exciting ways of enriching such experiences for students of different age groups. Common themes running through these chapters include the importance of making connections between writers and readers; conversing, reading, and writing in the L2 about important content; and helping students to build on their individual strengths.

Several authors address ways that computers can be used as tools in creating functional L2 learning environments. With the proliferation of computers in all education settings, ESL students are particularly at risk of being isolated and subjected to poor software (Johnson, 1985). These authors describe successful computer projects in which students use written language to communicate for real purposes with real audiences and in ways that promote L2 development.

Part II, "Rhetorical Concerns in Writing," moves from the broader contexts of L2 writing to address specific rhetorical issues for L2 writers. Because the cognitive processes students use in approaching L2 writing tasks involve solving complex rhetorical problems (Hayes & Flower, 1980), the eight authors in this section address the importance of considerations such as purpose, audience, and topic in composing. They present original research on how students develop as L2 writers and how classroom events affect writing processes and students' development as users of written English. They illustrate how teachers can structure a variety of situations in which cognitive and social processes interact to improve writing. Important themes running through this section are that teachers of L2 students, from the elementary school to the university, can help students gain a stronger sense of power over the use of the L2 for their purposes and a greater richness in their writing through the principles of authenticity, audience, topic, and purpose presented in this section.

In Part III, "Culture, Second Language Writing, and Creativity," five authors address cultural issues in the written discourse of ESL students. Because written language is culturally variable, cross-cultural differences in conveying meaning through writing are of great theoretical and practical importance (Widdowson, 1987). The topics students choose to write about, the ways they develop those topics, the kinds of information they include, the ways they organize the information, and the kinds of inferences they leave for the reader to make are all related to their own rich cultural experiences. The authors discuss these issues and suggest implications for teaching composition, for evaluating student writing, and for moving toward more pluralistic views of rhetoric.

We hope this book will contribute to further research on writing that takes account of students' rich cultural and linguistic backgrounds and that focuses on purposeful writing in rich contexts. We also hope the book will, in some small way, help lead the profession in the direction that people such as Raimes (1983) have advocated:

> In the classroom, teachers will ask questions about content and will
> seek out materials and methods that will allow their students the time,

space, and opportunity to generate and explore ideas by means of language. That could mean that learners will produce real instead of simulated discourse. It could also mean that with more questions being raised about writing as an authentic and valuable mode of learning, we might see writing become an integral part of every ESL program and of every class. (p. 549)

REFERENCES

Ashcroft, L. (1987). Defusing "Empowering": The what and the why. *Language Arts, 64,* 142–156.

Bach, K., & Harnish, R. (1980). *Linguistic communication and speech acts.* Cambridge, MA: MIT Press.

de Beaugrande, R. (1980). *Text, discourse, and process: Toward a multidisciplinary science of texts: Vol. 4. Discourse processes: Advances in research and theory.* Norwood NJ: Ablex.

Breen, M. P. (1987). Contemporary paradigms in syllabus design: Part II. *Language Teaching, 20,* 157–174.

Brown, H. D. (1987). *Principles of language learning and teaching* (2nd ed.). Englewood Cliffs, NJ: Prentice-Hall.

Celce-Murcia, M. (Ed.). (1985). *Beyond basics: Issues and research in TESOL.* Rowley, MA: Newbury House.

Connor, U., & Kaplan, R. B. (Eds.). (1987). *Writing across languages: Analysis of L2 text.* Reading, MA: Addison-Wesley.

Cook-Gumperz, J. (1986). Introduction: The social construction of literacy. In J. Cook-Gumperz (Ed.), *The social construction of literacy* (pp. 1–15). Cambridge: Cambridge University Press.

Day, R. R. (Ed.). (1986). *Talking to learn: Conversation in second language acquisition.* Rowley, MA: Newbury House.

Duran, R. P. (Ed.). (1981). *Latino language and communicative behavior: Vol. 6. Discourse processes: Advances in research and theory.* Norwood, NJ: Ablex.

Edelsky, C. (Ed.). (1986). *Writing in a bilingual program: Había una vez.* Norwood, NJ: Ablex.

Elbow, P. (1981). Note to the reader. *Writing with power.* New York: Oxford University Press.

Ellis, R. (1984). *Classroom second language development: A study of classroom interaction and language interaction.* Oxford: Pergamon.

Ellis, R. (1985). *Understanding second language acquisition.* Oxford University Press.

Fish, S. (1980). *Is there a text in this class? The authority of interpretive communities.* Cambridge, MA: Harvard University Press.

Flower, L. (1979). Writer-based prose: A cognitive basis for problems in writing. *College English, 41,* 19–37.

Flower, L., & Hayes, J. (1980). The cognition of discovery: Defining a rhetorical problem. *College Composition and Communication, 31,* 21–32.

Flower, L., & Hayes, J. R. (1981). A cognitive process theory of writing. *College Composition and Communication, 32*, 365–387.

Freedle, R. O. (Ed.). (1977). *Discourse production and comprehension: Vol. 1. Discourse processes: Advances in research and theory*. Norwood, NJ: Ablex.

Freedman, S. W. (Ed.). (1985). *The acquisition of written language*. Norwood, NJ: Ablex.

Freedman, S. W., Dyson, A. H., Flower, L., & Chafe, W. (1987). *Research in writing: Past, present, and future* (Technical Report No. 1). Berkeley and Pittsburg: University of California, Berkeley, and Carnegie Mellon University, Center for the Study of Writing.

Gardner, R. C. (1986). *Social psychological aspects of second language learning*. London: Edward Arnold.

Gass, S. M., & Madden, C. G. (1985). *Input in second language acquisition*. Rowley, MA: Newbury House.

Genesse, F. (1987). *Learning through two languages: Studies of immersion and bilingual education*. New York: Harper & Row/Newbury House.

Giles, H., & Byrne, J. (1982). An intergroup approach to second language acquisition. *Journal of Multilingual and Multicultural Development, 3*, 17–40.

Hakuta, K. (1986). *Mirror of language: The debate on bilingualism*. New York: Basic Books.

Halliday, M. A. K., & Hasan, R. (1976). *Cohesion in English*. London: Longman Group.

Halliday, M. A. K., & Hasan, R. (1985). *Language, context, and text: Aspects of language in a social-semiotic perspective*. Victoria, Australia: Deakin University.

Hayes, J. R., & Flower, L. (1980). Identifying the organization of writing processes. In L. Gregg & E. Steinberg (Eds.), *Cognitive processes in writing* (pp. 3–30). Hillsdale, NJ: Lawrence Erlbaum Associates.

Heath, S. B. (1986). Sociocultural contexts of language development. In California State Department of Education (Ed.), *Beyond language: Social and cultural factors in schooling language minority students* (pp. 143–186). Los Angeles: California State University, Evaluation, Dissemination and Assessment Center.

Hirsch, E. D. (1987). *Cultural literacy: What every American needs to know*. Boston: Houghton Mifflin.

Hudelson, S. (1984). Kan yu ret an rayt en Ingles? Children become literate in English as a second language. *TESOL Quarterly, 18*, 221–238.

Jernudd, B. H., & Jo, S. H. (1986). Bilingualism as a resource in the United States. In R. B. Kaplan (Ed.), *Annual Review of Applied Linguistics (Vol. 6)* (pp. 10–18). Cambridge: Cambridge University Press.

Johnson, D. M. (1985). *Using computers to promote the development of English as a second language: A report to the Carnegie Corporation*. Tucson, AZ: University of Arizona. (ERIC Document Reproduction Service No. ED 278 211)

Johnson, D. M. (1987). The organization of instruction in migrant education: Assistance for children and youth at risk. *TESOL Quarterly, 21*, 437–459.

Kaplan, R. B. (1986). Introduction. In R. B. Kaplan (Ed.), *Annual Review of Applied Linguistics (Vol. 6)* (pp. vii–ix). Cambridge: Cambridge University Press.

Krashen, S. D. (1982). *Principles and practice in second language acquisition.* New York: Pergamon.

Krashen, S. E. (1984). *Writing: Research, theory and applications.* New York: Alemany.

Langer, J. (1987, March). *Reading, writing, and studying across the curriculum.* Paper presented at the meeting of the Tucson Area Reading Council.

Lees, E. O. (1987). Proofreading as reading: Errors as embarrassments. In T. Enos (Ed.), *A sourcebook for basic writing teachers* (pp. 216–230). New York: Random House.

McKay, S. (Ed.). (1984). *Composing in a second language.* Rowley, MA: Newbury House.

McLaughlin, B. (1987). *Theories of second language learning.* London: Edward Arnold.

Moffett, J. (1968). *Teaching the universe of discourse.* Boston: Houghton Mifflin.

Moffett, J. (1981). *Active voice: A writing program across the curriculum.* Montclair, NJ: Boynton/Cook.

O'Malley, J. M., Chamot, A. U., & Walker, C. (in press). The role of cognition in second language acquisition. *Studies in Second Language Acquisition.*

Penfield, J. (1987). ESL: The regular classroom teacher's perspective. *TESOL Quarterly, 21,* 21–39.

Perdue, C. (Ed.). (1984). *Second language acquisition by adult immigrants: A field manual.* Rowley, MA: Newbury House.

Piaget, J. (1955). *The language and thought of the child* (M. Gabain, Trans.). New York: Modern Library. (Original work published 1926)

Purves, A. C. (1986). Rhetorical communities, the international student, and basic writing. *Journal of Basic Writing, 5*(1), 38–51.

Raimes, A. (1983). Tradition and revolution in ESL teaching. *TESOL Quarterly, 17,* 535–552.

Rose, M. (1983). Remedial writing courses: A critique and a proposal. *College English, 45,* 109–128.

Ruiz, R. (1984). Orientations in language planning. *NABE Journal, 8*(2), 15–34.

Ruiz, R. (1987). Criticisms of English language behavior in the United States. *Journal of Intensive English Studies, 1*(1), 65–85.

Saville-Troike, M. (1984). What really matters in second language learning for academic achievement? *TESOL Quarterly, 18,* 199–219.

Spack, R. (1984). Invention Strategies and the ESL college composition student. *TESOL Quarterly, 18,* 649–670.

Stern, H. H. (1983). *Fundamental concepts of language teaching.* Oxford: Oxford University Press.

Troike, R. C. (1983). *Developing America's language resources for the twenty-first century: Foreign language and bilingual education.* Unpublished manuscript.

Tucker, R. (1985). Introductory remarks. In R. B. Kaplan (Ed.), *Annual Review of Applied Linguistics (Volume 5)* (pp. 2–9). Cambridge: Cambridge University Press.

Vygotsky, L. S. (1962). *Thought and language* (E. Hanfmann & G. Vakar, Trans.). Cambridge, MA: MIT Press. (Original work published in 1934.)

Wells, G. (1981). *Learning through interaction: The study of language development*. Cambridge: Cambridge University Press.

Wells, G. (1986). *The meaning makers: Children learning language and using language to learn*. Portsmouth, NH: Heinemann.

Widdowson, H. G. (1983). *Learning purpose and language use*. Oxford: Oxford University Press.

Widdowson, H. G. (1987). Foreword. In U. Connor & R. B. Kaplan (Eds.), *Writing across languages: Analysis of L2 text* (pp. iii–iv). Reading, MA: Addison-Wesley.

Witte, S. P. (1985). Revising, composing theory, and research design. In S. W. Freedman (Ed.), *The acquisition of written language* (pp. 250–284). Norwood, NJ: Ablex.

Wolfson, N., & Judd, E. (Eds.). (1983). *Sociolinguistics and language acquisition*. Rowley, MA: Newbury.

Wong Fillmore, L. (1986). Research currents: Equity or excellence. *Language Arts, 63*, 74–81.

Yalden, J. (1987). *Principles of course design for language teaching*. Cambridge: Cambridge University Press.

Zamel, V. (1982). Writing: The process of discovering meaning. *TESOL Quarterly, 16*, 195–209.

PART I

Settings, Networks, Connections

John Hayes (1987) has recently observed that "the processes which a writer brings to bear on a writing task, and presumably what the writer learns from the task, depend critically on the situation and, in particular, on the teacher's strategy for managing the writing assignment" (p. 3). We, too, think that situation, or setting, is important for the teaching of writing. In keeping with this thinking, the authors in this first part of the book describe both general and specific settings for engaging ESL students in writing.

In the first chapter, Jim Cummins examines national settings by considering the effects of the more than 30 educational reform reports that have appeared since the publication of *A Nation at Risk* (National Commission on Excellence in Education, 1983). Cummins argues that while these alarmist reports attempt to remedy problems in U.S. education, they actually serve to disempower students, especially minority students, in several ways. First, these reform-movement documents imply, if not directly advocate, strongly teacher-centered approaches, which disempower not only students but teachers as well. Second, the reform movement confuses the relationship between equity and excellence, and may make equity impossible. Third, because the reform movement reflects an autocratic view of society, it may do little to enable students to think critically. Cummins discusses the historical context for the current reform movement, and then offers alternative proposals based on interactive teacher-student relationships, enriching linguistic and cultural resources, and abilities and attitudes that empower students to fully participate in a global community.

In Chapter 2, Donna M. Johnson focuses on one aspect of the context of situation for writing—interpersonal role relationships. She argues that second language (L2) students often have little power in communicative situations and are not often able to see the effects on readers of what they write. Therefore, in addition to having students write on a variety of topics to a variety of audiences for a variety of purposes, Johnson argues that teachers need to create literacy events in which ESL students have opportunities to write from various positions of power. She provides evidence that language use is related to factors such as interpersonal power and control in language use contexts. She then suggests specific ways that teachers can organize events to enrich writing through (1) arranging for student selection of topics, (2) building on students' social motivations, and (3) allowing students to teach their peers and teachers.

Luis C. Moll discusses the relevance of Vygotskian theory for promoting the development of L2 writing. He first provides an overview of Vygotsky's general theory and then discusses the zone of proximal development as a collective rather than individual construct. He shows how the concept of a zone has important implications both for assessment and for instruction. Because children's abilities at any one time vary in relation to the context in which they are performing, assessment of work in differing contexts, including collaborative contexts, represents a more dynamic, less static, view of development. In order to socially mediate children's interaction with content, teachers must create tasks and activities considering the collective, socially constructed zones of their students. Finally, Moll provides specific suggestions for ways that teachers can create and mediate the types of classroom social systems that lead to ownership and reorganization of literacy learning activities by children.

Mary M. Kitagawa describes a small but important setting for engaging ESL students in writing: her own fifth/sixth-grade classroom, in which more than 80% of her students are nonnative English speakers. Kitagawa focuses on the language use of three of her students: Loc, a native speaker of Vietnamese; Hector, a Spanish speaker from El Salvador; and Jeremy, a monolingual English speaker. Her observations of these three boys illustrate the theme of building upon learners' knowledge and concerns so as to empower students to gain control over choice of topics and genres. Kitagawa also describes the writing core of her class, consisting of journals; poetry; book-talk letters; expressive writing that interweaves literature, science, and social studies; and reports based on observations and oral history interviews. The chapter shows how teachers can help students shift from passive recipients to active participants in their own language learning. It also shows how all members of a class, including the teacher, need to become members of a "hungry audience" if they are to fully empower each other as writers.

Sarah Hudelson explores individual differences in the development of two Spanish speaking children as English writers during a school year. As she worked with the children outside of their regular classes once every two weeks over a period of one year, she encouraged them to write. Providing samples of their work, she describes the kinds of writing they did, how they used their Spanish as one resource for learning and writing in English, and how their engagement in conversation, drawing, and writing all contributed to their development. Hudelson shows how the two children differed in their approaches to the task of creating texts and, more importantly, how the nature of what was expected in the regular classroom formed their views about writing at school. She then makes recommendations about the kinds of supportive contexts children need to develop as writers in a new language.

The Kreeft Peyton and Mackinson-Smyth chapter represents the results of a collaborative researcher-teacher effort as well as an advance in the methodology of studying written L2 production as it occurs on line. The authors describe a computer network designed to improve the writing of hearing-impaired students learning English as a second language at Gallaudet University and its affiliated elementary school. They first provide an overview of what is involved in using English for students whose L1 is American Sign Language (ASL). The authors then explain how the network was used during their two-year research project to provide opportunities for students to engage in interactive written conversations with peers. Students print their work and later analyze and discuss (in ASL) strategies used in their English discourse, including those that help them learn from one another. Their literacy skills improve as they gradually incorporate these strategies into their own writing. Their data also illustrate how students, in a context of meaningful interaction, are able to vary their language to adapt to the communicative needs of different partners.

Dennis Sayers writes about a functional computer networking project for bilingual education in which distant sister classes in New Haven, Connecticut, and San Diego, California, collaborate in journalism projects. Students at two schools compose on word processors and use an asynchronous network to send composed material and related messages to students at the other school. Intra- and inter-school editorial boards develop policies for publishing a single bilingual news-paper. Sayers reports that although the teachers differed in their philosophies of writing instruction, they melded those philosophies "to more fully exploit the educational potential of the computer writing network." The project gave students control over the topics and forms for their writing. It also encouraged students to write for a wider audience than usual. Further, students learned to collaborate not only within a classroom but also between two classrooms in two distinct cultures. A key point is that the discussions among cooperating groups in the two connected classrooms helped to change the way that both students and teachers think about criteria for judging effective writing, the kind of writing they would want to publish in their joint newspaper.

In Chapter 8, Kate Mangelsdorf explores important connections between speaking and writing in L2 interactions, and she suggests methods for integrating these two modes of expression in college classrooms. Speaking and writing, as Ede (1987) has suggested, share numerous characteristics, including communicative purposes and strategies for constructing and negotiating meaning. These shared characteristics make possible the integration of writing and speaking classroom interactions to enhance second language acquisition. Mangelsdorf describes teaching strategies for such enriching integration, including dialogue journals, oral presentations, and peer group work in which students use both speaking and writing to negotiate meaning.

In the final chapter in the section, Ann Schlumberger and Diane Clymer describe a crucial setting for teaching writing to ESL students: the context in which teachers are trained. Schlumberger and Clymer describe a teacher training program built on principles of collaboration. In the program they describe, teach-ers collaborate in several ways. First, they work together to develop and use holistically scored essays for the purpose of placing new ESL composition students in appropriate courses. Second, they work cooperatively to construct activities and assignments for many or all sections of each course. Third, they contribute equally to in-class essay examinations. Fourth, teachers collaborate to design curricula for the courses. As teachers work together to discover appropriate strategies for engaging their ESL students in writing, they come to understand that teachers must be lifelong learners if they are to fully enrich the learning experiences of the people they teach.

REFERENCES

Ede, L. (1987). New perspectives on the speaking-writing relationship: Implications for teachers of basic writing. In T. Enos (Ed.), *A sourcebook for basic writing teachers* (pp. 318–327). New York: Random House.

Hayes, J. R. (1987). Integrating writing research. *The Quarterly of the National Writing Project and the Center for the Study of Writing, 9*(4), 1–3.

National Commission on Excellence in Education. (1983). *A nation at risk: The imperative for educational reform.* Washington, DC: U.S. Government Printing Office.

CHAPTER 1

The Sanitized Curriculum: Educational Disempowerment in a Nation at Risk

Jim Cummins
Ontario Institute for Studies in Education

During the past twenty years, a major thrust of federal educational policy in the United States has been toward promoting greater equity of educational outcomes for students from diverse socioeconomic and ethnic/racial backgrounds. Although there are many isolated examples of successful programs, there is little evidence that the reforms have been effective in reversing the pattern of widespread school failure among minority students. The dropout rate among Mexican-American and Puerto Rican students remains close to 50% (Jusenius & Duarte, 1982), achievement scores of black and Latino students are far below those of their Anglo peers (National Assessment of Educational Progress, 1981), and Latino students are still massively overrepresented in classes for the learning disabled (Ortiz & Yates, 1983).

Since 1983, the rhetoric of reform has shifted from equity to "excellence." Initiated by the report of the National Commission on Excellence in Education (1983), titled *A Nation at Rick: The Imperative for Educational Reform,* the reform debate has spawned more than 30 reports (Wiggins, 1986), and legislation promoting educational reform has been passed by a large number of states across the nation. The "imperative" for reform has been sparked by the widespread perception that educational standards in the United States have been in decline for a number of years and, as a result, American business interests are placed in jeopardy in an increasingly competitive world economy. As expressed by *A Nation at*

The author would like to thank Sonia Fiorucci for assistance in preparing this paper.

Risk: "Our once unchallenged preeminence in commerce, industry, science and technological innovations is being overtaken by competitors throughout the world" (1983, p. 1).

The recommendations of *A Nation at Risk* and most subsequent reports have focused primarily on raising standards and graduation requirements, eliminating the "curriculum smorgasbord" of "soft" subjects in favor of a common core curriculum for all students, and increasing the amount of time that students are expected to spend learning the "new basics." The thrust is toward "getting tough" with students and teachers in order to increase the rigor in curriculum materials and instruction. In several states, teachers must now pass "competency" examinations or lose their jobs, and promotion of students from one grade to the next is dependent on satisfactory performance on standardized tests.

A number of educators have expressed concerns that the drive for "excellence" and, in particular, the manner in which the construct of excellence has been made operational, represents a reduction of commitment to educational equity. They point to the fact that in states such as Arizona and Texas, a large proportion of minority teachers (Latino and American Indian) fail the teacher appraisal examinations and that the lock-step approach to curriculum and instruction promoted by the educational reform movement effectively excludes minority children's experience and learning styles from the classroom (see, e.g., Cuban, 1984; Lauderdale, 1987; Passow, 1984; Stedman & Kaestle, 1985).

This chapter analyzes the current educational reform movement within the context of a theoretical framework for the empowerment of minority students. The notion of empowerment implies the development of a sense of efficacy within the student with respect to his/her own learning and personal identity. Students who are empowered by their interactions with educators experience a sense of control over their own lives and they develop the ability, confidence, and motivation to succeed academically. They participate confidently in instruction as a result of having developed a secure cultural identity and appropriate strategies for accessing the information/resources they need to accomplish academic tasks to which they are committed. I argue that the reform movement as conceptualized and implemented will contribute to the disempowering of students, particularly minority students, because (a) the pedagogical relationship between teachers and students is virtually ignored in most reports, but the proposed reforms imply a traditional "transmission" approach to teaching that is fundamentally disempowering for both teachers and students; (b) equity issues are largely omitted from consideration, but the implied relationships between equity and excellence are conceptually confused and prejudicial to the attainment of equity; (c) the reforms reflect an autocratic, top-down image of society that is inconsistent with the development of a democratic citizenry; (d) paradoxically, the focus on "excellence" as it is being implemented is more likely to produce intellectually passive, compliant consumers than critical thinkers capable of solving the increasingly complex moral and environmental issues that our children's generation (and American business) will face.

I first briefly place the reform movement in historical context and then discuss the critiques that have been made of the current reform thrust, specifically, the four broad issues outlined above. Then I discuss an alternative conception of educational reform based on (a) a teacher-student relationship that requires reciprocal interaction between teachers and students and active use of written and oral language by students for exploration of ideas and development of critical and creative thinking skills; (b) the use of the linguistic and cultural resources that students bring to the classroom for enrichment of all students; and (c) a task analysis of skills and attitudes that our children's generation will need to participate effectively in both a democratic society and a global community in which the rate of technological change is matched only by that of global environmental deterioration.

EQUITY AND EXCELLENCE
IN HISTORICAL CONTEXT

The renewed call for a return to "the basics" echoes the attack, especially that of Vice Adm. Hyman Rickover (1959), on the assumed excesses of progressive education in the 1950s. As many commentators have pointed out, the pendulum of educational fashion has swung many times between traditional and progressive education, or teacher-centered versus child-centered pedagogies. The fundamentally different philosophical and psychological assumptions of traditional and progressive education are lucidly expressed by John Dewey (1963, pp. 18–19), widely regarded as the father of progressive education.

Now with the publication of *A Nation at Risk* and the subsequent reports, the pendulum has swung back to reemphasizing "the basics." The crisis to be overcome is the alleged decline in standardized test scores and its implications for the economy and security of the country. However, a careful analysis of the data suggests that the "crisis" has been fabricated to rationalize a conservative educational agenda that is already having a seriously damaging effect on the development of children's minds. This perspective is presented in the next section.

THE RHETORIC AND REALITY
OF EDUCATIONAL REFORM

In discussing the "imperative" for educational reform contained in the reports of 1983 and subsequent years, it is important to distinguish between those reports, such as *A Nation at Risk,* written by committees, which for the most part endorse an "effectiveness through rigor" philosophy, and the reports written by educators such as John Goodlad (1984), Ernest Boyer (1983), and Theodore Sizer (1984). These latter reports are considerably more carefully researched than the committee reports and they take greater account both of the views of educators and of the complexity of the processes of school reform (Albrecht, 1984; Cross, 1984; Howe, 1984). They also focus explicitly on the pedagogical relationship between teachers and learners, a concern that is virtually absent from most of the more influential committee reports. However, the reforms being implemented in many states mindlessly follow the mechanistic, quick-fix solutions recommended in *A Nation at Risk* and ignore the quality of interactions between teachers and students (see, e.g., Cuban, 1984).

The reform movement as it is being implemented is characterized by a series of logical and empirical contradictions. The rhetoric that decries what *A Nation at Risk* calls the "rising tide of mediocrity" and its presumed causes does not stand up to critical scrutiny. Specifically, the "crisis" of test score declines which gave rise to the imperative for reform is more apparent than real (Stedman & Kaestle, 1985); the alleged causes of the apparent decline (the erosion of educational quality due to the permissiveness of the 1960s and 1970s) are easily refuted (Stedman & Kaestle, 1985); the means recommended to reverse the decline are inconsistent with everything that is known about organizational reform (Bacharach & Conley, 1986; Cross, 1984; Cuban, 1984); the means are also inconsistent with the overt goals of promoting critical and creative thinking skills among students so that they can effectively contribute to the needs of business in a rapidly changing economy (Cross, 1984) and to the creation of a healthy democracy (Cohen, 1984; Giroux & McLaren, 1986; Sirotnike, 1983); the simplistic and rigid conception of the educational process in general and the reform process in particular sacrifices not only equity but also excellence (Albrecht, 1984; Howe, 1984; Lauderdale, 1987; Stedman & Kaestle, 1985).

All of these criticisms revolve around the implicit adoption of a transmission model of pedagogy in most of the reform reports and subsequent implementation attempts. I shall comment briefly on each of the specific points before outlining the central importance of the pedagogical interactions between teachers and students for any genuine educational reform directed at both excellence and equity.

Fabricating a Crisis: The Test Score Decline

Stedman and Kaestle (1985) point out that the picture of test score declines in the late 1960s and 1970s "is much more complex than critics claim, and the contradictory evidence is not easily explained" (p. 207). For example, most of the alarmist presentations of test score declines fail to take account of the very different populations of test takers in the early 1960s as compared with the 1970s and 1980s. Thus,

> During the 1970s a falling dropout rate among black students and increased immigration of Asian and Hispanic students increased the percentage of minority students in our high schools from one-sixth to nearly one-fourth. Such changes probably contributed to lower test scores . . . demographic changes may account for between 30% and 50% of the test score decline in standardized achievement tests during the 1970s. (Stedman & Kaestle, 1985, p. 205)

They go on to point out that data from the National Assessment of Educational Progress (NAEP), which are "probably the best indicators of national trends" (p. 207), showed that "13- and 17-year-olds maintained their overall reading scores and that 9-year-olds improved theirs in testing carried out in 1970, 1975, and 1980" (p. 207). Although 17-year-olds slipped in inferential comprehension, the drop was minor (from 64% correct in 1970 to 62% correct in 1980) and not universal, being limited to the Northeast and to boys.

Stedman and Kaestle point out that the decline in standardized test scores ended in the late 1970s, well before "the reformers issued their reports, and before the legislatures passed their post-1980 reform bills" (p. 209). Instead of dire warnings of "a rising tide of mediocrity," they argue, *A Nation at Risk* should have proclaimed "a rising tide of test scores." They attribute the upswing in test scores to a variety of factors, such as changed family configuration of test-takers (now more often first- or second-born children due to falling family sizes), the increasing dropout rate, which makes the high school population more selective, and the fact that instruction is focusing more on skills measured by standardized tests, a trend that they view with considerable concern.

Finding Scapegoats: "Permissiveness" as a Causal Factor

Many of the educational critics of the 1980s attribute the alleged fall in academic standards to the student-centered permissiveness and social unrest of the late 1960s. However, as Stedman and Kaestle point out, the greatest student protest took place between 1968 and 1971, whereas the greatest decline in standardized test scores occurred between 1971 and 1978:

> Blaming the decline on the effects of social unrest in the schools may be fashionable, but the middle to late 1970s were years of educational retrenchment, characterized by a renewed emphasis on the basics, the spread of statewide competency testing and moves to end social promotion. We can hardly blame the test declines of the 1970s directly on activist educators who, frustrated by their inability to change schools, had effectively abandoned their efforts by the mid-1970s. (1985, p. 208)

A further point is that virtually all the empirical data (e.g., Cuban, 1984; Goodlad, 1984; Sirotnik, 1983; Sizer, 1984) show that instruction in schools has changed very little over the course of this century. The process of teaching and learning, according to Sirotnik's analysis of more than 1,000 elementary and secondary classrooms, "appears to be one of the most consistent and persistent phenomena known in the social and behavioral sciences . . . the 'modus operandi' of the typical classroom is still didactics, practice, and little else" (Sirotnik, 1983, pp. 16–17). He notes that teacher lecturing or whole-class work on written assignments continue to emerge as the primary instructional patterns and suggests that "navigating back to the basics should be easy. We never left" (p. 26). Goodlad (1984, p. 106) similarly notes that in the classrooms he observed "traditional not progressive pedagogy dominated." He also notes that early elementary teachers attempted to individualize instruction and varied classroom procedures more than others and "the early elementary grades are those that have held up best, nationwide, on tests of pupil achievement!" (p. 106).

In short, the attribution of test score declines to "progressive" educational practices is pure scapegoating since traditional teacher-centered instruction continues to predominate in classrooms across the nation.

Organizational Reform: Top-Down Control and Disempowerment of Teachers

Several commentators have pointed out that the current reform movement in American education assumes the validity and efficacy of a top-down process of organizational change (e.g., Bacharach & Conley, 1986; Cross, 1984; Cuban, 1984). Bacharach and Conley, for example, point out that "reform in American education has been predicated on the assumption that the problem lies with teachers and their motivation to teach" (p. 641).

Consequently, in order to improve education, "we need to *control* teachers more effectively" (p. 641, emphasis in original).

This orientation to organizational change is the opposite of the organizational structure found effective both in business and educational settings. Cross (1984) provides an illuminating comparison of the recommendations for business in Peters and Waterman's (1982) best-selling book, *In Search of Excellence,* with recommendations that have emanated from the current educational reform movement. She points out that Peters and Waterman conclude that the single most pervasive theme in excellent companies is their profound respect for the individual worker. Individual workers will exert "extraordinary energy" above and beyond the call of duty when they are given even a modicum of control over their own destinies. However, with the exception of the reports by Sizer (1984) and Goodlad (1984),

> the reports on school reform show little inclination to give workers in education more control over their own destinies. In fact, they frequently recommend external control from the top as the proper antidote of the permissiveness of the 1960s and 1970s. The language of many of the recommendations implies an external authority charged with regulating, controlling, and seeing to it that the proper checkpoints are established and maintained.
>
> Peters and Waterman point out that less-than-excellent organizations take a negative view of their workers. "They verbally berate participants for poor performance. . . . They want innovation but kill the spirit of the champion. . . . They design systems that seem calculated to tear down their workers' self-image."
>
> That sounds a lot like the educational reform movement of the 1980s. Most reformers today are telling teachers that they are a sorry lot, because they score lower on college tests than their college classmates. The reformers . . . are telling students that they are losers who will be denied further educational opportunities if they don't shape up. It is very hard to feel like a winner anywhere in the system of education today. . . . Contemporary reformers . . . pay little attention to the creation of an atmosphere that stimulates enthusiasm for learning. (1984, pp. 169–172)

It is ironic that this bureaucratic management model (Bacharach & Conley, 1986) has been adopted by educational reformers who are primarily concerned about the future of American business interests at precisely the time when that model is increasingly being questioned within the business community itself.

The empirical evidence from the educational sphere also demonstrates clearly that coercive top-down orientations are ineffective both in the organization of schools and in the relations between teachers and students in the classroom. The process of top-down control is, almost by definition, disempowering for those being controlled. Cuban (1984, p. 214), for example, points out, "For years, research studies (all of them available to policymakers) have shown that districts conform to the letter of top-down directives but seldom move beyond simple compliance unless they are internally motivated to do so." Bacharach and Conley similarly cite research showing that administrators in effective schools have relinquished the notion that coordination of the activities of teachers and other school professionals requires control from the top down. Likewise, the teachers who work with these administrators have relinquished the notion that they are entitled to function as totally independent agents in their own classrooms. Bacharach and Conley note that

> The principals of effective schools are invariably characterized as "strong leaders," but their strength does not stem from their status or from their ability to control the activities of individual teachers. In fact, these principals make conscious efforts to *minimize* the differences in status that exist between themselves and their teachers and to *avoid* dictating solutions or otherwise limiting the discretion of teachers. Instead they assume primary responsibility for certain key processes, but they allow teachers to assist in those processes and to take part in decision making. (1986, p. 642, emphasis in original)

Seeley (1985), in reviewing Seymour Sarason's (1983) book *Schooling in America: Scapegoat or Salvation,* similarly attributes the failure of schools and school reforms to the delegation of "education" to hierarchically organized bureaucracies, which in turn delegate it to teachers who then deliver it in the form of "instructional services" to children. He argues that such a delegation process places the students and their families in a passive role, as recipients of education, when they should be participants in it. He goes on to argue that

> This helps explain why so many classes are "boring, boring, boring." While the teachers presumably know that they are supposed to "deliver instructional services," the students have nothing to do except "receive" the services—an inherently passive and often boring role and one that has little to do with learning. This delegation process places teachers in the role of lowest-rung bureaucratic functionaries when they should be leaders in the learning process. (1985, p. 350)

In short, the current top-down attempt to control teacher–student interactions contravenes what is known about effective organizational change. Extrinsic control (coercion) is exercised from top levels of the educational hierarchy (politicians and policymakers) to the levels below, with teachers and their students unfortunate enough to be at the bottom of this hierarchy. Both teachers and students are disempowered in this process in that they have lost control of their own lives within the classroom. The teacher's role is to transmit mindlessly a predetermined curriculum in a prescribed manner, while the students' role is to ingest skills and facts for later regurgitation on standardized tests.

Societal Reflections: Eliminating Critical Thinking from the Classroom and Society

Part of the rhetoric of the educational reform movement is the need to increase students' powers of critical thinking and higher-order cognitive skills generally. A concern expressed in a number of reports was the decline during the 1970s in higher-order thinking skills (e.g., inferential comprehension in reading, mathematics problem solving) evidenced in National Assessment of Educational Progress (1981) data. Thus, reform packages being implemented in several states include provision for the teaching of critical thinking skills. However, critical thinking is viewed as just another skill to be transmitted rather than an integral part of the teaching of all curricular content. In stark contrast to the rhetoric emphasizing the importance of critical thinking, the effect of the reforms has been to eliminate any kind of critical thinking on the part of either teachers or students from instruction in "the basics" and, in fact, to penalize any deviations from rote transmission, since such behaviors are "off-task."

In addition, issues of direct concern to students' future and current lives are seldom raised in the classroom. The curriculum has been sanitized such that students rarely have the opportunity to discuss critically or write about issues that directly affect the society they will form. Issues such as racism, environmental pollution, U.S. policy in Central America, genetic engineering, global nuclear destruction, arms control, and so forth are regarded as too "sensitive" for fragile and impressionable young minds. Instead, students are fed a neutralized diet of social studies, science, and language arts that is largely irrelevant to the enormous global problems that our generation is creating for our children's generation to resolve.

Critics of the current educational reform movement consistently point to the perversion of the learning process implied by the focus on transmission of facts and basic skills in isolation from critical evaluation of those facts and active utilization of skills for projects to which students are committed. Cohen (1984, p. 13), for example, talks of the "flat, arid, wasted hours" that students spend in most high schools; Albrecht (1984) laments the fact that as a result of *A Nation at Risk* and subsequent committee reports, the real keys to improving education, namely, involving students more actively in the learning process and paying more attention to the cultivation of higher thought processes, are difficult to get on the public agenda for discussion. Cuban (1984, p. 214) points to the contradiction between the types of schooling that state-level policymakers and corporate executives want for their own children and the type of schooling they have effectively mandated for others, consisting of "an assembly-line where teachers produce a predictable flow of well-behaved children, chock-full of facts and sporting ever-higher tests scores." He goes on to point out that policymakers expect that, as a result of the reforms, students leaving schools will possess problem-solving and reasoning skills; however,

> researchers know that pressures on teachers to cover course content swiftly and to raise student test scores have combined to produce classrooms in which teachers lecture for two-thirds of the time to the assembled class, ask most of the questions, and rely on the textbook as the sole source of information. Researchers also know that for students to cultivate critical thought, they need to ask questions often and freely, become actively involved for long periods with problems that makes sense to them, and engage in activities in which the teacher plays the role of coach. . . . Teachers are in a double bind. They are expected to instruct students in such a way as to cultivate critical thought, yet the state requires that they cover content and raise test scores. (1984, p. 214)

It should be noted that these goals are not necessarily in conflict since curriculum content can be covered probably more effectively in the long run by instruction that evokes students' higher-order thinking skills than by instruction that requires only mote memorization of facts or application of skills.

Since evaluation of teachers has become dependent on the extent to which they raise students' standardized test scores, there is no incentive for teachers to innovate, or to encourage students' critical and creative thinking skills. Although lip-service is paid to these objectives, they are not reflected on the standardized tests and are therefore not reflected in the interactions that children experience in the classroom. Albert Shanker (1987), president of the American Federation of Teachers, like other commentators, has noted these trends with concern:

> In response to this pressure teachers spend huge amounts of time drilling students in multiple choice questions and sample exams and teaching the strategies of test-taking. Wherever I go, I meet teachers who complain that they find it increasingly difficult to do real teaching. There's no time for concepts, for thinking, for stimulating discussions. All the time is spent on boosting test scores. . . . We may end up with a

generation whose heads are full of little bits and scraps of knowledge
and who are adept at picking from (a), (b), (c), or (d) but unable to write,
express, think or persuade. (p. 14)

A recent NAEP national study of students' writing provided empirical
documentation of this bleak scenario and linked students' inadequate
writing abilities to the "pervasive lack of emphasis" on higher-order skills
throughout the school curriculum (NAEP, 1986). The report, titled *The
Writing Report Card: Writing Achievement in American Schools,* found
that only about one-fifth of students write adequately and most students
have difficulty organizing their thoughts coherently in writing. Students'
performance on persuasive writing tasks, such as convincing the school
principal that a rule should be changed, was "dismaying," according to the
report. The NAEP also found that lack of extended writing in school was
directly related to students' poor performance; those students who reported writing three or more essays during a six-week period performed
better than students who reported doing no writing during that time.

The lack of emphasis on creative writing, critical thinking, and problem solving involving real rather than trivial issues contributes directly to
lack of interest and motivation on the part of students (and teachers). The
proposed reforms exacerbate rather than redress the one-way transmission of information and skills within the classroom.

The image of our future society implied by this type of education is a
society of compliant consumers who passively accept rather than critically analyze the forces that impinge on their lives. Sirotnik (1983) similarly points to the hidden curriculum being communicated to students in
the typical classroom that emerged from his analysis; this classroom
contains

> a lot of teacher talk and a lot of student listening . . . almost invariably
> closed and factual questions . . . and predominantly total class instruc-
> tional configurations around traditional activities—all in a virtually af-
> fectless environment. It is but a short inferential leap to suggest that we
> are implicitly teaching dependence upon authority, linear thinking, so-
> cial apathy, passive involvement, and hands-off learning. (p. 29)

The same perspective has been forcefully argued by Henry Giroux
and his colleagues (e.g., Aronowitz & Giroux, 1985; Giroux & McLaren,
1986), who maintain that the critical thinking skills necessary for meaningful participation in a democratic society are being eradicated by our
current models of schooling.

Even within the narrower context of the future needs of American
business, which was a prime concern of many of the reform reports, it is

clear that the reforms being implemented are counterproductive. Cross (1984) points out that

> the reports say very little about preparing people to live in a world in which the pace of change is escalating with each generation. Indeed, arguments about what constitutes the core of knowledge seem almost quaint, in the face of the current knowledge explosion. Between 6,000 and 7,000 scientific articles are written each day, and information doubles every five and a half years. By the time the average physician completes his or her training, half of all the information acquired in medical school is obsolete. (p. 172)

Within this context, our society (and business interests) requires individuals enthusiastic about actively engaging in learning throughout their lives and capable of critically interpreting and applying the vast amount of information available.

The current reform movement ignores the obvious fact that critical thinking skills can be developed in students only by teachers who are themselves critical thinkers. If teachers are not themselves critical thinkers willing to challenge the system within which they operate, they are unlikely to encourage their students to critically analyze and creatively resolve problems. However, as documented above, critical thinking and questioning of authority by teachers is seldom encouraged by those at higher levels of the eduational hierarchy. The thrust of reform has been to control teachers and to eliminate "off-task" classroom behaviors. Off-task behaviors effectively constitute all behaviors that are not assessed in typical standardized achievement tests, among which are creative and critical thinking, expressive writing in various genres, and cooperative problem-solving skills. In short, the rhetoric of current educational reform in the United States proclaims the goal of critical thinking and self-motivated learning, but the classroom reality reeks of disempowerment, both of teachers and students.

Equity and Excellence: A False Dichotomy

As documented by Stedman and Kaestle (1985), apparent test score declines and increases have been significantly influenced by the dropout rate of minority students. Specifically, the lowering of scores in the early 1970s was partly a function of a decrease in the dropout rate among minority students, while the more recent rise in scores partly reflects another increase in the dropout rate, which makes the composition of high schools more selective. Thus, if excellence is effectively defined in terms of standardized test scores, a major thrust toward increasing the amount of excellence in schools should be to increase the academic performance of low-achieving students, among whom minorities are significantly over-represented. Policymakers who proclaim an increase in excellence (i.e., standardized test scores) that has been brought about by pushing minority students out of school prior to high-school graduation manifest a level of reasoning skill and/or hypocrisy that reflects a nation that is truly "at risk."

A reform movement directed at minority students must begin by inquiring into the causes of minority students' underachievement, and intervention processes should be predicated upon this causal analysis. A framework for analyzing minority students' underachievement has been elaborated (Cummins, 1986) and will be summarized briefly here. The essentials of this analysis are consistent with the criticisms of the current educational reform movement discussed above in that the pedagogical relationship between teachers and students and between schools and the communities they serve are regarded as central. The focus is on empowering minority students, a process that can be accomplished only by educators who are themselves empowered; in other words, who are secure in their own personal and professional identity and confident that they have the ability and administrative support to help students succeed academically. Empowerment is a reciprocal process between educators and students that cannot take place in the closed hierarchically controlled bureaucracy promoted by current reform efforts.

A FRAMEWORK FOR EDUCATIONAL REFORM AMONG ESL STUDENTS

A considerable amount of data shows that power and status relations between minority and majority groups exert a major influence on school performance (Cummins, 1984; Ogbu, 1978). Minority groups that tend to experience academic difficulty (e.g., Finns in Sweden; Hispanic, Black, and Native American groups in the U.S.; Franco-Ontarian, Black, and Native groups in Canada) appear to have developed an insecurity and ambivalence about the value of their own cultural identity as a result of their interactions with the dominant group.

A central proposition of the theoretical framework (Cummins, 1986) is that minority students are disempowered educationally in very much the same way that their communities are disempowered by interactions with societal institutions. The converse of this is that minority students will succeed educationally to the extent that the patterns of interaction in school reverse those that prevail in the society at large. In short, minority students are empowered and disabled as a direct result of their interactions with educators in the schools. These interactions are mediated by the implicit or explicit role definitions (i.e., mind-sets) that educators assume in relation to four institutional characteristics of schools. These characteristics reflect the extent to which:

1. Minority students' language and culture are incorporated into the school program.
2. Minority community participation is encouraged as an integral component of children's education.
3. The pedagogy promotes intrinsic motivation on the part of students to use language actively in order to generate their own knowledge.
4. Professionals involved in assessment become advocates for minority students by focusing primarily on the ways in which students' academic difficulty is a function of interactions within the school context rather than legitimizing the locating of the "problem" within students.

Data supporting the importance of each of these dimensions have been reviewed in detail by Cummins (1986, 1987). Here I focus only on the pedagogical dimension within which the other three dimensions can be incorporated. The pedagogical dimension incorporates most of the issues already discussed with respect to the general educational reform movement and can be conceptualized along a continuum from interactive/experiential to transmission models of teaching.

ORIENTATIONS TO PEDAGOGY: INTERACTIVE/EXPERIENTIAL VERSUS TRANSMISSION

It is remarkable that few of the major commentators in the educational reform debate, who decry the mindless call for a return to basics, mention the parallel controversy within the sphere of language and literacy teaching that has raged for almost twenty years. Although still very much a minority movement, a significant shift has taken place with respect to our assumptions about how reading and writing ought to be taught. This shift in the sphere of applied linguistics started with the psycholinguistic approach to reading instruction, promoted by Frank Smith (e.g., 1978) and Kenneth Goodman and Yetta Goodman (e.g., 1977), which insisted that reading was an active process of constructing meaning from text. In Britain, similar assumptions were articulated by the enormously influential Bullock Report (1975) which emphasized that oral and written language skills are acquired through active use of the language and that language development should be integrated with *all* curricular subjects.

These assumptions regarding how language and literacy skills are acquired and ought to be taught gained momentum in the late 1970s and 1980s with the process writing (Graves, 1983) and cooperative learning movements (Kagan, 1986), and are also clearly reflected in recent computer networking projects (see Sayers, this volume). All of these approaches emphasize active use of language for genuine communication in the context of a task to which the student is intrinsically committed.

These approaches also represent a reaction against transmission models of pedagogy and reflect a set of assumptions regarding the teaching–learning relationship that are parallel to those endorsed by most critics of the current educational reform movement. A difference, however, is that the recommendations are based not so much on philosophical or political ideals but on empirical data regarding the nature of language and how it is acquired. Specifically, it has been argued that a transmission model of teaching contravenes central principles of language and literacy acquisition and that a model allowing for reciprocal interaction between teachers and students represents a more appropriate alternative (Cummins, 1984; Wells, 1982, 1986). This interactive/experiential model incorporates proposals about the relation between language and learning made by a variety of investigators, most notably, in recent years, in the Bullock Report (1975), and by Freire (1973, 1983), Barnes (1976), Lindfors (1980), and Wells (1982, 1986). Its applications with respect to the promotion of literacy conform closely to psycholinguistic approaches to reading (e.g., Goodman & Goodman, 1977; Smith, 1978) and to the recent emphasis on encouraging expressive writing from the earliest grades (e.g., Chomsky, 1981; Graves, 1983).

A central tenet of the interactive/experiential model is that "talking and writing are means to learning" (Bullock Report, 1975, p. 50). Its major characteristics, in comparison to a transmission model, are:

1. Genuine dialogue between student and teacher in both oral and written modalities.
2. Guidance and facilitation rather than control of student learning by the teacher.
3. Encouragement of student-student talk in a collaborative learning context.
4. Encouragement of meaningful language use by students rather than correctness of surface forms.
5. Conscious integration of language use and development with all curricular content rather than teaching language and other content as isolated subjects.
6. A focus on developing higher-level cognitive skills rather than factual recall.

7. Task presentation that generates intrinsic rather than extrinsic motivation.

In short, pedagogical approaches that empower students, encourage them to assume greater control over setting their own learning goals and to use written and oral language for active collaboration with each other in achieving these goals. The instruction is automatically "culture-fair" in that all students are actively involved in expressing, sharing, and amplifying their experience within the classroom. The approaches reflect what cognitive psychologists such as Piaget and Vygotsky have emphasized about children's learning for more than half a century. Learning is viewed as an *active* process that is enhanced through *interaction*. The stress on action (Piaget) and interaction (Vygotsky) contrasts with behavioristic pedagogical models that focus on passive and isolated reception of knowledge.

The relevance of these two pedagogical models for educational equity derives from the fact that a genuine multicultural orientation that promotes minority student empowerment is impossible within a transmission model of pedagogy. Transmission models exclude, and therefore effectively suppress, students' experiences. Consequently, these teacher-centered approaches do not allow for validation of minority students' experiences in the classroom.

This clearly implies that minority students' first languauge (L1) should be valued within the classroom and its development encouraged. It also implies that community resources that reflect students' experiences should be used and community participation encouraged within the classroom in either children's L1 or L2 (see Roen, this volume).

With respect to assessment, it is worth noting that assessment and pedagogy are closely linked in that classroom teachers have considerable opportunities to observe children undertaking a variety of cognitive and academic tasks when the instruction is individualized and interactional. This information can and should play an important role in assessment/ placement decisions. Within a transmission model, when the instructional tasks are teacher imposed rather than expressive of children's own experience, then the instruction tends to mirror the biases of standardized tests and consequently provides much less opportunity for observation of children's capacities. This further illustrates the subtle ways in which the transmission approach underlying the educational reform movement contributes to the disabling of students.

The image of the ESL learner within an interactive/experiential model is of an explorer of meaning, a critical and creative thinker who has contributions to make both in the classroom and in the world beyond; students interpret and analyze facts rather than just ingest them. They read to learn rather than simply learn to read; they engage in creative writing both to collaboratively explore with teachers, parents, and peers the horizons of their experience and to extend these horizons. Approaches such as critical literacy (Ada, 1986a, 1986b; Shor, 1987), process writing (Graves, 1983), cooperative learning (Kagan, 1986) and computer networking (Sayers, this volume) all embody the principles of interactive/experiential pedagogy.

The society implied by this type of education is one in which people have power, that is, control over their lives and the ability and confidence to make informed decisions about issues that affect their lives. When students do not experience this power within the classroom they will be less able to exercise it as adults, either in the workplace or in their personal lives.

CONCLUSION

It is clear that a pedagogy for the empowerment of ESL students is based on fundamentally different assumptions about the teaching-learning process than those that underlie the current educational reform movement. I have distinguished these two sets of assumptions in terms of interactive/experiential and transmission models of pedagogy. I have suggested that the academic difficulties of ESL students are, in part, a function of transmission models that exclude students' experience from the classroom and suppress the most basic function of language, namely, meaningful communication in both written and oral modes. Within this pedagogical orientation, students play their assigned role of receiving knowledge while teachers play their assigned role of transmitting it. Students and teachers are essentially passive in this process, both of them controlled and disempowered by higher levels of the educational hierarchy.

A practical "pedagogy for resistance" (see, e.g., Aronowitz & Giroux, 1985) designed to empower ESL students would incorporate at least two immediate goals. The long-term goal would be to rid the educational system of the straightjacket of standardized tests which, within the mandates of current conceptions of reform and accountability, essentially function as tools for the oppression of teachers and the suppression of learning.[1]

A more limited and perhaps more feasible goal would be for individ-

---

[1] Most U.S. educators take standardized tests so much for granted that they do not realize that most Canadian and European school systems do not assess their students in this way, because the narrow focus of such tests excludes important curriculum objectives related to topics such as critical thinking, creative writing, literature appreciation, and so forth.

ual educators and administrators to insist that any tests used in the school incorporate the full range of curriculum objectives emphasized within an interactive/experiential model of pedagogy. Thus, if commercial tests are not available that adequately assess objectives such as communicative use of language in both oral and written modalities, critical and creative thinking skills, cooperative problem solving, and so forth, then the school district itself should be pressured to develop such instruments, either as criterion- or norm-referenced tests. Such locally developed measures should be given at least as much weight in evaluation of students and teachers as the more restrictive commercial standardized tests.

In short, the process of reform must involve the individual classroom teacher and other professional educators actively challenging the educational structure within which they operate. When educators begin to critically analyze the forces that disempower them within the classroom, they automatically take the first steps toward the empowerment of their students.

REFERENCES

Ada, A. F. (1986a). *Creative reading: A relevant methodology for language minority children.* Unpublished paper, University of San Francisco.

Ada, A. F. (1986b). Creative education for bilingual teachers. *Harvard Educational Review, 56,* 386–394.

Albrecht, J. E. (1984). A Nation at Risk: Another view. *Phi Delta Kappan, 65,* 684–687.

Aronowitz, S., & Giroux, H. A. (1985). *Education under siege: The conservative, liberal and radical debate over schooling.* South Hadley, MA: Bergin and Garvey.

Bacharach, S. B., & Conley, S. C. (1986). Educational reform: A managerial agenda. *Phi Delta Kappan, 67,* 641–645.

Barnes, D. (1976). *From communication to curriculum.* Harmondsworth, England: Penguin.

Boyer, E. L. (1983). *High school: A report on secondary education in America.* New York: Harper & Row.

Bullock Report. (1975). *A language for life: Report of the committee of inquiry appointed by the Secretary of State for Education and Science under the chairmanship of Sir Alan Bullock.* London: HMSO.

Chomsky, C. (1981). Write now, read later. In C. Cazden (Ed.), *Language in early childhood education* (2nd ed., pp. 296–299). Washington, DC: National Association for the Education of Young Children.

Cohen, D. K. (1984). The conditions of teachers' work. *Harvard Educational Review, 54,* 11–15.

Cross, K. P. (1984). The rising tide of school reform reports. *Phi Delta Kappan, 66,* 167–172.

Cuban, L. (1984). School reform by remote control: SB 813 in California. *Phi Delta Kappan, 66*, 213–215.

Cummins, J. (1984). *Bilingualism and special education: Issues in assessment and pedagogy*. Clevedon, England: Multilingual Matters. Co-published in the United States by College-Hill Press, San Diego.

Cummins, J. (1986). Empowering minority students: A framework for intervention. *Harvard Education Review, 56*, 18–36.

Cummins, J. (1987). *Empowering minority students*. Monograph submitted for publication.

Dewey, J. (1963). *Experience and education*. New York: Collier Books. (Original work published 1938).

Freire, P. (1973). *Education for critical consciousness*. New York: Seabury.

Freire, P. (1983). Banking education. In H. Giroux & D. Purpel (Eds.), *The hidden curriculum and moral education: Deception or discovery?* Berkeley, CA: McCutcheon Publishing.

Giroux, H. A., & McLaren, P. (1986). Teacher education and the politics of engagement: The case for democratic schooling. *Harvard Educational Review, 56*, 213–238.

Goodlad, J. I. (1984). *A place called school: Prospects for the future*. New York: McGraw Hill.

Goodman, K. S., & Goodman, Y. M. (1977). Learning about psycholinguistic processes by analyzing oral reading. *Harvard Educational Review, 47*, 317–333.

Graves, D. (1983). *Writing: Children and teachers at work*. Exeter, NH: Heinemann.

Howe, H. (1984). Symposium on the year of the reports: Responses from the educational community. Introduction. *Harvard Educational Review, 54*, 1–5.

Jusenius, C., & Duarte, V. L. (1982) *Hispanics and jobs: Barriers to progress*. Washington, DC: National Commission for Employment Policy.

Kagan, S. (1986). Cooperative learning and sociocultural factors in schooling. In California State Department of Education (Ed.), *Beyond language: Social and cultural factors in schooling language minority students* (pp. 231–298). Los Angeles: California State University Evaluation, Dissemination, and Assessment Center.

Lauderdale, W. B. (1987). *Educational reform: The forgotten half.* Bloomington, IN: The Phi Delta Kappa Educational Foundation.

Lindfors, J. W. (1980). *Children's language and learning*. Englewood Cliffs, NJ: Prentice-Hall.

National Assessment of Educational Progress. (1981). *Literacy in America: A synopsis of National Assessment findings*. Denver: Education Commission of the States.

National Assessment of Educational Progress. (1986). *The writing report card: Writing achievement in American schools*. Princeton, NJ: NAEP.

National Commission on Excellence in Education. (1983). *A nation at risk: The imperative for educational reform*. Washington, DC: U.S Government Printing Office.

Ogbu, J. U. (1978). *Minority education and caste*. New York: Academic Press.

Ortiz, A. A., & Yates, J. R. (1983). Incidence of exceptionality among Hispanics: Implications for manpower planning. *NABE Journal, 7,* 41–54.

Passow, A. H. (1984). Tackling the reform reports of the 1980s. *Phi Delta Kappan, 65,* 674–683.

Peters, T. J., & Waterman, R. H. (1982). *In search of excellence: Lessons from America's best-run companies.* New York: Harper & Row.

Rickover, H. G. (1959). *Education and freedom.* New York: Dutton.

Sarason, S. B. (1983). *Schooling in America: Scapegoat or salvation.* New York: Free Press.

Seeley, D. S. (1985). Seymour Sarason and the problem of school change. *Harvard Educational Review, 55,* 342–353.

Shanker, A. (1987, January 14). Reforms need close look. *Education Week,* pp. 13–14.

Shor, I. (1987). *Critical teaching and everyday life.* Chicago: University of Chicago Press.

Sirotnik, K. A. (1983). What you see is what you get—consistency, persistency, and mediocrity in classrooms. *Harvard Educational Review, 53,* 16–31.

Sizer, T. R. (1984). *Horace's compromise: The dilemma of the American high school.* Boston: Houghton Mifflin.

Smith, F. (1978). *Understanding reading* (2nd ed.). New York: Holt Rinehart & Winston.

Stedman, L. C., & Kaestle, C. F. (1985). The test score decline is over: Now what? *Phi Delta Kappan, 67,* 204–210.

Wells, G. (1982). Language, learning and the curriculum. In G. Wells, *Language, learning and education.* Bristol: University of Bristol, Centre for the Study of Language and Communication.

Wells, G. (1986). *The meaning makers.* Portsmouth, NH: Heinemann.

Wiggins, S. P. (1986). Revolution in the teaching profession: A comparative review of two reform reports. *Educational Leadership, 44,* 56–59.

CHAPTER 2

Enriching Task Contexts for Second Language Writing: Power through Interpersonal Roles

Donna M. Johnson
University of Arizona

A stubborn continuity in the way teachers teach has persisted across decades. Traditional teacher-centered instruction, the most firmly entrenched teaching approach in the educational system, is rooted in many years of practice; young second language (L2) learners in elementary schools, as well as their monolingual peers, are recipients of this tradition. They spend their days in teacher-centered classrooms in which lecture, whole-class discussion, recitation, and individual seatwork prevail as the favored methods (Gage, 1985). Innovators have found it difficult to change these stable patterns. Yet theory and research in children's L2 acquisition in the last two decades indicate that these classroom interactional patterns may work against L2 development. Children's involvement in the meaningful and communicative use of language is central for both oral and written L2 development (Ellis, 1985; Krashen, 1985; Rigg & Enright, 1986; Wong Fillmore, 1985; Wong Fillmore & Valadez, 1986). But meaningful opportunities to understand and use their L2 occur less frequently for L2 learners when they must struggle to participate, along with fluent English speakers, in traditional, inflexible teacher-centered classrooms (Miller, 1982).

In this chapter I argue that teachers can empower students through explicit attention to and intentional modification of social role relationships in the writing tasks they arrange for students. By giving explicit attention to reader-writer social role relationships and consciously working to vary them, teachers can enrich written L2 use and thereby enhance development. I support these claims by providing converging evidence from linguistic theory, sociolinguistic theory, research in L2 use and acquisition, and studies of writing. In the second part of the chapter I provide specific suggestions for L2 writing activities.

A SOCIAL VIEW OF L2 USE

Teachers in most English as a second language (ESL) classes do not treat writing as a social activity focused on purposeful and meaningful communication with others. Yet a major part of the art and the science of L2 teaching in an elementary school should be to create the kinds of social contexts and conditions in which communicative interaction can and will flourish. Much recent research indicates that using and learning an L2 is a social activity; it is shaped by, and in turn affects, the social context of the classroom (Ellis, 1985; Enright & McCloskey, 1985; Fishman, 1977; Gaies, 1985; Johnson, 1983). We can view these school social contexts for L2 use at various levels. At the school level the contexts comprise the social and organizational structure of the school, various teachers and aides who work with children, various coexisting programs, other classrooms, and administrative structures (Chamot & O'Malley, 1987; Johnson, 1987; Penfield, 1987). The classroom social context includes features such as the roles and interactions of participants in the classroom. It also includes the way tasks for L2 use are organized socially.

Second language writing activities and writing development should be viewed as involving not only linguistic processes but social and cognitive processes as well (Edelsky, this volume; Urzua, 1987). These processes interact with one another and with features of the social context in complex ways that affect how students view L2 writing as well as how they develop as L2 writers. Just as children use a variety of cognitive, social, and linguistic strategies in learning to speak English as an additional language (Wong Fillmore & Swain, 1984), developing L2 writers also use various cognitive, social, and linguistic strategies to participate in the L2 literacy communities that they and their teachers create in the school environment. While researchers have studied social contexts for oral L2 use and development (Enright & McCloskey, 1985; Milk, 1985; Saville-Troike, 1984), few, until quite recently, have examined the social nature of L2 writing and the kinds of social contexts that enhance development.

The social structure for L2 writing assignments is usually limited to a common form of student–teacher interaction: the teacher initiates a topic, the students respond with a piece of writing, and the teacher responds to content and form. The teacher assumes the role of expert in content and language, the person with status who "knows," and the child remains in a subordinate role. For example, teachers often ask students to write a sentence or paragraph to practice using new vocabulary or a grammatical form, or they supply the first line of a paragraph about a reading in a content area and ask children to construct the rest of the paragraph. For many years teachers have used this common classroom interaction pattern for L2 students (Raimes, 1983). Yet relying on this pattern for L2 writing limits students' ways of using written language. To promote development in L2 literacy, we need to expand, not limit, students' ways of using written language to accomplish multiple purposes (Heath, 1986).

SOCIAL ROLES AND CLASSROOM DISCOURSE

In classroom contexts certain characteristics of oral and written language use tend to be linked to particular social roles that students and teachers enact. For example, researchers, through many studies of oral classroom discourse in monolingual classrooms, have documented teachers' tendency to rely on an initiation-response-evaluation (IRE) discourse structure as a kind of "unmarked" or "default" pattern for conducting lessons (see Cazden, 1986, 1987 for reviews). In this typical, three-part structure, teachers initiate questions (to which they usually already know the answers) in order to check students' knowledge, a student responds, and the student's response is evaluated with feedback from the teacher. This structure is linked to the roles teacher and students play; the teacher initiates and evaluates and the students respond. Similarly, researchers in L2 classrooms have demonstrated that teachers rely heavily on the use of the IRE structure and ask a high percentage of "known information" or "display" questions (Long, 1983). The "default" pattern, then, applies to oral interactions in L2 classrooms as well as to L1 classrooms. In fact, this interaction pattern may be more common for ESL students than for other, so-called mainstream, students (Farr, 1986).

However, research in both L1 and L2 use has illustrated that when students' social roles are expanded their language use changes accordingly. For example, Milk (1980) found that when students in bilingual classrooms worked in small groups, they talked more and produced a wider range of speech acts, particularly controlling and informing acts, than when they participated in teacher-directed instruction. Milk concluded that small-group settings can provide highly favorable contexts for L2 use, and that excessive teacher control of student talk may negatively affect language development because it limits the range of speech acts that children use. Long and Porter (1985) have summarized similar findings for the interlanguage talk of adult L2 learners.

Although these researchers examined spoken L2 discourse, their findings offer important implications for planning L2 writing experiences for ESL children. In both spoken and written language, the social roles that students play relate in systematic ways to the language they use. In reader-writer interactions, just as in conversational interactions, interpersonal factors in the context of situation are systematically related to the texts children create (Couture, 1986; Halliday & Hasan, 1985; Kreeft Peyton & Mackinson-Smyth, this volume; Williames, 1985). Placing students in limited roles as powerless responders will only lead to limited texts and limited growth.

POWER IN WRITTEN LANGUAGE USE

For L2 writers, we need to seek ways to expand their power as language users. Elbow (1981, p. viii) emphasizes two kinds of power in writing: (1) power over oneself in the writing process, and (2) control over the use of language as a communicative tool, as well as contact with and power over readers. For this discussion we will view the notion of power, in an L2 writing context, as a student's ability to obtain personal objectives through literacy events and written text. That the student's objectives are personal does not imply that they conflict with a teacher's goals. Skilled teachers attempt to arrange writing tasks in which their own teaching goals and students' agendas coincide. To help students gain power, in this view, teachers allow and encourage them to obtain and maintain a variety of personal objectives through their writing. These objectives might include, for example, receiving factual information they seek, influencing the social nature of classroom activities, finding out other children's opinions, or even changing school policy. Just as language use plays a crucial role in the attainment and/or exercise of personal power (Kedar, 1987), so do power and control in social relationships shape language use (Brown & Levinson, 1987, p. 33). It is to this issue that we now turn.

RELATIONSHIPS BETWEEN
SOCIAL ROLES AND TEXT

Children's social roles and the power attached to those roles, along with other features of the social context, shape language use. In functional views of language (Couture, 1986; Halliday & Hasan, 1985) the interpersonal role relationships among persons in a communicative situation (what Halliday and Hasan call "tenor of discourse") constitute one feature of the context of situation that is linked in a systematic way to the interpersonal semantic component of a text. These meanings are realized through particular grammatical and lexical choices. What writers convey and how they convey it depend partly, then, on their intentions with regard to the interpersonal relationships with persons involved in the literacy event. As Halliday and Hasan point out, these relationships might be either relatively permanent (teacher–student, for example) or temporary (group leader, for example). The importance of role relations in language use is so powerful, in fact, that Bell (1984) proposes, for sociolinguistic theory, that stylistic or intraspeaker variation can be accounted for through the notion of "audience design"; that is, style is essentially speakers' response to their audiences (p. 145). Similarly, researchers and theorists in composition and literacy have considered issues of audience an important topic of study because how writers construe, adapt to, and interact with their audiences influences not only style, but also writing quality (Edelsky, 1986; Elbow, 1981; Graves, 1983; Hillocks, 1986; Piché & Roen, 1987; Roen & Willey, 1988; Rubin, 1984).

Much recent work in L2 writing emphasizes the importance of having children write on a variety of topics, to a variety of audiences, for a variety of purposes (e.g., Hudelson, 1986). In addition, scholars urge teachers to engage students in creating a broad array of written texts, particularly genre structures (Halliday & Hasan, 1985, p. 69; Heath, 1986; Moffett, 1968). To empower ESL students in their use of written language, we also need to focus our attention on the role relationships that define tenor in the context of situation. We need to help students assume an appropriate variety of social roles as they use written language and the related oral language to accomplish various purposes. Richness in language use relates in part to the power involved in different social interactional roles, and increased power through a broader range of roles can result in richer language use in teacher-planned writing tasks, as well as richer language use in the unstructured, informal writing that occurs in classrooms. To gain control over a range of ways of using written language, and to achieve their social purposes, students need to learn to effectively and appropriately handle the demands of writing from varying positions on the dimension of interpersonal power. The implication for instruction is that we need to expand the range of social roles we allow and ask students to assume as L2 writers.

VARYING SOCIAL ROLES IN L2 WRITING

Teachers can vary social roles in writing tasks in many ways. I discuss three approaches that have value for L2 writing development: (1) arranging for student control of topics, (2) building on students' social agendas to link social and academic writing goals, (3) arranging for students to be teachers.

Control of Topic: The Comparative or the Carnival?

One way to give students some control is to allow and encourage them to take the initiative in generating topics for writing. If such a goal is not an explicit part of ESL instruction, however, many marvelous opportunities to empower students slip by. An example from an ESL program I recently evaluated illustrates this point. As I observed an ESL aide delivering an oral and written (worksheet) lesson focusing on the use of the comparative degree in adjectives to a small group of elementary school students, one boy began to tell her in animated Spanish about a carnival he had gone to over the weekend. Interested, she asked a few questions about it in Spanish, then returned to her drills on the comparative. Here was an excellent, but missed, opportunity to create a fascinating literary activity focusing on a topic from the child's own social and cultural life. Clearly this child was intensely interested in this topic and no doubt had much to say and write about it. I imagine that the richness of his production in isolated sentences aimed at mastering the comparative would not compare with what he might have created in writing about his carnival experience. Teachers need to intentionally structure situations in which children write about issues in which they are interested and about which they are informed and motivated to inform others. Part of this process involves capitalizing on those issues that emerge out of the students' own interests. As Graves (1986) has put it, we need to let children follow their "obsessions." These notions are consistent with current theories of socially constructed L2 curricula (see Breen, 1987, for example).

Mounting evidence from research in both oral and written language development suggests that a sense of control in using language contributes to richness in language use and better writing. Although there is little direct evidence from research in L2 writing, the value of giving ESL children some control in topic selection can be supported by work in L1 writing by Graves (1983), Calkins (1987), Atwell (1987), and others, and indirectly by research in oral L2 use. Scholars do not often link these two bodies of research; yet, to the extent that many of the processes involved in written L2 use and development are similar to those involved in oral L2 use and development, theory and research in one area can inform the other area.

Research in L2 acquisition indicates that development occurs as learners attempt to make sense when they comprehend and produce oral and written discourse (Ellis, 1985, p. 268). L2 development involves a gradual process of working out relationships between forms and functions encountered and used in a variety of meaningful contexts (Ellis, 1985, pp. 75–98). It is important for development, therefore, that language-use contexts be rich and varied. Cathcart's (1986; Cathcart-Strong, 1986) interesting work in situational variation in L2 use provides linguistic support for the notion that power, in the form of child-controlled conversational interactions, is associated with richness in language use. She studied L2 kindergarten children in a variety of situations with monolingual English speaking peers and adults and found that, when L2 children had control in conversational interactions, they produced a wider variety of communicative acts and syntactic structures in English. Her observations suggest that oral L2 use can vary as a function of the control dimension of interpersonal relationships, with richer functional and grammatical use associated with higher degrees of control. It is not difficult to see how these relationships between personal control and grammatical and functional aspects of linguistic production may also hold in written communication. In the most directly interactive kinds of writing, done in the context of literacy events that involve several modes of language use, ways of using both written and oral language will tend to be closely linked. Consequently, relationships that hold for oral language may hold for the associated written language.

Many scholars have emphasized that a sense of control over topics, subject matter, and meanings to be conveyed helps promote writing development (Goodman, 1986; Graves, 1986; Raimes, 1983; Zamel, 1982). Children do have a great deal of control over topics in interactive journal writing, and researchers have begun to document, in both formal and informal projects, the successful use of such journals for ESL students' writing development (Hayes, Bahruth, & Kessler, 1986; Kreeft, Shuy, Staton, Reed, & Morroy, 1984; Spack & Sadow, 1983). For some children, in fact, journals may provide the only means by which they initiate communicative interactions in English. Journals create a channel for communication that can accommodate personality differences among children who are just beginning to learn English. Reed (1986), for example, has written about a Vietnamese child's willingness to interact with his teacher in a dialogue journal long before he was willing to do so orally in front of classmates (see also Kitagawa, this volume). Similarly, Hughes (1986) provides a brief report of a child who, once his interest was captured in interactive journal writing, made impressive progress in reading and writing in his ESL pullout class.

Urzua (1987) also writes of the value of a sense of control in selecting topics. For six months she examined the oral and written interactions and texts of four Southeast Asian children who participated in writing activities such as dialogue journal writing and peer response groups. She observed that when children chose their own topics, their own voices came through more strongly and they were more effective writers. She found that allowing students some control over topics gave them the freedom to build on their own knowledge and to share that knowledge with others. Interest in their own topics led to richness in their writing.

Written conversations on computer networks can give children ownership of topics and can have benefits for L2 use and learning. Children can interact about social matters or academic matters, later discussing and analyzing their own written production (Kreeft Peyton & Mackinson-Smyth, this volume). They can also engage in journalism projects in which they write articles to be read by others, and negotiate tasks and strategies with distant audiences (Mehan, Moll, & Reil, 1985; Sayers, this volume). Collaborative writing tasks on topics that capture children's interest can also provide supportive contexts for L2 development. Through collaboration each child contributes to the text, negotiates meaning in the L2, and learns from the others (Daiute, 1986).

Giving students some control in selecting topics they write about represents no more than common sense to many teachers, and ample theoretical and empirical evidence supports the notion that unfamiliar topics negatively affect writing quality. Yet teachers do not always use this common sense and research knowledge with young ESL students. Because of former ideas about avoiding errors and strictly sequencing the L2 curriculum, some teachers are hesitant to let go of old guidelines and adopt new ones based on better information about language learning. To enrich L2 writing experiences and L2 learning we need to allow and encourage children to build on what they know, we need to appreciate what they want to learn about, and we need to structure tasks that give them freedom to take risks in drawing on their L2 competence to create their own new meanings. These goals should be explicitly central to a school's plan for second language and literacy development.

Building on Students' Social Purposes

Understanding and building upon children's social purposes for communicating through writing further empowers them and enriches their writing. Teachers can do this by observing the informal writing that children do. Dyson's (1987) ethnographic work in this area is particularly relevant for L2 learners. She has noticed in her observations of ethnically diverse classrooms that children construct an "underground writing curriculum" in addition to the teacher's agenda for writing. For example, children pass notes, copy stories, draw pictures, and write letters to one another. Dyson also describes ways in which children "unintentionally" help each other learn by monitoring one another and talking about various features of writing. They discuss spelling conventions, stylistic techniques, and even criteria for what makes good fiction. They do all of this, she points out, because they value writing, as does the teacher, and they want to establish and maintain their group membership as well as their own individuality (Dyson, 1987). Teachers, then, can recognize and incorporate these activities into their planning rather than separating children's academic and social lives. Dyson suggests that teachers can build on peer social networks and the lively unofficial writing curriculum to create academic structures that support growth in written language. Atwell (1987), for example, asks junior high students to write notes and letters to one another about books they are reading. Dyson and Atwell worked in monolingual classrooms, but the principles they used could also enhance writing tasks in an additional language. Teachers of ESL students can encourage drawing, talking, thinking, and sharing in L2 writing activities. Encouraging collaboration among students in pairs and small groups and establishing a postal system with student mailboxes effectively work toward these goals.

The interconnectedness among these three factors—how children react informally, how teachers structure communicative tasks, and how children develop in their L2—has theoretical importance and has been the subject of investigation in research on oral L2 acquisition. For example, we know that the way teachers structure oral content-based communicative tasks for monolingual English speakers and ESL children can influence the social-interactional environment of the classroom, resulting in ESL children's increased or decreased use of English (August, 1982; Johnson, 1983, 1988). Similarly, we may expect to find in future research on L2 writing that the way teachers structure literacy events involving reader-writer interactions between monolingual English writers and their bilingual or multilingual peers will affect L2 underground writing activities. If this proves to be the case, we need to take advantage of these potential relationships in several ways. First, we need to observe and build on the underground L2 writing activities that students engage in, as Dyson suggests for the settings she studied. Second, we need to interweave social and academic purposes for writing in the L2 by creating activities that work with, rather than against, the written communication that goes on in informal social interaction. And third, we need to create activities that will contribute to and enrich the informal communication system. A recognition of, and an intentional plan to build on, the interconnectedness of these factors should contribute significantly to development in L2 writing. These principles would be difficult to address in a static, rigid ESL program model. They can be important features of a more dynamic and flexible plan for L2 development that is built on a recognition of the importance of social factors in second language use and development.

Children as Teachers

I have mentioned traditional writing assignments in which children have little power, as well as tasks in which they have relatively equal status with peers. I have proposed that as we vary the amount of power children have in a communicative interaction, the language they use varies, and that to enrich writing we need to systematically increase children's power in reader-writer interactions. We can further increase their control in an L2 literacy event, and encourage them to achieve their purposes, by structuring situations in which children step into the role of teacher. As teachers or leaders, children have high status, their expertise is respected, and they have certain functions to carry out. Their role is then realized in the language they use.

It is difficult for some teachers to accept the suggestion that the child, especially the ESL child, can sometimes assume the role of teacher. Yet many teachers have used this kind of social structuring with success, and research supports the practice. Steinberg and Cazden (1979), for example, implemented and studied peer tutoring in "instructional chains." In this situation a child teaches to another child a concept or activity that he or she has learned from the teacher. Steinberg and Cazden report that children in their study display "surprising competence" in using language appropriately to deal with peer teaching tasks outside the teacher's direct control. Children were able to use their own versions of "teacher talk" in sophisticated and appropriate ways to accomplish multiple functions (p. 260). Steinberg and Cazden point out that teachers often underestimate children's competence, particularly when the children are not yet fluent English speakers. Yet after observing their students performing competently as teachers and using teacher-like register, the teachers drastically raised their estimations of what their students could do. "When we give children the chance to teach each other, if we truly examine how they do it, they can teach not only each other but us as well" (Steinberg & Cazden, 1979, p. 265; see also Díaz, Moll, & Mehan, 1986; Kitagawa, this volume).

Other studies of reciprocal and peer teaching provide support for the benefits of having ESL students assume the role of teachers. We found in two studies of L2 acquisition that children acquiring ESL could be competent teachers, successfully teaching a science or art activity to a fluent English speaking peer. After learning how to carry out the activity in teacher-led groups of peers, an ESL child assumed the role of teacher and taught the activity to a monolingual English speaking peer. ESL children who assumed the role of teacher showed statistically significant increases in L2 vocabulary comprehension (August, 1982; Johnson, 1983, 1988) compared to control groups in which ESL children did not teach their peers. For L2 writing, children can produce a set of instructions for other children to follow based on knowledge that they alone possess and wish to share, such as a recipe from a grandmother (see Kitagawa, this volume, for examples).

Teachers and researchers have successfully improved reading comprehension using a different model of reciprocal teaching. Palinscar and Brown (1984) conducted a number of reciprocal teaching experiments aimed at improving reading comprehension. In their model of reciprocal teaching, based on interpretations of Vygotsky's (1978) theories as well as concepts of expert scaffolding, an adult guides students to interact with a text in gradually more complex ways with students alternately assuming teaching roles. The teacher and students take turns generating summaries and questions, clarifying complex sections of texts, and making predictions about what might happen next. Students who engaged in reciprocal teaching performed better on a variety of measures of comprehension and production. Their teachers, skeptical at first about their students' ability to participate in reciprocal teaching, were impressed with the students' progress.

Students can assume the role of teacher in a variety of other L2 writing activities. Recall that power, as I am defining it for this chapter, refers to a child's ability to obtain objectives through what he or she writes. These objectives could relate to a peer, a teacher, or a community member. To accomplish objectives in relation to peers, children can engage in the peer review process in pairs or small groups. Peer review has strong theoretical bases and has come to be widely used (Gere, 1987; Gere & Stevens, 1985; Nystrand, 1986; Urzua, 1987). After reading or listening to another child's writing, children can write questions, stating what else they would like to know or what they would like clarified, for example, about a peer's paper. They may then see the information provided in a subsequent draft, accomplishing their purposes of finding out something and helping a peer improve his or her piece. L2 teachers can extend Palinscar and Brown's highly structured concept of reciprocal teaching to more creative L2 writing activities. For example, students can alternate leadership roles to direct writing activities centered on reading, activities such as predicting, constructing questions, summarizing, and so on, either with pencils or with computers as their writing tools. In other kinds of tasks, students can write instructions to other students for engaging in activities. Jigsaw tasks (Kagan, 1986) and report writing, in which children each have information that they teach to others to accomplish a joint goal, can be carried out using a great deal of L2 writing. Students can also write on a cultural topic on which they are expert in order to inform others, particularly an interested teacher (Freeman & Freeman, this volume;

Kitagawa, this volume). ESL students who develop computer expertise can serve as resources to teachers and peers through what they write. When students are in teaching, informing roles, they are viewed as experts; they feel a sense of responsibility to be accurate, interesting, persuasive, and appropriate. These roles motivate them to use language appropriate to the role.

Children studying English as a second language can teach not only their peers and their teachers but also others outside the school. Calkins (1987) has suggested that "writing isn't desk work but life work" and that for every writing task in which we engage students we need to ask: What might this become and where is it going to go? She suggests that to empower students, their writing needs to go beyond the folders or the board or the class library so that they can see its consequences. They can enter contests, inform community members, or give written work as gifts. In one school children wrote to a publisher to request paper for their school—a real purpose to achieve a real objective. The students of a local bilingual education teacher wrote to the Secretary of Education after he visited their class to inform him about bilingual classes and to urge his support. When children can see the effect of their writing on others, whether peers, teachers, or community leaders, they are motivated to use their L2 resources.

CONCLUSION

I have argued that L2 teachers need to adopt a more social interactional view of writing, recognizing that for L2 children, writing is best approached as communicative interaction that takes place in a defined context. To empower students in their use of written language it is useful to focus our attention on enriching the task contexts for writing, especially the role relationships that define tenor in the context of the writing situation. We need to help students assume a broader variety of social roles as they use written language to accomplish their purposes. I've provided evidence supporting the view that when children have more control or power in social interactional roles, when they are given opportunities to use language from varying positions on the power dimension, richer language use results. I've suggested also that teachers can promote richer language use in assigned tasks by building on children's social purposes and the informal, "underground" writing in which children engage. To promote the development of L2 writing we need to systematically expand the range of social roles, including the more powerful ones, we allow and encourage students to assume in writing activities.

REFERENCES

Atwell, N. (1987). *In the middle: Writing, reading, and learning with adolescents.* Portsmouth, NH: Heinemann.

August, D. L. (1982). *The effects of peer tutoring on the second-language acquisition of Hispanic elementary school children.* Unpublished doctoral dissertation, Stanford University.

Bell, A. (1984). Language style as audience design. *Language in Society, 13,* 145–204.

Breen, M. P. (1987). Contemporary paradigms in syllabus design. Part II. *Language Teaching, 20* (2), 157–174.

Brown, P., & Levinson, S. C. (1987). *Politeness: Some universals in language usage.* Studies in Interactional Sociolinguistics 4. Cambridge: Cambridge University Press.

Calkins, L. (1987, November). *Writing with purpose and consequence.* Paper presented at the meeting of the National Council of Teachers of English, Los Angeles.

Cathcart, R. (1986). Situational differences and the sampling of young children's school language. In R. R. Day (Ed.), *Talking to learn: Conversation in second language acquisition* (pp. 118–140). Rowley, MA: Newbury.

Cathcart-Strong, R. (1986). Input generation by young second language learners. *TESOL Quarterly, 20,* 515–530.

Cazden, C. B. (1986). Classroom discourse. In M. C. Wittrock (Ed.), *Handbook of research on teaching* (3rd ed., pp. 432–463). New York: Macmillan.

Cazden, C. B. (1987). Language in the classroom. In R. B. Kaplan (Ed.), *Annual Review of Applied Linguistics (Vol. 7)* (pp. 18–33). Cambridge: Cambridge University Press.

Chamot, A. U., & O'Malley, J. M. (1987). The cognitive academic language learning approach: A bridge to the mainstream. *TESOL Quarterly, 21,* 227–249.

Couture, B. (1986). *Functional approaches to writing: Research perspectives.* Norwood, NJ: Ablex.

Daiute, C. (1986). Do 1 and 1 make two? Patterns of influence by collaborative authors. *Written Communication, 3,* 382–408.

Díaz, S., Moll, L. C., & Mehan, H. (1986). Sociocultural resources in instruction: A context-specific approach. In California State Department of Education (Ed.), *Beyond language: Social and cultural factors in schooling language minority students* (pp. 143–186). Los Angeles: California State University, Evaluation, Dissemination and Assessment Center.

Dyson, A. H. (1987). *Unintentional helping in the primary grades: Writing in the children's world* (Tech. Report No. 8). Berkeley: University of California, Center for the Study of Writing.

Edelsky, C. (1986). *Writing in a bilingual program: Había una vez.* Norwood, NJ: Ablex.

Elbow, P. (1981). *Writing with power.* New York: Oxford University Press.

Ellis, R. (1985). *Understanding second language acquisition.* Oxford: Oxford University Press.

Enright, D. S., & McCloskey, M. L. (1985). Yes talking! Organizing the classroom to promote second language acquisition. *TESOL Quarterly, 19,* 431–453.

Farr, M. (1986). Language, culture, and writing: Sociolinguistic foundations of research on writing. In E. Z. Rothkopf (Ed.), *Review of research in education* (Vol. 13, pp. 195–223). Washington, DC: American Educational Research Association.

Fishman, J. A. (1977). The social science perspective. In Center for Applied Linguistics (Ed.), *Bilingual education: Current perspectives* (Vol. 1, pp. 1–49). Arlington, VA: Center for Applied Linguistics.

Gage, N. L. (1985). *Hard gains in the soft sciences: The case of pedagogy.* Bloomington, IN: Phi Delta Kappa.

Gaies, S. (1985). *Peer involvement in language learning.* Orlando, FL: Harcourt.

Gere, A. R. (1987). *Writing groups: History, theory, and implications.* Carbondale: Southern Illinois University Press.

Gere, A. R., & Stevens, R. S. (1985). The language of writing groups: How oral response shapes revision. In S. W. Freedman (Ed.), *The acquisition of written language: Response and revision* (pp. 85–105). Norwood, NJ: Ablex.

Goodman, K. (1986). *What's whole in whole language?* Portsmouth, NH: Heinemann.

Graves, D. (1983). *Writing: Teachers and children at work.* Portsmouth, NH: Heinemann.

Graves, D. (1986, November). *Reading and writing power for teachers, for kids: Resources, reflections, beginnings.* Keynote address presented at the Teachers Applying Whole Language Conference, Tucson, AZ.

Halliday, M. A. K., & Hasan, R. (1985). *Language, context, and text: Aspects of language in a social-semiotic perspective.* Victoria, Australia: Deakin University.

Hayes, C. W., Bahruth, R., & Kessler, C. (1986). The dialogue journal and migrant education. *Dialogue, 3* (3), 3–5.

Heath, S. B. (1986). Sociocultural contexts of language development. In California State Department of Education (Ed.), *Beyond language: Social and cultural factors in schooling language minority students* (pp. 143–186). Los Angeles: California State University, Evaluation, Dissemination and Assessment Center.

Hillocks, G., Jr. (1986). *Research on written composition: New directions for teaching.* Urbana, IL: National Conference on Research in English and ERIC.

Hudelson, S. (1986). ESL children's writing: What we've learned, what we're learning. In P. Rigg & D. S. Enright (Eds.), *Children and ESL: Integrating perspectives* (pp. 23–54). Washington, DC: Teachers of English to Speakers of Other Languages.

Hughes, L. (1986). Making language connections: Writing in ESL pull-out classes. *Dialogue, 3*(2), 6–7.

Johnson, D. M. (1983). Natural language learning by design: A classroom experiment in social interaction and second language acquisition. *TESOL Quarterly, 17,* 55–68.

Johnson, D. M. (1987). The organization of instruction in migrant education: Assistance for children and youth at risk. *TESOL Quarterly, 21,* 437–459.

Johnson, D. M. (1988). ESL children as teachers: A social view of second language use. *Language Arts, 65*(2), 154–163.

Kagan, S. (1986). Cooperative learning and sociocultural factors in schooling. In California State Department of Education (Ed.), *Beyond language: Social and cultural factors in schooling language minority students* (pp. 143–186). Los Angeles: California State University, Evaluation, Dissemination and Assessment Center.

Kedar, L. (1987). *Power through discourse*. Norwood, NJ: Ablex.

Krashen, S. (1985). *The input hypothesis: Issues and implications*. New York: Longman.

Kreeft, J., Shuy, R. W., Staton, J., Reed, L., & Morroy, R. (1984). *Dialogue writing: Analysis of student-teacher interactive writing in the learning of English as a second language* (Report No. 83-0030). Washington, DC: National Institute of Education. (ERIC Document Reproduction Service No. ED 252 097)

Long, M. (1983). Native speaker/non-native speaker conversation in the second language classroom. In M. A. Clarke & J. Handscombe (Eds.), *On TESOL '82: Pacific perspectives on language learning and teaching* (pp. 207–225). Washington, DC: Teachers of English to Speakers of Other Languages.

Long, M. & Porter, P. (1985). Group work, interlanguage talk, and second language acquisition. *TESOL Quarterly, 19,* 207–228.

Mehan, H., Moll, L., & Reil, M. (1985, June). *Computers in classrooms: A quasi-experiment in guided change*. Final report to the National Institute of Education. La Jolla, CA: University of California, San Diego.

Milk, R. (1980). *Variation in language use patterns across different group settings in two bilingual second grade classrooms*. Unpublished doctoral dissertation, Stanford University.

Milk, R. (1985). The changing role of ESL in bilingual education. *TESOL Quarterly, 19,* 657–670.

Miller, W. (1982). Language learning opportunities in bilingual and all-English classrooms. In L. Wong Fillmore & S. Ervin-Tripp (Eds.), *Sources of individual differences in second language learning*. Berkeley: University of California.

Moffett, J. (1968). *Teaching the universe of discourse*. Boston: Houghton Mifflin.

Nystrand, M. (1986). *The structure of written communication: Studies in reciprocity between writers and readers*. Orlando, FL: Academic Press.

Palinscar, A. S., & Brown, A. L. (1984). Reciprocal teaching of comprehension-fostering and comprehension-monitoring activities. *Cognition and Instruction, 1,* 117–175.

Penfield, J. (1987). ESL: The regular classroom teacher's perspective. *TESOL Quarterly, 21,* 21–39.

Piché, G. L., & Roen, D. H. (1987). Social cognition and writing: Interpersonal cognitive complexity and abstractness and the quality of students' persuasive writing. *Written Communication, 4,* 68–89.

Raimes, A. (1983). Tradition and revolution in ESL teaching. *TESOL Quarterly, 17,* 535–552.

Reed, L. (1986). Sheltered English applied to writing, *Dialogue, 3*(2), 3–4.

Rigg, P., & Enright, D. S. (1986). *Children and ESL: Integrating perspectives*.

Washington, DC: Teachers of English to Speakers of Other Languages.

Roen, D. H., & Willey, R. J. (1988). The effects of audience awareness on drafting and revising. *Research in the Teaching of English, 22,* 75–88.

Rubin, D. L. (1984). Social cognition and written communication. *Written Communication, 1,* 211–245.

Saville-Troike, M. (1984). What really matters in second language learning for academic achievement? *TESOL Quarterly, 18,* 199–219.

Spack, R., & Sadow, C. (1983). Student-teacher working journals in ESL freshman composition. *TESOL Quarterly, 17,* 575–593.

Steinberg, D., & Cazden, C. (1979). Children as teachers—of peers and ourselves. *Theory into Practice, 18,* 258–266.

Urzua, C. (1987). "You stopped too soon": Second language children composing and revising. *TESOL Quarterly, 21,* 279–297.

Vygotsky, L. S. (1978). *Mind in society: The development of higher psychological processes.* (M. Cole, V. John-Steiner, S. Scribner, & E. Souberman, Eds. and Trans.). Cambridge, MA: Harvard University Press.

Williames, J. (1985). The interactive nature of the newspaper letter. *M.A.L.S. Journal, 10,* 108–140.

Wong Fillmore, L. (1985). When does teacher talk work as input? In S. M. Gass & C. G. Madden (Eds.), *Input in second language acquisition* (pp. 17–50). Rowley, MA: Newbury.

Wong, Fillmore, L., & Swain, M. (1984, March). *Second language acquisition in children: Theoretical perspectives from the field.* State-of-the-art paper presented at the Research Symposium of the 18th Annual Meeting of TESOL, Houston.

Wong Fillmore, L., & Valadez, C. (1986). Teaching bilingual learners. In M. C. Wittrock (Ed.), *Handbook of research on teaching* (3rd ed., pp. 648–685). New York: Macmillan.

Zamel, V. (1983). Writing: The process of discovering meaning. *TESOL Quarterly, 16,* 195–209.

CHAPTER 3

Teaching Second Language Students: A Vygotskian Perspective

Luis C. Moll
University of Arizona

This chapter examines practical implications of the ideas of L. S. Vygotsky for the teaching of writing to ESL students. Much has been written recently about Vygotsky, and several excellent accounts of his work are available (see, e.g., Cole, 1985; Kozulin, 1986; Laboratory of Comparative Human Cognition, 1983; Minick, 1985; Riviere, 1984; Vygotsky, 1978, in press; Wertsch, 1985a, 1985b). Therefore, rather than present a general account of his theory, I elaborate upon one of his major theoretical concepts, the zone of proximal development, and illustrate its pedagogic potential through the use of examples gathered from classroom observations. I begin with an overview of Vygotsky's ideas. I then review the concept of the zone of proximal development, relating it to other aspects of Vygotsky's theory. The point here is to avoid divorcing the concept, as an analytic unit, from major elements of Vygotsky's approach. Following this discussion of the zone, I present examples from recent classroom research that illustrate why I think this theoretical concept is of great importance to the schooling of limited English proficient children. Instead of presenting the zone as an individual construct, I stress thinking of the zone as a collective construct—that is, as a way of helping teachers think about the social organization of instruction and assess the cognitive consequences of their arrangements.

A VYGOTSKIAN PERSPECTIVE

Vygotsky built on the idea that human beings are thoroughly social. From the moment of birth we enter into social relations that shape and mold us, relations that make us complex and dynamic *social* individuals. Our lives emerge and develop through activities that these social relations create or facilitate, and it is also through social relations that we influence and change others.

Vygotsky emphasized that human learning is always mediated through others, such as parents, peers, and teachers, and these interactions themselves are mediated. Humans use cultural tools and artifacts (e.g., speech, literacy, mathematics, computers) to mediate their interactions with each other and with their surroundings. These artifacts, as Vygotsky observed, are social in origin and use. A fundamental property of these tools is that they are first used to communicate with others, to mediate contact with our social worlds; later, with practice, much of it occurring in schools, as we use these tools to mediate our interactions with self, to help us think, we internalize their use. Therefore, from a Vygotskian perspective, a major role of schooling is to create social contexts for mastery of and conscious awareness in the use of these cultural tools. It is by mastering these technologies of representation and communication (Olson, 1986) that individuals acquire the capacity, the means, for independent intellectual activity: what Vygotsky called higher psychological functions. Thus, Vygotskian theory posits a strong, dialectic connection between external (social), practical activity mediated by the use of cultural tools, such as speech and writing, and individuals' intellectual activity.

Vygotsky's point, however, wasn't solely to remind us of the social- and tool-mediated nature of learning. His claim was much more context specific: The intellectual skills children acquire are directly related to how they interact with others in specific problem-solving environments. He posited that children internalize and transform the kind of help they receive from others and eventually use these same means of guidance to direct their own subsequent problem-solving behaviors. In Vygotskian terms, the same mediational means are used interpsychologically (in communication) and intrapsychologically (in thinking). Here his concept of the zone of proximal development becomes important.

Clarifying the Zone

Vygotsky (1978) defined the zone of proximal development in a deceptively simple way: the distance between the actual developmental level as determined by individual problem solving and the level of potential development as determined through problem solving under adult guidance or in collaboration with more capable peers (p. 86). The idea, put briefly, is that children differ in their current state of development in ways that cannot be determined by techniques that only analyze their performance when working alone (Minick, in press). The essence of this concept, and its importance for ESL instruction, is the qualitatively different perspective one gets by contrasting a student's performance alone with his or her performance in collaborative activity. It is important to keep in mind that both individual tests or tasks and collaborative activities are ways of sampling students' behaviors in specific contexts; therefore, one may think of the zone as referring to the importance of considering contextual variability in assessing performance. Vygotsky, in part, developed the concept to counter the uses of static measures, such as IQ tests, in determining children's abilities. The zone, then, in my interpretation, is a way of building diversity into assessment practices; it functions as a safeguard against underestimation of students' intellectual capabilities when assessed through standard, static measures or when observed in highly constrained instructional environments.

Vygotsky also drew instructional implications from his concept. He suggested that instruction should be directed at students' proximal development, at the future, at behaviors in development. The role of teachers, be they adults or peers, is to create and support social activities that help students to master behaviors that are in advance of what they can already perform independently. That is, from a zone or proximal development perspective, instruction should lead students, stretch them, be prospective, create models of the future. Thus, in this view, the zone facilitates a critical assessment of the individual and of the social system created for the individual to learn. It provides teachers, as I will argue below, with a much more realistic and positive view of children's "potential for instruction," to use Vygotsky's term; a potential that is revealed most clearly by children's strengths as displayed in collaborative activities, as opposed to weaknesses manifested in individual or static assessments (Cole & Griffin, 1983; Díaz, Moll, & Mehan, 1986).

The Zone in Context

I now discuss three aspects of Vygotsky's theory to clarify how I am using the concept here and how it fits into Vygotsky's more general framework (for more elaborate discussions, see Griffin & Cole, 1984; Minick, in press; Wertsch, 1984).

Whole Activity. Among the most neglected aspects of Vygotsky's theory, particularly as it relates to applications of the zone, are his warnings against atomistic, reductionist approaches (see Vygotsky, in press). He argued against reducing the phenomenon of interest, whatever it may be, into separate elements that are studied in isolation; instead, he insisted on the study of what we could call "whole activities." For example, he wrote as follows:

> . . . a psychology that decomposes verbal thinking into its elements in an attempt to explain its characteristics will search in vain for the unity that is characteristic of the whole. These characteristics are inherent in the phenomenon only as a unified whole. Therefore, when the whole is analyzed into its elements, these characteristics evaporate. In his attempt to reconstruct these characteristics, the investigator is left with no alternative but to search for external, mechanical forces of interaction between elements. (Vygotsky, in press, p. 9)

Accordingly, he proposed partitioning the whole into what he called units. In contrast to atomistic elements, units designated a product of analysis that possess all the basic characteristics of the whole. The unit, then, is a vital and irreducible part of the whole.

It is important to consider how this proposition relates to the concept of the zone of proximal development. One way is to reject conceptualizing the zone as the teaching or assessment of discrete, separable skills and subskills. As Cole and Griffin (1983) have pointed out, from a Vygotskian or sociohistorical perspective,

> We should be trying to instantiate a basic *activity* [italics added] when teaching reading and not get blinded by the basic *skills*. Skills are always part of activities and settings, but they only take on meaning in terms of how they are organized. So, instead of *basic skills,* a sociohistorical approach talks about basic activities and instantiates those that are necessary and sufficient to carry out the whole process of reading in the general conditions of learning. (p. 73)

The same point about basic activities applies to the teaching of writing or other subject matter (see Moll & Díaz, 1987; for a compatible perspective, see Edelsky, this volume; Freeman & Freeman, this volume; Goodman, 1986; Hudelson, this volume). It is easy to miss this point when applying the concept of the zone to the study of classroom learning because a "skills" perspective is so pervasive that, as Edelsky (1986) points out, it is taken for granted that those skills and subskills are instantiations of literacy. By focusing on isolated skills and subskills, the essence of reading or writing as a "whole activity" evaporates, to use Vygotsky's metaphor. Within this skills context, as we have written elsewhere (Moll & Díaz, in press), it is very easy to underestimate the ability of LEP or ESL students and to assume that they cannot engage in advanced English literacy activities until they master lower order basic skills, such as decoding. The intellectual level of lessons, therefore, is constrained accordingly.

The first step, then, in creating a zone of proximal development for writing is to make sure that writing takes place as a whole activity; activities in which the full social and communicative goals of writing should always be present.

Mediation. Vygotsky placed great emphasis on the nature of the interaction between adult and child, particularly as it relates to formal instruction. He wrote about the "unique form of cooperation between the child and the adult that is the central element of the educational process," and how by this interactional process "knowledge is transferred to the child in a definite system" (Vygotsky, in press, p. 156). Thus, central to his concept of the zone are the specific ways that adults (or peers) socially mediate or interactionally create circumstances for learning.

It would be misleading to claim, however, that Vygotsky's emphasis on adult mediation means that the adult is active and the child is a passive recipient of the adult's machinations. On the contrary, central to his analysis is the view of the child as an active organism helping create the very circumstances for his or her own learning. He wrote:

> a central feature of the psychological study of instruction is the *potential the child has to raise himself* to a higher intellectual level of development through collaboration. . . . The zone of proximal development determines the domain of transitions that are accessible to the child. (Vygotsky, in press, p. 206, emphasis added)

He viewed children as active learners and the teacher as a mediator who provides children, through both oral and written communications, with the means necessary, with the assistance, to perform intellectual activities. Social mediations, therefore, constitute the zone of proximal development and represent the central unit of analysis within this framework.

It is thus incorrect to think of the zone as solely a characteristic of the child or of the teaching, but rather of the child engaged in collaborative activity within specific social environments. The focus is on the social system within which we hope children learn, with the understanding that this social system is mutually and actively created by teacher and students. Central to a Vygotskian analysis of teaching is recognizing how the adult, through the mechanism of social interactions, creates and regulates those social systems for learning that we call lessons.

Change. The most common way to conceptualize change within a zone of proximal development is as individual change—that the child is able to do something independently today that he could do only with assistance yesterday. This is what I call the "transmission" or the "transfer" model of the zone, and it is in part Vygotsky's examples that have led to this conceptualization. For example, he wrote:

> That which lies in the zone of proximal development at one stage is realized and moves to the level of actual development at a second. In other words, what the child is able to do in collaboration today he will be able to do independently tomorrow. (Vygotsky, in press, p. 206)

The work of Campione and colleagues (Campione, Brown, Ferrara, & Bryant, 1984) is a good example of research trying to elaborate this conceptualization of the zone. The goal in their work is to assess how much children of different characteristics benefit from training that provides structured guidance on completing a task. Change is assessed by examining how much a particular child transfers the training to a similar task when working alone. The emphasis is on the zone of proximal development as a "metric" of individual change, on determining how well children are able to assimilate help that is transmitted by the adult.

I propose a different approach to thinking of change within a zone of proximal development, an approach that may be more useful for classroom instruction, what I call the "re-creation of meaning" model of the zone. It emphasizes the appropriation and mastery of mediational means, such as writing, assessed not only or necessarily through independent performance after guided practice, but by the ability to participate in qualitatively new collaborative activities. The focus is not on transferring skills as such, but on the collaborative use of mediational means to create, obtain, and communicate meaning. The role of the adult is not necessarily to provide structured cues, but rather, through exploratory talk and other social mediations, to assist children in appropriating or taking control of their own learning. The key here is to help children create meaning through their participation in diverse literacy activities. The goal is to make children consciously aware of how they are manipulating the literacy process and applying this knowledge to reorganize future experiences or activities. The emphasis, then, is not on transmitting knowledge or skills in pre-packaged forms in the hope that these skills will be internalized in the form transmitted; the emphasis is on joint literacy activities mediated by the teacher and intended to help children express and obtain meaning in ways that will enable them to make this knowledge and meaning their own. This perspective is similar to what Wertsch (1984) proposed as shifts in children's (and I would add adults') situation definition representing change in the zone. That is, children, with the assistance of others, create new meaning. This approach is also similar to what Goodman (1986) calls facilitating students' "ownership" of learning and of language.

In the examples provided below, I illustrate how some teachers create and mediate the type of social system in their classrooms that leads to this ownership and reorganization of learning activities by children, and in which the elements summarized above are prominent features of the literacy learning activities.

ZONES FOR WRITING: EXAMPLES FROM OUTSTANDING TEACHERS

The examples here are taken from observations we conducted in three classrooms located in a major Southwest city.[1] We selected these teachers for observation because they had been judged by peers and administrators as outstanding, effective teachers of Hispanic children. We conducted participant observations in these classrooms for six months and interviewed the teachers, formally and informally, throughout the project to get a thorough understanding of their teaching methods. In total, we collected approximately 100 hours of observations, which we supplemented with about 10 hours of videotaping per classroom.

The three teachers we studied held similar instructional views. They followed what is known as a "whole language" approach (see, e.g., Freeman & Freeman, this volume; Goodman, 1986). Central to this approach is a view of literacy as the understanding and communication of meaning, so that both comprehension and expression are built and developed collaboratively by students and teachers through functional, relevant, and meaningful language use. Therefore, a major instructional goal of the teachers was to make their classrooms literate environments in which many language experiences could take place and different types of "literacies" could be practiced, understood, and learned. This approach rejects fitting reading and writing into skill sequences taught in isolation or in a successive, stage-like manner. Rather, it emphasizes the creation of social contexts in which children learn to try out, use, and manipulate language in the service of making sense or creating meaning. The role of the teacher in these social contexts is to provide the necessary guidance—mediations, in a Vygotskian sense—so that children, through their own efforts, assume full control of diverse purposes and uses of oral and written language.

It is this process of social mediation that I want to highlight here. Not the creation of *individual* zones of proximal development, but of *collective,* interrelated zones of proximal development as part of a teaching

---

[1] Maria Harper collected most of the observations described herein as part of the Project on Effective Schooling for Hispanics. This project was funded by a grant to Eugene Garcia from the Inter-University Program for Latino Research and the Social Science Research Council.

system: the social mediations of teachers as they arrange, rearrange, change, improve, or dissolve social situations for learning. The curriculum was learned through different types of social relationships that teachers facilitated. This process was mediated in the sense that the teachers shifted it strategically to engage students or to give them practice with different aspects of the process. Regardless of individual differences in teaching or in children, including differences in English language proficiency, the teachers mediated in similar ways the children's interaction with the classroom content. All of the teachers facilitated learning through the creation of related tasks or activities, rather than controlled learning by imposing a single model of learning for the children to follow. None of the classrooms included essential component practices as found in learning models (Heath, 1986); rather, each classroom used a strategic mix of social resources, activities, and tasks to teach different aspects of literacy. Similarly, these teachers resisted reducing the intellectual level of the curriculum to match English as a second language (ESL) children's real or perceived oral language difficulties, a practice that is quite common in working-class, Latino classrooms (Moll, 1986; Oakes, 1986). Instead, the teachers provided differential assistance in helping the students accomplish comparable academic goals. These practices, I argue, are good examples of providing zones of proximal development for learning: The teacher holds in abeyance the "higher order" goals of the lessons while searching, in the interaction, for ways to support at the highest level possible the students' performance. Further, the goal is simultaneously to create future contexts in which children can apply in new ways what they are learning.

Example 1: Diversity and Meaning

We were impressed by the way these teachers coordinated, most often successfully but sometimes unsuccessfully, the students' interactions with the curriculum. These interactions occurred within social arrangements in which the students dealt with content in varying ways. This diversity of instruction was most prominent in language arts. For example, reading and writing took place in many ways, and they were usually integrated as part of a broader activity: reading individually, being read to, reading to others, reading to prepare a report, writing to be read by others, reading what others had written, reading and writing for fun, reading to prepare for a written test, reading to teach others, writing to read to others, reading and writing to prepare a project, reading for text editing, writing in journals and logs. In short, the teachers consciously tried to provide the children with practice in the greatest possible range of oral and written language uses to obtain and communicate knowledge. And I would argue that each of these activities represented zones of proximal development for learning; they were social situations in which the teacher could assess children by contrasting their performance in contexts where they received differential assistance to perform. As the teachers pointed out, most of their assessments were conducted by observing the students in various contexts; that is how they got to know the children and assess how they were doing, what type of assistance they needed, and whether the children were taking over the activity, making it their own—in our terms, whether there was movement in the zone.

Clearly, the most prominent characteristic of these classrooms was not the transfer of specific skills, but the constant emphasis on creating meaning. It was the key barometer to movement in the zone. Every observation we collected had notations of the teachers' efforts at creating, clarifying, expanding, and monitoring the students' understanding of the activities and tasks. This making of meaning permeated every instructional activity in these classrooms, regardless of topic, theme, or purpose, and regardless of the children's English language competence. There are two aspects of this meaning making that I want to elaborate as examples of what I have called collective zones of proximal development: first, how comprehension was always the dominant goal of reading; second, how these teachers helped the students understand and make sense of strategies authors use to convey meaning. Through their questioning, the teachers always made the students examine the writer's strategies in some depth: how we interpret what we read, how we feel about the characters and why, our predictions and guesses about what is going to happen, and how writers manipulate words, phrases, descriptions, or dialogue to influence readers. Consider the following example; the story being read is about a panther that kills a little boy's (Lonny) dog. The teacher asked the group what they thought would happen next:

MARY: I think Lonny is going to kill the cat.

JOHN: I think Lonny is not going to kill the cat. . . .

BARB: The reason why he is not going to kill the cat is because she has babies.

JUAN: I think that he is going to kill the panther and his dad is going to help him.
    (Other children give their opinions about whether Lonny is going to kill the panther.)

TEACHER: (interrupting) I just want to explain what we just did in the group.

The teacher proceeded to explain that Mary (the first student to respond) offered a prediction, the panther would be killed, and others shared their ideas on what they thought was going to happen to the panther. She then emphasized to the group that, as readers, we are always predicting. The children nodded affirmatively.

The teacher continued the lesson by asking, "We have been predicting what will happen. How about anything else? Anything about the author or something that struck you about the story?"

Roberto raised his hand and said that he liked the way the author described the dog's death because he could "see" exactly how it happened and "see" the wound in the dog. Manuel said that he could feel the sadness because Lonny's tears were dropping on the dog's body.

The purpose of the teacher's questioning was to make the children aware of writing strategies. She also encouraged the children to develop their own strategies and to borrow strategies from authors to use in their own writing. In the next example, the teacher asked the class if anyone wanted to share what they were writing, an activity that formed part of the students' writing routines. Lisa and Ernesto volunteered. The rest of the class moved to the front of the room. The teacher asked Lisa to read first and also asked, "Why are you doing this?" Lisa responded, "To see if it [the piece she has written] is o.k." Lisa then read a fairly lengthy story. After she had finished reading, the teacher asked, "What worked well?" Some of Lisa's peers responded that she let them know her characters by providing a physical description and used the dialogue to describe the characters' thoughts. Another student commented that she did not start the story with the typical "Once upon a time. . . ," but rather with "The bus was coming. . . ," a much more interesting beginning. Others commented that by having her characters use different languages (Spanish and English) she interested her readers and defined her characters.

Most of these comments occurred with limited prompting from the teacher. It was clear that the children were used to commenting on writing by pointing out strategies used by authors, including themselves. In a Vygotskian sense, these children had "internalized" ways of analyzing language use and its effects on readers. Meaning and how it came about through the use of language were permanent topics of discussion in all activities involving written language, whether the children were readers or writers, ESL students or not. This is what I mean by the zone as the re-creation of knowledge. The students used strategies they had appropriated through use and analysis of language to shape their own activities, to present more sophisticated or clearer texts, to make sense of more complicated texts, or simply to derive more enjoyment from literacy. The children displayed in various ways how they were mastering literacy.

Example 2: Strategic Bilingual Groupings

The teachers in the study did not group students by ability; instead, they grouped them by interests or activities, and the composition of the groups changed frequently. The teachers also experimented with grouping children by language. In the example presented below, the teacher grouped three students for a writing activity: two fluent bilingual children and a limited English speaker. The teacher hoped that by grouping a struggling ESL student with biliterate peers, this student would get some help in completing the writing assignment. I include this example because it helps make a point that we have emphasized in previous writings: the importance of building on first language oral and literacy development in planning second language instruction (Moll & Díaz, 1985). Just as creating zones provides teachers with a qualitatively different perspective on students, knowing what they are capable of doing in their first language is equally valuable in helping teachers avoid erroneous interpretations of children's abilities or potential for instruction.

The three students in the example, all girls, were asked to collaborate in an assignment that consisted of writing the dialogue for a "Peanuts" cartoon. The teacher grouped an ESL student, Sylvia, with two fluent bilingual girls, Gloria and Ana. Gloria was the scribe in English, while Sylvia wrote in Spanish. Initially, the bilingual girls took the lead and dominated the assignment. They created the dialogue, gave names to the characters, and told Sylvia what to write. Progressively, however, Sylvia became more active, offering bits of dialogue. As they started to write the words for a new cartoon frame, the following interaction took place:

ANA: *Sylvia, piensale uno.* [Sylvia, think of one.]

SYLVIA: Okay.

GLORIA: (creating dialogue) "Boy, is this hard. . . ."

ANA: ". . . hard work."

SYLVIA: (almost leaping from her seat) *¡O, ya sé! Ya sé! "Esta bola de* (inaudible) *se hace más grande y más pesada."* [Oh, I know! I know! This (inaudible) ball is getting bigger and heavier.]

ANA: Oh, yea, that's very good.

GLORIA: *De veras.* . . . wait, look, "Boy is this hard work." *"O . . . este, este es trabajao muy duro."* [Oh, this, this is very hard work.]

SYLVIA: (starting to write what Gloria said) *¿O, a ver, va una "h" con la "o"?* [Oh, let's see, does an "h" go with the "o"?]

GLORIA: *No, no mas sola.* [No, by itself.]

SYLVIA: (while waiting) *Este . . .* [This . . .]

GLORIA: *"Este trabajo es, está, muy duro."* [This work is, is very hard.]

SYLVIA: (asserting herself) *No, mejor le deberiamos de poner, "Esta bola de nieve está muy pesada."* [No, we should write, "This snowball is very heavy."]

After suggesting her dialogue, Sylvia taps her hand with her pencil and looks at Gloria as if to affirm that she wants her dialogue used. She then points at the illustration to show that her suggestion makes sense. Ana seems to agree; Gloria acquiesces. The girls agree to write it as Sylvia has suggested. But Gloria then tries to reword the dialogue slightly: *"Esta bola está muy pesada."* [This ball is very heavy.] Sylvia won't go for it; she states: *No, mira, yo le estoy poniendo, "Esta bola de nieve está muy pesada."* [No, look, I am writing, "This snowball is very heavy." Gloria finally agrees: *No, está bien,* Okay. [No, it's all right, Okay.] The girls move on to the next cartoon frame.

By observing the girls working collaboratively, the teacher could determine that Sylvia, the ESL student, not only understood the assignment but had the necessary writing competence in Spanish to participate in the activity. Observations such as this one lead this teacher to allow her ESL students to write assignments in Spanish, while she provided assistance with their English fluency. As the year progressed, it was common to observe students reading in English but writing reviews of books and other assignments in Spanish. In such a bilingual arrangement, the teacher ensured that the ESL children participated in tasks at the same intellectual level as the rest of the class while monitoring and assisting the children's English development.

But what of a teacher who is not fluent in Spanish? An English monolingual teacher in our study provided us with a description of how she used bilingual groupings to create a different zone of proximal development, one in which she would remediate her teaching through peer interactions. She described the sequence of groupings she used with an ESL student:

1. She placed the ESL students with other students who knew Spanish well; her goal here was to make the students comfortable and to allow them to learn the classroom routine.
2. She asked the bilingual students to help her teach the other children by clarifying content and procedures. Her observations here consisted of determining what content the different ESL students liked and getting an indication of how well they could handle the work in Spanish. She would also ask other students to read stories to the ESL students in Spanish or in English. I should mention that students reading aloud to one another formed part of the usual classroom routine, so it was not a way of singling out the ESL students for special remedial help.
3. Once the students became active participants in the class, she would then start sampling what the student could do in English to determine the nature of the help the student needed in that language.
4. Finally, she would place the student in an all-English context,

knowing that the student who really cared about the content of study would make his or her voice heard; lessons were now not a matter of language or the lack of it per se but of communicating beliefs, ideas, and knowledge. And she had the faith that in such a context the students would apply their ample social and intellectual resources to the task.

The routine described above will of course vary depending on the instructional circumstances, especially the characteristics of the students and teachers. However, what is important is not the specific sequence, but that the teacher's primary concern was organizing social routines that involved the student substantively in the class. As Genesee (1986) has suggested, second language learners will learn the second language to the extent that they are motivated by the curriculum to learn academic material. In our terms, the teacher used the classroom resources, in this instance bilingual peers, to create zones of proximal development that allowed the student to participate, as did the rest of the class, in activities that had a real academic purpose, activities that had meaning, that made intellectual sense.

DISCUSSION

I now summarize some of the implications of the ideas described above for teaching ESL students. I have presented examples of classroom practices that, although not guided specifically by Vygotsky's ideas, are nevertheless compatible with such a perspective: the holistic emphasis, the focus on language as social and communicative activity, the practice of creating meaningful literacy activities, and the role of the adult's and peer's social mediations in facilitating mastery and ownership of mediational means.

The analysis of such practices also has implications for how we think about Vygotsky's zone of proximal development. The major importance of this concept for ESL teaching is that it provides a constant, critical perspective on the social organization of instruction. The examples provided suggest that the zone is not only a matter of design, that is, of coordinating structural arrangements and means of action, but a matter of content and meaning. Children must make sense of an experience to be able to re-create their own version of it; and this making sense is not an independent but a collaborative achievement, it is mediated in zones of proximal development. Further, zones of proximal development need not be created individually for each student; rather, they can be created collectively, as children interact with a diverse social system of instruction, with mutually supporting zones of proximal development, and continually display what they know, what they are learning, and how they are using what they know to deal with new and more advanced instructional situations. And it is in transforming new situations with the teacher's help that children actively transform themselves.

REFERENCES

Campione, J., Brown, A. L., Ferrara, R. A., & Bryant, N. R. (1984). The zone of proximal development: Implications for individual differences and learning. In B. Rogoff & J. Wertsch (Eds.), *Children's learning in the "zone of proximal development"* (pp. 77–92). San Francisco: Jossey-Bass.
Cole, M. (1985). The zone of proximal development: Where culture and cognition create each other. In J. V. Wertsch (Ed.), *Culture, communication and cognition: Vygotskian perspectives* (pp. 146–161). New York: Cambridge University Press.
Cole, M., & Griffin, P. (1983). A socio-historical approach to re-mediation. *Quarterly Newsletter of the Laboratory of Comparative Human Cognition, 5*(4), 69–74.
Díaz, S., Moll, L. C., & Mehan, H. (1986). Sociocultural resources in instruction: A context-specific approach. In California State Department of Education (Ed.), *Beyond language: Social and cultural factors in schooling language minority children* (pp. 187–230). Los Angeles: California State University Evaluation, Dissemination and Assessment Center.
Edelsky, C. (1986). *Writing in a bilingual program: Había una vez.* Norwood, NJ: Ablex.
Genesee, F. (1986). The baby and the bathwater or, what immersion has to say about bilingual education. *NABE Journal, 10,* 227–254.
Goodman, K. (1986). *What's whole in whole language?* Portsmouth, NH: Heinemann.
Griffin, P., & Cole, M. (1984). Current activity for the future: The Zo-ped. In B. Rogoff & J. Wertsch (Eds.), *Children's learning in the "zone of proximal development"* (pp. 45–64). San Francisco: Jossey-Bass.
Heath, S. B. (1986). Sociocultural contexts of language development. In California State Department of Education (Ed.), *Beyond language: Social and cultural factors in schooling language minority children* (pp. 143–186). Los Angeles: California State University Evaluation, Dissemination and Assessment Center.
Kozulin, A. (1986). Vygotsky in context. In L. S. Vygotsky, *Thought and language* (A. Kozulin, Ed., pp. xi–lxi). Cambridge, MA: MIT Press.
Laboratory of Comparative Human Cognition. (1983). Culture and cognitive development. In W. Kessen (Ed.), *Handbook of child psychology* (Vol. 1, pp. 295–356). New York: Wiley.
Minick, N. (1985). *L. S. Vygotsky and Soviet activity theory: New perspectives on the relationship between mind and society.* Unpublished doctoral dissertation, Northwestern University.
Minick, N. (in press). The zone of proximal development and dynamic assessment.

In C. S. Lidz (Ed.), *Foundations of dynamic assessment*. New York: Guilford Press.

Moll, L. C. (1986). Writing as communication: Creating strategic learning environments for students. *Theory into Practice, 25,* 102–108.

Moll, L. C. and Díaz, R. (1987). Teaching writing as communication: The use of ethnographic findings in classroom practice. In D. Bloome (Ed.), *Literacy and schooling* (pp. 55–65). Norwood NJ: Ablex.

Moll, L. C., & Díaz, S. (1985). Ethnographic pedagogy: Promoting effective bilingual instruction. In E. Garcia & R. Padilla (Eds.), *Advances in bilingual education research* (pp. 127–149). Tucson: University of Arizona.

Moll, L. C. and Díaz, S. (in press). Change as the goal of educational research. *Anthropology and Education Quarterly.*

Oakes, J. (1986). Tracking, inequality, and the rhetoric of school reform: Why schools don't change. *Journal of Education, 168,* 61–80.

Olson, D. (1986). Intelligence and literacy: The relationship between intelligence and the technologies of representation and communication. In R. Sternberg & R. Wagner (Eds.), *Practical intelligence: Nature and origins of competence in the everyday world* (pp. 338–360). New York: Cambridge University Press.

Riviere, A. (1984). La psicología de Vygotski. *Infancia y Aprendizaje, 27–28* (3–4), 7–86.

Vygotsky, L. S. (1978). *Mind in society: The development of higher psychological processes.* (M. Cole, V. John-Steiner, S. Scribner, & E. Souberman, Eds. and Trans.). Cambridge, MA: Harvard University Press.

Vygotsky, L. S. (in press). Speech and thinking. In L. S. Vygotsky, *Collected Works, Vol 1.* (N. Minick, Trans.). New York: Plenum.

Wertsch, J. V. (1984). The zone of proximal development: Some conceptual issues. In B. Rogoff & J. Wertsch (Eds), *Children's learning in the "zone of proximal development"* (pp. 7–18). San Francisco: Jossey-Bass.

Wertsch, J. V. (1985a). *Vygotsky and the social formation of mind.* Cambridge, MA: Harvard University Press.

Wertsch, J. V. (Ed.). (1985b). *Culture, communication and cognition: Vygotskian perspectives.* New York: Cambridge University Press.

CHAPTER 4

Letting Ourselves Be Taught

Mary M. Kitagawa
Richey Elementary School, Tucson

Loc, Jeremy, and Hector had very different personalities, but all three boys taught me the same truth about writing education: Students write and learn best in the accomplishment of their own agenda. Since the agenda of a writer includes such diverse purposes as self-discovery, self-expression, recording, reporting, entertaining, and persuading (see, for example, Britton, Burgess, Martin, McLeod, & Rosen, 1975; Moffett, 1968), the vital need is for a context in which to carry out those intentions. Because of their linguistic and cultural adjustments, writers who are second language (L2) learners need that context most of all. If we put their texts through templates of acceptable syntax or semantics before we respond to the intentions of the writer, the L2 writer perceives that the invitation to write was fraudulent. Even a very inarticulate story carries something of its writer's intentions to a determined reader. Students learning to express themselves through writing, or learning to do so in English, need such determined readers instead of diagnosticians (cf. Britton, et al., 1975, who call for reading student compositions as a "trusted friend"; also Krashen, 1982; Raimes, 1983; Zamel, 1985).

This chapter describes how students can maintain agendas of their own within the framework of writing education. The setting described is primarily that of my regular intermediate elementary school classroom, which is not designated as ESL but happens to be populated by students who are nearly all L2 (or L3) learners. There is no special program in our school for these students so I, with my bilingual aides, have full responsibility for their ESL instruction along with the rest of the curriculum.

Loc, Jeremy, and Hector varied as much in their approaches to language learning as they did in their personalities (see Hudelson, this volume; Wong Fillmore, 1983). Each had his own language agenda. Loc, a native speaker of Vietnamese, took charge of his language learning as if I were an apprentice serving under his direction. Jeremy, a monolingual English speaker, apparently adopted the local language patterns of his new neighborhood and classmates to signal that he wanted a place in their social setting. Hector, a Spanish speaker, set up a resistance effort that, while passive, created a formidable speech barrier, although he expressed himself in writing. It was by trading my teacher role for what Thad Sitton (1980) calls an ethnographer approach to these student-informants that I could participate according to the agenda that each brought with him.

An ethnographic attitude reveals a student's agenda. Furthermore, the willingness to be informed in an ethnographic fashion sets up a teacher-student relationship that empowers students in their writing and learning. After describing the three boys, I will describe how certain methods and philosophical strands of education provide students with access to their own agendas.

THREE BOYS APPROACH LANGUAGE LEARNING

Loc

When Loc came to my fourth-grade class some years ago, his English was limited to phrases he had learned on the way from Vietnam to his new home in Tucson. He began on the very first day to make a place for himself among his classmates. He leafed through a book of science experiments and pointed to an illustration for demonstrating static electricity. Indicating a comb and plastic wrap, he asked me, "You have?" Loc soon had a crowd watching as he made bits of paper dance. When his audience began to drift away, he shifted to a book of origami directions and regained their attention. His audience was hooked.

Within a few weeks he began to write, painstakingly, a few lines a day, about how he had left Vietnam in a small boat. Although some of it was garbled, the class responded to the importance he placed upon his story by listening as if each new addition were an episode in a serial. An important factor in this stage was that Loc was under no assignment or time constraints. He was neither demonstrating his grasp of a certain genre nor creating a piece of literature; he was simply communicating something that he alone had to offer others. The class format of a writing workshop in which everyone worked on individual projects allowed him to acquire skills as part of his actual communication in English.

Loc persistently trained me to help him. One day, for example, he stopped writing and stood up. He put one hand over his eye and grabbed his ankle with the other, holding his leg up in back. "Teacher, what is man—one eye, one leg?" I was so dense that no amount of repetition gave me the answer. Finally he went to the school office and found someone with a better imagination. When he returned he explained, "Teacher, man—one eye, one leg—is pirate. Write it down." It turned out that he wanted to explain about "pirate" ships that sometimes preyed upon escapees.

Loc's aggressive efforts to learn English enabled him to make rapid progress. His motivation to master English and his self-confidence made my job easy. Besides the specific assistance his classmates and the aides and I could provide when he asked for help, the primary contribution we made was of ourselves as an audience determined to be informed, entertained, and persuaded by what he had to offer (see Mittan, this volume).

In contrast to Loc, who clearly saw himself as an L2 learner, most students in my school are Mexican Americans or Yaqui Indians (a small tribe with origins in Mexico, now recognized officially by the United States government as American Indians) who would bristle at the idea that they need special lessons in English. Yet, according to the various tests they fall prey to, many do not measure up to native speaker norms. They are categorized as L2 learners because they learned English as part of adjusting to the world beyond their families, including the school setting. Besides Spanish, some also have a measure of receptive knowledge of the Yaqui language used by their grandparents. For most, English came so closely upon the heels of their L1 that they claim it solidly as their own.

Jeremy

When Jeremy, my only Anglo student that year, moved into this neighborhood from another part of Tucson, he set himself an agenda that included adjustment of his speech to meet social needs. He seemed to recognize that there was a group code in operation. Within a few months of his arrival, he adopted two local interjections for reaction to disconcerting information. These are a nasalized "Eh?" with a certain pattern of sharply rising intonation and a Yaqui interjection, b^we (shortened form of ab^we) "look, my goodness."[1] Jeremy's timing and pronunciation seemed to duplicate his new friends' exactly. What do we say of the linguistic sensitivity by which a ten-year-old, who has some notoriety with teachers for not being attentive to classroom instruction, adapts himself to the social

[1] I am indebted to Eloise Jelinek and Fernando Escalante, a professor and a graduate student at the University of Arizona, respectively, for information about this expression.

nuances of a local dialect? A bilingual classmate paid tribute to his achievement when, apparently unconciously, he reminded Jeremy of his turn in a game by saying in Spanish, *"Tu vas"* ("You go").

Jeremy's adjustment is a preview of the sorts of adaptations the rest of my students, as seventh graders, will face when they are bused to a junior high school across town. Just as Jeremy did upon entering this cultural setting, they will leave behind their majority status as Hispanics and Native Americans when they enter into the predominantly white, mainstream culture of their secondary education. They will have to learn to balance themselves on feet planted in two worlds at the same time.

The Jeremys and the Locs readily reveal how much I can count on what the learners will teach themselves. I am challenged to trust also the less self-assured students such as Hector.

Hector

Unlike Loc, who aggressively took charge of his own language learning on the first day, Hector still agonized over even answering roll call during his third year in this country. I was calling roll only to try to get Hector to start each day with an utterance in either English or Spanish, but this Salvadoran boy was both shy and stubborn. He would station himself near the water fountain and duck for a drink as the alphabetical listing came to his name. In that way he could preclude answering verbally and just account for his presence with a waving hand. If the drinking fountain was occupied, he would stand behind me and tap me on the shoulder to grin and wave when I called his name.

He would murmur minimally in Spanish but not speak at all in English. He was shy even in conversation with native speakers of Spanish. Like his classmates, he and I had dialogues in the journal he kept. His entries, in Spanish, were personal narratives and descriptions that revealed poetic sensitivity. I answered as best I could in my limited Spanish, which he was too polite to correct in spite of my requests. Later, I asked him to try to write his introductory sentences in English. I truthfully explained how much easier I could read Spanish once I recognized the general topic. Hector began to accommodate my needs in this way, sometimes continuing the entire text in English. His writing revealed enough L2 communicative competence to maintain our written dialogue, even though he never really broke the speech barrier he had set up.

Telling Their Own Stories

In spite of their diverse approaches to L2 acquisition, all three boys had stories only they could tell (see also Urzua, 1987). And they told those stories because they perceived their audience to be a receptive one. Jeremy usually wrote accounts of play interactions in which social inclusion or exclusion was an underlying theme. By teaching me of his passionate desire for full acceptance, he gained for himself extra tolerance of his attention-getting mischief in class.

Hector poured his homesickness into poignant essays that brought home to me the personal cost of the strife in his homeland. In one he compared the interactions of doves he watched at his uncle's home to relationships with family members left behind in El Salvador. "They are my sisters," he wrote, straining my limited Spanish to accommodate metaphors.

If I checked my translations of any part of his texts with Spanish speakers, I did so without Hector's knowledge because I wanted him to feel responsible for me as his reader. When he accepted the obligation to inform me and participate in a written dialogue with me, he had to yield to my need for some English. He had to shift out of his own domain and take on an interdependent writer–reader relationship (cf. Flower, 1979). Donald Graves (1983) claims that it is this vision of the imprint of information on others that is a basic source of the energy that motivates writers and leads to breakthroughs in their writing. So, one of our roles as teachers is to make conspicuous our desire to be informed. Through modeling that behavior myself, the writer's classmates join me in being a "hungry audience."

Unlike Hector and Loc, whose stories clearly represent other world views, most of my students have not yet pitted their identities against other norms. The neighborhood is an entity distinct enough to be called a "village," even though it is almost downtown Tucson. In the evenings people gather to chat outside and children commandeer the streets for play. In this cohesive atmosphere, students sometimes think there is nothing newsworthy to write. To help them realize that it is their individual perceptions that make experiences unique, I need to make of myself an audience interested in the way the world looks through their eyes. This task is made easier in my school by the fact that our students have enjoyed teacher interest in their self-selected topics as early as first grade, even before they learned to form all the letters or spell in conventional ways.

The whole language (Goodman, 1986) milieu of their first experiences with written language empowered these students to write in real, not artificial, self-expression. As first graders they accomplished their own communicative purposes for writing because, no matter how limited their skills, their teacher did not treat their writing as a "dry run." Even a student who wrote "Mi tf kam ot" got more attention to her missing tooth than the missing letters.

As a norm for curriculum planning, I too lean heavily upon the philosophical tenets of whole language, especially the requirement of authentic language use as much as is possible in a school setting (Goodman & Goodman, 1981). The research my husband and I did on an educational model from Japan also influenced the way I try to centralize writing in the curriculum. There are many parallels between whole language and *seikatsu tsuzurikata* (SAY-KAH-TSOO TSOO-ZOO-REE-KAH-TAH) 'life experience writing' (see Kitagawa & Kitagawa, 1987). Although neither of these approaches was developed specifically for second language learners, both can serve such students because both are based upon the purposeful, functional needs of first, second, or third language users (Goodman, 1986; Halliday, 1973, 1974; Kitagawa & Kitagawa, 1987).

RESPONDING AS A PERSONAL READER

One key element of the Japanese model which I have tried to implement in my teaching is a way of responding to writing that neither evaluates nor alters the focus. In *seikatsu tsuzurikata* this response is symbolized by the *akapen* (AH-KAH-PEN) 'red pen', but this English translation is misleading because, unlike the connotation of criticism associated with a "red pen," the *akapen* in the *seikatsu tsuzurikata* model reflects a reader who is subjectively biased toward the writer. It is meant to mirror and nurture the writer at work, rather than to extend, correct, or evaluate the text. The writer's exposure to the reader's intense desire to be informed, rather than the reader's power to evaluate or correct, drives the writer to tell the story well. In the writer–*akapen* dialogue, the writer's perspective is the single focus of attention and the reader role is played out in detailed response along the margins of the page. Giving specific responses, almost line by line, has the effect of convincing students that their everyday lives are full of stories worth articulating fully. I am a novice at *akapen* responding, but here is an entry Genara, one of my Yaqui students, and I shared:

GENARA'S ENTRY	*MY* AKAPEN
Once me, Cruzita and Lydia were outside at lunch time, after a while we walked around the field. Suddenly Lydia stopped and I slid on the grass. Then I cut myself so Lydia and Cruzita picked me up and took me to the nurse's office.	Maybe last year. Lydia's stopping made you fall on a rock, I guess.
My grandma came and looked at my cut closely. After she finished looking the nurse wrote a note for me to get stitches. I said I	

didn't want stitches. It was my choice to have my grandma heal my cut with the medicine called yerba colorada. She gets it from the roots of a plant. My grandma puts water in a glass and it gets red from the roots. By a week later the pain was gone and all I had was a scar.

Oh, your grandma is one who heals people. These details are what you've seen. Genara, this is an important memory!

BEGINNING WITH THE WRITER'S KNOWLEDGE BASE

We need to stress real writer–reader interactions for ESL learners to assure that these students are not excluded from the best possible educational environments (Wong Fillmore, 1986). There is a danger that their inability to sound native in English will delude administrators and teachers into believing that it is merciful to siphon them off into remediation programs which deny them the resources of their own stories. Kits, writing formulae, and fragmentation of language tasks into workbooks and computer programs all purport to prevent failure by isolating writing tasks into components. But forcing students to write on decontextualized topics and distracting their attention to language patterns drains their personal commitment to the content of their writing. And it is personal commitment that fosters what we call voice: that evidence of the self of the writer which, even when hidden, vitalizes a piece of writing (Britton, 1975).

Writing that begins with the knowledge base of the writer resounds with the author's voice (Graves, 1983). Because it is the writer who teaches and the reader who is taught, we can see the link between the words *author* and *authority*. Just as Genara informed me about her grandma's healing abilities, another ESL student, Marco, let me in on the mess he made trying to cook.

MARCO'S ENTRY

. . . When I was done [fixing tortillas and other ingredients] I put the enchiladas in a plate and had to heat up the sauce cause it was cold. When I turned it on I went to watch tv. I couldn't wait to taste it so I went to the kitchen and put it high and went to the table to wait. When I turned around there was cheese on the ground and everywhere so I thought it was ready. And when I ate them I only ate five because I made five for my big dog and three for my small dog and they were

MY AKAPEN

It is hard to get everything hot at the same time.

You're impatient at this point. Cheese boiled over, I guess. Your dogs sure appreciate your

| good but I saw the mess and cleaned it up before my mom got here. | cooking, but maybe your mom doesn't. |

From journals, students easily branch into more formal descriptions, profiling and grandmother or writing cooking instructions. The journal that provides student-to-teacher information becomes a launching pad for reaching a wider audience, including all who have access to classroom publications of student writing (cf. Moffett, 1968, on expansion of audience and heightening of abstraction).

WIDENING THE RESOURCE BASE

As the audience widens, so must the resource base. Collecting oral histories from elders and recording traditional aspects of cultural background are research tasks that help students bridge from first-person narratives to writing from primary sources in the third person. One year we published a booklet on the history of our school with writing based primarily on memories described by local guest speakers. The next year we recorded descriptions of the favorite games parents and other relatives recalled from their childhood.

A SIXTH-GRADE RESEARCH UNIT

After using primary sources of the neighborhood to write oral history reports, sixth graders can read about a topic of their own choosing and write a research paper with the same authority with which they previously wrote personal narratives and interview-based research. They can write authoritatively from second-hand data only if they first take the time to inform themselves adequately, so I set a timetable to keep them from trying to write prematurely.

Topic

During the choosing and delineating of a topic, students take on ownership of the subject (see also Roen, this volume; Johnson, this volume). Even when writing in their journals, students are used to taking a little time to consider alternative topics before plunging into an entry. Although I had seen some *seikatsu tsuzurikata* students in Japan keeping lists of potential topics, I started encouraging lists only after I experienced Donald Graves's encouraging conference participants to do the same in a workshop (Tucson, Arizona, October 31, 1986). Once I started asking students to use a few minutes in that way, the writing seemed focused in more instances, as if the selection process had heightened commitment to the subject itself. For the research paper, students spent about a week scanning materials on possible topics and writing introspectively with one purpose: to ascertain what topic had enough inner appeal to last throughout about a month of daily sessions of study and writing. Macrorie (1980) describes a good topic as an itch you just have to scratch. I model my own topic search and share the reasons for my choice, and then I go through the whole process as one of the class.

The Writer Becomes Informed

During data collecting, a sense of authority begins to reveal itself. Sergio is surprised and obviously pleased when he discovers that he can teach me things I never knew about space shuttles. Leticia makes a chart of all the Greek gods and then revises the chart to include only the gods she will cover in her report: "They [fellow students] probably won't be as interested as I am in the rest." Loc's cousin, Duyen, interviews her parents about Vietnam and gains new perspectives on the magnitude of the decision her parents made when they decided to leave. She writes in her journal, and later in her text, "Now I know what the price of my freedom is." When the students work on their research, there is an air of concentration in the room that is not typical during teacher-directed activities.

I want students to maintain themselves in a discovery mode until they attain authority on the topic, so I try to hold off the beginning of their text production. Most of them, if allowed to take notes, will actually begin to write their reports. Yet there are details they will need to retrieve later. I give students little notepads of self-sticking papers to attach to the edges of key pages as flags. Labeling these with a word or phrase provides a trail back through the data and allows the students to concentrate on their own understanding.

WRITING TO INFORM OTHERS

Students who become "expert" about their topics can easily write from that authority, if it is genuine. Once writing begins, the dichotomy between those who are really informing an audience and those who are mock-informing shows in the sorts of difficulties that arise. The mock-informers refer back to their sources to "lift" phrases and sentences, making a patchwork quilt that is original only in the sense that language has been rearranged. They also are the ones who keep checking with others, especially with the teacher, to find out, "Is this good enough?" The real informers check back for details and test their writing against the knowledge they have acquired. Graves (1983) relates the contrast to the difference between being a homeowner and making repairs willingly or being only a tenant. Without that sense of ownership, the student may be committed to the assignment, but not to the topic.

BOOK-TALK LETTERS

Instead of formal summaries or evaluations, which 10- to 12-year-olds seem to find very difficult, I usually have my students write in their journals informal letters to me about the library books they are currently reading. This is genuine information to me, whether they describe the plot, the characters, or their reactions, predictions, confusions, associations and other experiences with the text. They know that, even with books I have read, I have a fellow bibliophile's interest in their own perspectives. I learn more from hearing about their personal interaction with the text than from a glossy presentation they might make about it as literature. This is closer to the way adults normally inform each other about reading experiences. Nancie Atwell (1987) similarly models her reading classes after what she calls "dining room table" book discussions; these discussions occur in conferences and in written dialogues in her eighth graders' reading logs.

Although I am primarily acting as a sounding board, I am also using these natural interactions in book-talk letters to keep tabs on each student's reading development. For example, Rolando complained about William Armstrong's (1969) *Sounder* that the dog was the only character given a name. His writing showed that he appreciated fully that the author was presenting the lives of the sharecroppers as bleak. He simply had not connected those two facts yet.

When the same journal–notebook provides space for writing authoritatively in both personal narrative style and also in book-talk letters, students begin to take on a sense of autonomy that is basic to both processes, reading and writing. We cannot hope to empower their writing without also activating the text-creation role by which readers personalize reading experiences. Book-talk letters allow students to highlight in writing those aspects of the text that they respond to most keenly, even when that response is idiosyncratic to that particular reader. How could answers to predetermined comprehension questions, as in a basal reading series, give the teacher the same information?

I have to confess that, by way of preparing students for the customary requirements for book reports in junior high school, I do require a few— but I try to ease them into the experience by having them write about a book I have read aloud in class, so it is clearly just an exercise in summary and evaluation.

READING ALOUD TO STUDENTS

Reading aloud provides many benefits, linguistic as well as social. It provides a common knowledge base upon which the classroom community interaction can draw (as, for example, when students suggested naming our goldfish Old Ann and Little Dan, an in-joke created by transposing the parts of the names of the dogs in Wilson Rawls' (1975) *Where The Red Fern Grows*. Also, especially for students who have not been read to, or who have not been read to in English, listening to stories read aloud is an effective way to become acquainted with the literary language that they need in order to gain access to English in all of its forms (see Goodman, 1986; Graves, 1983).

EXPRESSIVE WRITING IN CONTENT AREAS

Students also write to inform me about their reactions to audiovisual materials used in science and social studies lessons. Again, it is easy for them to write authoritatively because I am asking to be informed about something that only they can know: their own thinking and feeling. When they teach me in this way, they usually solidify their impressions and surprise me at the same time. After seeing a film about the millions of years in which the Grand Canyon evolved, one student wrote, "It made me wonder if there really was an Adam and Eve." I cringed at the possibility of parental wrath until I realized it was Duyen, whose Buddhist parents probably would not object.

CONVENTIONS AND USAGE

Instead of formal spelling, grammar, punctuation, and handwriting lessons, I provide mini-lessons on each of these in the course of dictation exercises. I write or select the text to exhibit whatever aspects of language I want to present, and I try to make it something that has currency in our study or mutual experiences. It takes only about 60 minutes per week because the lessons are short and most of the study is homework; but it has proved to be the most efficient formal instruction device I have used, especially in a class of students of widely mixed language proficiencies. I can use the same materials but vary the expectations for those who find it more difficult.

I also consider these dictation-based lessons to be an opportunity for me to model standard written English without making a frontal attack on students' language use. For example, I can include "ask" used in standard ways even though the students will probably continue to use "tell" in its place, as in "When you write to your pen pal, tell her how old she is" or "I told my mother if I could bring cookies." The students are not likely to alter their speaking habits much until they move into circles where their peers do not accept that usage. I have tried in the past to make a lesson about the distinction between the two words, with no noticeable result except my own sense of having made myself an outsider. "Letting ourselves be taught" includes observing the language use in its social contexts as well.

There are instances of Spanish transfer which I have noticed primarily when students are basing their writing upon information from interviews they conducted in Spanish. When I read "She *had* (was) ten years (old)" or "My uncle hit *her* (his) sister," it is usually because the student is directly translating an interview; it is unnecessary for me to focus upon these instances since the same students form equivalent sentences in standard English when they are not translating. And if I do focus upon the "medium" instead of the "message," the writer also will focus upon the superficial aspects of language, to the detriment of his or her ability to inform an audience.

A CONCLUDING EXAMPLE

When he visited my class (October 30, 1986) Donald Graves demonstrated his way of maintaining the role of one who is determined to let himself be taught. He listened intently to Gerald's narrative and said, "Let me see. I want to be sure I got that right. . . ." Then he began to report the story back to Gerald: "First you heard a noise, and then you went outside, but. . . ." As soon as he detected in Graves' voice some uncertainty over how the cat in the story made a rattling noise, Gerald interrupted quickly to clarify that the cat had knocked cans from a shelf. Gerald saw himself as the only one who could supply the missing information to satisfy Graves' genuine desire to get the story straight. An audience who listens as Graves does or responds with the nurturing bias of the *akapen* is an audience that sincerely wants to "get it right." Whether or not the writer reworks that text, the experience of having actually informed an audience is a heady motivator for future improvement (Koch, 1982). There is an enhancement of the writer's domain that seems to be the most effective way to promote authority and voice. With ESL writers these are the critical elements of writing prowess. Far from being a passive role, the phrase "letting ourselves be taught" represents an active challenge for teachers, in writing education for ESL students and in the entire milieu of the educational scene.

REFERENCES

Armstrong, W. (1969). *Sounder.* New York: Harper & Row.

Atwell, N. (1987). *In the middle: Writing, reading and learning with adolescents.* Upper Montclair, NJ: Boynton/Cook.

Britton, J., Burgess, T., Martin, N., McLeod, A., & Rosen, H. (1975). *Development of writing abilities (11-18).* London: Macmillan Education.

Britton, J. (1975). Now that you go to school. In Richard L. Larsen (Ed.), *Children and writing in the elementary school* (pp. 3–16). New York: Oxford University Press.

Flower, L. (1979). Writer-based prose: A cognitive basis for problems in writing. *College English, 41,* 19–37.

Goodman, K. (1986). *What's whole about whole language?* Portsmouth, NH: Heinemann.

Goodman, K., & Goodman, Y. (1981). *A whole-language comprehension-centered view of reading development* (Position Paper #1). Tucson: University of Arizona School of Education.

Graves, D. H. (1983). *Writing: Teachers and children at work.* Exeter, NH: Heinemann.

Halliday, M. A. K. (1973). *Explorations in the functions of language.* London: Edward Arnold.

Halliday, M. A. K. (1974). *Language and social man.* (School Council Programme in Linguistics and English Teaching Papers Series II, S. Lushington, Gen. Ed.) Vol. 3. London: Longman Group, Ltd.

Kitagawa, M. M., & Kitagawa, C. (1987). *Making connections with writing: An expressive writing model in Japanese schools.* Portsmouth, NH: Heinemann.

Koch, R. (1982). Syllogisms and superstitions: The current state of responding to writing. *Language Arts, 59,* 464–471.

Krashen, S. D. (1982). *Principles and practice in second language acquisition.* Oxford: Pergamon.

Macrorie, K. (1980). *Searching writing.* Upper Montclair, NJ: Boynton/Cook.

Moffett, J. (1968). *Teaching the universe of discourse.* Boston: Houghton Mifflin.

Raimes, A. (1983). Anguish as a second language? Remedies for composition teachers. In A. Freedman, I. Pringle, & J. Yalden (Eds.), *Learning to write: First language/second language* (pp. 258–272). New York: Longman.

Rawls, W. (1975). *Where the red fern grows.* New York: Bantam Books.

Sitton, T. (1980). The child as informant: The teacher as ethnographer. *Language Arts, 57,* 540–545.

Urzua, C. (1987). You stopped too soon. *TESOL Quarterly, 21,* 297–304.

Wong Fillmore, L. (1983). The language learner as an individual: Implications of research on individual differences for the ESL teacher. In M. A. Clarke & J. Handscombe (Eds.), *On TESOL '82 Pacific Perspectives on Language Learning & Teaching* (pp. 157–174). Washington, DC: Teachers of English to Speakers of Other Languages.

Wong Fillmore, L. (1986). Research currents: Equity or excellence? *Language Arts, 63,* 474–481.

Zamel, V. (1985). Responding to student writing. *TESOL Quarterly, 19,* 79–101.

CHAPTER 5

A Tale of Two Children: Individual Differences in ESL Children's Writing

Sarah Hudelson
University of Miami

In classrooms for native speakers (NS) of English, whole language approaches to literacy involve children in reading experiences with whole, authentic texts and in writing experiences in which they create whole texts for varying purposes and for varied audiences (Milz, 1985). The perspective taken is that children learn to read by reading and learn to write by constructing their own meanings in written form and by having other people react to what they have written. Proponents of whole language approaches to literacy (Bissex, 1980; Calkins, 1986; Goodman & Goodman, 1977; Goodman, 1987; Graves, 1983; Jagger & Smith-Burke, 1985; Newman, 1985; Smith, 1983 and many others) maintain that children are willing and even eager to write about topics of their own choice and that skill as a writer develops within the context of authentic, purposeful writing rather than through practicing isolated skills.

In the last few years, numbers of educators have suggested that such learning environments are appropriate for second language (L2) acquirers, and that writing process strategies effective for NS make sense in an L2 (Allen, 1986; Edelsky, 1982, 1986; Flores et al., 1985; Goodman, Goodman, & Flores, 1979; Hudelson, 1984; Lindfors, 1987; Rigg & Enright, 1986; Urzua, 1980, 1987). This theoretical perspective on writing, and interest in the writing of beginning English as a second language (ESL) users, led me to carry out the work reported here.

For approximately one day a week for a school year I served as a classroom volunteer, participant observer, and ESL tutor in a second-grade classroom in a Dade County, Florida, public school. My goal was to understand better the development of ESL writing in some native Spanish speaking children (I chose Spanish because I am fluent in Spanish and I wanted to be able to use the children's native language if needed.) I spent one day a week observing and taking notes in the children's classrooms, helping children with school assignments, conversing with teachers, conducting regular audiotaped sessions with my tutees, and collecting reading and writing samples. I had planned simply to document what I was seeing. However, a personal commitment to a whole language view of literacy resulted in my making direct efforts to encourage children's writing from this perspective on language development. The teacher asked me to tutor two children new to the school, Roberto and Janice, and I have chosen to tell their stories.

THE CHILDREN

Roberto was a "Marielito," a designation applied to the 125,000 people who left Cuba during the April to August 1980 exodus from the port of Mariel. A small, slight child, with two front teeth missing, Roberto had attended kindergarten in Cuba. He had spent his first year in U.S. schools in a classroom populated solely by non-English speaking Mariel children like himself. The curriculum for these entrants, according to school officials, had focused on teaching the English that would be needed in school and on socializing children to American schools, by which was meant teaching classroom participation rules, cafeteria etiquette, and so on. Then Roberto was transferred to the school where I met and worked with him. Roberto tested a Level 1 on an adaptation of the Michigan Oral Language Test, the language assessment instrument administered by the district to determine ESOL placement (Dade County uses the term ESOL, English for Speakers of Other Languages, rather than ESL).

Roberto was a quiet child, not unfriendly, but not an initiator of interactions with other children. He was serious about school, a trait that came from his father. Roberto's father was eager for his son to do well academically and visited the school on several occasions to see how his son was doing. Roberto's classroom style was to listen and to take everything in but not to volunteer an answer orally or commit something to paper unless he was sure that he had the right answer. His classroom teacher thought of Roberto as a good student. His ESOL teacher found him to be a child reluctant to participate orally.

Janice was a student in the same classroom. In September she had just arrived from Puerto Rico with her mother. She also tested at Level 1 on the English Proficiency test. At first a seemingly shy girl homesick for Puerto Rico, Janice gradually became more outgoing. By the end of the school year she was a popular child, surrounded by others during activities. Initially, Janice's style was to sit quietly, taking in everything and mimicking what others were doing. Later she became more talkative, and sometimes the teacher would scold her for talking. She soon overcame her reticence to use English. She was clearly not the perfectionist Roberto was. She was not as reluctant as Roberto was to guess, to make mistakes. Her classroom teacher saw her as a satisfactory student. In ESOL she made rapid progress and moved at midyear from her first placement to a group that was progressing more quickly. By the end of the year, Janice was more comfortable with and more willing to use English than Roberto was.

Individual differences among child L2 learners, traced to varying social and cognitive styles, have been documented by researchers concerned with oral language development (for example, Strong, 1983; Ventriglia, 1982; Wong Fillmore, 1976, 1983). In watching these children, it became apparent that individual differences could influence rate of literacy growth as well.

THE CLASSROOM CONTEXT

Roberto and Janice were both in a second-grade class, in which half the students were native Spanish speakers designated as of limited English proficiency (LEP). Of the others, three were fluent Russian-English bilinguals, five were NS of English, and four were fluent English-Spanish bilinguals. Their teacher, a native Spanish speaker, used English in classroom instruction.

School opened at 8:15 A.M. with morning announcements and exercises. At 8:30 most of the Spanish speakers left the room for an hour of instruction in Spanish reading and writing. The materials, the Spanish Curriculum Component (Dade County Board of Public Instruction, 1973), used a phonics approach to Spanish reading. Writing consisted of copying syllables and words. The children did no original writing in Spanish. From 9:30 to 11:30 everyone was involved in English language arts and math. After lunch the class participated in science, social studies, and films or art activities. However, the LEP students, Roberto and Janice included, attended pullout ESOL classes three times a week from 12:15 to 1:15. Dismissal from school was 1:45 P.M.

Janice and Roberto received English literacy instruction both in their classroom and in the ESOL class. The regular classroom teacher used a combination of board work and basal readers. The board work involved spelling words to copy, sentences to copy and illustrate, and incomplete sentences with a choice of words to complete each sentence. The teacher used a basal reader for oral reading practice focused on accurate pronunciation. Most "reading time" consisted of completing workbook pages. The children did none of their own writing in the regular classroom.

In the ESOL class the teacher used the *Miami Linguistic Readers* (Robinett, Rojas, & Bell, 1970), progressing from formal English reading readiness to reading phonics-patterned readers such as *Nat the Rat*. The ESOL teacher did not permit the children to use Spanish in the ESOL room. Writing instruction consisted of copying letters. Original writing did not occur.

I categorized both literacy situations as teacher directed and skills based, a categorization which corresponds with DeFord's (1985) analysis of skills orientation in reading instruction. Daily activities, directed by the teacher, came only from text materials. The teacher evaluated the children on the basis of how well they performed on workbook tasks. Reading instruction focused almost exclusively on sounds, syllables, and words, rather than on connected text. The teachers did not ask children what they might want to read, nor did they ask children to create their own message. In fact, the teachers expressed the view that the children had to learn how to pronounce and write letters, words, and sentences before they could be asked to write on their own.

Obviously this view of literacy development differed significantly from my own. For this reason I asked the teacher if I could experiment with some ESOL writing activities for my tutees. I received permission to work individually with Roberto and Janice on other than school curriculum once or twice a month. On those occasions, we would leave the room to work. I would bring some writing implements, including lined and unlined paper, pencils, crayons, and magic markers. I allowed the children to draw whatever they wanted (since they would write only after drawing), to talk about what they had drawn, and to write something about their drawing. My intent was to encourage the children to express themselves as they were able. I hoped that they would begin to see writing as text construction. The pieces the children produced in our sessions together helped me to appreciate their individual struggles to become English writers.

ROBERTO AS A WRITER OF ENGLISH

Late in October, when I asked Roberto if he could write, he told me that he could write a little in both Spanish and English. He then wrote and read the following:

ROBERTO'S READING	ROBERTO'S WRITING
casa se cae carro	casa secage carro
luces refrigerador no verde	losese referaro no mege
el nino esta en la casa	elgego es ta en la casa
el perro esta en la casa	el pe ro es ta en saca
el nino boto	casa el elgego moco
un papel	un pa paplg
Tiff is sitting *mi mama esta*	Tiff is sitting *mema esta*
limpiando where is a car in	*le pago wer es e car in*

In November his English writing and reading was similar:

ROBERTO'S READING	ROBERTO'S WRITING
Nat the rat is drinking milk	Nat the rat is drikig milk
A dog is drinking milk Yes	e dog is drikig e milk Yes
A lady is eating cake	e lege is etie cake

The sentences came from *The Miami Linguistic Readers* (Robinett, Rojas, & Bell, 1970) and from the county-developed Spanish materials. These early samples demonstrated that the English writing that this Spanish dominant child produced approximated much more closely standard adult English than did the Spanish. This may have been the result of the amount of class time devoted to English. Another factor may have been Roberto's developing phonetic and syllabic hypotheses about how to write Spanish (Edelsky, 1986; Ferreiro & Teberosky, 1982; Hudelson, 1981–82). Most significant, however, is that Roberto viewed writing as the production of sentences and words already practiced in a workbook.

This view of writing continued into December, when Roberto drew and then wrote reproductions of reading workbook sentences, complete with illustrations:

ROBERTO'S READING	ROBERTO'S WRITING
A cat is in a chair	A cat is in a her
King Kim is sitting	
and napping	King Kim is sitting and napping
A rat is digging around	rat is drigging rarcot

In December, however, Roberto also began to create detailed, multicolored drawings which he talked about at length in Spanish and briefly and simply in English. I persuaded him to write a little in English about each drawing. To accompany a picture of a strange-looking figure with a fat body and huge arms, Roberto wrote the word *sateco* and read "Santa Claus."

On another day Roberto and Janice discussed (in Spanish) Roberto's arrival in the United States from Cuba by boat. Then each child drew a picture and wrote something. Roberto drew a picture of a boat flying the Cuban flag and wrote the word *CUNA* ("Cuba") on the boat. Then he hesitantly wrote the sentence *This boat is cuna* and read to me "This boat is Cuba." Roberto repeatedly asked for help in spelling the word *boat*. Only reluctantly did he invent his own spelling. (Invented spelling refers to the children's creations of their own spellings of words based on developing hypotheses about orthography. These hypotheses may be based on letter names, sound-letter correspondences, phonetic pronunciation, saliency and perceptibility of particular sounds, and an individual's idiosyncratic pronunciation of a word. See Bissex, 1980; Edelsky, 1986; Graves, 1983; Hudelson, 1981–82.)

Roberto's cycle of drawing, sharing, and limited writing, accompanied by protestations about lack of knowledge of conventional forms, continued from January through May. In January he drew a vivid, multicolored picture of a fire and a fire engine. As he drew he told me, in Spanish, about a car that had been on fire in his neighborhood. When I asked him if he could write about what had happened, he wrote: *The car is in the* faro and read "The car is on fire."

From February through April he wrote only phrases or lists of words. A drawing of a house resulted in the words *I little house,* read as "one little house." The creation of a color chart was accompanied by the words *red* and *green* next to the appropriate colors. Even when he experimented with cursive writing, he wrote only the labels *fara* (fire), *man, sun, car, miami, Dragen* and *rat* to accompany detailed illustrations.

Finally, in May, Roberto created a drawing of some of the superheroes, identified and labeled Superman *(superman)* and the Hulk *(uok)*, and described the Hulk's actions as "Hulk is fighting with Superman" (written as *is faring with Superman*). Roberto followed this writing and reading with a detailed drawing of and comments about another character, Spiderman, but he refused to write any more.

Several patterns emerged in Roberto's writing as the year progressed. (1) Roberto enjoyed drawing as a means of self-expression as well as a rehearsal for writing, a phenomenon noted with native English speakers (Calkins, 1986; Dyson, 1982a). (2) Roberto consistently created drawings that were more complex and complete than the writing that accompanied them, a feature of the early writing of many young native English speakers (Bissex, 1985; Dyson, 1981). (3) Roberto was eager to share what he had drawn, and he created narratives about his creations (see Dyson, 1981, for examples of English speaking children using a similar strategy). (4) Roberto often began in or switched quickly to Spanish as he created stories about his drawings. (5) After he provided a narration, he could be persuaded to write a little in English about what he had drawn. However, this did not happen voluntarily or as an integral part of the drawing, as is the case with some native speakers (Bissex, 1985; Dyson, 1981; Giacobbe, 1981). (6) Roberto consistently talked much more about his drawings than he wrote. Most of Roberto's meanings were carried by his pictures rather than by his writing (Calkins, 1986).

Over the year Roberto remained reluctant to express himself in writing in English. If the task was copying or reproducing from memory, he did well and performed willingly. If asked to send his own message, however, he produced only a few words and asked repeatedly for assistance. His drawings and narrations made it clear that he did have a variety of ideas, but drawing remained his primary medium of expression.

There are probably many reasons why Roberto developed as he did. Undoubtedly Roberto's limited English had an effect on his written products. He was not a fluent English speaker even at the end of the school year. Moreover, he lacked confidence in his English abilities. While evidence suggests that L2 learners do not need to have complete control over the oral systems of their L2 before they begin to read and write it (Hudelson, 1984), we must acknowledge that the more ability one has in the language the easier reading and writing will be. Roberto's limited English made it difficult for him to write extensively in the language.

Undoubtedly, too, his classroom writing experiences contributed to his reluctance to send his own messages. Investigations of native English speaking children becoming readers and writers have documented that teachers' beliefs about how children learn reading and writing have an effect on the products children generate (DeFord, 1981, 1985; DeFord & Harste, 1982; Dyson, 1982a). It seems likely that Roberto's classroom experiences affected his perceptions of the writing process and therefore the products he produced.

It also seems plausible that Roberto's generally cautious approach to tasks and his lack of willingness to take risks in any academic area of school played a role in his development as an English writer. His personal style had an effect on his rate of growth. This claim, I believe, is strengthened through a comparison of Janice's and Roberto's work over the same period of time.

JANICE AS A WRITER OF ENGLISH

Janice's first reaction to being asked to write in English was that she didn't know any English. She had with her a picture of some people. When asked who they were she replied first in Spanish and then in English that they were a father and a mother. She then wrote the phrase: *myjaus maymodel yamaypader.* This she read as "my house, my mother, and my father."

She refused to write any more. Here Janice exhibited characteristics noted in young native language writers, invented spelling and unconventional segmentation of a word. While Janice's invented spelling reflected a heavy use of Spanish orthography (for example, spelling the word *house* using Spanish sound-letter correspondences and coming up with *jaus*), she also demonstrated an awareness of English orthography in the standard spelling of *my*. Unconventional segmentation refers to children's use of their own ideas, rather than conventional norms about using spaces between written elements, for example, running together the words *myhouse* rather than inserting a space between the words.

In December, after listening to Roberto explain his boat trip from Cuba to the United States, Janice drew a picture of a ship on some waves and a child next to the ship. But when asked to write something about what she had drawn, she created:

JANICE'S READING	*JANICE'S WRITING*
The cat is drinking	Do cat si durinking
Dog sit Tiff is sitting	DogsiTiffsitting

Instead of writing something related to her picture, Janice produced sentences from the *Miami Linguistic Readers* (Robinett, Rojas, & Bell, 1970). Janice's writing strategy was to attempt to reproduce a text she had learned to copy in her workbook. While she used drawing as a vehicle for self-expression, she did not view writing in the same way.

As did Roberto, Janice came to enjoy creating intricate drawings as a prelude to composing a graphic message. In January, after drawing pictures of a television with a human figure and a house on the screen, Janice labeled the pictures in Spanish with these words: *un televisino y una nina y una casa.* When I asked her if she could write something in English she produced the words: *un TV and ges and jaus* and read this as "one tv and girl and house." Janice was willing to try to send a short message in English as well as in Spanish.

Janice preceded her writing in February and March by creating multicolored drawings of houses complete with lawn, flowers, and apple trees. She then wrote on lined paper rather than on the picture:

FEBRUARY

Janice's reading	*Janice's writing*
My house is red	My Haus is red
My car is black	My car is black
My flowers	My faured
trees	three

MARCH

Janice's reading	*Janice's writing*
My house is red and	My Haus is Red and
blue and I got	dlue and Iigat
flowers and trees	faurr and trree
and I got apples	and I gat aporl
that is house my	dad is Haus my
	garnmo (crossed out)
grandmother	Grandmotho

Until February, Janice's development paralleled Roberto's in many ways. The classroom context influenced Janice to view writing in a certain way. Janice passed through a phase in which she equated writing with the accurate reproduction of workbook sentences. She protested frequently that she couldn't write in English either because she didn't know how to say what she wanted to say or because she didn't know how to spell the words. Janice demonstrated a continuing concern for correctness by asking for spellings, but she did invent spellings. But where Roberto ended this year producing word lists or single sentences, Janice moved beyond this stage. By February Janice wrote more than a single sentence in connection with her drawing. And beginning in March, Janice, unlike Roberto, interacted with me about her writing and, taking the reader into account, added to what she had written. Two examples illustrate this interaction.

Janice's March piece initially concluded with "My house is red and blue and I got flowers and trees and I got apples." When she stopped I asked, "Is this your house, Janice?" Janice shook her head no and told me in Spanish that it was her grandmother's house, after which she wrote: "That is house my grandmother." She crossed out her first attempt at *grandmother,* informing me, in Spanish, that she had spelled the word incorrectly. Then she spied a basal reader from which she had recently read a story about a grandmother. She found the word *grandmother* and copied it from the text.

In April, Janice silently drew two buildings, one at the top of the paper and one at the bottom. She connected the buildings by a winding road, and on the road she drew a vehicle. She also drew a bench at the roadside and a person standing by the bench. Then she wrote:

JANICE'S READING	*JANICE'S WRITING*
I got a Hotel	I gad a hotel
and one tree	and ono tree
and one bus	and ono bus
and one street	and ono Street
and one house	and ono house

and one girl	and ono gere
waiting	ueeirin
the bus	the Bus
take to the hotel	take to the hotel
visit him grandmother	dezit him gamer

Initially Janice stopped writing after the words *one girl* and read what she had written. I asked her what the girl was doing. Janice replied in Spanish that the girl was waiting for the bus. I repeated, "Oh, she's waiting for the bus," and Janice added to her effort: "waiting the bus." When I asked why the girl was waiting for the bus, Janice protested in Spanish that she didn't remember how to say in English that the bus was going to take her to the hotel. I replied, "Oh the bus is going to take her to the hotel." Janice then reread everything she had already written and added: "take to the hotel." A final query as to why she was going to the hotel resulted in this: "visit him grandmother."

As Janice responded to my questions, she added information to what she had written, a strategy that may be seen as the beginning of revision (Calkins, 1986). As Janice added information, she was conscious of mistakes but willing to make them. In addition, Janice did not let her limited English stop her. She used her Spanish to get information about how to say things in English. As Janice did this, she grew as a writer. In contrast, Roberto did not use oral input to add to his writing, nor did he ask for information about how to say something in English.

In May, Janice used the Mercer Mayer wordless pictures book *A Boy, A Dog, A Frog and a Friend* (1971) to create a story, which she read as she constructed:

JANICE'S READING	*JANICE'S WRITING*
The boy is fishing	The Boe is fisehing
He going to fall down	He going to fo daun
He fall down	He fo daun
He trying to get out	Hear toaring to gereout
the water	the wetre
the turtle got his fishhook	the therin gad has fish
The dog going fighting	the Dog going fairing
With the turtle	wit the thernr
bite the dog	dait the dog
The boy going to	the boe going to
take the dog and the turtle	thek the dog and tha thernr
going bite the dog	goig dat the Dog
The boy take the dog	The Boethek the Dog
He take the dog	He thek the Dog
He put he tail in the water	He put the tel in the wetre
He fall down	He fo daun

He going jump to take	He going jump to thek
the dog to the water	the Dog to the wetre
The turtle dies	the theringr dais
He going to take xxxout	he going to take rafaa
The boy take the	the Boe thek the
turtle in his	thernic and hes
hand and the frog and	had and the forg and
dog going walking	dog going walking
the boy digging the hole	the boe dieing the ho

Janice stayed with this task for more than half an hour. Frequently she described a picture first in Spanish and then in English. Often she asked for translations of words and phrases that she did not know in English (for example, *fishhook, bite, take out, tail, die*). She spelled unfamiliar words as she thought they should be spelled. She sounded out a lot of words as she wrote them. Repeatedly she reread what she had just written before going on to a new page. Janice produced a description of what was happening on each page. As she struggled with this new task, she paid less attention to handwriting. All of these behaviors reminded me of descriptions of young monolingual English speakers experimenting with writing (Bissex, 1985; Calkins, 1986; Dyson, 1982b; Giacobbe, 1981).

This effort demonstrated clearly that Janice saw herself as an individual willing to take risks to construct meaning, a language user aware of mistakes but willing to make them, a bilingual who used her native language to ask for help with English. These behaviors were quite different from Roberto's.

CONCLUSIONS AND CLASSROOM IMPLICATIONS

I have reported a school year's worth of work with Janice and Roberto. Certainly the children's classroom writing experiences had an influence on their perceptions of writing and on their pieces. Initially the children viewed writing as copying, reproducing workbook material, or using spelling words to construct sentences. Both moved beyond this view. Each child responded to an environment quite different from that of the classroom, an environment that believed that ESL children could and should produce English texts while still learning the language (Edelsky, 1986; Flores et al., 1985; Hudelson, 1984; Urzua, 1987). In this environment Janice made more progress than Roberto. Janice probably would be classified as the "better" or more successful language learner (Rubin, 1975; Strong, 1983; Wong Fillmore, 1976, 1983). Roberto's tentative, cautious, non-risk-taking behavior probably had an effect on his rate of progress both as a speaker and as a writer of English. Janice was more willing than Roberto to guess at answers, to use what she knew at a particular time, to make mistakes, to ask for information from sources outside herself. These characteristics probably contributed to her more rapid rate of progress as a user of English.

Roberto and Janice are typical of ESL children in public schools who need to learn English to succeed in English-medium schools. They also show that ESL children do display individual differences in personality traits and in cognitive and social styles. These individual differences mean that ESL children respond in different ways to school language experiences.

Most ESL teachers hope that all their students would respond to an environment that encourages written expression as Janice did. But some children will respond more like Roberto. This does *not* mean that writing opportunities should be discontinued. Rather, it calls for even more such opportunities on a regular (e.g., daily) basis. Writing needs to be viewed as an integral part of second language development, and children need to write different kinds of pieces for varied purposes and audiences.

ESL children will need to receive continued support of what they are doing, acceptance of what has been produced, and gentle but persistent encouragement to continue to express themselves. Early in their schooling, priority should be given to establishing fluency and willingness to write. Rejection of the writer's efforts or a focus on what is wrong may only serve to make the writer even less confident and less willing to take the risks necessary to construct a text.

Part of acceptance and focus on what children are doing involves understanding drawing as integral to the composing process, and as sometimes more important to the writer than the writing itself. Calkins (1986) notes that for many beginning writers, "The act of drawing and the picture itself both provide a supporting scaffolding within which the piece of writing can be constructed . . ." (p. 50). She also suggests that ". . . during their early forays into writing, they [children] often embed much of their meaning in the picture rather than in the text" (p. 51). Acceptance of children's drawing seems especially relevant for L2 learners struggling not only with written forms but also with the oral expression that is so integral a part of the NS's early writing (Dyson, 1981).

Drawing may also serve as a tool to promote talk. As children describe and narrate their drawings, they use their developing language to communicate with others. As part of interactions, children receive comprehensible input (Krashen, 1982) that they may use to construct oral or written messages.

Also crucial to both understanding and encouraging children's language development is an acceptance and utilization of one of their greatest strengths, their native language(s). Allowing the use of the native language in an ESL setting continues to be a controversial practice. From my perspective, encouraging English while allowing children to use their native language if needed gives a more accurate picture of what children do and what their needs are. If children feel free to use their native language, they may write more than if they feel constrained not to use it. Feeling comfortable narrating stories in a language children speak fluently provides a natural and authentic opportunity for fluent speakers to repeat their words in English, thus providing a model of fluent English and needed comprehensible input, which may later be used for further production. Allowing the native languages may make children feel comfortable and give them access to more input than they would have otherwise, thus contributing to, rather than retarding, their growth as users of English.

This volume demonstrates repeatedly that teachers have a powerful impact on L2 learners' development. Many ESL teachers work in pullout situations where they are not the only teacher working with the ESL child. Often other teachers hold differing views of language teaching and learning. This situation makes it vitally important that we share our perspectives on and our understandings of effective learning environments for second language learners. We need to share what we know and use examples from children such as Janice and Roberto to make our points. We need to become advocates for our ESL students to ensure them the best possible education (Cazden, 1986). We need to act on what we know, rather than "go along with" the prevailing classroom or district philosophy.

Finally, we must understand that children ultimately are in control of their own learning, including their learning of writing. While we may support, encourage, and facilitate children's development, we cannot control it. When children determine that they are able, they will write. Writing will grow according to individual timetables, when it feels right for the children, not just for us as adults. Roberto proved this to me when I visited him in his third-grade classroom a year after we had met. I was no longer a school volunteer tutor, but I wanted to see Roberto and Janice again, so I arranged a visit. Roberto asked if I was going to take him out of the room so that he could draw and write. The teacher gave permission and we left the room. Robert voluntarily narrated a wordless picture story to me in English and wrote and read to me a brief summary of some of the pictures in the story.

ROBERTO'S READING	*ROBERTO'S WRITING*
The duck is in the nest She have many eggs in the nest. Father and Mother was	The deuk is in the nest. She have many eggs in The nest. Father and

| happy and they and xxx and | Mather was happy and day |
| happy | and natg and happy |

After this first piece Roberto drew a picture of a dragon breathing fire onto a tree. Behind the tree was a rock. In the sky, the sun was shining on the creature. Then Roberto wrote and read:

ROBERTO'S READING	*ROBERTO'S WRITING*
Sun is hot. The fire is in	Sun is hot. The fire is in
the tree. The rock is in	The tree. The rock is in
fire too. The lawn is blue.	fire too. The lonw is blue.
The dinosaur is brown.	The danasorn is down.
The dinosaur has fire in	The danasorn has fire in
his mouth.	his mouth.

When I asked Roberto about writing in his room, he said that he wrote spelling lists and English book sentences. But he was willing to create this text for me. Apparently, Roberto finally had determined that he could express himself in English, that he knew enough English and enough about writing to risk his own expression. While I could encourage and cajole him, only Roberto could do the composing. Once again I, the teacher, became the learner as Roberto taught me that he was in charge of the situation, and that I needed to have patience and trust in each learner's individual pattern of growth. That was the most important lesson of all.

REFERENCES

Allen, V. (1986). Developing contests to support second language acquisition. *Language Arts, 63,* 61–67.

Bissex, G. (1980). *GYNS AT WK: A child learns to write and read.* Cambridge, MA: Harvard University Press.

Bissex, G. (1985). Watching young writers. In A. Jagger & M. T. Smith-Burke (Eds.), *Observing the language learner* (pp. 99–113). Newark, DE: International Reading Association.

Calkins, L. (1986). *The art of teaching writing.* Portsmouth, NH: Heinemann.

Cazden, C. B. (1986). ESL teachers as language advocates for children. In P. Rigg & D. S. Enright (Eds.), *Children and ESL: Integrating perspectives.* Washington, DC: Teachers of English to Speakers of Other Languages.

Dade County Board of Public Instruction. (1973). *Spanish curriculum development component.* Miami: Dade County Board of Public Instruction.

DeFord, D. (1981). Reading, writing and other essentials. *Language Arts, 58,* 652–658.

DeFord, D. (1985). Validating the construction of theoretical orientation in reading instruction. *Reading Research Quarterly, 15,* 351–367.

DeFord, D., & Harste, J. (1982). Child language research and curriculum. *Language Arts, 59,* 590–600.

Dyson, A. (1981). Oral language: The rooting system for learning to write. *Language Arts, 58,* 776–784.

Dyson, A. (1982a). The emergence of visible language: Interrelationships between drawing and early writing. *Visible Language, 16,* 360–381.

Dyson, A. (1982b). Teachers and young children: Missed connections between teaching/learning to write. *Language Arts, 59,* 674–680.

Edelsky, C. (1982). Writing in a bilingual program: The relation of L1 and L2 texts. *TESOL Quarterly, 16,* 211–228.

Edelsky, C. (1986). *Writing in a bilingual program: Había una vez.* Norwood, NJ: Ablex.

Ferreiro, E., & Teberosky, A. (1982). *Literacy before schooling.* Exeter, NH: Heinemann.

Flores, B., Garcia, E., Gonzales, S., Hidalgo, G., Kaczmarek, K., & Romero, T. (1985). *Holistic bilingual instruction strategies.* Chandler, AZ: Exito Publishing Company.

Giacobbe, M. E. (1981). Who says that children can't write the first week? In R. D. Walshe (Ed.), *Donald Graves in Australia: Children want to write . .* (pp. 99–103). Exeter, NH: Heinemann.

Goodman, K. (1987). *What's whole in whole language?* Portsmouth, NH: Heinemann.

Goodman, K., & Goodman, Y. (1977). Learning to read is natural. In L. Resnick & P. Weaver (Eds.), *Theory and practice of early reading* (Vol. 1, pp. 137–154). Hillsdale, NJ: Lawrence Erlbaum Associates.

Goodman, K., Goodman, Y., & Flores, B. (1979). *Reading in the bilingual classroom: Literacy and biliteracy.* Rosslyn, VA: National Clearinghouse for Bilingual Education.

Graves, D. (1983). *Writing: Teachers and children at work.* Portsmouth, NH: Heinemann.

Hudelson, S. (1981–82). An introductory examination of children's invented spelling in Spanish. *NABE Journal, 6,* 53–67.

Hudelson, S. (1984). Kan yu ret an rayt en ingles: Children become literate in English as a second language. *TESOL Quarterly, 18,* 221–238.

Jagger, A., & Smith-Burke, M. T. (Eds.). (1985). *Observing the language learner.* Newark, DE: International Reading Association.

Krashen, S. (1982). *Principles and practice in second language acquisition.* Oxford: Pergamon Press.

Lindfors, J. (1987). *Children's language and learning* (2nd ed.). Englewood Cliffs, NJ: Prentice-Hall.

Mayer, M. (1971). *A boy, a dog, a frog and a friend.* New York: Dial Press.

Milz, V. (1985). First graders' uses for writing. In A. Jagger & M. T. Smith-Burke (Eds.), *Observing the language learner* (pp. 173–189). Newark, DE: International Reading Association.

Newman, J. (Ed.). (1985). *Whole language: Theory in use.* Portsmouth, NH: Heinemann.

Rigg, P., & Enright, D. S. (Eds.). (1986). *Children and ESL: Integrating perspectives*. Washington, DC: Teachers of English to Speakers of Other Languages.

Robinett, R., Rojas, P., & Bell, P. (1970). *The Miami linguistic readers*. Boston: Heath.

Rubin, J. (1975). What the good language learner can teach us. *TESOL Quarterly, 9*, 41–51.

Smith, F. (1983). *Essays into literacy*. Portsmouth, NH: Heinemann.

Strong, M. (1983). Social styles and the second-language acquisition of Spanish-speaking kindergarteners. *TESOL Quarterly, 17*, 241–258.

Urzua, C. (1980). A language learning environment for all children. *Language Arts, 57*, 38–44.

Urzua, C. (1987). "You stopped too soon": Second language children composing and revising. *TESOL Quarterly, 21*, 279–304.

Ventriglia, L. (1982). *Conversations of Miguel and Maria: How children learn a second language*. Reading, MA: Addison-Wesley.

Wong Fillmore, L. (1976). *The second time around: Cognitive and social strageties in second language acquisition*. Doctoral dissertation. Stanford, CA: Stanford University.

Wong Fillmore, L. (1983). The language learner as an individual: Implications of research on individual differences for the ESL teacher. In M. Clarke and J. Handscombe (Eds.), *On TESOL '82: Pacific perspectives on language learning* (pp. 157–174). Washington, DC: Teachers of English to Speakers of Other Languages.

CHAPTER 6

Writing and Talking about Writing: Computer Networking with Elementary Students

Joy Kreeft Peyton
Center for Applied Linguistics

JoAnn Mackinson-Smyth
Kendall Demonstration Elementary School

MEGAN:	Hello Helen, are you ready?
HELEN:	yes
MEGAN:	Good, I got alots of presents.
HELEN:	what dose?
MEGAN:	Please repeat, I dont understand what you mean.
HELEN:	oh "what you did dose"?
MEGAN:	What dose?
HELEN:	i mean what you did got christmas?
MEGAN:	Oh okay, I got clothes, shoes, and some toys!! And some cabbage patch dolls too.
HELEN:	i got clothes, puppy pound, fluppy dog, and etc.
MEGAN:	I got six newborn pound puppies for christmas too.
HELEN:	i don't know true or false about pound puppies?
MEGAN:	Oh, thats part of toys.
HELEN:	false

The research reported here is part of a three-year project to implement and study the use of classroom networking with hearing-impaired elementary school and university students. The project is funded by a grant from the President of Gallaudet University.

We are grateful to Donna Christian, Rachel Harris, and Jana Staton for very helpful comments on earlier drafts of this chapter.

MEGAN: Yes, right, you know all toys are false.

HELEN: i have a cabbage path's clothes

MEGAN: Oh, that nice, I got two cabbage patch kids dolls.

HELEN: oh, i got three cabbage patch kids doll.

MEGAN: very close. My real cat was very bad during the vacation.

HELEN: what your did cat do?

MEGAN: OOOHh terrible thing, she toilet on moms favorite sofa, etc.

HELEN: yes, bad cat. i want more know etc.

MEGAN: ok he mess my moms favorite plant, destroyed my moms old sofa as her stachting post, put her claws on washing machine, dryer things at unitily room. VVEERRYY BBAADD CCAATT!!!!

HELEN: your mom say kick out the cat?

MEGAN: Plus she ruined one of my favorite hat. No, she understand that she hated to be alone in house for two weeks without us, thats why she do that.
Bye i have to get off, i really enjoyed talking to you, hope to talk to you again at here.

HELEN: ohoh. my kitty only out and cacht rat
time stop bye good lucky bye

MEGAN: yeah me too, one boy cat out and one girl in, I have to go we will talk in way.

HELEN: bye!!!

MEGAN: bye!!

In an elementary classroom in Washington, D.C., five conversations like this one are taking place at once, but the only sound in the room is the clicking of computer keys and an occasional chuckle. These students, aged 7 to 9 years, are hearing impaired and are conversing in writing on a local area network.[1] They are part of a larger program of networked classrooms at Gallaudet University, a liberal arts university in Washington, D.C., for hearing-impaired students. Each networked class is equipped with about 12 computer terminals, with the networking capability and software that allow real-time interaction. The students and teacher each sit at a terminal and type what they want to say into a private area at the bottom of the screen, not visible to other members of the class. When they press a key, the message moves from the lower to the upper part of the screen and is immediately transmitted to all of the screens in the class,

---

[1] Networked conversations are reproduced here as the children produced them, without corrections to spelling, capitalization, etc. However, names of students and teachers have been changed. In some ways, the children's network writing does not adequately reflect their competence with the use of writing conventions since, to make typing easier, they often omit capitalization and punctuation, even though they know how to use them and do use them in their other writing.

tagged with the name of the person sending it. As new messages are typed and sent, the screen scrolls to make room for them, approximating the kinds of discussions that would occur in any class, except that they are written. The computer stores the entire discussion, which can be reviewed at any time in the class, or printed out in its entirety at the end. Figure 6.1 shows the screen configuration, with one message in the lower private area and two in the upper public area.

For two years we have been working with these students as they converse on the newtork (Mackinson-Smyth as the teacher and Kreeft Peyton as the researcher), observing them in class as they write on the network and during their later discussions of the printed transcripts, and analyzing the transcripts they produce. Our observations have revealed some important processes in literacy development among these students and some conclusions about the role that writing on the network seems to play in this development. When writing conversationally on the network, the students experience "writing" not simply as the act of composing autonomous text, but as a natural, functional, and communicative activity and as an opportunity to negotiate meaning and learn from each other. They write in collaboration with other writers, who provide models of written English and continual feedback. As they write over time and develop as writers on the network, they begin to explore new ways to express themselves in writing and to learn the conventions of written text. They learn to write to various audiences and to make their writing clear, interesting, and appropriate for their audience. Writing becomes another important means for expressing their ideas.

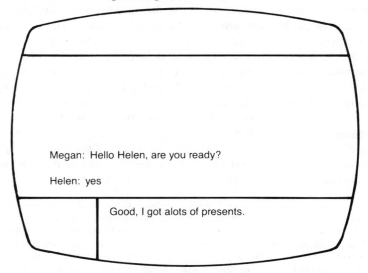

Figure 6.1. Computer Screen in Networked Classroom

Each conversation results in a printed transcript that is later reread, edited, and discussed. Thus the students' literacy development involves not simply writing and reading what others have written on the network, but also reflecting about that writing and about themselves as effective communicators. As they develop as readers and writers they develop as well the metalinguistic ability to talk about writing, also an important aspect of literacy development (Heath, 1985; Heath & Branscombe, 1984).

In this chapter, we describe how the network is used with these students, show some of the features of their network writing and its relation to their literacy development, and discuss some of the writing development we have seen in the two years the children have been writing on the network. To provide a more in-depth look into the process, we then focus on the writing of two students in the class, one of the most and one of the least proficient in English. Although the students in the study are hearing-impaired, the approach can be used with hearing students as well (and is now being used with various populations of hearing students across the country). We believe, therefore, that the approach we describe here and the results we have seen are relevant for those working with any students learning English as a second language (ESL) (with appropriate modifications to suit the needs of the student population).

MAKING THE SPEECH–WRITING CONNECTION: LOCAL AREA NETWORKS AND WRITING DEVELOPMENT

The local area computer networks at Gallaudet University were established in an attempt to facilitate the reading and writing development of hearing-impaired students. Because of their hearing impairment, they have limited exposure to spoken English. Apart from captioned TV and movies and conversations via TDD (a telecommunications device that allows typed telephone conversations), hearing-impaired students have little opportunity to use or observe the use of English in a conversational context and to receive immediate feedback about their production. This lack of exposure to spoken English and minimal use of English in interaction affects their written English skills and their confidence as writers (Charrow, 1981; Ivimey & Lachterman, 1980; and cf. Powers & Wilgus, 1983, for a review of other studies).

In some ways, the difficulties that hearing-impaired students have with writing are very different from those of ESL students who are hearing. Lack of access to spoken English has already been mentioned as an important factor. American Sign Language (ASL, the first language of most of the students in this study), a visual-gestural language, has all of the syntactic and semantic features of a fully developed language, but its structure is very different from that of English.[2] When hearing students learning ESL move from speech to writing, they are working within the same language. When hearing-impaired students move from face-to-face interaction to written English, they are often moving from one language to another.

However, in other ways, the processes of learning to write are similar (Ewoldt, 1985), as are some of the problems. A blank piece of paper can silence the most fluent and expressive of speakers, even when English is their native language (Elbow, 1981; Rose, 1984; 1985). The writing of many ESL students even at the college level can be "dry, flat, mechanical prose, full of unsupported generalizations, repeated concepts, and errors . . . not only filled with grammatical errors but empty of life and content" (Raimes, 1983, p. 258).

Therefore, interactive writing on a local area network, originally conceived for use with hearing-impaired students, can be used with hearing students as well to give them opportunities to use written English in an interactive, communicative, and functional context. As scholars studying writing development point out, writing seems so difficult in part because it is considered to be so different from speech. Speech is thought of as an ability that is acquired at home, whereas writing is taught at school. Speech is considered casual, social, and interactive; writing is considered formal, solitary, and monologic (Elbow, 1985; Shuy, in press). Students are often encouraged to remove "speech-like" qualities from their writing. However, Elbow argues that "writing of the highest quality—writing as good as any of us could possibly hope to achieve—not only can but should have many of the essential qualities misguidedly labeled 'inherent in speech'" (1985, p. 291). Rather than treating speech and writing as mutually exclusive abilities, we need to "exploit the speech-like qualities of writing . . . capitalizing on the oral language skills that students already possess and helping [them] apply those skills immediately and effortlessly to writing . . ." (1985, p. 290).

Recent writing theory and pedagogical approaches beginning with Moffett (1968), have attempted to make a closer connection between speech and writing. Kroll (1981), for example, proposes a developmental writing model that builds on speaking abilities and integrates them into the writing process. Interactive writing in letters (Heath & Branscombe, 1984), in dialogue journals (Staton, Shuy, Kreeft Peyton, & Reed, in press), and through electronic mail (Levin, Riel, Rowe, & Boruta, 1985; Sayers,

---

[2] Cf. Charrow (1981) for discussion and Stokoe (1971, 1972) and Baker and Cokeley (1980) for more complete definitions of ASL and descriptions of its features. ASL does not have a written form.

this volume) takes writing out of its isolated, formal niche and allows lively and spontaneous written exchanges. As Heath and Branscombe point out,

> just as the development of oral language depends on the context of the rich interaction between child and adults, so the development of written language depends on a rich responsive context. . . . Young children acquiring language search for units of symbolic behavior, construct systems of elements and relations, and try to match their production to those of selected others in recurrent situational contexts; the new writer must follow similar steps to generate internal rules for writing to communicate. Responsive, interactive writing frequently occurring over a period of time provides the data from which students may search out meaningful units and systems in writing. (1984, p. 30)

Writing on a local area network takes these approaches one step further. On a network, all classroom communication—from informal chitchat and classroom management details at the beginning of class, to focused discussions of course content, readings, and papers written by students, to the collaborative writing of compositions—can be done in writing. These activities can be placed along two continua (following Cummins, 1981)—one moving from personal to academic and the other from interactive to monologic (Figure 6.2). Traditionally, the activities listed on the interactive end of the continuum have been conducted in speech, with writing reserved for those near the monologic end. In a networked classroom, rather than discussing ideas or each others' writing orally or in sign and then stopping to write only to compose or revise, written discussion can lead to written composition. All activities are accomplished in writing, and the gap between speech and writing can be closed.

DEVELOPING EARLY LITERACY: COMPUTER NETWORKING WITH ELEMENTARY CHILDREN

With young deaf children in elementary school, the network is used to enhance literacy development. It was first used by six eight-year-olds from Kendall Demonstration Elementary School (affiliated with Gallaudet University). All the students had deaf parents, and their first language (L1) was American Sign Language (ASL). They had considerable proficiency in written English, were reading at the second- and third-grade level, and were on or near grade level in all academic subjects. After a year they were joined by a class of younger students who were less proficient in English (the new members were 7 and 8 years old; members of the original group were 9 years old at the time). Language backgrounds of the new group of

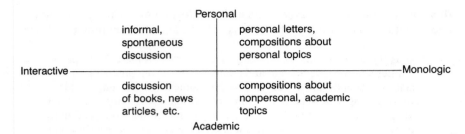

Personal

informal,	personal letters,
spontaneous	compositions about
discussion	personal topics

Interactive ——————————————————————————— Monologic

discussion	compositions about
of books, news	nonpersonal, academic
articles, etc.	topics

Academic

Figure 6.2. Two Continua for Language Tasks (adapted from Cummins, 1981).

students were mixed. Two had deaf parents; four had hearing parents (and therefore were not exposed to ASL in the home). One student's family was from Asia and did not speak English. These students were below grade level in reading and in most academic areas.

Both classes are self-contained; each had the same teacher all day. Once a week they leave their regular classrooms to go to the computer lab to converse on the network for about an hour. Because they are slow typists and their attention span is short, they work in pairs or in groups of two or three rather than as a whole class. The teacher assigns the pairs or groups, but the students are encouraged to decide among themselves, on their way to the lab, a topic for discussion and the kind of writing they will do. Sometimes the negotiation about the topic takes place on the network itself:

ROBIN: hello, robin here
          lets talk about star wars

MARCIE: I prefer to talk about trip going to your house then star wars

ROBIN: No I don't want to talk about trip little trip and not important I prefer to talk about star wars

MARCIE: ok promise that we talk about star wars then talk about trip to your house

ROBIN: ok fine

MARCIE: ok write your question

Initially, members of the original class were paired or grouped with one another, and one student each week was paired with the teacher. When the new class joined, the original students alternated between being grouped with each other, with the less proficient students, and with the teacher.

At the end of each session the conversations are printed and retyped in large type exactly as students produced them. Students are given retyped dialogue to take home and edit. Later that week, in the regular classroom, the edited transcript becomes the basis for discussion (in sign language) of content, interaction patterns, manners of written expression, and language form. Students identify topics discussed on the network and determine whether the speakers stayed on a topic or strayed from it, looking for linguistic cues to support their decisions. They discuss how the speakers began, ended, and maintained their conversations: Was there a greeting? Did they check to make sure they both wanted to proceed with the agreed-upon topic? Did they politely close the conversation? Were there smooth topic transitions? They discuss whether a particular question or response was clear and how various responses might be improved. They also do some further editing, focusing on punctuation, capitalization, spelling, and grammar (a sheet used to guide these discussions is shown in Figure 6.3). The teacher of the more proficient students suggests strategies they might use to work with the less proficient ones to encourage writing development, and over time they have been able to identify these strategies in their own writing.

INTERACTING ON THE NETWORK

As they write to each other on the network, the children work together to develop their ability to express themselves in written English: keeping each other focused on a topic, modeling structures and vocabulary for each other, and requesting elaboration if a contribution is uninformative or clarification if it is unclear. In this example, Nancy reprimands Andy for ignoring her response to his question about animals (line 4) and persists in getting him to focus his writing on *one part* of a movie (lines 6 & 7, 9, 11, 13). (Lines are numbered here for easy reference.)

ANDY:	1	I love dog and cat and pony.
NANCY:	2	Oh, I see I love kitties, puppies, dog and cat.
ANDY:	3	What do you like kind of animals????????
NANCY:	4	I SAID KITTIES, PUPPIES, DOG, AND CAT
ANDY:	5	OHHHHH! how stupid I am!
NANCY:	6	Well, talk about star wars . . . star wars is good movie
	7	and what part do you love in star wars?
ANDY:	8	starwars is my favorite movie!!!!!!!!!!
NANCY:	9	what part?
ANDY:	10	(RETURN TO JEDI) what is your?
NANCY:	11	I said what part in only one movie
ANDY:	12	(STAR WAR)!!!!!!!!!!!!! AND (E.T.)!!!!!!!!!!
NANCY:	13	sample I like to see luke fighting with mean star wars

Name _____

Date   _____

1. Who are the speakers?
2. What is the topic of the conversation?
3. How do you know?
4. How did the speakers begin their conversation?
5. Does the topic change? If so, why?
6. How did the speakers end their conversation?
7. List some things that each speaker remembers to do.

Speaker: _____   Speaker: _____

8. List some ways that each speaker would improve communication.

Speaker: _____   Speaker: _____

Figure 6.3. Networking Follow-up Sheet

ANDY:	14 I like to see hansolo and luke are driving the pilot
	15 around the !!!!!!!!!!
NANCY:	16 perfect how stupid are you? i just tease you that's
	17 all . . .

Below, Marcie and Kate discuss Kate's Christmas vacation. Marcie models for Kate the (almost) correct structure, vocabulary, and spelling for "i have scare dream" (line 3) and later teaches her a new word, "nightmare" (line 8). She also attempts to get Kate to elaborate more about why she didn't enjoy the hotel she stayed in (lines 11–13).

MARCIE:	1 then what happen on that night?
KATE:	2 i have scare drem
MARCIE:	3 you mean you had bad dream?
KATE:	4 yes
MARCIE:	5 oh i see did you swim at hotel?
KATE:	6 no it is snow
MARCIE:	7 oh i mean inside you are right you can not swim in the snow
	8 and i want to teach you new word for bad dream is nightmare
	9 did you enjoy at the hotel?
KATE:	10 no
MARCIE:	11 why you did not? can you explain?
	12 explain mean to tell someone about something
	13 then why did you did not enjoy the trip to the hotel?

KATE:　　14 I AM MISUNDERSTAND YES I HAVE ENJOYIN HOTEL

In the conversation that opens this chapter, Megan persists in requesting that Helen clarify the meaning of "what dose" until Helen explains, "I mean what did you get for Christmas?"

Conversations between the more and the less proficient writers have many of the features that have been documented in studies of oral interactions between caretakers and children learning a first language (Cross, 1977; Snow, 1977; Wells, 1981, 1986) and between native and nonnative speakers of a language (Allwright, 1984; Hatch, 1978a, 1978b) in which the primary focus is on meaning and more proficient speakers create opportunities for less proficient speakers to participate, model language for them and expand on their contributions, and request clarification and elaboration. The following conversation between Robin and Pam illustrates some of the dynamics that can occur on the network to promote literacy acquisition. Robin is one of the most proficient writers in the original class, a 10-year-old prelingually deaf (deaf at birth) child of deaf parents. Her L1 is ASL, and she has developed a high level of proficiency in her L2, English. She is a strong student, working above grade level in all academic areas. Pam is one of the least proficient writers in the second class, an 8-year-old prelingually deaf child of hearing parents, who are native to Asia and speak mostly Vietnamese in the home. Pam has some knowledge of ASL and beginning proficiency in English. She was working below grade level in all academic areas when she started writing on the network.

PAM:　　1 hello robin

ROBIN:　　2 hi Pam　how are you

PAM:　　3 fine.

ROBIN:　　4 oh i am fine too　do you have any pets?

PAM:　　5 yes i have my pet is fish.

ROBIN:　　6 oh i see　i have a pet too　i have a dog.

PAM:　　7 oh you have baby dog?

ROBIN:　　8 no before that dog was baby　baby dogs are called puppies.

PAM:　　9 no

ROBIN:　　10 My dog is girl. She is 4 years old.

PAM:　　11 oh

ROBIN:　　12 Do you want to know what's her name?

PAM:　　13 yes i want your name.

ROBIN:　　14 Okay, Her name is Tina. Do you like cats?

PAM:　　15 who is's cats.

ROBIN:　　16 No I dont have cats　I want to know if you like cats?

PAM:　　17 oh i like cats yes

ROBIN: 18 Do you like kittens? Kittens are baby cats.
        19 favorite.
PAM: 20 but i favorite kittens baby.
ROBIN: 21 Oh I see. I cant have kittens or cats. They make my dad have
            cold.
PAM: 22 i not understand.
ROBIN: 23 My dad is allergy to cats. Allergy mean that people cant use or
            touch
        24 If i drink milk i become sick.
        25 Do you understand?
PAM: 26 your father home? robin and dog doing out or in.
ROBIN: 27 no, my dog doing in. do you like bear?
        28 afraid.
        29 bite.
PAM: 30 no i afraid bear because will be bite.
ROBIN: 31 Well, Bears is my favorite animal. what is your favorite animals?
PAM: 32 my favorite is bear baby.
ROBIN: 33 oh they are called cubs.
PAM: 34 oh.
ROBIN: 35 what color bear do you like? black or white or brown or yellow.
PAM: 36 i like white.
ROBIN: 37 oh me too   they are polar bears   bye   time to stop
        38 i enjoy talking with you.

Robin clearly demonstrates the ability to facilitate Pam's participation
in the discussion (an ability that she probably learned in part during her
network discussions with the teacher and in-class discussions of effective
strategies). She focuses on topics that are familiar to Pam, pets and
animals in general. She maintains discussion of these topics by asking Pam
questions. Her questions are primarily yes-no (e.g., "do you have any
pets?", lines 4, 12, 14, 16, 18, 27), in which the vocabulary needed to
formulate an answer is provided in the question (and Pam uses that
vocabulary in her response in line 5, "yes i have my pet is fish"). When she
asks *wh* questions (such as "What color bear do you like?"), which do not
provide the vocabulary needed for formulating a reply, she provides a
model upon which Pam can build her answer (line 31, "Bears is my
favorite animal. what is your favorite animals?"; line 35, "what color bear
do you like? black or white or brown or yellow."). Robin checks on Pam's
comprehension of what she has written (line 25), and shifts topics with
Pam when Pam turns from the discussion of allergies back to the discussion of pets (line 26). She accepts Pam's rather unclear contribution (line
26, "robin and dog doing out or in," which, as far as we can tell, means,

"Does your dog go outside or stay inside?") and replies to it (line 27). She introduces new vocabulary that Pam then uses in her turns, moving from general to more specific terms—from cats (lines 14 & 16) to kittens (18); from pets (4 & 6) to dog (6) to puppies (8); from bears (27) to cubs (33) and polar bears (37). She explains new words as she introduces them (*puppies,* line 8; *kittens,* 18; *allergy,* 23; *cubs,* 33; *polar bears,* 37). When Pam wants to use words that she doesn't know how to write, she stands up and signs to Robin the word she needs, and Robin provides the word in writing (line 19, *favorite;* 28, *afraid;* 29, *bite*). With Robin's help, Pam is able to produce a relatively complex statement, "No, I am afraid of bears because they bite" (line 30).

These interactions on the network provide abundant opportunities for developing English literacy in a context that scholars now argue is essential for beginning writers, both native English speakers (Calkins, 1983, 1986; Goodman, 1984; Graves, 1983) and ESL students (Hudelson, 1984; Kreeft, Shuy, Staton, Reed, & Morroy, 1984). Reading and writing grow out of the students' own experiences and interests. Writing is used to communicate real messages to real audiences. As they attempt to express their thoughts to another person in writing, the students are pushed to attempt structures they have not yet mastered and given models of structures on which they can build their messages. Although they are not composing autonomous text, they are developing abilities essential for writing, including choosing a topic and writing at length about it in a way that is coherent to a reader and learning to produce the spelling, vocabulary, structures, and conventions of written English.

DEVELOPING LITERATE BEHAVIORS

When they had become more accustomed to writing on the network, usually after about six months, some of the more proficient children, without teacher prompting, began to display greater metalinguistic and literate awareness. They played word games that require knowledge of the structure of English and collaboratively produced stories such as this one written by a group of three students.

MARCIE: hello, let start our topic is "coming into my night mare"
Once upon a time there was a boy named Tom he went to sleep he had night mare   he . . .

ANNA: what mare mean is?

ROBIN: it means a bad dream.

MARCIE: she is right

ANNA: oh i see. his mare is about an vamprie. a vamprie want to eat he. he not want the vamprie to eat he.

ROBIN: he ran into a house that is haunted and he was in. The door slammed.

MARCIE: he started to be afraid he had alot of imagion that mean he think what shall hapeen then he thought he was at the movies with alot of doors that slammed. There is other mean to mare is a female horse   night mare mean bad dreams

ANNA: but he saw many vamprie. then he thought it is a false vampries. but it is real vampries!!!!!!!

ROBIN: he ran and ran and fainted

MARCIE: then he woke up with blood on neck and say "ohhhhh vvaammp-piirree hhaadd bitt me"
do you understood me?

ANNA: then he ran to his mom but when he saw his mom and his mom is deid!! . . . [etc.]

This kind of collaborative story writing exemplifies a student-initiated move toward a different type of reading and writing, the production of extended, autonomous text. However, Heath (1985) argues that "becoming literate is not the same thing as learning to read and write; it is learning to talk reading and writing" (p. 15). "Learners must, before they can become successful in using language for many functions, pay attention to the forms and structures of types of discourse" (p. 24). Students learning to read and write must be able to examine their own and others' writing, analyze and manipulate their written text, and develop different uses of written English for different contexts and with different audiences (Heath & Branscombe, 1984).

In sessions that follow the network discussions, the group of more proficient students reviews, discusses (in sign language), and edits the resulting transcripts (the process is described earlier in this chapter and the discussion guidelines used in the follow-up are provided in the Appendix). In these discussions, their written English "becomes the object . . . of study" (Heath, 1985, p. 25), as these children reflect about and analyze together what they have written on the network. As these discussions have continued over the two years, the children have shown an increased sense of ownership of their writing and an improved ability to analyze it. They have also come to consider themselves as experts about the language of the networked discussions, since they were the ones who produced it.

After the students had been having these follow-up discussions for about a year, they reviewed the transcript of the conversation about pets between Robin and Pam above. They were able to identify some of the strategies that Robin had used to help Pam. Different students mentioned that she was "explaining," "making her writing more clear," and "giving her new words." They also talked about the overall structure of the conversation and the connections between the contributions of the two participants. Some students felt that Pam had changed the topic to introduce two new ones in line 26 when she wrote, "your father home? robin and dog doing out or in." But others argued that she was instead tying her turn to Robin's previous one, asking if Robin's father was at home sick because of his allergies. Then she returned to the discussion of pets.

In these sessions, the children are developing the metalinguistic ability to "talk . . . about language as such" (Heath, 1985, p. 27). When they return to the network later, they incorporate into their writing suggestions made during the discussions—clearly establishing a topic and attempting to stick to it; making smooth transitions to new topics; requesting clarification when they don't understand; attempting to interpret what their partner means, in the context of what they themselves have said and the flow of the entire conversation; and using appropriate writing conventions.

WRITING VARIATION AND WRITING DEVELOPMENT: FOCUS ON ROBIN AND PAM

As we discussed earlier, Robin and Pam represent the most and the least English proficient students in the two classes. Therefore, we decided to examine their writing development on the network over time as two extremes along the range of writing abilities demonstrated by all of the students. The problem with following Robin's writing development became quickly evident, however, as we read consecutively through the transcripts of her interactions. The most striking and interesting feature of her writing over time was the marked change in its nature depending not so much on the time she was writing, but on the topic of conversation and whom she was writing with.[3] In her conversation with Pam discussed earlier, Robin writes short, syntactically simple entries (an average of 5.1 words per T-unit,[4] excluding openings and closings), focuses the conversation on concrete things (pets and animals), and uses the present tense throughout the conversation.

In contrast, when she writes on the network with the older students who are more proficient in written English, her writing is very different. The following conversation took place between Robin, Marcie, and Megan three months earlier than Robin's conversation with Pam. Marcie and Megan, with Robin, were in the first group of students using the network.

---

[3] Our study of Robin's writing development over time remains to be done.

[4] A T-unit is "a main clause plus all subordinate clauses and nonclausal structures attached to or embedded in it" (Hunt, 1970, p. 4).

At the time this conversation took place they were preparing to change to a new school.

(after greetings; Megan has gotten onto the network late and thinks she has been left out of some of the conversation)

MEGAN: Hello, Why did you go ahead without me now im mad!!!!

ROBIN: well not really we did not talk about anything yet or about langley school. . . .

MEGAN: Please repeat what you said before, My computer broked! Now it is my second time that computer broked. Wow!!! I dont care. We are suppose to talk but you both go ahead without me, it is not fair. Ok I dont like you both!!!!!

ROBIN: no i just said hello marcie are you on. Should we go ahead talking about Langley school or arguing all afternoon!!!!

MEGAN: I wont talk unless you tell me what you said before period!!!! . . .

ROBIN: Well, my dad told me that he saw many motivated children wanting to learn about different cultures.

MARCIE: my dad told me the same things as what you say   well also my dad say that there is four boy in class and one girl   when we join itll be four girls and four boys and the teacher name is mr. browning and my mom saw the music this morning   "im special"   ever morning they do sing that song and i pledge to america . . .

ROBIN: My dad told me that he saw about 28 kids. . . . well you should be lucky to have a chance to go to Langley school. All of the children most of them are looking forward to see us. . . .

In this conversation, Robin and the other two girls are talking about a more abstract topic, attending a different school. Robin writes syntactically more complex entries, an average of 10.1 words per T-unit, excluding openings, closings, and turn-taking cues, twice as many as with Pam. (This figure is based on the whole conversation, from which this text is excerpted.) While she uses simple present tense verbs when writing with Pam, here she uses past tense, progressives ("most of them *are looking* forward to see us"; "you *are wasting* my time"; ". . . saw many motivated children *wanting* to learn about different cultures"), adverbial complements ("should we go ahead *talking* about Langley school or *arguing* all afternoon"), and modals ("*Should* we go ahead . . ."; "you *should* be lucky . . .").

Since this conversation took place before the conversation with Pam, these differences are clearly not a result of Robin's language development over time, but of language variation related to audience. Robin is demonstrating her sensitivity to different kinds of audiences and her ability to adjust her writing accordingly, an important aspect of learning how to write (Moffett, 1968; Park, 1986; Rubin, 1984).

We were better able to track Pam's development. We were particularly interested in doing so, since she began working on the network with little knowledge of English (as mentioned earlier, Vietnamese is the language used at home by her hearing parents) and could do little conversational writing alone. Most of her early network conversations were accomplished with a teacher continually present, helping her to read what was written to her and to write a response. Thus, her early conversations were very short (the conversation below, one of her first, in September, took 45 minutes to produce), because most of her time was spent signing questions and explanations with the teacher.

MARCIE:	1	hello everybody
PAM:	2	hi
MARCIE:	3	hello pam marcie here how are you?
PAM:	4	i ma fine
MARCIE:	5	i am fine too
PAM:	6	i ma go vilneae mother and father
MARCIE:	7	you will do what with mom and dad
PAM:	8	yes we will go mom and dad
MARCIE:	9	to where?
PAM:	10	i ma monmy me serae mare
MARCIE:	11	you type it wrong and the correct way is i made mistake and i change
	12	my mind
PAM:	13	i go your home wite play
MARCIE:	14	do you mean you want to play my home today?
PAM:	15	yes
MARCIE:	16	well, you cant not to go to my house because my mom is working
PAM:	17	oh me not know
MARCIE:	18	oh i enjoy to talk with you!! bey for now ok
PAM:	19	i not know tawt watw bey
MARCIE:	20	oh i am sorry i mean bye
PAM:	21	OK I BYE TO YOU
MARCIE:	22	ok bye

Pam's contributions are short (an average of 4.6 words per turn), consisting of simple clauses and phrases. She does not maintain a topic for long. In line 13 she changes the topic ("i go your home wite play," meaning "I want to go to your home to play"), and much of her writing is incomprehensible (Marcie found out what Pam meant to say in line 10, and writes it for her in line 11, because Pam explained its meaning in sign language). Pam alternates between "i" and "me" as first person subject (using "me" as subject in lines 10 and 17) and uses no punctuation. She does, however, incorporate some of Marcie's language ("mom and dad" in line 8, "bye" in line 20) and answers Marcie's questions (lines 4, 8, and 15), indicating that she is reading (with the teacher's help).

Pam's writing is much different five months later, in February, in her conversation with Robin (above). At this point she is reading and writing on the network with very little teacher help. The conversation is longer and focuses throughout on the topic of pets and animals. Although the overall length of her contributions is not longer (an average of 4.1 words per turn), in two of her entries she writes two propositions (line 5—"yes i have my pet is fish"; line 26—"your father home? robin and dog doing out or in"). Rather than simply responding to questions, she also asks them (line 15—"who is's cats"; line 26—"your father home?"). She is using Robin's language model extensively as a basis for her own writing, and with Robin's help with vocabulary manages to produce an embedded clause (line 30—"no i afraid bear because will be bite"). She consistently uses "i" as first person subject, and although she does not use capitalization (few of the children do on the network), she is using some punctuation.

Near the end of a year of networking, Pam added collaborative story production to her writing on the network, an activity that initially only the more proficient students had engaged in.

PAM: hi ellie

ELLIE: hello pam LETS YOU START STORY NOW
        WHAT TITTLE DO YOU WANT ??

PAM: you first story now . . .

ELLIE: NO YOU START STORY WHAT TITTLE DO YOU WANT ??

PAM: "monster"

ELLIE: OHHHH I SEE OKAY GO ON

PAM: one day my class go to camp time for night all sleep tomorrow
        morinig go to pool that is fun so time for bus then monster come here
        and helen see a monster helen say ahhh then my class see a monster
        then run go to bus faster arrive in school my class under a ect. . . .
        [Translation: One day my class went to camp. At nighttime, we all
        went to sleep. The next morning we went to the pool. That was fun.
        When it was time to go to the bus, a monster came. Helen saw the
        monster and said "ahhh." Then the class saw the monster and ran
        fast to the bus. We arrived at school and then my class was under a
        etc. . . .]

Pam concludes her part of the story with "a [and] ect. . . ." when Ellie loses patience waiting for her to finish her part of the story, and tells her (in sign language) to send it. Here, Pam has gone along with Ellie's suggestion that they write a story. Later, she begins initiating story writing herself.

Pam is still far from being a proficient writer of English, but she is steadily moving toward that point as she continues to use writing to communicate with various members of the class and to experiment with various kinds of writing.

CONCLUSION

These students have many opportunities in their classes, besides the network conversations, for using reading and writing for communicative purposes. Both teachers attempt to provide a wide range of authentic reading and writing activities for their students (similar to whole language approaches discussed by Freeman & Freeman, this volume). Students write often, both in dialogue journals (interactive writing between individual students and the teacher in bound notebooks) and in the production of stories and compositions. They conference about their writing with peers and teachers and publish their works within the class. But on the network they experience an extended time during which their primary identity is established through writing. They are "let loose" to find a written identity and create a written manner of expression in a lively, creative, and spontaneous context. During this time their attention is not focused on the acts of "reading and writing," but on communicating.

Frank Smith argued:

> writing gets into our head like much of our knowledge of spoken language and indeed of the world in general, without awareness of the learning that is taking place. The learning is unconscious, effortless, incidental, vicarious, and essentially collaborative. It is incidental because we learn when learning is not our primary intention, vicarious because we learn from what someone else does, and collaborative because we learn through others helping us to achieve our own ends. (1983, p. 561)

The use of networked computers has allowed the concept of "writing" to break out of the confines of narrow views of "composing" and to become, instead, a natural and essential way of communicating in many and varied situations. It allows these children to learn to write without even realizing it.

REFERENCES

Allwright, R. (1984). The importance of interaction in classroom language learning. *Applied Linguistics, 5,* 156–171.

Baker, C., & Cokely, D. (1980). *American sign language: A teacher's resource text on grammar and culture.* Baltimore: TJ Publishers.

Calkins, L. (1983). *Lessons from a child*. Exeter, NH: Heinemann.

Calkins, L. (1986). *The art of teaching writing*. Exeter, NH: Heinemann.

Charrow, V. R. (1981). The written English of deaf adolescents. In M. F. Whiteman (Ed.), *Writing: The nature, development, and teaching of written communication* (pp. 179–187). Hillsdale, NJ: Lawrence Erlbaum Associates.

Cross, T. G. (1977). Mothers' speech adjustments: The contribution of selected child listener variables. In C. Snow & C. Ferguson (Eds.), *Talking to children: Language input and acquisition* (pp. 151–188). Cambridge: Cambridge University Press.

Cummins, J. (1981). The role of primary language development in promoting educational success for language minority students. In *Schooling and language minority students: A theoretical framework* (pp. 3–49). Los Angeles: California State University, Evaluation, Dissemination and Assessment Center.

Elbow, P. (1981). *Writing with power*. New York: Oxford University Press.

Elbow, P. (1985). The shifting relationships between speech and writing. *College Composition and Communication, 36,* 283–303.

Ewoldt, C. (1985). A descriptive study of the developing literacy of young hearing-impaired children. *The Volta Review, 87,* 109–126.

Goodman, Y. (1984). The development of initial literacy. In H. Goelman, A. Oberg, & F. Smith (Eds.), *Awakening to literacy* (pp. 102–109). Exeter, NH: Heinemann.

Graves, D. (1983). *Writing: Children and teachers at work*. Exeter, NH: Heinemann.

Hatch, E. (1978a). Discourse analysis, speech acts and second language acquisition. In W. Ritchie (Ed.), *Second language acquisition research* (pp. 137–155). New York: Academic Press.

Hatch, E. (1978b). Discourse analysis and second language acquisition. In E. Hatch (Ed.), *Second language acquisition: A book of readings* (pp. 401–435). Rowley, MA: Newbury House.

Heath, S. B. (1985). Literacy or literate skills?: Considerations for ESL/EFL learners. In P. Larson, E. Judd, & D. Messerschmidt (Eds.), *On TESOL '84* (pp. 15–28). Washington, DC: Teachers of English to Speakers of Other Languages.

Heath, S. B., & Branscombe, A. (1984). "Intelligent writing" in an audience community: Teacher, students, and researcher. In S. W. Freedman (Ed.), *The acquisition of written language: Revision and response* (pp. 3–32). Norwood, NJ: Ablex.

Hudelson, S. (1984). Kan yu ret an rayt en ingles: Children become literate in English as a second language. *TESOL Quarterly, 18,* 221–238.

Hunt, K. W. (1970). *Syntactic maturity in school children and adults*. Society for Research in Child Development (monograph serial No. 134). Chicago: University of Chicago Press.

Ivimiy, G., & Lachterman, D. (1980). The written language of deaf children. *Language and Speech, 23,* 351–377.

Kreeft, J., Shuy, R. W., Staton, J., Reed, L., & Morroy, R. (1984). *Dialogue writing: Analysis of student-teacher interactive writing in the learning of English as a second language* (Report No. 83-0030). Washington, DC: National Institute of Education (ERIC Document Reproduction Service No. ED 252 097)

Kroll, B. (1981). Developmental relationships between speaking and writing. In B. M. Kroll & R. J. Vann (Eds.), *Exploring speaking–writing relationships: Connections and contrasts* (pp. 32–54). Urbana, IL: National Council of Teachers of English.

Levin, J. A., Reil, M. M., Rowe, R. D., & Boruta, M. J. (1985). Muktuk meets jacuzzi: Computer networks and elementary school writers. In S. W. Freedman (Ed.), *The acquisition of written language: Revision and response* (pp. 160–171). Norwood, NJ: Ablex.

Moffett, J. (1968). *Teaching the universe of discourse*. Boston: Houghton Mifflin.

Park, D. P. (1986). Analyzing audiences. *College Composition and Communication, 37,* 478–488.

Powers. A., & Wilqus, S. (1983) Linguistic complexity in the written language of deaf children. *Volta Review, 85,* 201–210.

Raimes, A. (1983). Anguish as a second language? Remedies for composition teachers. In A. Freedman, I. Pringle, & J. Yalden (Eds.), *Learning to write: First language/second language* (pp. 258–272). New York: Longman.

Rose, M. (1984). *Writer's block: The cognitive dimension*. Carbondale: Southern Illinois University Press.

Rose, M. (Ed.). (1985). *When a writer can't write*. New York: Guilford Press.

Rubin, D. (1984). Social cognition and written communication. *Written Communication, 1,* 211–245.

Shuy, R. W. (in press). The oral basis of written language acquisition. In J. Staton, R. W. Shuy, J. Kreeft, & L. Reed (Eds.), *Interactive writing in dialogue journals: Practitioner, linguistic, social, and cognitive views*. Norwood, NJ: Ablex.

Smith, F. (1983). Reading like a writer. *Language Arts, 60,* 558–567.

Snow, C. E. (1977). Mothers' speech research: From input to interaction. In C. Snow & C. Ferguson (Eds.), *Talking to children: Language input and acquisition* (pp. 31–49). Cambridge: Cambridge University Press.

Staton, J., Shuy, R. W., Kreeft, J., & Reed, L. (in press). *Dialogue journal communication: Classroom, linguistic, social, and cognitive views*. Norwood, NJ: Ablex.

Stokoe, W. C., Jr. (1971). *The study of sign language*. Silver Spring, MD: National Association of the Deaf.

Stokoe, W. C., Jr. (1972). *Semiotics and human sign languages*. The Hague: Mouton.

Wells, G. (1981). *Learning through interaction: The study of language development*. Cambridge: Cambridge University Press.

Wells, G. (1986). *The meaning makers: Children learning language and using language to learn*. Portsmouth, NH: Heinemann.

CHAPTER 7

Bilingual Sister Classes in Computer Writing Networks

Dennis Sayers
University of Hartford
New England Multifunctional Resource Center (MRC)

Computer writing networks are so new in today's schools that we often have no choice but to fall back upon familiar metaphors as we seek to understand this innovation. The typical reaction of a puzzled teacher when he or she first tries to envision the educational potential of these networks goes something like this: "Oh, yeah . . . I get it. You mean pen pals over the computer." Indeed, much of the initial writing exchanged between students falls squarely into the pen pal genre. Letters are quickly composed at computers and immediately sent via modems to distant classes. Yet teachers and researchers have noted that the early excitement of writing letters to "computer pen pals" soon becomes boredom; moreover, pen pal letters offer young writers few opportunities for the development of more complex composition skills such as revision (Riel, 1983).

This chapter gives details of one aspect of an effort to restructure writing activities between two upper elementary-level bilingual classes, one taught by Arturo Solis at Truman School in New Haven, Connecticut and the other taught by Michelle Gonsalves of the Valley Center School in San Diego, California. These classes had previously exchanged pen pal letters only through a computer writing network called *De Orilla a Orilla* or, translated from the Spanish, "From Shore to Shore" (Sayers & Brown, 1987). The goal of this restructuring was to create a functional writing environment: a jointly published classroom newspaper guided by an editorial board in each classroom. In particular, this chapter focuses on the deliberations of two student editorial boards in arriving at a joint editorial policy.

Using computers as a medium of communication, rather than trying to program the machines to teach students or getting the students to program the machines, is a recent concept. The earliest student writing network that utilized computers extensively was established by the Interactive Technology Laboratory at the University of California at San Diego (UCSD) in 1983. One of the principal governing images for the exchange of writings in the UCSD network was student journalism (Levin, Riel, Boruta, & Rowe, 1984; Levin & Riel, 1984; Rosa & Moll, 1985). The model of the computer as electronic mail carrier delivering pen pal letters was replaced by that of the computer as classroom teletype. Student journalism is a particularly effective governing image because of the clear definition of roles it provides young writers: they are reporters when they write articles for local newsletters, editors while revising and polishing articles for publication, and correspondents when they send the best writings to other classes (Mehan, Moll, & Riel, 1985; Riel, 1985).

Clearly this model advances a concept of local journalism, sprinkled with articles from foreign correspondents. Local student-editors give feedback only to fellow classmate-reporters. Articles received from "foreign correspondents" are selected and edited locally according to the editorial policy of that classroom's newsletter. In other words, peer feedback for young authors is limited to that provided by fellow students within the context of each classroom. Although the computer writing network has the potential for providing peer feedback on a draft from many distant readers, this promise is rarely realized. Margaret Riel (personal communication, 1987) hypothesizes that this is due to the difficulty of coordinating timely feedback between several classes in a computer writing network.

DE ORILLA A ORILLA: A GRASSROOTS APPROACH TO COMPUTER NETWORKING

Arturo Solis and Michelle Gonsalves participate in *De Orilla a Orilla,* an interlocking network of electronic bulletin boards which matches pairs of "sister classes." The one-on-one structure of this network offers some unique possibilities for examining alternatives to the local journalism model. As we shall see, the pairing of sister classes also provides the two teachers with a supportive context for reflecting upon, challenging, and redefining their classroom strategies for writing instruction. Thus, a few words about *de Orilla a Orilla* should help establish a context for the later discussion of joint editorial boards between sister classes.

De Orilla a Orilla is the multilingual special interest group of a large and growing confederation of electronic bulletin boards called Computer Mail System—SchoolNet (CMS—SchoolNet), which attempts to bring asynchronous computer networking within the reach of most school districts' budgets. An electronic bulletin board, in this case an Apple II computer running special software and plugged into a phone outlet, may be likened to a computerized post office which teachers and students can call (a) to pick up messages from their personal mailbox, (b) to leave messages for another user, and (c) to send copies of a message to a group of users. CMS—SchoolNet was founded during the 1985–86 school year by Al Rogers, formerly of the San Diego County Teacher Education and Computer Center (TECC). The network now includes over 500 teachers and students in 13 states and in Argentina, Japan, Israel, Mexico, Puerto Rico, and Spain.

De Orilla a Orilla began by linking classes in Mexico and Puerto Rico with Latino students enrolled in bilingual programs in the United States. The goal was to improve students' educational achievements—especially writing skills—both in the United States, where Spanish is a minority language, and in Mexico and Puerto Rico, where it is the dominant or majority language. In November of 1985, I worked with Andres Menendez of the Laboratory High School at the University of Puerto Rico and Enid Figueroa of Project CEMI at the University of Turabo to connect students in New England bilingual programs with their Puerto Rican counterparts. By the spring of 1986, Kristin Brown of San Diego State University had involved classes in California and Mexico. The *De Orilla a Orilla* network was growing quickly.

Typically, sister classes have been partnerships between two U.S. bilingual classes or between a bilingual class here and a class from the "mother" culture. Recently, however, students who study Spanish as a foreign language at a California high school have been paired with a class in Puerto Rico. Another fascinating exchange occurred between deaf high school students in San Diego, most of Mexican heritage, and a secondary class of hearing students in Rio Piedras, Puerto Rico. Thus students from two language backgrounds, American Sign Language and Spanish, learned about their sister class through their shared second language, English.

Communication is accomplished primarily through writing. Word processors are used to plan, compose, revise, and edit texts, and telecommunications to send the writings quickly to faraway readers. Students typically write with *FrEdWriter,* Al Rogers' public-domain educational software or its companion *Spanish FrEdWriter,* a simple bilingual program that permits Spanish accents both on the screen and in the printed copy. Writings are exchanged by posting them on an electronic bulletin board program. Every afternoon the teachers leave their computers connected by modem to a phone line, turn off their monitors and head for home. The next morning, students read and print out the "mail" that has been delivered overnight.

How have the messages been exchanged? The local electronic bulletin boards are communicating through an interlocking network of similar boards. An electronic bulletin board may be a "node" or a "gateway." A node located in a local school calls and exchanges messages with another bulletin board acting as a regional gateway. The gateway acts as the relay point for many other local nodes. After midnight, when telephone rates are lower, the various gateway computers automatically dial their closest neighbor and messages are passed along in two directions, much like full and empty buckets in a fire brigade. Participating schools pay nothing for the local call that connects them to the CMS—SchoolNet. The gateway computers share costs over the entire system as each relay point pays the phone bill—usually under a dollar—for one leg of the overnight mail delivery service. The result is next-day delivery to each participating classroom of large batches of student writings.

Using this technology, students write much more than electronic pen pal letters. The most successful projects have been those that have a life of their own away from the computer and can be amplified by the participation of the sister class, such as the production of local newsletters mentioned earlier. Teachers discover myriad ways to exploit the learning potential of computer writing networks, some of which employ other media and the "old-fashioned" postal service. The steady stream of student writings is often supplemented with culture packets—"time capsule" packages including photos, maps, lists of proverbs, items of local interest, and audio- or videotape recordings. Teachers have found that both the number and quality of texts shared over the computer increases as culture packets are regularly exchanged between sister classes.

De Orilla a Orilla is expanding. Soon more countries (Argentina, Canada, and Cape Verde) and language groups (Cape Verdean Creole, French, Jamaican Creole, Portuguese, and Puerto Rican Sign Language) will join. The goal of *De Orilla a Orilla*—for bilingual education and second language students in the United States as well as for their colleagues in other nations—is to promote literacy by linking developing writers to a wide world of language learners.

NEGOTIATING A JOINT EDITORIAL POLICY IN A COMPUTER WRITING NETWORK

After communicating through the *De Orilla a Orilla* network for several months, Gonsalves and Solis met face-to-face for the first time on March

23, 1987, at the first Collaborative Writing Across Cultures Conference sponsored by the New England Multifunctional Resource Center (MRC). This center is one of 16 MRCs funded by Title VII through the U.S. Office of Education to provide staff development for ESL/bilingual education programs. Like many other pairs of sister class teachers who attended the conference, Solis and Gonsalves met to plan future collaborative projects. The two teachers were not content to remain at a pen pal stage of writing exchange, and student journalism through newsletter writing seemed an attractive alternative. However, they felt that there would be few opportunities to explore the potential of collaborative writing if they set their sights no higher than the publication of two separate newsletters with articles included from each class. From the discussion grew a project that focused on student editorial boards and the development of a common editorial policy.

A number of educational researchers have suggested that the functional writing environment provided by computer writing networks may promote the development of writing skills both in the students' mother tongue and in English, their second language (Cummins, 1986a, 1986b; Rosa & Moll, 1985; Sayers, 1986; Sayers & Brown, 1987). Joint student editorial boards seemed just such a functional writing context. The teachers and I expected that as students in the sister classes negotiated an editorial policy for a jointly published newsletter, they would establish criteria (a) to aid in the planning of articles, (b) to structure peer feedback, and (c) to encourage revising. We planned to implement this student-generated editorial policy by channeling peer feedback on rough drafts written by students in one class through an editorial board in their sister class. The remainder of this chapter focuses on the intricate negotiations that led to the creation of a functional writing environment, mediated by computer networking, in which subsequent student writings were embedded. It centers on the social context in which texts were produced.

The teachers' role was to facilitate students' efforts at defining and implementing a common editorial policy. We proposed that:

1. Both teachers select five or six students to serve on editorial boards for a jointly produced newspaper.
2. Students at each site conduct a meeting to come up with a list of points for an editorial policy. This meeting would be tape recorded.
3. A list of editorial policy suggestions be typed into word processors and exchanged between sister classes over the computer bulletin board network.
4. The teachers set a mutually convenient time to conduct a "live chat" between editorial boards. (A live chat is a real-time, written conversation using computers linked to phone lines via modems.)

During this exchange, differences would be ironed out and a common editorial policy agreed upon. The live chat would be "captured" both as a text file and on audiotape.
5. To test their policy, editorial board members write drafts of articles using *FrEdWriter* and send them over the bulletin board network to students on the editorial board in the sister class.
6. Each editorial board meet to critique the texts they received. Texts would be returned to the sister class editorial board with suggestions for revision.
7. If necessary, a second live chat would be convened to refine the editorial policy.
8. The remainder of the students in both sister classes submit drafts for review by the corresponding editorial board.
9. A single bilingual newspaper would then be jointly published by the sister classes.

We were surprised at the results; as Solis put it, *"Uno propone y Dios dispone"* (One proposes, but God disposes). The teachers and I had envisioned this project as a student-directed effort. Yet it is clear from the data we collected that the activities were in large part facilitated—indeed at times forcefully directed—by the teachers. Each instructor has a particular teaching style and an individual philosophy of writing instruction. Although our initial expectation was that the students would independently negotiate a joint editorial policy, what actually occurred was quite different. It appears that the editorial policy deliberations provided a common ground for a meeting of minds between the groups. Each group of students, whose concept of an ideal text had been influenced by their teacher over the course of the school year, accommodated their list of revision criteria to the list submitted by their sister class's editorial board. Both teachers found themselves fully involved in the decision making that led to a joint editorial policy. As a closer look at the exchanges between teachers and editorial boards will show, the two teachers appeared to accommodate their personal philosophy of writing instruction to that of their sister class colleague *to more fully exploit the educational potential of the computer writing network.*

On Friday, May 8, 1987, the editorial board at Valley Center School in San Diego (Tony, Nichole, Carlos, Ian, and Hugo) met with their teacher, Michelle Gonsalves, to discuss an editorial policy. The Valley Center school district employs an alternate-week model of bilingual instruction, in which classes are conducted entirely in one language during one week, and instruction is provided in the other language the following week. Since this was English week, the meeting was conducted primarily in English. The criteria were:

1. Good order or sequence of events.
2. Good enough spelling and punctuation to read, but editorial board will correct it.
3. Honesty.
4. Articles do not have to be perfect since editorial board will give advice.
5. Articles should be fairly long, but not too long.
6. Topics should be decided on by those who write the articles.

After listing these criteria, Ms. Gonsalves probed each student for reasons for the criteria they had selected. Nichole spoke about honesty: "Well, if you were reading a friend's story, and one of their sentences didn't make sense, but they were your best friend, and you told them it made a lot of sense, but didn't just tell them that because they were your best friend . . . you have to be honest and tell them what's wrong with the story and what isn't." Tony's comments on order and continuity were: "It has to make kind of sense. . . . If you talk of something and then you talk of something else and then you talk again of the same thing, it doesn't sound right." Carlos spoke about selecting topics important to the author: "If we choose something and they don't like it, they won't do a good job on it. And they won't like to copy it." Students were already thinking of ideas that they wanted to write about: Ian on music, Nichole about a party animal story, Tony on a story about a devil that took a kid.

The Valley Center students then sent a message to the students on the editorial board in Arturo Solis' class at Truman School in New Haven, Connecticut. This message differed somewhat from the initial list produced in the editorial board meeting, both in order and emphasis. Especially noteworthy is the expansion of the original one-word "honesty" point into a more operational definition, item 6 below. Their criteria, translated from Spanish, were:

1. Something that is important to the author.
2. Not too long.
3. Does not have to be perfect, because the editorial board will make the corrections.
4. Should use a logical sequence.
5. Correct spelling for good comprehension.
6. The editorial board should make comments directed to the article, not the author of the article.
7. Correct punctuation.

In fact, the San Diego editorial board students were so eager to get started that they decided not to wait for agreement on a joint editorial policy with their New Haven counterparts. Instead, they wrote drafts on their chosen topics over the weekend and sent them off on Monday. Significantly, as we shall see later, Gonsalves also included a draft of an article written by Nichole about Disneyland.

The New Haven editorial board at Truman School consisted of Wanda, Marilyn, Linda, John, Zuleima, and Vanessa. Their discussion of editorial policy was led by Arturo Solis on Tuesday, May 12, and conducted in English and Spanish. In Solis's district, instruction is provided in either language at the discretion of the teacher. The editorial board meeting was taped. Solis led the meeting by soliciting contributions from the students. All but one of the criteria were proposed by the students. The teacher, however, did control the amount of time spent discussing each point. The criteria of the New Haven students were:

Topics
1. Stories that happen in both of the schools.
2. Something that happens in the state.
3. Interviews of people.
4. Differences of life style.
5. Exchanges that have gone on between schools.
6. Safety patrol.

Mechanics
7. Four paragraphs.
8. Indentation.
9. Without a lot of spelling mistakes.
10. Punctuation marks.
11. Things that make sense.
12. Time order should be correct in the correct sequence.
13. Having good main idea in a paragraph.
14. Capitalization.
15. (teacher adds) Facts and opinions.
16. Subject and predicate and complete sentences.

Having completed their suggestions for the joint editorial policy, the New Haven students next turned their attention to the list submitted by their colleagues in San Diego. Although they ratified unanimously all the suggestions sent by the Valley Center students, the tape transcript suggests that their decision was not merely a rubber-stamp approval. This can be inferred from the strategies the teacher uses to manage the discussion of the Valley Center criteria (see above). As Mr. Solis summarizes points 2, 4, 5, and 7 of the Valley Center list, he notes how these criteria match those that had just been brainstormed by the New Haven students. However, he restates—three or four times—and illustrates for the children only those points (1, 3, and 6) that are distinct from his class's list of criteria.

Thus, the stage had been set for the fourth step, the live chat between editorial boards on Wednesday, May 13. Mr. Solis had sent a message that morning to San Diego saying that his students had ratified the Valley Center suggestions. He also included a copy of the New Haven criteria and asked for comments from the San Diego students. The setting for the live chat was similar in each classroom: the teacher typed at the computer, surrounded by the children on the editorial board. Sometimes each teacher merely typed what students dictated, while at other times he or she summarized the gist of the lively discussion taking place around the computer. A translation of what appeared on both computer screens follows.

SAN DIEGO: We are here. ga [Note: GA means "Go ahead," a ham radio convention.]

NEW HAVEN: [. . .] the kids are here, are there any questions or comments? ga

SAN DIEGO: Many comments and questions. [. . .] Let's begin with the policy. [. . .]

NEW HAVEN: Well then, are you in agreement with the points we sent you this morning? ga

SAN DIEGO: We agree with certain points that you sent us. As to articles about the school, the community, the state, . . . well, the children said they didn't really like that, but they understood it was important. We could agree with a little bit of persuasion. As far as the correct use of paragraphs . . . "that might be a little hard" was the comment of the group. The rest of the policy was fine. ga

NEW HAVEN: Well, what they meant to say by the correct use of the paragraphs was that you shouldn't write a story from start to finish "in one blow" *(de un solo golpe)* without giving the reader an idea that in that story there are several important points. We'll send you another little rabbit if you say yes. ga [Note: A live rabbit (!) had actually been sent by one of the New Haven students to the San Diego class.]

SAN DIEGO: Now we understand and we agree. Especially we see the point of stories that are written in "in one blow" (good analogy). ga

NEW HAVEN: As far as the first point, the children want to know about you, about your community, your school, your people, your teachers, (some that are somewhat crazy and others that are nice). They want you to know of the things that happen to us here, and how they see them, since they don't see things the same as we adults see them. For them this means sharing and coming to know one another better. Some of what their teacher thinks has rubbed off on them. ga

SAN DIEGO: YES YES YES now you owe us four rabbits. We didn't tell you that YES we liked the idea of interviews a lot and now with your magnificent explanation of the other points, we're in agreement with them. They say that they want to interview the crazy Mr. Perdue [the Valley Center computer coordinator] and the Pretty One, Profesora Gonsalves, since they don't know me well enough by now. They know more about my life than I do sometimes, ga

NEW HAVEN: Yes, that's what they want to know. Already they have the teacher on the front page (what a scandal!) then they want you to interview the principal of the school and to know his points of view. They want to know more of the teacher who breaks guitars over the heads of students if they act bad. [Mr. Perdue appeared with a guitar in one of the video tapes exchanged between the sister classes.] And also they want to know of the young woman (in other rooms they say Missy, but not in mine, they have to learn correct Spanish) (laughter from the children). [Mr. Solis refers to the use of "Missy" by Puerto Rican students to address teachers, a carry-over from the 1920s and 1930s when U.S. policy required English as the official language of instruction in Puerto Rico.] Are we in agreement over the policy [. . .]? Tomorrow afternoon (my afternoon here) we will try to send the first articles. We can't promise but we will try. You should have them after you finish your lunches in the sunny fields of your school, next to the swimming pool. While we have to eat in our hot cafeteria!!! ga

SAN DIEGO: We agree on the name and the policy. But who is Missy? ga

NEW HAVEN: To all the women teachers they use Missy (short for Miss plus the name). Many people permit this. Just like they say Mister to the male teachers . . . without their name following. [A similar throwback to U.S. educational policy in Puerto Rico.] But this is only when they are allowed to, as I said before, some teachers let them. They shouldn't but. . . . So who is the Missy there? The curtain rises and it's Miss Gonsalves. ga

SAN DIEGO: "Ms." please, and not because of my liberation. We'll try to send our articles tomorrow also. The students now have a clearer idea of what to write. The articles that we sent will be changed, except for the one on Disneyland. ga

NEW HAVEN: Right, chief!!! [. . .] Wanda Machado is making a note so we don't forget.

SAN DIEGO: [. . .] The children had to go back to the room. Nicole is still here. She's our secretary and is writing some notes about this communication. We have to go back too. ga

NEW HAVEN: YES, they're going to throw us out of here also, since it is 3:45 and we have to load our bookbags up and leave for where the sun doesn't shine. [. . .] Bye ga

SAN DIEGO: BYE. But Mr. Solis, we know very well that you never have only one last comment. BYE

The live chat may be divided into four parts: (a) introductions, (b) discussion of the criteria submitted by the New Haven students, (c) an explanation of forms of address used by Puerto Rican students and (d) leave taking. Of particular interest is the negotiation evident in the discussion of editorial board criteria.

The San Diego group agrees with "certain points." But they also note two clear areas of difference. First, the New Haven students had been quite specific and cryptically brief in their list of acceptable topics (school, local, state news, and interviews) while the San Diego students had left topic choice open to the author ("something that is important to the author"). The California students, however, admit somewhat reluctantly that they see the value of the Connecticut students' suggestions, though they don't say why. Second, the San Diego students feel that "correct use of paragraphs" (presumably the specification of a limit of four paragraphs) "would be a little hard" to conform to.

The New Haven group briefly explains their rationale for the second point of discussion, which is basically an argument for a full and logical development of a "story," and this explanation is readily accepted by the San Diego editorial board (and the teacher). However, the discussion of topic yields richer evidence of collaboration.

Mr. Solis and his students explain that their vision of the joint newsletter has to do with "sharing and coming to know one another better." For the first time in the chat he makes reference to the social environment in which this writing project is taking place, and specifically to the fact that teachers are playing a role in this supposedly student-led decision-making process by adding, "Some of what their teacher thinks has rubbed off on them." Immediately a lively discussion begins which stimulates several suggestions for topics: interviews with teachers, principals, and others which would further the process of sharing over the network.

What seems to have occurred is that a common ground has been reached by both groups, led by each teacher, as to appropriate topics for this joint newsletter, topics which will stress "sharing and coming to know one another better." Through the negotiation of the live computer chat, the California group appears to have modified their conception of this joint writing project to a view that more fully exploits the potential resources for learning between sister classes in computer networks. They have accepted Solis' challenge to write "about you, about your community, your school, your people, your teachers." The seemingly casual remark by

Ms. Gonsalves about the Disneyland article is a strong piece of evidence that common ground has in fact been reached.

The reader will recall that the topics originally selected by the San Diego editorial board members for their own writings were very much in a creative writing vein, stressing themes of personal interest to student authors, with the exception of the Disneyland piece, which focused on a topic of presumably high interest to their distant audience in Connecticut. In this connection it is noteworthy that Gonsalves mentions in the chat that "the articles that we sent will be changed, except for the one on Disneyland." Indeed, the brief discussion about "forms of address" used by Puerto Rican students could also be viewed as evidence of the newly implemented joint editorial policy that stresses "coming to know one another better."

The process approach (Calkins, 1983; Calkins, 1986; Graves, 1983) to writing instruction, which stresses purposeful writing on student-selected topics for real audiences with many opportunities for revision, peer feedback, and teacher conferencing, has been embraced by a number of teachers very enthusiastically. However, many teachers are unacquainted with or have only a passing familiarity with the process approach to writing instruction. From my observations of Solis' class and discussions with Gonsalves, I would characterize the San Diego teacher's approach as very much within the process writing model, while the New Haven teacher employed a more traditional method of writing instruction, including assigned topics and written teacher comments, with fewer opportunities for peer feedback and teacher-student writing conferences.

The negotiation evidenced in the editorial board deliberations can be seen as a process of mutual accommodation of these two approaches to writing instruction made possible by the necessity of discovering new forms of collaboration appropriate to computer writing networks. Gonsalves' group changed their editorial criterion on newsletter topics from one which permitted students to write on any topic whatsoever to one which stressed a more focused range of topics centering on the real lives and daily concerns of students. In turn, Solis' group modified their insistence on the arbitrary "four paragraph essay" criterion by invoking a rationale based on a potential reader's expectations, signaling a shift from an approach to writing instruction based on ideal models to one concerned with audience awareness. In summary, the technological innovation encouraged both groups, led by their teachers, to question and adapt their approaches to writing with a view toward more fully exploiting the potential for learning offered by this new medium of communication.

The process of implementing the editorial policy continued, resulting in the first issue of *Computer Capers* which, in keeping with the decision of the joint editorial boards, included articles that revealed much about the day-to-day life of students at both schools. The two editorial boards critiqued, and in some cases copy-edited, writings submitted by students in their sister class. Clearly, the editorial boards became a palpable force in the shaping of student writings during all stages in the writing process. For example, Tony Vera, one of the San Diego students, asked for guidance from the New Haven editorial board prior to conducting an interview with their school principal.

The purpose of this chapter has been to chronicle the collaborative creation of a functional writing environment by students and teachers in bilingual sister classes. Students in bilingual education programs need authentic *contexts* for mother-tongue writing if they are to develop and maintain basic literacy skills, and then transfer them to English academic settings. In fact, these networks keep alive the ties to the mother culture, nourishing literacy for bilingual students. Second language students need authentic *contacts* with native speakers and plenty of practice in a range of language skills, including reading and writing, if they are to develop cultural awareness and communicative competence (Rosa & Moll, 1985). Computer networks like *De Orilla a Orilla* can help meet these needs by speeding students' writings across an ocean or a continent—maybe both— overnight.

REFERENCES

Calkins, L. M. (1983). *Lessons from a child*. Portsmouth, NH: Heinemann.
Calkins, L. M. (1986). *The art of teaching writing*. Portsmouth, NH: Heinemann.
Cohen, M., & Riel, M. (1986). *Computer networks: Creating real audiences for students' writing* (Technical Report #15). La Jolla, CA: Interactive Technology Laboratory, University of California at San Diego.
Cummins, J. (1986a). Cultures in contact: Using classroom microcomputers for cultural exchange and reinforcement. *TESL Canada Journal/Revue TESL du Canada, 3*(2), 13–31.
Cummins, J. (1986b). Empowering minority students: A framework for intervention. *Harvard Educational Review, 56,* 18–36.
Graves, D. (1983). *Writing: Teachers and children at work*. Exeter, NH: Heinemann Educational Books.
Levin, J., & Riel, M. (1984, April). *Educational electronic networks: How they work (and don't work)*. Paper presented at meeting of the American Educational Research Association, Chicago.
Levin, J., Riel, M., Boruta, M., & Rowe, R. (1984). Muktuk meets jaccuzi: Computer networks and elementary schools. In S. W. Freedman (Ed.), *The acquisition of written language* (pp. 160–171). New York: Ablex.
Mehan, H., Moll, L., & Riel, M. (1985). *Computers in classrooms: A quasi-experiment in guided change* (NIE Report 6-83-0027). La Jolla, CA: Interactive Technology Laboratory.

Riel, M. (1983). Education and ecstasy: Computer chronicles of students writing together. *The Quarterly Newsletter of the Laboratory of Comparative Human Cognition, 5*(3), 59–67.

Riel, M. (1985). The computer chronicles newswire: A functional learning environment for acquiring literacy skills. *Journal of Educational Computing Research, 1,* 317–337.

Rosa, A., & Moll, L. C. (1985). Computadores, comunicacion y educacion: una colaboracion internacional en la intervencion e investigacion educativa (Computers, communication and education: An international collaboration in educational intervention and investigation). *Infancia y Aprendizaje, 30,* 1–17.

Sayers, D. (1986). From journals to journalism: ESL writers. *Puerto Rico TESOL-Gram, 13* (3), 7–8

Sayers, D., & Brown, K. (1987). Bilingual education and telecommunications: A perfect fit. *The Computing Teacher, 17*(7), 23–24.

CHAPTER 8

Parallels between Speaking and Writing in Second Language Acquisition

Kate Mangelsdorf
University of Arizona

A few years ago I couldn't get one of my ESL composition classes to stop talking. The students were university freshmen; their major writing assignment was a response to Orwell's (1949/1982) novel *1984*. Big Brother intrigued them. Some hated him; a few admired him; still others were fascinated by the machinations of his society. Some class days I'd plan for a 20-minute discussion of part of the book, and after 45-minutes the students would still be at it, debating and explaining, pointing to parts of the book for evidence, relating Big Brother to governments they had experienced. I was worried that I hadn't spent enough time on organizational strategies or transitions; I expected their drafts to be rambling, possibly even incoherent. But these papers turned out to be the best I'd ever received in that course. They were rich with ideas developed in the class discussions; they had a strong sense of audience and voice far removed from the careful textbookish language I was used to reading. The rest of the semester I covered writing techniques briefly in class or in individual conferences. In the classroom I wanted to hear more of the students' voices.

What I discovered that semester was that despite differences between speaking and writing—for example, between the informal give and take of my students' class discussions and the more formal explication in their papers—the two ways of communicating could enrich each other: The voices that speak in the classroom can empower the voices struggling to be heard in the papers. In this chapter I describe the parallels between speaking and writing that explain why teaching these modes of language use together can strengthen second language acquisition. I also suggest ways to combine speaking and writing in second language (L2) classrooms and curricula.

SEPARATION OF SPEAKING AND WRITING

The tradition of separating speaking and writing in L2 curricula is rooted in the historical development of second language instruction. One major influence on teaching in the 1940s and 1950s was structural linguistics, which focused on describing the recurring surface forms of spoken rather than written language (Diller, 1978, p. 10). "Because through the ages written language in many cultures has been (or is) nonexistent, the spoken language was regarded by the structuralists as of primary importance, writing being considered 'merely a way of recording language by means of visible marks'" (Rivers, 1983, p. 3). Other recent influences on L2 instruction have their basis in ideas about child language acquisition. Versions of the direct method, such as the natural approach, stress oral language acquisition because of theories about the way children acquire their first language (L1) and the fact that children learn to speak before they learn to write (Krashen & Terrell, 1983). In fact, Krashen's theory of L2 acquisition (1982) is based on the idea that L2 learners acquire the target language through subconscious processes similar to those involved in L1 acquisition. Speech act theory has also influenced the discipline, resulting in new emphases on oral language use (Spolsky, 1980). The teaching of common speech acts, such as greetings or disagreements, is an important goal in courses based on functional syllabi (McKay, 1979).

Because of these influences, writing is often introduced in the early stages of instruction not as a meaningful way of communicating ideas, but as a way of reinforcing what was taught in the speaking classroom. Writing instruction is generally left for the later stages of development, much as my university level L2 writing classroom when, it is hoped, most students are fluent speakers of English.

Partly because of this separation between spoken and written language, the process of speaking can appear very different from the process of writing. For instance, when my students talked with each other in class, they, just as all people do, used nonverbal communication such as gestures and facial expressions; as writers, however, they expressed themselves only through the words they put upon the page. In class discussions, the participants in the conversation were immediately present and interrupted, disagreed, questioned, affirmed, or otherwise told them how their message was being received. When they sat down to write their papers, though, they had to imagine audience response; no reader was looking over their shoulder. Finally, when my students explained themselves to their classmates, they could make mistakes in syntax, diction, and usage; however, mistakes such as these in their papers lowered my evaluation of their writing ability.

Applying speaking processes directly to writing processes can indeed interfere with writing development. For example, because they are used to the immediate feedback of their listeners, inexperienced writers can overestimate the reader's ability to understand their ideas (Flower, 1979; Perl, 1979). Additionally, inexperienced writers often transfer conventions of speech, such as register, diction, or tone, to their writing, where it may be inappropriate (Halpern, 1984). Differences between oral and literate cultures can also affect writing development. Oral cultures often use thought processes different from the kinds of analytical thought processes found in literate cultures (Ong, 1978). Students whose dominant culture is orally based might have difficulty adjusting to modes of expression common to other cultures.

These differences between speaking and writing, however, do not have to result in the segregation of these ways of using language—listening and reading as well as speaking and writing—in the curricula. After all, students can learn to be aware of differences between language modes. Segregation of language skills into different courses, moreover, can prevent teachers from drawing on the important similarities between speaking and writing in order to enhance L2 acquisition.

SPEAKING AND WRITING AS COMMUNICATION

When I listened to my students argue about Big Brother in the classroom, and when I read their essays on the same topic, the same process was going on: communication through the construction and negotiation of meaning. Before my students had reached my classroom, they had developed some fluency in speech, including grammatical competence, or mastery of the linguistic code (Canale & Swain, 1981). In addition to being grammatically competent, many of my students were competent in other areas of oral language use, for communicative competence involves not only control of the phonology, grammar, and semantics of a language, but also the conventions concerning language use in various settings aimed at different audiences in order to convey a variety of messages (Spolsky, 1980). Additionally, in order to successfully convey and understand messages, my students had mastered not only discourse structures and sociolinguistic rules, but also strategies for changing their discourses when communication breaks down (Tarone, 1980).

My students had to learn communicative competence in their writing as well as in their speech. Writers need to do more than simply produce correct language forms. Taylor (1981) notes that "the emphasis in [a writing program] must be on communicating meaning. Simply put, the writer must have something to say" (p. 8). He suggests encouraging student-generated material in the early stages of writing instruction in order to draw on the students' originality and motivation. Similarly, Raimes (1980, 1987) has developed techniques for allowing students to develop their own responses to material while at the same time selecting from a range of language forms. In other words, students select the language forms that will best communicate their message, instead of choosing a message—any message—that will fit the particular form that is being taught that day in class.

In addition to communicative intent, the concept of communicative competence in writing includes appropriate language use. Just as my students had learned how to politely debate each other in an academic setting, they had to learn how to argue their point in an academic paper. Achieving appropriate language use involves audience awareness, or moving from writer-based prose (in which writers are mainly addressing themselves) to reader-based prose (in which writers have altered their text to adapt to the needs and expectations of readers). Reader-based prose "creates a shared language and shared context between writer and reader," while writer-based prose often simply reveals the process of the writer's thinking (Flower, 1979, p. 20). Zamel's (1983) case study of advanced ESL writers indicates the importance of audience awareness; she found that many of the skilled writers tried, while revising, to reread their papers from the point of view of a reader so that they could anticipate and meet their reader's responses and informational needs.

In my lesson on *1984*, I encouraged audience awareness by asking the students to write drafts of their papers, which were then read by one or more of their peers. I tried to pair students who disagreed with each other's theses to help the writers see how well their arguments were anticipating and responding to the reader's objections. Only after the students had generated their drafts did I attempt to teach the more formal aspects of academic writing, such as the use of cohesive devices and appropriate tone. I found, however, that most students were able to at least identify problems in these areas according to the responses of their peers. (For a discussion of peer reviews, see Mittan, this volume.)

SPEAKING AND WRITING AS INTERACTION

The importance of audience awareness during composing indicates that communication, whether oral or written, does not consist of a message being delivered, in a single coherent piece, to a receiver. Instead, communication is interactive; meaning is constructed, predicted, and negotiated by communicators. In my class discussions, for instance, a student would begin a sentence, falter, begin again, be interrupted by a student with another idea, respond to that idea, try again to finish the original idea, be assisted by another student, and so on. Other conversational "adjustments" include confirmation checks, comprehension checks, clarifications, requests, repetitions, expansions, and questions (Porter, 1986). Because negotiation of meaning is believed to be a crucial factor in L2 acquisition, conversational negotiation can aid language acquisition when the focus of the message is on content (Ellis, 1984). These content-based messages provide learners with comprehensible input that is contextually meaningful and "embedded in other language [the learners can] understand" (Long & Porter, 1985, p. 214). Authentic classroom communication, such as our discussions on *1984,* forces students to develop strategies for talking and listening when they make mistakes, just as they would in "real" communication (Johnson & Morrow, 1981). "No, this is what I mean," my students would tell each other—and me—as we struggled to communicate our ideas.

This frustrating but important struggle also occurred when the students and I read drafts of essays. Frequently when they read each other's papers, the students would stop to ask each other what a certain phrase meant. They also filled their peers' papers with question marks and comments such as, "I don't understand." In my conferences with students and in my written comments, I would do the same. Just as often, however, a reader would guess the meaning of a phrase or would simply continue to read, satisfied with understanding the general idea of the text. Any interaction between reader and writer is filled with such guesses and confusion as "readers . . . use their own knowledge about language and their experiences to predict and construct meaning as they read" (Goodman, Goodman, & Flores, 1979, p. 27).

Teaching students about the interactive nature of reading and writing, and its similarities with listening and speaking, can help them read their texts as readers rather than as writers. For instance, demonstrating reading processes with students by asking them to predict parts of a text can show the importance of textual redundancies (Troyka, 1987). Writers also need to develop strategies to anticipate their readers' informational needs (Roen & Willey, 1988). However, even experienced writes have difficulties anticipating their readers' reactions, for as Ong (1975) has claimed, "the writer's audience is always a fiction" (p. 9). The peer reviews and multiple drafts in my unit on *1984* helped students come closer to this "fiction" by allowing them to test and change their writing according to their readers' responses—just as they tested and changed what they said in class according to their listener's reactions.

HYPOTHESIS TESTING IN
SPEAKING AND WRITING

The process of testing and revising language according to audience feedback in the context of interaction is an important element in both L1 and L2 acquisition (Brown, 1987; Falk, 1979; Wells, 1986). This hypothesis testing can range from the phonemic level (as when learners modify sounds according to feedback) to the discourse level (as when writers develop culturally appropriate rhetorical strategies). In my classroom discussions, for instance, hypothesis testing occurred when students corrected their classmates' pronunciation or word choice. Another kind of hypothesis testing happened when students tried out their ideas—not just their language forms—on each other. For instance, a heated debate broke out when a student defended the use of censorship in Big Brother's society, a debate which ended when the student clarified his idea by saying that in instances of societal instability or crisis, censorship can be justified. In this case, the student changed his original hypothesis when he hears alternative ideas which made him rethink his position.

In writing, hypothesis testing can be seen in errors that result from experimenting with language forms based on the learners' internalized system of language forms (Bartholomae, 1980; Brown, 1987; Shaughnessy, 1977). For example, students recently introduced to rules governing the use of commas might begin to make more errors with commas as they try to apply the rule to their own writing (Horning, 1987). Just as my students corrected each other's language in class discussions, they also tried to correct each other in their peer reviews, and I did the same. Furthermore, their responses to each other's ideas (such as the thesis on censorship mentioned above) in their peer reviews also allowed them to test hypotheses about their topics.

In a sense, my students also tested hypotheses with themselves as they explored and refined their ideas. This sometimes happened in the class discussions, when students thought about what they wanted to say before they said it—and also changed what they were saying as they said it. It also happened in the generative writing the students did as they were reading *1984* for the first time and as they returned to the book for evidence to support their ideas. For example, I assigned free-writing exercises after the students had finished a section in the novel so that they could write about their reactions to the text so far. I also focused some of the free-writing on important quotations from the book so that the students would examine closely textual elements, such as the use of words or symbols. In this free writing the students would often begin with one idea but end up writing on a completely different one as the act of writing itself engendered more thoughts, more writing. This kind of hypothesis testing indicates that the process of writing is a way to learn about ideas as well as a way to demonstrate learning; that it is not simply "a matter of making and correcting errors or recapitulating what everyone already knows," but also a way "of finding and conveying meanings" (Knoblauch & Brannon, 1983, p. 466). L2 acquisition, oral as well as written, can be as much a matter of cognitive growth as it is a matter of structural accuracy.

SPEAKING AND WRITING AS DIALOGUES

When language learners test hypotheses, they adjust their language and ideas according to feedback from their respondents—correction or affirmation, for example. The back-and-forth nature of this kind of language use is similar to a dialogue in which communicators engage in social as well as cognitive interaction. According to Berthoff (1981), "all speakers and writers have listeners and readers" (p. 119). Even language that is seen primarily as monologue, such as the thinking described by Vygotsky (1934/1986) as inner speech or the egocentric speech Piaget observed in young children (Ginsburg & Opper, 1969), can be seen as having dialogic qualities in that, as Schafer (1981) points out, "questions are asked and then answered, problems are posed and then solved, opposing views are presented and then refuted" (pp. 25–26).

When I started to teach *1984*, I was prepared for dialogues in the form of free writing, drafts, peer reviews, and final drafts; students dialoguing with themselves, their peers, and me as they discovered and expressed their ideas. I had not, however, considered how oral classroom interaction parallels and contributes to the written dialogues and how, in fact, the oral and written language together produce interaction in which we—students and teacher—work together to find and express ideas in English. By integrating our focus on speaking and writing (as well as listening and reading) in the L2 classroom, we can provide students with opportunities to engage in dialogues which can enrich the development of all aspects of language learning.

INTEGRATING SPEAKING AND WRITING IN THE CLASSROOM

The same semester I taught this unit on *1984* to my talkative class, I taught another composition class with the opposite problem: The students didn't like to talk at all. After I had realized the importance of using speech in the writing classroom, I began to devise methods for combining speaking with writing in classroom interaction. One activity that addressed critical reading as well as other aspects of language use involved asking a small group of students to read a particular text—short story, poem, essay, a graph—and then to produce an analysis of the text. Each student in the group was assigned an aspect of the analysis; for instance, to describe the purpose of a symbol or to explain an element on the graph. The students shared their writing with each other, pooled their ideas, and worked together to produce a comprehensive analysis.

This activity is an example of the kind of group work that can provide students with practice in using the target language to solve problems or make decisions (Doughty & Pica, 1986). Tasks such as this one which require an exchange of information can lead students to adjust their interactions in a way that can promote their language acquisition (Long & Porter, 1985). Another group work task, giving students scenarios to respond to, integrates spoken and written language use, presents students with problems to solve, and is also appropriate for all levels of instruction. For instance, a teacher of a beginning language class can give groups of students scenarios concerning visitors to their campus. In the scenarios, the visitors need directions to find a certain building. The groups first discuss how to give directions, and every member of the group writes down the directions. The group then selects the best set of directions and reads the directions to the class, which decides if a visitor would be able to understand the directions.

Another group (or pair) activity that combines speaking and writing is the peer review, in which students read drafts of each other's essays and make suggestions for revisions. I have already discussed how peer reviews played an important role in my unit on *1984*. Peer reviews can also be used successfully with lower levels of instruction and with children (Kitagawa, this volume; Roen & Willey, 1988). Responses to drafts, both oral and written, help to extend the dialogic nature of communication as readers/listeners ask for clarifications and extensions and add their own ideas. Teachers who make dialogic responses (rather than only correcting structural errors and evaluating the final product) also help students communicate their ideas rather than simply try to produce correct language forms (Gere & Stevens, 1985; Sommers, 1982; Zamel, 1985). Furthermore, the conversational interactions which take place in peer response groups and student-teacher conferences aid oral acquisition by giving students opportunities to engage in simple conversations on topics with which they are concerned.

Instructors can also integrate speaking and writing by asking students to make oral presentations on subjects they care about. In a writing classroom, these presentations can be about the topic of an essay students are planning to write or are in the process of writing. Students can receive feedback from their peers and their instructor about their ideas so that two-way interaction occurs. (In my *1984* class, some of the most involved and wide-ranging discussions came out of this activity.) More formal speeches can also be given in a variety of content areas and levels. Groups of students can practice and revise their speeches, as they would their writing in a response group; the resulting interaction helps them understand their own ideas as well as their classmates'. Asking students to give a variety of oral presentations helps them become more aware of their audience and gives them practice in both formal and informal language use.

One forum which allows students to express opinions and feelings in written, informal language is dialogue journals, in which students write back and forth with another person, often another student and/or the teacher. This kind of dialoguing, which can occur not only in journals but also on computer networks, has been used from beginning to advanced levels of lanugage and content instruction (Heath, 1984; Kreeft Peyton & Mackinson-Smyth, this volume; Sayers, this volume; Spack & Sadow, 1983). Because these journals usually supplement classroom work, they give students the chance to write about matters, in and outside of the classroom, that are not typically addressed in formal instructional settings. Since the writers correspond directly with each other, their awareness of their readers increases. Also, these journals enable students to write informally, usually in conversational structures, which is not often the case in classroom settings. In these informal, conversational journals, students can practice, in writing, the kinds of interaction they use in speech. Teachers can also use dialogue journals as a bridge from speaking to writing with students who have already achieved some oral proficiency.

In my *1984* class, I did not have to devise activities such as those discussed above to stimulate discussion which would enrich the students' writing; the students did this for me, despite my initial misguided efforts to silence them. The students spoke up because they were interested in the content of the class, not because they wanted to practice expository and argumentative strategies, which was my curricular agenda. Because of this emphasis on content, the students naturally used target language forms to express their ideas. Using content- or thematic-based curricula can avoid what Widdowson (1978) has called "language put on display" (p. 53), or artificial classroom language where the focus is more on structure than meaning. Teaching language through content integrates all aspects of communication in order "to use language . . . the way language is normally used" (p. 158). Moreover, content-based academic writing instruction can aid understanding of content material (Shih, 1986). The students who read and wrote about *1984* learned not only about analyzing a text critically and expressing that analysis in an essay; they also learned about their own reactions and views to the issues in the novel.

My unit on *1984* certainly did not produce overall excellent work; the process of developing written (and spoken) proficiency in an additional language is more complicated than that. But because I could not silence my students' voices, I unknowingly gave them more ways to discover and explore ideas, to find the right words to express these ideas, and to negotiate with their audience about these ideas—all of which are critical in second language acquisition and cognitive growth.

REFERENCES

Bartholomae, D. (1980). The study of error. *College Composition and Communication, 31,* 253–269.

Berthoff, A. E. (1981). *The making of meaning.* Upper Montclair, NJ: Boynton/Cook.

Brown, H. D. (1987). *Principles of language learning and teaching* (2nd ed.). Englewood Cliffs, NJ: Prentice-Hall.

Canale, M., & Swain, M. (1981). A theoretical framework for communicative competence. In A. S. Palmer, P. J. M. Groot, & G. A. Trosper (Eds.), *The construct validation of tests of communicative competence* (pp. 31–36). Washington, DC: Teachers of English to Speakers of Other Languages.

Diller, K. C. (1978). *The language teaching controversy.* Rowley, MA.: Newbury House.

Doughty, C., & Pica, T. (1986). "Information gap" tasks: Do they facilitate second language acquisition? *TESOL Quarterly, 20,* 305–325.

Ellis, R. (1984). *Classroom second language development.* Oxford: Pergamon Press.

Falk, J. S. (1979). Language acquisition and the teaching and learning of writing. *College English, 41,* 436–447.

Flower, L. (1979). Writer-based prose: A cognitive basis for problems in writing. *College English, 41,* 19–46.

Gere, A. R., & Stevens, R. S. (1985). The language of writing groups: How oral response shapes revision. In S. W. Freeman (Ed.), *The acquisition of written language* (pp. 85–105). Norwood NJ: Ablex.

Ginsburg, H., & Opper, S. (1969). *Piaget's theory of intellectual development.* Englewood Cliffs, NJ: Prentice-Hall.

Goodman, K. S., Goodman, Y., & Flores, B. (1979). *Reading in the bilingual classroom: Literacy and biliteracy.* Rosslyn, VA: National Clearinghouse for Bilingual Education.

Halpern, J. (1984). Differences between speaking and writing and their implications for teaching. *College Composition and Communication, 35,* 345–357.

Heath, S. B. (1984). Literacy or literacy skills? Considerations for ESL/EFL learners. In D. Larson (Ed.), *On TESOL '84* (pp. 15–28). Washington, DC: Teachers of English to Speakers of Other Languages.

Horning, A. S. (1987). *Teaching writing as a second language.* Carbondale: Southern Illinois University Press.

Johnson, K., & Morrow, K. (Eds.). (1981). *Communication in the classroom.* Essex, England: Longman Group, Ltd.

Knoblauch, C. H., & Brannon, L. (1983). Writing as learning through the curriculum. *College English, 45,* 465–474.

Krashen, S. D. (1982). *Principles and practice in second language acquisition.* Oxford: Pergamon Press.

Krashen, S. D., & Terrell, T. (1983). *The natural approach: Language acquisition in the classroom.* Oxford: Pergamon Press.

Long, M. H., & Porter, P. A. (1985). Group work, interlanguage talk, and second language acquisition. *TESOL Quarterly, 19,* 207–228.

McKay, S. (1979). Towards an integrated syllabus. In K. Croft (Ed.), *Readings on English as a second language* (pp. 72–84). Boston: Little, Brown.

Ong, W. J. (1975). The writer's audience is always a fiction. *Publications of the Modern Language Association, 90,* 9–21.

Ong, W. J. (1978). Literacy and orality in our times. In T. Enos (Ed.), *A sourcebook for basic writing teachers* (pp. 45–55). New York: Random House.

Orwell, G. (1982). *1984.* In I. Howe (Ed.), *Orwell's 1984: Text, sources, criticism* (2nd ed.). New York: Harcourt, Brace, Jovanovich. (Original work published 1949).

Perl, S. (1979). The composing processes of unskilled college writers. *Research in the Teaching of English, 13,* 317–333.

Porter, P. (1986). How learners talk to each other: Input and interaction in task-centered discussions. In R. R. Day (Ed.), *Talking to learn: Conversation in second language acquisition* (pp. 200-222). Rowley, MA: Newbury House.

Raimes, A. (1980). Composition: Controlled by the teacher, free for the student. In K. Croft (Ed.), *Readings on English as a second language* (pp. 386–398). Boston: Little, Brown.

Raimes, A. (1983). Tradition and revolution in ESL teaching. *TESOL Quarterly, 17,* 535–552.

Raimes, A. (1987). *Exploring through writing: A process approach to ESL composition.* New York: St. Martin's Press.

Rivers, W. (1983). *Communicating naturally in a second language: Theory and practice in language teaching.* Oxford: Cambridge University Press.

Roen, D. H., & Willey, R. J. (1988). The effects of audience awareness on drafting and revising. *Research in the Teaching of English, 22,* 75–88.

Schafer, J. (1981). The linguistic analysis of spoken and written texts. In B. M. Kroll & R. J. Vann (Eds.), *Exploring speaking-writing relationships* (pp. 1–31). Urbana, IL: National Council of Teachers of English.

Shaughnessy, M. (1977). *Errors and expectations.* New York: Oxford University Press.

Shih, M. (1986). Content-based approaches to teaching academic writing. *TESOL Quarterly, 20,* 617–648.

Sommers, N. (1982). Responding to student writing. *College Composition and Communication, 33,* 148–158.

Spack, R., & Sadow, C. (1983). Student-teacher working journals in ESL freshman composition. *TESOL Quarterly, 17,* 575–593.

Spolsky, B. (1980). What does it mean to know a language? In K. Croft (Ed.), *Readings on English as a second language* (pp. 26–42). Boston: Little, Brown.

Tarone, E. (1980). Communication strategies, foreigner talk, and repair in interlanguage. *Language Learning, 30,* 417–431.

Taylor, B. (1981). Content and written form: A two-way street. In S. McKay (Ed.), *Composing in a second language* (pp. 3–15). Rowley, MA: Newbury House.

Troyka, L. Q. (1987). The writer as conscious reader. In T. Enos (Ed.), *A sourcebook for basic writing teachers* (pp. 307–317). New York: Random House.

Vygotsky, L. (1986). *Thought and language.* (A. Kozulin, Ed. and Trans.). Cambridge, MA: MIT Press. (Original work published 1934).

Wells, G. (1986). *The meaning makers: Children learning language and using language to learn.* Portsmouth, NH: Heinemann.

Widdowson, H. G. (1978). *Teaching language as communication.* Oxford: Oxford University Press.

Zamel, V. (1983). The composing processes of advanced ESL students: Six case studies. *TESOL Quarterly, 17,* 165–187.

Zamel, V. (1985). Responding to student writing. *TESOL Quarterly, 19,* 79–99.

CHAPTER 9

Teacher Training through Teacher Collaboration

Ann Schlumberger and Diane Clymer
University of Arizona

In the United States, interest in professional preparation of English as a second language (ESL) teachers emerged in the late 1960s and early 1970s, accompanied by the birth of the TESOL organization in 1966. During that period, competency-based teacher education (CBTE) was touted as a means of making training programs "accountable" by specifying skills that program graduates should exhibit. Although this approach did result in the identification of a repertoire of teaching behaviors, ESL professionals were concerned that CBTE promoted the notion of "pat answers" to classroom problems (Jarvis, 1972), misrepresented teaching as a simple stimulus-response situation (Diller, 1977), and implied that teacher education could be fully accomplished during the "discrete period" of the novice teacher's training program (Blatchford, 1977).

Blatchford's concern was that teachers were being educated to be technicians, when the reality of their post-training situation would demand that they choose among the plethora of theories and methodologies of ESL instruction to accommodate a variety of student needs and teaching contexts. Jarvis, too, urged teacher education that emphasized

> flexibility, acceptance of alternatives, and decision-making . . . [with] no attachment to any single methodology, philosophy, or set of objectives. . . . [with] inherent respect for the uniqueness of each teacher, each learner, and the interactive result of their collaboration. (1972, p. 177)

Echoing these goals, Larsen-Freeman (1983) distinguished the linear nature of teacher training from the open-ended concept of teacher education. In her article, she discusses the need for teachers to make informed choices in the classroom, listing "awareness," "a positive, open attitude," "transformation and accumulation of knowledge," and "skills development" as prerequisites of such choice making.

But how can we design teacher education programs to promote a responsive teaching style? Rivers (1983) recommends that novice ESL teachers experience "a cooperative, supervised apprenticeship where they are involved in course development, teaching, and testing" (p. 332). Most recently, Richards (1987) has called for giving prospective ESL teachers experience in "practice teaching," "observing experienced teachers," "self- and peer observation," and "seminars and discussion activities" (p. 222).

As coordinators of the nonnative speaker (NNS) strand of the English Composition Program at the University of Arizona, our primary concern has been the instruction of the NNS students. Clearly, though, the quality and consistency of instruction rests upon the ongoing professional development of the graduate assistant teachers (GATs) who teach our courses. Although we incorporate some of the direct supervision recommended by Rivers and Richards,[1] the core of our in-service education for ESL composition teachers is to provide them with a collaborative context for their teaching. This chapter describes the GATs' major collaborative experiences: working together to place students in courses, developing course materials, evaluating students' final examinations, contributing to curriculum design, and making in-service presentations.

RATIONALE FOR COLLABORATIVE APPROACH

Not surprisingly, our collaborative approach to teacher education derives from our experiences teaching English composition. We have found that assigning group work and peer critiques of compositions allow students to

---

[1] Even with all of their experience, many of the GATs chosen to teach NNS composition initially express anxiety about working with ESL writers. Our challenge with these new ESL GATs is to provide them with support without taking away their autonomy. Two or three times during their first semester teaching NNS composition, a coordinator or experienced ESL GAT visits their classes and reviews graded papers. But we consciously reduce the dichotomy between experienced and less experienced ESL GATs through the policy of at least once a year having everyone in the program, including coordinators, visit another's class and be visited in return. Then we celebrate either our successes or salvaging strategies during that month's off-campus meeting.

pool their knowledge and experience as they generate and evaluate their written texts, leading ultimately to self-assessment of their projects. (See Mittan, this volume, for a fuller description of student collaboration.) We believe that an analogous approach is appropriate to teacher training. By making activities requiring teacher collaboration a part of the NNS composition program, we enable our GATs to develop their ability to respond to the exigencies of the classroom while at the same time developing responsibility to their university colleagues and the wider professional community.

Collaborative learning is not new to professional education. Bruffee (1984) cites M. L. J. Abercrombie's (1964) use of it in the 1950s and 1960s in the training medical students in the art of diagnosis. During hospital rounds, rather than require each student to venture a diagnosis of a patient, Abercrombie encouraged the students to discuss the case and arrive at a consensus diagnosis. Comparing the instructional value of requiring individual versus collaborative diagnoses, she found that the consensus approach resulted in students developing sound medical judgment more quickly. Could not such a collaborative approach be appropriate for teachers who, like physicians, must consider many variables in making judgments?

We believe that providing our GATs with opportunities for collaborative learning encourages them to make informed choices and, in Bruffee's words, "models how knowledge is generated, how it changes and grows" (1984, p. 647). Before we describe the collaborative features of our teacher education program, however, we provide a synopsis of the GATs' previous preparation and a description of the ESL composition courses they teach.

GAT PREPARATION AND
ESL TEACHING ASSIGNMENTS

Table 9.1 provides a flowchart of the complete GAT education program at the University of Arizona. Only about half of the ten or so graduate students who teach in the NNS composition program report that they have taught before entering the university's Master's Program in Teaching English as a Second Language. Their previous teaching experience runs across all levels of public school to college, in subjects ranging from English to foreign languages. However, we are fortunate that all of these GATs have benefited from a year's experience teaching in the native English speakers' (NS) freeman composition sequence; this experience and a year of course work in the ESL master's program are prerequisites for teaching in the NNS composition program. Although the course work varies to some extent, most GATs come to us with a background in linguistics, English grammar and usage, and history of the English language, in addition to an introductory course in teaching English as a second language.

During their apprenticeship in the NS freshman composition sequence, new teachers are exposed to current research in composition, and attend workshops and lectures by nationally renowned academicians in the field. This theoretical knowledge is reinforced by supervisors who visit GATs' classes and review GATs' responses to student papers. Further support is offered in weekly small-group meetings in which the GATs exchange teaching strategies, compare assignments, and vent their reaction to the vicissitudes of teaching freshman composition. Their supervisors encourage them also to gather student essays to submit for the annually published *A Student's Guide to Freshman Composition* (Shropshire, Siebert, & Gungle, 1987), to attend the meetings of professional organizations, and to transform the insights they gain into published articles (Diogenes, Roen, & Swearingen, 1986).

After a year of experience teaching NS composition, ESL GATs are assigned to teach the NNS sequence of composition classes. Table 9.2 gives more detailed information about the NS and NNS composition courses. The University of Arizona offers three NNS undergraduate courses that parallel the NS freshman composition sequence. In addition, the university provides two advanced composition courses for NNS graduate students. Three hundred students progress through one or more of these writing courses, which are designed according to Moffett's (1968) and Britton, Burgess, Martin, MacLeod, and Rosen's (1975) insights into audience and purpose. At all levels, reading, listening, and speaking activities are integral parts of writing assignments (Schlumberger & Clymer, 1987).

During the ESL GATs' presemester orientation workshop, they receive an overview of the NNS program, including a description of the major assignments in each course. Thus, early on we strive to instill in GATs a sense of pedagogical purpose that transcends the course they are teaching. We hope that they will see themselves, their colleagues, and their students as participants in a writing process that extends beyond one semester. Then, having become acquainted with the purpose and context of the courses they will be teaching, the GATs are given a preview of their "audience" when they participate in sessions for holistically assessing placement essays.

PARTICIPATION IN PLACEMENT

There is no better way to heighten a sense of professional responsibility than to give people decisions to make, decisions for which they will

TABLE 9.1. TEACHER PREPARATION OF ENGLISH AS A SECOND LANGUAGE (ESL) GRADUATE ASSISTANT TEACHERS (GATS) OF COMPOSITION, DEPARTMENT OF ENGLISH, UNIVERSITY OF ARIZONA

First Year		Second Year		Beyond Second Year	
Academic Work in ESL	*Professional Development: Teaching Native Speaker (NS) Composition*	*Academic Work in ESL*	*Professional Development: Teaching Nonnative Speaker (NNS) Composition*	*Academic Work in Doctoral Field*	*Professional Development: Teaching NNS Composition*
May include: Introduction to Teaching English to Speakers of Other Languages History of English language Grammars Linguistics Cultural	Teaching of English (101, 102) Six classroom observations (3/ semester) by supervisor Weekly lectures on composition theory and rhetoric OR small	May include: TESOL methodology and second language acquisition Internship at pre-university ESL center Advanced seminar (L2	Teaching of English (106, 107, 108) Some 2–3 classroom observations by supervisor (usually only first semester); exchange of classroom visits	Varies according to field (Some GATs may be finishing M.A. in ESL.)	Teaching of English (106, 107, 108; also graduate courses 407A, 407B) Possible supervision of new ESL GATs; exchange of classroom visits

anthropology	group meetings	theory and research)	GAT-led monthly workshops	Leading of monthly workshops
Teaching of reading	Training in holistic scoring of NS essays	Comprehensive examination	Holistic scoring of NNS placement essays	Holistic scoring of NNS placement essays
Teaching of composition		Thesis on ESL issue (optional)	Participation in materials development	Participation in materials development
			Collaborative writing of final exam questions	Collaborative writing of final exam questions
			Holistic exchange grading of final exams	Holistic exchange grading of final exams
			Participation in curriculum development	Participation in curriculum development
			Presentations at local ESL conferences	Presentations at local, regional, and national conferences

TABLE 9.2. ASSIGNMENTS IN COMPOSITION COURSES TAUGHT BY ENGLISH AS A SECOND LANGUAGE (ESL) GRADUATE ASSISTANT TEACHERS (GATS), DEPARTMENT OF ENGLISH, UNIVERSITY OF ARIZONA

First Year	Second Year	Beyond Second Year
Composition for Native Speaker (NS): Undergraduates	*Composition for Nonnative Speaker (NNS): Undergraduates*	*Composition for NNS: Graduates (Taught by ESL GATs with M.A. Degrees)*
English 100: *Preparatory Course* (Parallel to 106 but NOT taught by first year GATs) 2 analytical, expository essays (2-draft process for each) 1 analytical persuasive essay (3-draft process)	English 106: *Preparatory Course* Essays on culture and community Narration, description, classification, cause/effect	English 106: *Preparatory Course* (Taken with undergraduates)
English 101: *First Semester Freshman Composition for NS* Essay on a remembered event Documented informational essay on topic of choice Documented argumentative essay based on informational essay written previously	English 107: *First Semester Freshman Composition for NNS* Expanded definition of an abstract term Essay on an aspect of culture Rhetorical analysis of student essay on culture Documented argumentative essay on topic of choice	English 407a: *Advanced Composition For NNS Graduate Students (I)* Expanded definition on topic in student's field (lay audience) Essay on ethics in student's field (semi-expert audience) Documented argumentative essay on issue in student's field (expert audience)
English 102: *Second Semester Freshman Composition for NS* Critical analysis of student essay 3 critical analytical essays about literature (2 novellas; 1 novel with documentation of secondary sources)	English 108: *Second Semester Freshman Composition for NNS* Analysis of advertisement Rhetorical analysis of essay Critical analyses of 2 novels	English 407b: *Advanced Composition for NNS Graduate Students (II)* Informal proposal for 407b project Analysis of published article in student's field 407b project (technical): review of literature, empirical report, chapter of thesis, etc.

experience the consequences. The students the GATs place will be their own, and participating in the holistic evaluation of placement essays is their first communal task in the NNS composition program. The placement examination for incoming NNS students is similar in format to the NS exam: In both cases, students are asked to write a thirty-minute impromptu essay on an assigned topic.

All first-year GATs of NS students are initiated to holistic evaluation practices (Myers, 1980), examining the content, organization, expression, and mechanics of sample NS freshman placement essays. However, our ESL GAT graders undergo additional training in weighing syntactical and rhetorical aspects of NNS papers. They need to determine, for instance, whether an English 106 or 107 placement is appropriate for a student who is fluent at the sentence level, but whose paragraph development relies on repetition instead of exemplification or causal analysis.

The GATs' ability to discern features important in NNS placement evolves during a discussion, led by a coordinator, in which graders arrive at consensus evaluations of 10 sample papers. The discussion reflects what Fanselow (1986) calls "the Socratic idea of teaching: aiding each other to remember what each already knows, helping each of us to see what is within each" (p. 243). Experienced ESL GATs contribute what they have learned about NNS students at the various course levels; novice GATs share the way the previous year's insights into composition theory and developing writers pertain to the task at hand. GATs also receive a synopsis of Homburg's (1984) criteria for categorizing expression and mechanical errors, roughly, those that are hardly noticeable, those that are annoying, and those that render meaning incomprehensible.

But transcending the instructional aspect of holistic paper assessment is the *espirit de corps* that is forged. The session marks the beginning of an ongoing professional conversation about how to lead students to write with clarity, if not grace. Such conversation characterizes collaborative learning. Bruffee (1984) links the two: "Besides providing a particular kind of conversation, collaborative learning also provides a particular kind of social context of conversation, a particular kind of community—a community of status equals: peers" (p. 642).

MATERIALS DEVELOPMENT

In writing classrooms, teachers activate student conversation/collaboration through assignments that elicit student interaction. Just so, in our training program, we have endeavored to give our teachers opportunities for collaborative learning by requiring them to interact in working out their course syllabi. Before the semester begins, the GATs gather in groups according to the course they are teaching so that a more experienced peer can answer questions about what to expect. At this point, GATs actively collaborate in working out the details of a particular semester's course. For instance, the first assignment in English 107 (the first-semester NNS freshman composition course) requires students to write an expanded definition of an abstract concept. Each semester the assigned concept changes in order to keep the assignment fresh. The idea students write about might be "hero" one semester, "friend" another, "justice" a third. Once the English 107 teachers agree on a topic they find an essay that will provide students with some background reading about the concept. Then, following the format used in the 107 reader, *Making Connections: Readers for Writers* (Adams & Smith, 1985), they develop a series of journal exercises that will prompt students to develop their own definitions using a variety of rhetorical strategies. The GATs' collaboration on the first assignment sets the stage for continued collaboration throughout the semester.

The English 108 collaborative project begins the previous spring when book orders are due. By then, a coordinator has identified GATs who want to teach the second-semester undergraduate composition course, which engages students in critical analysis of an advertisement, fiction, and nonfiction. The teachers, together with a coordinator of the program, choose a unifying theme that will characterize what students will read—for example, family and community, heroism, quests. Once this theme and the two novels students will read have been approved by the director of composition, the new 108 teachers begin compiling the short fiction, essays, and poems that the students will read as background to the novels. The GAT who teaches the summer section of 108 pilots these materials and reports back to the others before the fall semester begins. Those who will teach 108 in the fall then revise the compilation as needed and collaborate on writing the fall syllabus, utilizing what worked well during the summer.

Collaborating to develop materials for courses has resulted in GATs' undertaking other peer group projects upon their own initiative. For instance, the teachers of the preparatory course discovered that they needed an index to the grammar exercises in their text and collaborated in writing one, which is now on file for future English 106 teachers. At all course levels, informal sharing of successful assignments and peer analyses of what went wrong in class on Monday are frequent occurrences. GATs became accustomed to having a support group while teaching NS composition during their first year, and early emphasis on teacher collaboration in the NNS sequence encourages them to continue seeing their peers as professional resources.

FINAL EXAMINATIONS

The delicate balance between program control by coordinators on the one hand and GAT independence on the other is particularly apparent in the preparation of final examinations. Three-fourths of the way through the semester, the GATs begin their collaboration on the writing and, at the end of the semester, exchange grading of the final examinations for the NNS undergraduate writing courses. Students at each course level take a common final, writing an essay of their own in response to a "prompt essay" they are given to read either before the examination (106, 107) or during the examination (108). Choosing prompt essays and writing study questions and examination questions are the responsibility of the GATs. Our main intention has been to provide the GATs, caught in the end-of-semester rush, with a context for collaborative reflection on what their classes have accomplished during the semester. However, the progress of the GATs through these tasks—as one of them once observed—also serves as an end-of-the-semester model for how to sequence assignments. The following progression is one possibility:

1. The program coordinators lead a workshop on what makes good examination questions, during which GATs examine successful and unsuccessful questions and placement-essay prompts from previous semesters. Often, second-year GATs can provide insights on how the students typically answered successful questions—and on what may have misled them in unsuccessful questions.

2. During the following week, the GATs at each course level review possible prompt essays and agree upon one they consider appropriate for their students. They talk over their selection with a coordinator who determines that the prompt essay relates to a theme the students have been writing about all semester and is not too lengthy, too subtle, or too culturally biased. (One rejected submission dealt with American soap operas!)

3. Once an essay has been selected, each group begins drafting the examination questions which are then commented upon by a coordinator and revised further if necessary. Among other points, the coordinator asks the GATs to provide a rationale for their questions, and she also makes sure that the audience and purpose for the students' responses are clearly specified in the examination directions. (At this time, GATs also write study questions for their students but do not submit them to a coordinator.) Finally, copies of the examinations are reviewed by the director of composition.

Of course the proof of an effective examination is in the responses it elicits from the students. In contrast to the placement exams at the beginning of the semester, the holistic grading of the finals is not supervised. Immediately after the exam, the teachers reclarify what they expect in response to the essay questions. They pass two or three papers around to derive benchmarks for assigning grades; then, in the process of evaluating the papers, they evaluate the exam itself. A secondary benefit is that such collaborative reading of papers helps maintain consistency in grading.

CURRICULUM DESIGN

"Collaborative learning naturally challenges the traditional basis of the authority of those who teach" (Bruffee, 1984, p. 649) and those who design curricula! In fact, curriculum design is generally considered the responsibility of the director or coordinator of a program, but we have found it benefits our program if the GATs have a role in instigating as well as implementing curricular changes. Therefore, we have several policies to insure that we hear the voice of the GATs in these matters.

First of all, the coordinators pass on prospective textbooks for collaborative review by GATs with experience teaching the courses in which the books would be used. Second, ideas derived from GATs' course work, teaching experience, and research are incorporated into the program. For instance, one GAT who took a number of reading courses in the pursuit of his doctorate presented an excellent rationale for assigning "free reading" to students in English 106. Other 106 GATs liked the idea; their students' self-chosen reading material is now the basis for many journal entries. Another example is our incorporation of rhetorical analysis into the 107 and 108 courses. GATs originated these assignments to focus students' attention on form while teaching the skills of critical analysis. Finally, the most encompassing presentation of the program's curriculum is the result of GAT collaboration. In *The Student's Guide to ESL Composition* (1987), GATs Taylor and Mangelsdorf articulate the policies of the program in addition to presenting samples of students' work, a description of grading criteria, and a cross-cultural comparison of rhetorics. Similar to the *Guide* produced for NS freshman composition, this book is tailored to the NNS student audience.

IN-SERVICE ACTIVITIES

Through their collaboration on testing, generating materials, and curriculum design, the GATs come to recognize each other as important resources. These resources are tapped in monthly meetings. Instead of featuring lectures given by a teacher trainer or by the prescriptive outside expert so decried by teacher educators (Blatchford, 1977; Fanselow, 1986; Jarvis, 1972), meetings are either roundtable discussions of common pedagogical concerns or in-service workshops given by GAT peers who, through their own research and experience, have insights they wish to share.

At the beginning of each semester, we ask the GATs to tell us what aspects of teaching NNS composition they would like to focus on in the monthly meetings. Among the pedagogical and cultural presentations they request, responding to papers is a major concern which is addressed early in the semester. This workshop, usually led by a coordinator and a senior GAT, builds on discussion from the grading sessions and focuses on how the teacher's process of responding to papers can complement the student's process of writing them. Other presentation-discussions led by GATs themselves have covered providing students with instruction in reading, making students aware of audience in their writing, designing journal exercises that will support major theme assignments, and designing useful peer review exercises. The presenters are as eager for feedback as their colleagues are for information. Often, the presentations are revised for audiences at local, regional, or national professional conventions. By holding their ideas up to outside scrutiny, the GATs enlarge their sense of responsibility to encompass the wider teaching community as well as their own classroom and program. As Bruffee (1984) points out,

> We establish knowledge . . . collaboratively by challenging each other's biases and presuppositions; . . . and by joining the larger, more experienced communities of knowledgeable peers through assenting to those communities' interests, values, language, and paradigms of perception and thought. (p. 646)

CONCLUSIONS

The consensus of the teacher educators cited in this chapter is that teaching is a dynamic process requiring more than a set pattern of responses. In "Training Teachers or Educating a Teacher," Larsen-Freeman (1983) defines learning as "a willingness to examine and often risk one's beliefs and patterns of actions and thought" (p. 267). This is exactly what teachers are continually required to do, for teachers are—first, foremost, and forever—learners. Because we believe there is evidence that collaboration fosters learning, we have embedded collaboration in our teacher education program. We find that collaborative activities engage our GATs in an analytic dialogue in which their theoretical and experiential knowledge is sifted and synthesized. But as Brown (1987) points out, intuition plays as much a part in teaching and risktaking as does analysis (pp. 248–50). To this end, collaboration can also confirm a GAT's gut feeling of how to handle a classroom situation, with other GATs encouraging him or her to act on it. Then too, if a bright idea does not work out, a supportive peer group is the ideal context in which to examine why not.

Teachers who apply collaborative learning strategies in their classrooms are aware that collaboration takes time, discipline, and diplomacy. Nevertheless, incorporating teacher collaboration into a writing program has several benefits. First of all, collaboration heightens teacher consciousness of the recursiveness of learning at various course levels, thus building program coherence. Also, when teachers work together to develop materials and evaluate student work, consistency in course content and grading practices is encouraged. Finally, the intellectual stimulation resulting from engaging in collaborative tasks energizes both the teachers and the program. How enriching it can be when the professional collaboration and cooperation nurtured while earning teaching credentials continues to promote growth in educational systems outside the university.

REFERENCES

Abercrombie, M. L. J. (1964). *Anatomy of judgment*. Harmondsworth, England: Penguin.

Adams, W. R., & Smith, G. D. (1985). *Making connections: Readers for writers.* New York: Holt Rinehart & Winston.

Blatchford, C. H. (1977). Some questions on CBTE from TESOL. In J. F. Fanselow & R. L. Light (Eds.), *Bilingual, ESOL and foreign language teacher preparation: Models, practices, issues* (pp. 191–194). Washington, DC: Teachers of English to Speakers of Other Languages.

Britton, J., Burgess, T., Martin, N., McLeod, A., & Rosen, H. (1975). *The development of writing abilities 11–18*. London: Schools Council Research Studies, Macmillan Education.

Brown, H. D. (1987). *Principles of language learning and teaching* (2nd ed.). Englewood Cliffs, NJ: Prentice-Hall.

Bruffee, K. A. (1984). Collaborative learning and the "conversation of mankind." *College English, 46,* 635–652.

Diller, K. C. (1977). Linguistics and ESOL teacher preparation: some questions about competency-based teacher education. In X. Y. Zee (Ed.), *Bilingual, ESOL and foreign language teacher preparation: Models, practices, issues* (pp. 195–202). Washington, DC: Teachers of English to Speakers of Other Languages.

Diogenes, M., Roen, D. H., & Swearingen, C. J. (1986). Creating the profession: The GAT training program at the University of Arizona. *Writing Program Administrator, 10,* 51–59.

Fanselow, J. F. (1986). You call yourself a teacher? An alternative model for discussing lessons. In D. Tannen & J. E. Alatis (Eds.), *Georgetown University*

round table on languages and linguistics 1985: The interdependence of theory,
data and application (pp. 237–248). Washington, DC: Georgetown University
Press.

Homburg, T. J. (1984). Holistic evaluation of ESL compositions: Can it be vali-
dated objectively? *TESOL Quarterly, 18,* 87–105.

Jarvis, G. A. (1972). Teacher education goals: They're tearing up the street where I
was born. *Foreign Language Annals, 6,* 198–205.

Larsen-Freeman, D. (1983). Training teachers or educating a teacher. In J. E.
Alatis, H. H. Stern, & P. Strevens (Eds.), *Georgetown University round table on*
languages and linguistics 1983: Applied linguistics and the preparation of
second language teachers—Toward a rationale (pp. 264–274). Washington, DC:
Georgetown University Press.

Myers, M. (1980). *A procedure for writing assessment and holistic scoring.*
Urbana, IL: National Council of Teachers of English.

Moffett, J. (1968). *Teaching the universe of discourse.* New York: Houghton
Mifflin.

Richards, J. C. (1987). The dilemma of teacher education in TESOL. *TESOL*
Quarterly, 21, 209–226.

Rivers, W. M. (1983). Preparing college and university instructors for a lifetime of
teaching: A luxury or a necessity? In J. E. Alatis, H. H. Stern, & P. Strevens
(Eds.), *Georgetown University round table on languages and linguistics 1983:*
Applied linguistics and the preparation of second language teachers—Toward a
rationale (pp. 327–341). Washington, DC: Georgetown University Press.

Schlumberger, A., & Clymer, D. (1987, March). *What to do in composition classes*
when you have ESL students and no ESL expertise. Paper presented at the
Conference on College Composition and Communication, Atlanta.

Shropshire, S. M., Siebert, B. G., & Gungle, B. W. (1987). *A Student's Guide to*
Freshman Composition (8th ed.). Edina, MN: Bellwether Press.

Taylor, V., & Mangelsdorf, K. (1987). *A student's guide to ESL composition.*
Tucson, AZ: University of Arizona.

PART II

Rhetorical Concerns in Writing

At first glance, the title of this second section may seem odd. After all, to most people, particularly to those who work in second language teaching, rhetorical concerns are those matters that interested Aristotle, Plato, Corax, Tisias, Protagoras, Lysias, Gorgias, Isocrates, Cicero, and Quintilian—the great thinkers, rhetoricians, and rhetors of ancient Greece and Rome. These men and others, whose influence has persisted, spent much time analyzing persuasive and argumentative discourse.

But this section comprises chapters that take a broader, more catholic view of rhetorical concerns in discourse, beyond those particular to argument and persuasion. In general terms, the authors in this part do what the classical rhetoricians did: They perform "the systematic analysis of human discourse for the purpose of adducing useful precepts for future discourse . . ." (Murphy, 1983, p. 3). As they adduce useful precepts for teachers, they define rhetorical problems as Flower and Hayes (1980) do: any concern that a writer might need to negotiate, including development, purpose, organization, support, ethical stance, logic, audience expectations, sentence structure, punctuation, spelling, and even deadlines. As the authors in this section deal with these and other rhetorical challenges facing writers, they help all of us who teach to realize that "our responsibility is to control and vary the rhetorical demands of writing tasks to give students practice in adjusting relationships among writer, reader, subject, manipulating more and more complex variables" (Lindemann, 1987, p. 193).

For students learning to use English as an additional language, there is an increasing awareness that the constructing, addressing, and solving of rhetorical problems should emerge from a context in which there is a focus on important and meaningful communication in the L2. It is our responsibility as educators to draw on the rich linguistic, cultural, and intellectual resources that L2 students bring to

161

writing activities as we guide them in their growth. Creating L2 writing environments and tasks such as those suggested by these authors will help to "build a rich history for each student through a rich present" (Graves, 1986).

Each of the authors in this section writes about rhetorical concerns in basically the same way. That is, each discusses ways to engage students in rhetorical problem solving in the context of meaningful communication. Each offers suggestions for teaching writers to gain awareness of both rhetorical problems and tools for solving those problems. Each, then, offers means for guiding writers to awareness and from awareness to solutions. They each make it possible for writers to see and solve the problems that face them.

In the first chapter of this section, Carole Edelsky reports on a year-long study of the writing of 26 children in a bilingual program. Her study provides evidence countering three erroneous beliefs: (1) bilingualism is a limitation in learning written language, especially if the linguistic varieties are nonstandard; (2) young writers are insensitive to the needs of their audiences and to the demands of different types of texts and contexts; and (3) any graphic display is writing and any decoding of print is reading. She provides evidence of ways children use their strengths in two languages to make meaning, as well as ways they show sensitivity to audience, text, and context. Edelsky makes a distinction between authentic writing, in which all cueing systems are interacting, and mere simulations of writing, pointing out that the kinds of writing children do greatly affects their written language growth. In short, Edelsky demonstrates that young bilingual writers can, when engaged in authentic writing tasks, handle more rhetorical situations than many educators believe.

In Chapter 11, Yvonne S. Freeman and David E. Freeman draw on theory and research in child development and child language acquisition to show how whole language approaches to teaching can help secondary students of English as a second language (ESL) to define and address rhetorical issues. Freeman and Freeman describe an interesting lesson in a high school content reading ESL class for students who use a variety of languages. They interpret the lesson in relation to six principles of a whole language approach, illustrating how the lesson exemplifies each of the principles. The six principles are: (1) language classes should be learner centered; (2) language is learned best when kept whole; (3) language instruction should employ all four modes: listening, speaking, reading, and writing; (4) language in the classroom should be meaningful and functional; (5) language is learned through social interaction; and (6) language is learned best when teachers have faith in the learners. In the rich high school classroom environment that Freeman and Freeman describe, writing activities are content based and real rather than artificial.

Duane H. Roen, in Chapter 12, draws on theories of and research into composing and cognition to argue that teachers need to consider several factors when constructing writing assignments at any level. First, teachers need to guide students to address authentic audiences, purposes, and topics in their writing. Second, teachers can use process approaches to help students define and solve the many rhetorical problems that any writing entails. Third, teachers can make it possible for students to receive appropriate feedback or evaluation as they write, not only after they have finished writing. Roen describes specific preschool, elementary, secondary, and college writing activities that exemplify the principles he explores.

While Roen and other authors in this collection discuss peer review activities in general terms, Robert Mittan, in Chapter 13, focuses on them in great detail. Mittan demonstrates how peer review work allows students to use and develop their existing communicative powers. After reviewing theory supporting peer review activities, Mittan draws on his university ESL teaching experience to offer many practical suggestions for using such activities. He presents peer review work as the kind of meaningful social interaction that other authors in this collection advocate. He also represents peer review as a way of building on students' existing strengths as writers, readers and especially, collaborators.

In the penultimate chapter of the section, Joy M. Reid provides many ideas for those preparing university students for the writing tasks they will encounter in their academic course work. Reid bases her chapter on schema theory and contrastive rhetoric to point out that foreign students come to the United States with different sets of experiences and cultural expectations about academic work. ESL composition teachers need to make students aware of these differences and expand students' repertoires of options and strategies for communicating through writing. Reid provides specific suggestions for teaching ESL students how to talk about writing and how to prepare for a variety of writing tasks in a variety of disciplines. Reid further describes methods that teachers can use to persuade students that an academic audience expects specific strategies and formats, and that teachers are not trying to change the way that students think, but rather the way that students present thoughts.

In the final chapter of this section, Bruce W. Gungle and Victoria Taylor describe how they modified the Daly-Miller Writing Apprehension Test, a test frequently used with native English speakers. They administered the test to university students enrolled in composition courses specifically designed for ESL writers. Gungle and Taylor correlated apprehension scores with several variables: attention to form, attention to content, students' perceptions of writing requirements in their majors, and students' interest in taking advanced writing courses. They discovered that ESL students seem to have patterns of writing apprehension different from native speakers. Gungle and Taylor suggest that the Daly-Miller test may not be appropriate for ESL students; that scholars may need to construct alternative methods of assessing ESL students' writing apprehension. Gungle and Taylor also offer suggestions for classroom practices that may lessen ESL students' writing apprehension.

REFERENCES

Flower, L., & Hayes, J. (1980). The cognition of discovery: Defining a rhetorical problem. *College Composition and Communication, 31,* 21–32.

Graves, D. (1986, November). *Reading and writing power for teachers, for kids: Resources, reflections, beginnings.* Keynote address presented at the Teachers Applying Whole Language Conference, Tucson, AZ.

Lindemann, E. (1987). *A rhetoric for writing teachers* (2nd ed.). New York: Oxford University Press.

Murphy, J. J. (1983). The origins and early development of rhetoric. In J. J. Murphy (Ed.), *A synoptic history of classical rhetoric*. Davis, CA: Hermagoras Press.

CHAPTER 10

Bilingual Children's Writing: Fact and Fiction

Carole Edelsky
Arizona State University

Teachers, administrators, parents, children, politicians, even researchers have theories about reading and writing; beliefs that help establish expectencies, shape perceptions, and influence decisions (Harste & Burke, 1977). Often these beliefs are unexamined which, if anything, increases the likelihood they will be found under the surface and between the lines in school district mandates, curriculum guides, instructional materials, and syllabi in teacher education programs. When it comes to the education of non-English speaking children, the beliefs often find their way into law (e.g., requirements for bilingual teacher certification, establishment of particular testing programs, etc.).

A study of the written productions of young children enrolled in a bilingual program in a settled migrant, semirural school district in Arizona produced data that counter many beliefs about writing (Edelsky, 1982). A few of the erroneous beliefs (or theories or myths) presented here, along with the counter evidence, are:

- Bilingualism is a limitation in learning written language, especially if the linguistic varieties are nonstandard.
- Young writers are insensitive to the needs of their audiences and to the demands of different types of texts and contexts.

The full report of these data appears in Edelsky (1982). Presentation of changes in the children's written productions, changes in my own theoretical notions about writing, and changes in the bilingual program appear in Edelsky (1986).

This study was also one of the catalysts for bringing a pervasive underlying belief to the surface and for developing a theoretical proposal to counter it. That belief is:

* Any graphic display is writing and any decoding of print is reading.

At the time of this study, I believed our data were examples of writing. Through analysis of these samples and subsequent analyses of other data, however, I now believe that most of the pieces were examples of *simulations* of writing. After briefly describing the 1982 study, I address this third myth (confusing writing look-alikes with writing), followed by those two listed earlier.

THE STUDY

The intent of the 1982 Arizona study was to describe the writing of bilingual children enrolled in a bilingual program. The program was unusual for the late 1970s and early 1980s. Unlike the majority of bilingual programs which, at that time, equated literacy instruction with teaching reading, and which offered fill-in-the-blank workbook pages and an occasional half hour of "creative writing" as a nod to writing, here was a program in which children wrote (or so we thought). For the study, the regular in-class written work of 26 children (nine first, nine second, and eight third graders) was collected four times during one school year. The intent was not to specify in advance particular aspects of writing to investigate—from the more local and technical (such as letter formation) to the more global and literary (such as story quality)—but to derive categories and coding systems from the data themselves. Thus the study was an effort of qualitative research in which a team of researchers analyzed more than 500 written pieces from three different classrooms for codeswitching, invented spelling, nonspelling conventions (punctuation, segmentation), stylistic devices, structural features (e.g., beginnings, endings, links between clauses), and quality of content, in order to note changes over time as well as to make cross-sectional comparisons. We also examined these pieces and others, gathered unsystematically from several primary-grade classrooms, to find evidence for or against 30 beliefs about literacy. Other data, including teacher and aide interview responses, children's and siblings' school records, notes from parent meetings, administrative meetings, classroom observations, and a language situation survey permitted our analyses to move back and forth between the written pieces and larger and smaller contexts.

One of these contexts was the classroom and how writing happened there. Despite the official program philosophy, which included the use of whole texts, a focus on frequent writing for real purposes to varied audiences, the child's choice of which language to use for reading and writing, and an emphasis on meaning making, actual practice was considerably different. Although children did produce print daily for extended periods of time, were told frequently that the meaning was what mattered, were permitted to write in either Spanish or English, and several of the teachers did assign a variety of genres (journals, letters, invitations, reports, stories); nevertheless, the teacher was the audience for almost all the pieces. Journals were not answered. There were no conferences focusing on children's ideas. Nothing was revised (although a few pieces were edited). A piece was usually produced and checked off. (For a contrast in treating classroom writers and writing, see Calkins, 1982. For contrasts in handling journals, see Staton, Shuy, Kreeft, & Reed, in press. Rubin, 1984, reviews relationships between writing and audience.)

Occasionally, children wrote unassigned pieces that were different from their other productions. For example, the genres of unassigned writing included songs and jokes; they did not include journal entries or reports. Unassigned pieces were shorter. They had more sophisticated endings (assigned pieces often simply stopped, with no verbal closure), used far fewer punctuation marks, contained genuine queries, complaints, and pleadings, and often had a more poetic quality.

Occasionally, too, children became caught up in assignments. They may have begun them perfunctorily, but at some point they became engaged, presumably changing purpose from complying with the assignment to, perhaps, "one-upping" peers or teasing the teacher or entertaining themselves. (Hudson, in press, found similar responses to some assignments in mainstream English language classrooms. She called them "curriculum-surpassed writing.") In other words, what began as a writing exercise, a simulation of "writing," became an act of *writing*. What exactly is the difference?

Clearly, in the case of authentic writing (rather than "writing"), the language is being used to make meaning for some purpose (Edelsky & Smith, 1984). A student is less likely to be writing and more likely to be simulating writing when he or she is filling in blanks on a worksheet, finishing a story starter, or producing a story that includes the week's spelling words. The source of the contrast between writing and "writing" in school may lie in what Erickson (1984) refers to as the nature of the power relations between teacher and student, allowing each part more or less influence on task formulation. It may reside in Hudson's (in press) adaptation of the idea of control over the initiation versus the composition of a piece. Whatever the source of the difference between writing and "writing," it still remains to identify the difference—in other words, to characterize the act. It is time to turn to a discussion of the key erroneous beliefs regarding the nature of reading and writing.

ERRONEOUS BELIEF 1

Any graphic display is produced through writing (and any decoding of print occurs through reading).

Instead, extrapolating from Goodman's (1969), Harste's (1980), and Smith's (1978) models of the reading process, we find that writing is simultaneously a social, psychological, and linguistic process for making meaning. Language, oral or written, is predictable (Harste, Burke, & Woodward, 1982; Smith, 1978), with predictions, ultimately, being about meaning. Knowing a language means knowing the rule-governed systems of cues for making predictions. In written language, these cueing systems are the graphic and graphophonic, the syntactic, the semantic, and the pragmatic. The systems of cues work together—they are both interactive and interdependent. For example, in American English, pragmatic conventions for the genre recipe occur together with particular syntactic cues (imperatives, deletion of function words), orthographic cues (abbreviations), and page layout. In any instance of language in use, whether oral or written, cues from all systems interrelate and are present (or can be inferred). If a system is missing or if normally interactive and interdependent systems are severed or distorted, then the activity occurring is not writing (or reading) but something that merely resembles writing (or reading) because a graphic display is involved. (See Edelsky, 1986, for a more extensive discussion of authenticity in reading and writing.)

The act of writing may result in a novel or a note on a message board. It may be exquisitely penned or dashed off; it may be something one does with sorrow or with joy, intense effort or nonchalance; it may concern the sacred or the profane. It is not prestige or topic or form that distinguishes writing from writing exercises. The difference between *writing* one word in a blank on a job application form and putting one word in a blank on a worksheet has to do with the difference in interactivity between meaning options and pragmatic considerations (genre, purpose, audience, etc.). On one hand, what is to go in the blanks on the job application (past jobs, place at which to be reached, etc.), has some meaningful connection to the writer's purpose for filling out the application (to get a job). On the other hand, the semantic content needed for the blanks on the worksheet (e.g., miles to Grampa's house, reason for Grampa's sadness, etc.) has no particular relation to the purpose for filling out the worksheet (to complete the assignment; to get a good grade). What makes filling in blanks in a worksheet a case of simulation of writing (and not *writing*) is that cueing systems are either missing entirely or the normal interactivity among systems is distorted (especially the connection between the pragmatic system and each of the others).

Even when workbooks are abandoned and teachers ask children to write invitations, reports, journals, and stories—as they did in the study of 26 children in a bilingual program—there is no guarantee that writing is what will take place. If the children do not take the assignment and make it their own, if their purpose remains to fulfill the assignment rather than to invite or inform or entertain or some purpose reasonably tied to that particular genre, if the assignment prevents the audience and the purpose from being compatible—in other words, if the connections between systems are distorted or cut off, then what is happening is a simulation of writing and not writing.

As I said, it became clear after these data were collected and analyzed that it was not that we had a simple division between assigned writing and unassigned writing, but that, of more than 500 pieces, we had 34 pieces of unassigned writing, an unknown number of pieces of writing that had been initiated through assignments, and probably over 400 pieces of simulations of writing.

Why then, am I presenting some of these data in a book on writing? I have two main reasons: for comparision with much of the existing research literature; and for comparison with what is yet to come. In the first place, the work of these 26 children provides interesting contrasts to findings from other studies supposedly about writing but more likely about simulations. Much research on classroom writing uses data produced in response to prompts or assignments or pieces produced in "writing process" classrooms in which conferences are lesson-like (Florio-Ruane, no date) and children's purposes remain linked to compliance. Thus, much of what is known about children's writing is actually about children's simulations of writing. (The research of Calkins, 1982, and Graves, 1983, are notable exceptions. Additonally, some researchers, such as Hudelson, 1986, make a point of noting the artificiality of the pieces they have analyzed.) Because the analyses of simulations as well as of writing in the 1982 Arizona study both corroborate and counter findings from other studies of simulations of writing, and because findings from studies of simulations affect policy and research, the interpretations of the Arizona data are important additions to understanding children's writing.

The second major reason for presenting the data from this study is to offer them as a potential for comparison with *authentic* writing in future studies of written language development in bilingual classrooms. Simply because simulations of writing are pervasive in schools does not mean schools inherently require them. Some bilingual education teachers are now beginning to generate authentic writing as the rule rather than the exception. Some genres (e.g., dialogue journals) along with certain conditions of classroom climate regularly elicit genuine writing from monolingual, bilingual, and second language students (Staton, Shuy, Kreeft, and Reed, in press).

The theoretical proposal countering this first belief (that anything a person does with print constitutes writing or reading) will figure prominently in the discussion of the following myths. It was the basis for a post hoc analysis for this present discussion. That is, I sorted the counterevidence discovered during the original analysis into authentic writing and "writing" and then compared the two. Because I do not believe "anything a person does with print constitutes writing or reading," I avoid the term *writing* in the following discussion (unless I believe the referent to be real writing based on the criteria of simultaneously present and interacting cueing systems) and substitute *written productions, pieces,* or other circumlocutions.

ERRONEOUS BELIEF 2

Bilingualism is a limitation in learning written language, especially if the linguistic varieties are nonstandard.

A more accurate characterization based on these data is that the children had language strengths, with their bilingualism increasing their options for meaning-making with print. In both their genuine writing and their simulations of writing, even first graders used advanced vocabulary (e.g., *encerrado* 'isolated'; *se emborrachó* 'he got drunk'; *en ese instante* 'in that instant'; *aplacar* 'to calm'; *travesuras* 'pranks'—certainly not words that would appear in first grade readers). In both their writing and their "writing," these bilingual children spontaneously used sets of words which are often subject to drills in "language development" classes (e.g., sets of animal names, body parts, articles of clothing, foods, directional terms, and onomatopoetic words). A few children's writing and also their "writing" displayed use of questions as a stylistic device. One second grader wrote to her pen pal and used questions to add weight to the information that followed.[1]

(1) *Querida Yolanda,*
    A nosotros los gustaron las galletas. Estaban buenas. Quieren a
    tener un contest para ver quién agarra 1,000,000 popsicle sticks. ¿Y

---

[1] All examples of children's writing are presented with conventional spelling and punctuation.

sabes qué? ¡Yo tengo una mona bien bien grande y mi hermana dice que se parece a mí!
(Dear Yolanda,
We liked the cookies. They were good. They want to have a contest to see who gets 1,000,000 popsicle sticks. And do you know what? I have a really really big doll and my sister says it looks like me!)

A similar use of questions as a signal or excuse for offering information was found in reports to the teacher. *(¿Y SABES CUÁNTAS CARAS TENÍA? Tenía siete caras. ¿Y SABES DE QUÉ COLOR ES? Es azul y verde y color rosa . . .* "And do you know how many faces it had? It had seven faces. And do you know what color it is? It's blue and green and pink. . . .')

Complex tenses such as subjunctives and conditionals appeared in both writing and "writing." Example 2 is an excerpt from a get well letter written by a second grader.

(2) *. . . ¿Por cúal calle es para su casa? Yo no sé donde vive. Si* supiera *donde* viviera, *yo cuando* saliera *de la escuela me iba para su casa con la bike . . .*
(. . . What street is your house on? I don't know where you live. If I knew where you lived I, when I left school, I would go to your house with my bike. . . .)

Assigned topics such as If I Were Magic, If I Were a Penny, and If I Were the Principal elicited conditionals and subjunctives in writing exercises too. Children used adverbial clauses to begin sentences in simulations (. . . *DE LA TIENDA me voy a la escuela. Me voy a comer, DE COMER a jugar, DE JUGAR me voy a dormir. . . .* '. . . From the store I go to school. I go to eat; from eating to play; from playing I go to sleep . . .)'. They also used them in *writing* stories (. . . *Y EN ESTE MOMENTO QUE ESTABA PENSANDO, salió el conejo de repente y la niña se asustó y gritó* '. . . and at the moment she was thinking, the rabbit came out suddenly and the girl got scared and screamed)'.

The children could disambiguate anticipated ambiguities with description. For example, in distinguishing two rabbits, a third grader wrote *la otra que tenía los huevos mágicos* (the other one that had the magic eggs) as opposed to *él que no era mágico* (the one that wasn't magic).

One language strength appeared in genuine writing that did not appear in writing exercises. That was the invention of words based on morphological rules. In writing about eating hot chilis and needing to drink cold water, a first grader explained *ME ENCHILÉ la boca* (I chili-peppered my mouth).

Regardless of whether they were writing or "writing," then, these children showed that though their dialects of both Spanish and English were nonstandard, they had clear language strengths. Additionally, rather than limiting them, their bilingualism was a resource that increased their ability to make meaning. They were often assigned to "write" a report about a movie or program they had just seen. Interestingly, the movie was always in English; the report was in Spanish. In these reports, however, if they used direct quotes from the movie, these were in the language originally spoken (. . . *y el Popeye dijo "YAY"* '. . . and Popeye said, "Yay" '). With one strategically codeswitched item, they signalled the language of the movie and the character.

Within the same piece, translation pairs often appeared: *sad* and *triste, raccoon* and *mapache, tricked* and *engañado*. Codeswitching to English to match address term to ethnic identity was a similar phenomenon. Clearly, then, codeswitching was no indication of lack of knowledge of a term in a particular language. Instead, knowing both terms offered the children an increase in the number of synonyms for an idea as well as a resource for providing additional social information. It also provided them with another means for indicating emphasis. Not only could they write *fin* (the end) with increasing size and switch to all capital letters, but they could compound the message by switching to English *(el fin, El Fin. THE END)*.

In both writing and "writing," children showed signs that their bilingualism was not a source of confusion. In spelling the /k/ phoneme, they used *k, c,* and *ck* in English, *c, q,* and *qu* but never *k* in Spanish; tildes and accents appeared in Spanish but never in English.

As a whole, the children's productions dispute the notions that bilingualism in nonstandard varieties indicates language deficiencies or that it limits one's learning of written language. We need to demonstrate this point with more examples of genuine writing.

ERRONEOUS BELIEF 3

Young children are insensitive to the needs of their audiences and to the demands of different types of texts and contexts.

In fact, many pieces of writing as well as writing simulations showed considerable sensitivity to both audience and text demands. In writing exercises, there were arrows and notations to the reader (*atrás*→ on the back→) to direct the reader to turn the page over. Children inserted parenthetical remarks when they knew they could not supply the precise information the reader might want (*Después cantaron NO ME ACUERDO COMO SE LLAMA LA OTRA CANCIÓN QUE CANTARON* 'Then they sang I don't remember the name of the other song they sang').

Children produced writing exercises for their true audience—the teacher—no matter who was named as ostensible audience. They used Spanish in letters nominally addressed to English speakers but actually intended for the teacher-as-direction-giver because they knew the teacher valued Spanish writing. (However, they spontaneously translated Spanish texts when reading them to monolingual English speaking adults.) The second-grade teacher equated quality with length. Her students complied by producing twenty-page pieces filled with overly large printing, big spaces and repetitions (*y estaba bien bien bien bien bien grande* 'and it was very very very very very big)'.

The childrens' authentic writing also showed evidence of awareness of their audiences. Some made explicit attempts to establish rapport in letters, suggesting that they shared interests with their audiences.

> (3) *Querido Mr. F.,*
> *Yo te quiero decir feliz compleaños tuyos y la maestra me dijo que a*
> *tí te gusta pescar y cazar y a mí me gusta cazar también y pescar y*
> *ojalá que tengas una fiesta.*
> (Dear Mr. F.,
> I want to say happy birthday to you and the teacher told me that you
> like to fish and hunt and I like to hunt also and to fish and I hope you
> have a party.)

They scolded pen pals, offered medical advice in get well letters, and gave directions to Santa Claus on the best way to deliver a motorcycle.

> (4) *Yo le voy a llevar esta carta a usted, Santa Clos, para que me de una*
> *moto. Y la casa tiene un cuartito y allí puede meter la moto para que*
> *no batalle mucho metiéndolo por una ventana. Y mi casa es 13574.*
> *Gracias.*
> (I am going to send this letter to you, Santa Claus, so you'll give me a
> motorcycle. And the house have a little room and you can put the
> motorcycle there so you don't have to struggle a lot putting it
> through a window. And my house is 13574. Thanks.)

The children were similarly sensitive to the demands of texts and contexts. They honored the fundamental distinction between oral and written texts. Codeswitching was frequent in their speech (as Grosjean, 1984, has reported in the speech of bilingual communities generally) yet rare in either writing or writing exercises. Assignments for different genres had distinct layouts, beginnings, and endings. Stories had titles, journals and letters did not. Dialogue appeared in stories and journals, but not letters. Letters contained the name of the author; journals did not. Children even seemed to be aware that the graphic forms of words were affected by the context.

The huge *K* on the K-Mart sign or the circled *K* over the Circle K in their neighborhood was not what appeared in their journal entries about going to these stores. Instead, they spelled out *ceimart* or *ceimar* for K-Mart and *circocei* or *ceircoci* for Circle K. Apparently they had some sense of difference between logos and prose.

When they really wrote, there were also signs of sensitivity to context. First graders chose color topics and wrote for the sheer pleasure of it when many colored markers were placed at a free-time writing center, producing pieces about skirts, flags, and houses of *color rosa* (written in pink marker), *azul* (written in blue marker), *verde* (written in green), and so forth. Whether writing or "writing," the children did attend to text constraints, contextual variation, and audience needs.

CONCLUSION

Beliefs about writing have tremendous influence on educational practice. The most critical belief concerns what writing is, its nature. Even if people are unaware of the distinction I have drawn between writing and simulations of writing, they do differentiate between the more and the less artificial (though still not the genuine article). For instance, controlled writing and free writing, writing skills and creative writing are divisions of both ESL and mainstream language education. Although the most artificial exercises can never become real writing, can never surpass the curriculum (Hudson, in press), the less artificial simulations (e.g., stories on assigned topics) can sometimes, midstream, turn into the real thing. Even if they do not, as most of the time they did not during the year of this study, certain exercises (movie summaries, stories begun with story starters) did offer an opportunity for young children to write better than when they produce such artificial simulations as word lists and sentence completion tasks. At least with something approaching (if not constituting) real writing, the children in this study showed that they did in fact have language strengths, that their bilingualism was not a barrier to displays of written language competence, and that they could indeed account for audience needs and text demands.

The bilingual program in this study, a pioneer in the late 1970s, required almost none of the most artificial writing exercises; instead it offered children daily opportunities to do less artificial simulations and occasional opportunities to really write. Second and third graders were let loose from the confines of ditto sheets and workbooks; first graders were not fed the usual steady diet of phonics; thus, all the children had opportunity to orchestrate most of the cueing systems—and they blossomed. At first. But although segmentation, punctuation, and spelling conventions continued to develop, the dramatic initial flowering soon seemed to wither in the most crucial areas. The spectacular growth in written meaning making and conceptions of self as writer reported by Graves (1983) and Calkins (1982) was not evident here. Simulations had their limits.

If this bilingual program was a pioneer, so was this study. It was undertaken to fill a void in the literature. There had been no investigations of bilingual children's *writing*. To do such a study, it was necessary to find classrooms where children *write*. That study is still needed.

REFERENCES

Calkins, L. (1982). *Lessons from a child*. Exeter, NH: Heinemann.

Edelsky, C. (1982). *Development of writing in a bilingual program* (Report No. NIE G-81-0051). Washington, DC: National Institute of Education.

Edelsky, C. (1986). *Writing in a bilingual program: Había una vez*. Norwood, NJ: Ablex.

Edelsky, C., & Smith, K. (1984). Is that writing—or are those marks just a figment of your curriculum? *Language Arts, 61,* 24–32.

Erickson, F. (1984). School literacy, reasoning, and civility: An anthropologist's perspective. *Review of Educational Research, 54,* 525–546.

Florio-Ruane, S. (no date). *Teaching as response: The problem of writing conferences*. Unpublished manuscript.

Goodman, K. (1969). Analysis of oral reading miscues: Applied psycholinguistics. *Reading Research Quarterly, 5*(9), 9–30.

Graves, D. (1983). *Writing: Teachers and children at work*. Exeter, NH: Heinemann.

Grosjean, F. (1984, October). *The bilingual as a competent but specific speaker-learner*. Paper presented at the Boston University Conference on Language Development, Boston.

Harste, J. (1980, April). *Language as social event*. Paper presented at the annual meeting of the American Educational Research Association, Boston.

Harste, J., & Burke, C. (1977). A new hypothesis for reading teacher research: Both teaching and learning of reading are theoretically based. In P. D. Pearson (Ed.), *Reading: Theory, research and practice. Twenty-sixth yearbook of the National Reading Conference* (pp. 32–40). St. Paul, MN: Mason.

Harste, J., Burke, C., & Woodward, V. (1982). *Children, their language and world: Initial encounters with print* (Report No. Nie G-79-0132). Washington, DC: National Institute of Education.

Hudelson, S. (1986). ESL children's writing: What we've learned, what we're learning. In P. Rigg & D. S. Enright (Eds.), *Children and ESL: Integrating perspectives* (pp. 23–54). Washington, DC: Teachers of English to Speakers of Other Languages.

Hudson, S. (in press). Children's perceptions of classroom writing: Ownership within a continuum of control. In B. Rafoth & D. L. Rubin (Eds.), *The social construction of written communication*. Norwood, NJ: Ablex.

Rubin, D. L. (1984). Social cognition and written communication. *Written Communication, 1,* 211–245.

Smith, F. (1978). *Understanding reading* (2nd ed.). New York: Holt Rinehart & Winston.

Staton, J., Shuy, R., Kreeft, J., & Reed, L. (in press). *Interactive writing in dialogue journals: Linguistic, social and cognitive views.* Norwood, NJ: Ablex.

CHAPTER 11

Whole Language Approaches to Writing with Secondary Students of English as a Second Language

Yvonne S. Freeman and David E. Freeman
Fresno Pacific College

> *My memories of Ban Vinay in Thailand is very sad. When we live in Ban Vinay my brother is very sick. He almost died there. We were very poor. We have to get in a line to get our food. I was very small at that time. When we get in line, all the older people always step over me, because I was so small they couldn't see me. . . .*

This is the introduction to a piece written by Mai, a ninth-grade Hmong student in Lonna Deeter's high school content reading ESL class in Fresno, California. Mai's response was one of many made by Lonna's ninth- through twelfth-grade students as they reacted to a newspaper article about Ban Vinay, a well-known refugee camp in Thailand (Pyle, 1987). In the first few lines, Mai is able to share an important personal experience in her second language. Her writing is an example of an activity promoted in a classroom where the teacher employs whole language principles to help students develop literacy skills in content areas including English, social studies, math, and science.

First language (L1) researchers and theorists have drawn upon what is known about language acquisition and learning to develop the whole language approach to teaching children (Cochrane, Cochrane, Scalena, & Buchanan, 1984; Altwerger, Edelsky, & Flores, 1987; K. Goodman, Smith, Meredith, & Y. Goodman, 1987; Harste, Woodward, & Burke, 1984; Rich, 1985; Watson, 1982). Second language educators have also developed theories and approaches that are consistent with what whole language advocates propose for students (Enright & McCloskey, 1985; Franklin, 1986; Hudelson, 1984; Krashen, 1985; Rigg & Enright, 1986). When teachers of limited English proficient students have applied whole language principles, they have found that their students respond positively and enjoy success that they sometimes have not previously experienced in school (Freeman, Freeman, & Gonzalez, 1987). The classroom experiences provided by whole language teachers engage students, drawing on their strengths, knowledge, and potential.

K. Goodman (1986) explains that learning takes place "in the context of reading and writing real language," and that in order to develop literacy, students need ". . . to use just enough print, language structure, and meaning, and to keep it all in the proper personal and cultural perspective . . ." (p. 43). When Lonna put the newspaper article about Ban Vinay on the bulletin board for her students, Mai and her classmates clustered around the article, read it to each other, and shared memories. Most chose to accept the invitation the teacher gave them to respond in writing as well. Those responses, posted around the article, promoted further reading and discussion. The students were developing literacy in the context of reading and writing real language. They drew upon their culture and personal experiences as they used the print and structure of their second language to get and construct meaning.

In this chapter we first present six whole language principles that we believe are important for second language (L2) learners. Because Mai's teacher, Lonna, shared a whole language philosophy of education, we describe the principles in the context of her lesson. This lesson, in which students responded to the newspaper clipping about Ban Vinay, demonstrates how the six principles can be applied in classrooms. Next we describe the physical environment of a whole language classroom to demonstrate the importance of a positive language learning environment. Finally, we discuss writing activities that have been successful with secondary second language students, including routine, daily writing activities, and specific activities centered on content-area themes.

PRINCIPLES OF WHOLE LANGUAGE

Language Classes Should Be Learner Centered

Lonna chose the Ban Vinay article for display on her response board because she knew that many of her students had had direct experience with the camp. In this way she centered the lesson on the learners. Teachers like Lonna are what Y. Goodman (1978) calls "kid-watchers."

They are aware of student interests and activities, and they draw on those interests and activities to create lessons meaningful to their students.

Only when teachers know a good deal about their students can they create truly learner-centered lessons. Lonna knew that Mai and many of her students had had direct experiences with the refugee camp featured in the newspaper article. Because she asked students to write about something they were interested in and had direct experience with, the students produced some of their best writing.

At the beginning of the year, when teachers do not know the interests or experiences of most of their students, one of the best ways to devise learner-centered lessons is to give students choices in their daily writing activities. As students write, teachers learn about their students' lives and interests. Teachers can then affirm student interests and experiences and encourage students to expand upon what they already know and begin to write about what they want to learn. The result, as Lonna found, is often better quality and greater quantity of writing. Allowing students to choose their own topics individualizes lessons. At the same time, teachers become aware of common interests among groups of students, and this awareness allows them to plan future group activities.

Language Is Best Learned When Kept Whole

Lonna applied the second principle of whole language in her lesson when she created an activity in which learning could move from whole to part. Too often, language activities in classrooms for limited English proficient students move from part to whole rather than from whole to part. In part-to-whole lessons, students work with bits and pieces of language instead of with full texts. Since the assumption is that language is easier for students if it is broken into bite-sized chunks with one chunk presented at a time, students seldom read or write complete pieces. Often the teaching scope and sequence of skills are determined by school curriculum guides and textbooks. In these L2 classrooms, students are treated as if they were on an assembly line passively waiting in school factories for the pieces of knowledge to be stuffed into them (Nattinger, 1984).

This part-to-whole approach is logical, but lacks psychological validity (K. Goodman, 1986). Studies of child language acquisition suggest that learning involves a gradual differentiation of the whole into parts, not a building up of parts into the whole (Vygotsky, 1978). Thus, teachers or curriculum writers who attempt to make learning easier by breaking it into parts actually make it harder by reducing the available context cues (Halliday & Hasan, 1976; Heath, 1984; Pakenham, 1982; Widdowson, 1978). Whole language teachers always attempt to keep the language whole and thus provide rich contexts for language activities in their classrooms.

The response to the Ban Vinay article was part of a larger unit on newspapers. The unit began with a general discussion of the purpose and value of the newspaper. A speaker from the local paper came and explained to the class the various parts of a paper such as headlines, the masthead, the index, and the different sections. During this talk, students were able to examine the various sections of the newspaper, since the school had purchased enough newspapers so each student could have one. In addition, the students toured the newspaper offices.

In the Ban Vinay lesson, students responded to a whole article, not part of an article or an adapted version of an article. Full, unadapted texts provide more comprehensible input than do adapted or simplified texts (D. Freeman, 1986; Y. Freeman, 1987). The students' written responses were full pieces of writing, not constrained or limited to a particular form by the teacher. Both Graves (1983) and Calkins (1986) have argued that only when writers produce whole texts from the start can they develop an adequate understanding of the writing process.

Language Instruction Should Employ All Four Modes: Listening, Speaking, Reading, and Writing

Whole language teachers believe that learning is easier when lessons include speaking and listening as well as reading and writing. Carolyn Burke (Harste, Burke, & Woodward, 1982) suggests that each language encounter, whatever the modality, feeds a common data pool. Each time a person listens, speaks, reads, or writes, he or she adds data to the language pool, and those data are available the next time the person listens, speaks, reads, or writes.

In Lonna's class, the students read the article and talked about it informally. They shared memories and experiences with their classmates, some of whom had not had direct experiences with refugee camps such as Ban Vinay. After the students had written about the article, Lonna put their responses up for other students to read and talk about. Thus, when Mai read the article and talked about it with her friends, she was adding to her pool of knowledge, and that led her to write about her own experiences. Mai's writing then became a language source for other students' reading as well as her own.

Language in the Classroom Should Be Meaningful and Functional

Whole language teachers also operate on the principle that learning occurs when students see a purpose for their activities. Rather than "making assignments," such teachers offer students invitations to read and write. As a result, when students choose to accept these invitations, they take ownership of the reading and writing processes. They elect to read and write for their own purposes, not simply to satisfy a requirement imposed by the teacher or the program. What they produce is "authentic writing" (Edelsky, 1986) that serves a number of different personal and social purposes.

Mai responded to her teacher's invitation by recording a memory of her experience in the refugee camp. The writing served a personal function (Cochrane et al., 1984; Halliday, 1975). Such writing allows students to express their individual awareness. Mai also knew that her writing would be read by other students (not just by the teacher), and that she would talk with them about it, so her piece also served an interactional function. Later, she might take this writing home to read to a younger brother or sister born in the United States to help them learn English. In this way the writing would serve a heuristic function. Finally, she might talk with her parents about their memories of the camp and then incorporate their comments into a revision of her piece. As a result, the writing would serve what Cochrane and co-workers (1984) refer to as the perpetuation function of language. In various ways, then, Mai's piece served her own personal and social purposes.

Language Is Learned through Social Interaction

The Ban Vinay activity also reflected a fifth principle of whole language: learning occurs through social interactions. Lev Vygotsky (1978) proposed that certain developmental processes "are able to operate only when the child is interacting with people in his environment and in cooperation with his peers" (p. 90). Gordon Wells (1986), as the result of his longitudinal study of children's language development, found that meaningful interaction leads to school success. M. A. K. Halliday (1975), basing his arguments on the study of his son, concluded that children develop language in order to function in social interactions. Social interaction has also been shown to be important for cognitive development of adults (Luria, 1979; Wertsch, 1985). Similarly, research has shown the importance of interaction for L2 development (Enright & McCloskey, 1985; Johnson, 1983; Wong Fillmore & Valadez, 1986). Yet in many classrooms, students are afforded few opportunities for social interaction as they sit quietly in straight rows.

Often teachers hesitate to allow students to talk with one another. Classrooms in which social interaction is promoted are often viewed as undisciplined. Sometimes students seem to be talking about everything except the assignment. Whole language teachers, who believe that social interaction is crucial to learning, work hard to create a highly structured environment within which individuals can interact (Calkins, 1986; Hubbard, 1986). This is often accomplished by establishing classroom routines. In the process writing classes Calkins describes, students keep their pieces in a folder that they pick up as soon as they enter class each day. The whole class meets briefly for a mini-lesson covering a particular aspect of their writing. The teacher also reviews what each student will be working on that day. Then students break into groups for drafting pieces, conferring with the teacher or peers, or for editing. Toward the end of the period, students meet in groups to share their pieces and respond to one another's writing. Students know that they will have time to read, write, and confer each day, and they know that there are acceptable and unacceptable ways to accomplish these tasks. The teacher's role is to establish an orderly environment in which social interactions can and will take place.

The writing in Lonna Deeter's classroom was not an isolated, individual enterprise. Instead, it was embedded in a network of social interactions. The students clustered around the bulletin board, eagerly reading and discussing the article. As they talked, they built concepts and developed vocabulary necessary for their writing. During their writing they conferred with one another and the teacher, trying to find ways to express the meanings they wished to share. Before revising, they had the opportunity to talk with friends and relatives about their experiences in Ban Vinay. The final pieces the students produced were tacked up on the board where they provided stimulation for further social interactions including further writing.

Lonna told her students before they began writing that their responses would not be graded. She noted that this lack of grading made her students more relaxed about putting their feelings on paper, especially the less able writers. Lonna did not need to use grades to motivate her students to write because the writing in her class served a natural function of enabling her students to interact socially.

Language Is Learned When Teachers Have Faith in Learners

The first five principles that whole language teachers follow would not work without this sixth principle. These teachers believe their students want to learn and are capable of learning. They refuse to operate on assumptions that would limit the potential for learning. Harste, Woodward, and Burke (1984) have pointed out that all teachers operate on certain assumptions. "The assumptions we make limit what can be learned. Alter those assumptions and the potential for learning expands" (p. 70).

Some assumptions block teachers from having faith in their students. One of these is the assumption that adults know what is best. These adults may be teachers, curriculum writers, or state education officials. Because they assume they know what is best, they also assume they can best decide what students need and when they need it. Then they assume that learning is easier if knowledge is broken up into manageable parts to be presented in a certain sequence and at a certain rate. They may further assume that certain modalities should be developed before others. For example, reading may be delayed until oral language is fully developed. In this process, adults often assume that the knowledge or skills will serve necessary functions for the learner. Finally, if knowledge is simply to be transmitted from the adult to the child, adults assume that social interaction between students will only slow the learning process.

On the other hand, whole language teachers take their cues from the students because they feel classes should be learner centered. Because whole language teachers believe learning is easiest when lessons move from whole to part, they develop integrated units. They promote activities in which students engage in social interactions and use all four modalities to serve their own purposes, working together as they read, write, and talk about full texts. Whole language teachers believe that learning is intrinsically motivating under these conditions, so students can and will learn.

The response board with the Ban Vinay article motivated the students because the content was learner centered. Students used all four modalities and interacted socially in natural, authentic ways. The teacher did not have to make up vocabulary lists or skill sheets to go with the lesson. Instead, reading and writing flowed naturally out of the topic.

Because whole language classes operate on principles different from traditional classes, they frequently look different from traditional classes. In the following sections we describe Lonna Deeter's classroom and then look at some routine and specific writing activities that occur in that classroom.

WHAT A WHOLE LANGUAGE CLASSROOM LOOKS LIKE

The environment of the classroom can encourage students to do lots of speaking, listening, reading, and writing. The content area reading classroom in Fresno, California, where Mai and her classmates discussed and wrote about the refugee camp, is an excellent example. Everything in the room encourages students to read and write as they interact with each other and the teacher.

Over the door of the classroom is a large poster announcing "Happy

Easter." To the left of the door is a bulletin board labeled "Important" in English, Laotian, Hmong, and Spanish. Notices relating to the students are posted there. To the right on the door, next to the blackboard, is a large calendar again labeled in English and other languages. Student writing and drawing is arranged around the blackboard.

Another large bulletin board announces the unit theme being worked on: "Why read the newspaper?" and then answers the question with sections displaying "news," "entertainment," "advertising," and "opinion." A pocket chart hanging on the wall entitled "Newspaper Parts— What's There?" lists in detail the sections of a newspaper and the types of writing found in each.

The article about the refugee camp, Ban Vinay, is displayed next on the Response Board. Student written responses are posted around the article. Under this display there is a bookshelf of content area magazines for young people, including *World, Zoobooks,* and *Ranger Rick.*

Assignments This Week is another bulletin board and displays the activities planned for the week. Next to the assignments is a display where students can locate school information such as the "Daily Schedule," "Weekly Bulletin," "Daily Bulletin," and cafeteria "Menu."

The back of the room has windows; the middle is a large sign designating the "Library." On the table below the sign are sets of fiction books, dictionaries, and writing supplies. Two racks of paperback books for students to browse through are next to the library table.

The remaining wall of the room has "Haiku Poetry by Students," all written in calligraphy on laminated color paper. Under the poetry, on the counter along the wall, students find encyclopedias, a globe, writing materials, and a book return basket. As an added touch, there is a basket of laminated bookmarks that have sayings from the students' native countries written in the first language on one side and translated into English on the other.

Literacy in the L2 is promoted in a number of ways within this literate environment. Students read, discuss, and write using what they find available to them in the classroom. With this type of positive language learning environment, students regularly engage in a number of specific and routine writing activities. Specific activities emerge as thematic units develop. Routine writing is done throughout the year on a daily basis.

SPECIFIC WRITING ACTIVITIES

Much of the environmental print in the room reflects and enhances particular writing activities the students are engaging in. For example, before the teacher had the students write poetry, she first displayed Haiku poetry around the room. After several days, she asked students if they had noticed it and encouraged them to talk about it. She then shared some Haiku poetry written by students during the Vietnam War. After some discussion the teacher and the students agreed that they could also write Haiku poetry. Lonna drew on principles of cooperative learning (D. Johnson, R. Johnson, Holubec, & Roy, 1984; Kagan, 1986) and had her students work with a partner to produce a poem. Then they read their poems to the class. Though the poems did not follow the strict rules of Haiku, four different examples show that they produced powerful images:

1. The birds leave their nest
   As we left our beautiful home
   Tears will never end.
2. Strong trees growing high
   Seeds falling from its branches
   New life is here again.
3. The day is so bright
   Night comes very quickly
   Leaving my heart lonely.
4. Tears fall from her eyes
   He lied and broke her young heart
   People love and lose.

The teacher and students also worked together to create the newspaper displays. Students brainstormed to list the sections of a newspaper, looked at newspapers in groups to confirm their lists, and then determined the function of each section of the paper. They assembled their findings into the bulletin board display. Thus, the bulletin board was not simply put up by the teacher; it was created by the students under the teacher's guidance.

Classroom activities based on the newspaper emerged naturally from student interest. For example, groups in one class chose newspaper ads of interest to them, wrote up questions about the ads, passed the questions to others to answer and then discussed the questions and answers.

Another class followed a particular court case, involving a surrogate mother, that interested them for several months. In one lesson, the teacher asked students to first list what they remembered about the case. The students and teacher put these remembered facts on the blackboard. Then the students read the latest court results from a recent article and discussed them in small groups. Each group wrote a summary of the article when they finished the discussion. The success of this activity is vividly reflected in Lonna's comment:

> Frankly, the surrogate mother case has created the most excitement this year. It has been on-going, thought-provoking, and a wonderful learning

experience. We've been able to include a discussion of biology, court-room procedures, laws, and morals. We've had speakers come in and even visited a courtroom to fully understand how they function. Students are even bringing me articles I've missed (from other sources) and asking me to share them with the class. It's wonderful! (personal communication)

The Ban Vinay article posted on the Response Board was perhaps the most effective activity in the newspaper unit. The teacher had often posted an article from the newspaper on the Response Board to generate discussion and writing, but this article received even more response than usual. The local newspaper ran a long article on the refugee camp because so many of the Fresno residents are familiar with the camp and know people still living there. The description of the article was detailed and the pictures graphic. All of the students, including those who were not Southeast Asians, were interested in the article. Although the vocabulary was difficult, the students' background knowledge allowed them to read, discuss, and write about the article.

In the case of the Haiku poetry and the newspaper article, bulletin boards served both to promote student writing and to display finished pieces. In other cases, students wrote in response to class activities and the finished products were then posted around the room. One successful lesson involved the use of wordless books.

Lonna began the lesson on wordless books by asking the students to discuss a topic they had obviously discussed before: "How can you help your younger brothers and sisters or other relatives this summer? What can you do to help them be better students in school next year?" Students suggested taking younger siblings to the library, reading to them, talking to them, and writing with them.

Next, the teacher told the students that she had a series of pictures with no words for them. She divided the students into groups and asked each group to take a set of pictures from a wordless book, sequence them, talk about the sequence of events in the story, and then write a story about the pictures.

Once students had sequenced the pictures, they began to collaborate to write their stories. Students were encouraged not to describe the pictures, but to write a story their younger relatives would "find interesting, funny, and exciting." After the students wrote their stories, they read them to the class, took suggestions for revision, and rewrote the stories. They put the words underneath the pictures and designed and illustrated covers for the books so they really could read their stories to children later.

Pen pal letters caused perhaps the biggest sensation of the year in

Lonna's content reading English as a second language (ESL) classroom. Ninth through twelfth graders got involved when the teacher suggested that the morning class students in one high school write to her afternoon class at a different high school. Students drew names of pen pals and wrote enthusiastically. The first exchange was tentative, but by the second letter, students were exchanging pictures, phone numbers, and addresses. A party was planned for the end of the year so the pen pals could meet one another.

Although the teacher had initiated this activity simply to give her students a purpose to practice letter writing, the project became much more than letter-writing practice. Almost all the students wrote longer pieces than they had all year, and they wrote with more enthusiasm. They worked harder at revising and editing their letters for their peers than they ever had for any writing their teacher had assigned to be turned in to her. In addition, the students showed more initiative in this assignment than in any other. They instigated the picture exchange, and they suggested and helped plan the end-of-the-year party.

ROUTINE WRITING ACTIVITIES

Besides specific activities such as these, Lonna incorporated writing on a routine daily basis, primarily by using various types of journals (Calkins, 1986; Hansen, Newkirk, & Graves, 1985; Zamel, 1985).

The Daily Personal Journal

Though there are variations, this kind of journal writing usually allows students to write about what is important to them personally. Students write daily, sharing their personal experiences. In her classroom, Lonna suggests topics, but also gives students an option: ". . . or write about anything you would like to write about."

But even the topics Lonna gives students come originally from them. For example, at Christmas time her students discussed how Christmas was celebrated in the United States and in other countries. The class read an article about Kwanzaa, an African celebration lasting from December 26 to January 1. In this celebration, one of seven candles is lit each day to represent ideas or beliefs about a successful life, such as having faith in oneself or learning to get along with others. After students read the article they brainstormed a list of their beliefs about getting along in life. The teacher then used those student suggestions as possible topics for daily journal entries.

Two examples of these entries show ESL secondary students expressing their opinions in English. The topic for these examples came from the brainstorming list and centered on the importance of saying nice things to others. The first example is from Jesus, a tenth-grade student whose L1 is Spanish, and the second from Chansamone, a ninth-grade Laotian student. In both cases, the students' responses show an understanding of the topic and an ability to express their opinions in English. Chansamone even attempted to use a vocabulary word encountered in a reading.

> Friday, March 13, 1987
> I think talk badly to other is not the good way to do. If you act that way everyone thought that you're strange person. I don't want to talk badly to other because I'm not smart at all. so I want everyone help me and care about me. if I don't smart but I be nice and share thing with other then they will care and help me if I have same problem. I think talking badly to other is not good to say.
> Friday, March 13, 1987
> Talking about other is not very nice. If you are talking about someone you are being acrimonious. You would not like it if they say something bad about you. So don't talk about other. It is easy to be friends with them.

In journal entries such as these, students work on fluency rather than accuracy in their writing. Lonna does not correct journal entries because she wants students to take risks and to have opportunities for natural writing development (Calkins, 1986; Flores, et al., 1985; Graves, 1983; Sampson, 1977). When students write pieces such as their responses to the Ban Vinay article, that writing is extensively revised and edited. Thus, Lonna's corrections are selective.

Literature and Content Response Journals

In this type of journal, students write a reaction to the reading they are doing in class. When students read stories or fiction, the literature response journal allows them to share their understanding of what they read as well as their personal involvement with the text. Personal involvement in the text has been shown to be important for second language learners (Hudelson, 1986; Rigg & Enright, 1986; Stevick, 1976). Jesus' literature response to his reading demonstrates his personal involvement with his reading.

> Tuesday, April 7, 1987
> I want to read my storybook that book call *Alone With Another.* I very like that book it help me alot of things to be alone with another. I also

like to read about, because when I was very lonely I read that book then it warm me up it have many interesting in there. this my book that I like to read every day.

Content journals are similar to literature journals. Students react to the expository reading they do by summarizing the ideas, writing questions, and suggesting related topics. For example, students read a section of their social studies book, summarize what they think are the main ideas, and write down questions they have for discussion.

Student Interactive Journals or Written Conversations

Generally, teachers respond to the personal, literature, and content response journals. However, students can also share their personal journals with fellow students who write reactions or questions, and they can write to one another about their reading in content area classrooms.

Written conversations are especially good for beginning students. Students write a line or a question in their journal. They pass their journal to another student who writes a response. If students are insecure about their writing they can read aloud to each other what they have written and explain if necessary. The atmosphere should be relaxed, and students should understand that it is the message, not the mechanics, that is important in their journals. This type of written communication encourages students to put into writing what they wish to say to one another about their personal lives or about something they have read and discussed in the class.

Another option that is similar to written conversations is the message board. This is a section of bulletin board space where students leave notes for each other and the teacher. There are always plenty of tacks and slips of paper near the board so students can write and receive messages easily. For years teachers have discouraged students from passing notes; yet notes are excellent means of written communication. Both written conversations and message boards are a kind of legal classroom note passing.

Journals, written conversations, and messages allow students to explore their ideas through their L2. These informal, routine writing activities can also help students discover ideas they wish to write about in more formal contexts. Interactive journal writing is especially helpful for teachers who deal with large numbers of students and find themselves overwhelmed as they try to respond to each writer individually. Students can respond to each other and at the same time teach each other.

When students write daily, their development as writers can be evaluated. It is helpful to have students date all journal entries so that both teachers and students can evaluate progress. As students and teachers look back over journal entries, they can see progress in both the quantity and the quality of the writing.

CONCLUSIONS

The new California *English Language Arts Framework* (1987) expresses well the need for a different curriculum for ESL students:

> One of the greatest challenges to English-language arts programs in California today is extending the crucial language skills of listening, speaking, reading and writing to the increasing numbers of students in the schools for whom English is a second language. . . . Limited English-proficient students need a rich linguistic environment in which the use of repetitive skill-based worksheets and exercises is limited, and frequent opportunities are provided for students to speak, listen, read, and write in meaningful contexts. (p. 22)

Immersing LEP students such as Mai, Jesus, and Chansamone in a literate environment where they have daily opportunities to read and write about things that are important to them and that serve their purposes helps them become literate in our complex, literate society.

Lonna Deeter's classroom is not a typical classroom for second language students. Mai and her classmates are engaged in meaningful, communicative activities daily. They see a purpose in these activities and in coming to school. Many of the students are learning English so they can help their parents function in a new society and so they can prepare their younger brothers and sisters to succeed in school. Lonna uses every opportunity to engage her students in meaningful, whole language activities that not only improve their abilities to use English but also empower those students to communicate effectively.

REFERENCES

Altwerger, B., Edelsky, C., & Flores, B. (1987). Whole language: What's new? *Reading Teacher, 41,* 144–154.

Calkins, L. M. (1986). *The art of teaching writing.* Portsmouth, NH: Heinemann.

Cochrane, O., Cochrane, D., Scalena, S., & Buchanan, E. (1984). *Reading, writing and caring.* Winnepeg: Whole Language Consultants Ltd.

Edelsky, C. (1986). *Writing in a bilingual program: Había una vez.* Norwood, NJ: Ablex.

English-Language Arts Curriculum Framework and Criteria Committee. (1987). *English language arts framework for California public schools kindergarten through grade twelve.* Sacramento: California State Department of Education.

Enright, D. S., & McCloskey, M. L. (1985). Yes, talking! Organizing the classroom to promote second language acquisition. *TESOL Quarterly, 19,* 431–454.

Flores, B., Garcia, E., Gonzalez, S., Hidalgo, G., Kaczmarek, K., & Romero, T. (1985). *Holistic bilingual instructional strategies.* Tempe, AZ: Exito.

Franklin, E. A. (1986). Literacy instruction for LES children. *Language Arts, 63,* 51–61.

Freeman, D. (1986). *Use of pragmatic cohesion cues to resolve degrees of pronoun reference ambiguity in reading.* Unpublished doctoral dissertation, University of Arizona, Tucson.

Freeman, D., Freeman, Y. S., & Gonzalez, R. D. (1987). Success for LEP students: The Sunnyside sheltered English program. *TESOL Quarterly, 21,* 361–367.

Freeman, Y. (1987). *The contemporary Spanish basal in the United States.* Unpublished doctoral dissertation, University of Arizona, Tucson.

Goodman, K. S. (1986). *What's whole in whole language?* Portsmouth, NH: Heinemann.

Goodman, K. S., Smith, E. B., Meredith, R., & Goodman, Y. M. (1987). *Language and thinking in school: A whole-language curriculum.* New York: Richard C. Owen.

Goodman, Y. M. (1978). Kid watching: An alternative to testing. *National Elementary School Principal, 57,* 41–45.

Graves, D. (1983). *Writing: Teachers and children at work.* Portsmouth, NH: Heinemann.

Halliday, M. A. K. (1975). *Learning how to mean: Explorations in the development of language.* London: Edward Arnold.

Halliday, M. A. K., & Hassan, R. (1976). *Cohesion in English.* London: Longman Group, Ltd.

Hansen, J., Newkirk, T., & Graves, D. (1985). *Breaking ground: Teachers relate reading and writing in the elementary school.* Portsmouth, NH: Heinemann.

Harste, J. C., Burke, C. L., & Woodward, V. A. (1982). Children's language and world: Initial encounters with print. In J. Langer & M. Smith-Burke (Eds.), *Reader meets author/bridging the gap: A psycholinguistic and sociolinguistic perspective* (pp. 105–131). Newark, DE: International Reading Association.

Harste, J. C., Woodward, V. A., & Burke, C. L. (1984). *Language stories and literacy lessons.* Portsmouth, NH: Heinemann.

Heath, S. B. (1984). Literacy or literate skills? Considerations for ESL/EFL learners. In P. Larson, E. L. Judd, & D. S. Messerschmitt (Eds.), *On TESOL '84* (pp. 15–28). Washington, DC: Teachers of English to Speakers of Other Languages.

Hubbard, R. (1986). Structure encourages independence in reading and writing. *The Reading Teacher, 40,* 180–185.

Hudelson, S. (1984). Kan yu ret an rayt en ingles: Children become literate in English. *TESOL Quarterly, 18,* 221–238.

Hudelson, S. (1986). ESL children's writing: What we've learned, what we're learning. In P. Rigg & D. S. Enright (Eds.), *Children and ESL: Integrating perspectives* (pp. 23–54). Washington, DC: Teachers of English to Speakers of Other Languages.

Johnson, D. M. (1983). Natural language learning by design: A classroom experiment in social interaction and second language acquisition. *TESOL Quarterly, 17,* 55–68.

Johnson, D. W., Johnson R., Holubec, E. J., & Roy, P. (1984). *Circles of learning: Cooperation in the classroom.* Alexandria, VA: Association for Supervision and Curriculum Development.

Kagan, S. (1986). Cooperative learning and sociocultural factors in schooling. In California State Department of Education (Ed.), *Beyond language* (pp. 231–298). Los Angeles: Evaluation, Dissemination and Assessment Center.

Krashen, S. (1985). *Inquiries & insights.* Hayward, CA: Alemany.

Long, M. H., & Porter, P. A. (1985). Group work, interlanguage talk, and second language acquisition. *TESOL Quarterly, 19,* 207–225.

Luria, A. R. (1979). *The making of mind: A personal account of Soviet psychology.* Cambridge, MA: Harvard University Press.

Nattinger, J. R. (1984). Communicative language teaching: A new metaphor. *TESOL Quarterly, 18,* 391–408.

Pakenham, K. J. (1982). Developing expectations for text in adult beginning ESL readers. In M. A. Clarke & J. Handscombe (Eds.), *On TESOL '82* (pp. 149–161). Washington, DC: Teachers of English to Speakers of Other Languages.

Pyle, A. (1987, March 8). Waiting in Thailand. *Fresno Bee,* pp. A1, A8–A9.

Rich, S. (1985). Whole language—a quick checklist. *Whole Language Newsletter, 3,* 5–6.

Rigg, P., & Enright, D. S. (1986). *Children and ESL: Integrating perspectives.* Washington, DC: Teachers of English to Speakers of Other Languages.

Sampson, G. P. (1977). A real challenge to ESL methodology. *TESOL Quarterly, 11,* 241–255.

Stevick, E. W. (1976). *Memory, meaning & method: Some psychological perspectives on language learning.* Rowley, MA: Newbury House.

Vygotsky, L. S. (1978). *Mind in society: The development of higher psychological processes.* (M. Cole, V. John-Steiner, S. Scribner, & E. Souberman, Eds.). Cambridge, MA: Harvard University Press.

Watson, D. J. (1982). What is a whole-language reading program? *The Missouri Reader, 7,* 8–10.

Wells, C. G. (1986). *The meaning makers.* Portsmouth, NH: Heinemann.

Wertsch, J. V. (1985). *Vygotsky and the social formation of mind.* Cambridge, MA: Harvard University Press.

Widdowson, H. G. (1978). *Teaching language as communication.* New York: Oxford University Press.

Wong Fillmore, L., & Valadez, C. (1986). Teaching bilingual learners. In M. C. Wittrock (Ed.), *Handbook of research on teaching* (3rd ed., pp. 648–685). New York: Macmillan.

Zamel, V. (1985). Responding to student writing. *TESOL Quarterly, 19,* 79–101.

CHAPTER 12

Developing Effective Assignments for Second Language Writers

Duane H. Roen
University of Arizona

Young (1978) and Hairston (1982), in their frequently cited descriptions of recent changes in first language (L1) composition instruction, note that traditional views of composing had little to do with communication. In the traditional L1 classroom, students were simply expected to produce final products with little if any guidance for producing them. Further, teachers, and consequently students, in those traditional classrooms were preoccupied with style and usage as well as with expository essays and research papers.

I used the past tense in the preceding paragraph, but that belies the fact that in many schools today tradition lives on—not only in English composition classes of children whose L1 is English but also in English as a second language (ESL) composition classes and more general ESL classes (Raimes, 1983). To call these views traditional belies another fact, for the word *traditional* implies that these views have been around for eons. But if we turn the clock back 2,300 years to Greece, we find that Aristotle's (ca. 333 B.C./1954) *Rhetoric* is filled mostly with invention strategies—strategies for generating ideas. If we turn the clock back even further—to almost 2,400 years ago—we find that Plato's (ca. 370 B.C./1956) *Phaedrus* focuses on such matters as the writer/speaker's commitment to the topic. Ideas were important to the Romans and Greeks; they should be important to us, too.

To help L1 or L2 composition teachers move back to the old-time religion that rhetoricians and compositionalists rediscovered several decades ago, in this chapter I, discuss three crucial features of successful writing assignments. First, I examine ways that we and our students—L1 or L2—can and should consider the audiences, purposes, and topics for their written discourse. Second, I argue that process approaches to composing can help writers work more skillfully and more confidently to solve the rhetorical problems (Flower & Hayes, 1980) that writing entails. Third, I discuss the importance of appropriate feedback or evaluation, especially from peers, all through the process of composing, again, so that writers can more easily solve rhetorical problems. As I work through these features, I hope to argue successfully that at times we should forget about students' learning to write for the sake of their writing to learn. I also hope to make clear that while some assignments may be more appropriate at one level (elementary, secondary, college) than another, many assignments can be adapted for use at more than one level.

AUDIENCE, TOPIC, AND PURPOSE

Choosing an audience, a topic, or a purpose may not be the first thing writers will or should do as they compose. It is often the case that writers set out to do one thing in writing, only to discover (Flower & Hayes, 1980; Murray, 1968) as they work that they want to do another. Even though audience, topic, and purpose may not come first, they are very important to the success of an inexperienced writer.[1] The problem in many classrooms is that language teachers do not fully appreciate the role of audience, topic, and purpose in students' writing. Consequently, many teachers either do nothing with this inseparable trio of concerns or mishandle the trio by giving students a constant diet of artificial audiences, topics, and purposes.

Consider for a moment the kinds of writing that people generally do in their leisure time. Exclude from your considerations any writing that teachers or employers require. Also exclude writing that people need to do to get other work done in the world: shopping lists or consumer complaint letters. Further, exclude the writing that language teachers do in our leisure time; we are, after all, professional wordsmiths—people with a

---

[1] When I refer to inexperienced writers I am appropriating Sommers' (1980) sense of what it means to be a student writer. It is not a pejorative sense, but rather one that neutrally denotes the acumen with which these writers solve rhetorical problems (Flower & Hayes, 1980; Zamel, 1985b) as they compose in English. That acumen varies as students move from one cultural and linguistic setting to another. I am not suggesting that all student writers are inexperienced at composing in English. When I refer to inexperienced writers, I am also embracing Raimes' (1986) argument that L1 and L2 composing problems are more similar than different. Finally, my use of the term includes Rose's (1983) observation that facility with one discourse type does not necessarily mean facility with other discourse types.

special affection for writing. Most people do not share our love for the written word.

Without exception, every time I ask people about the types of writing they do in their leisure time, I get two kinds of responses. In every group one or two people tell me that they keep a journal or diary, but most tell me that they write personal letters to close friends and relatives.

Think about personal letters for a moment. Think about an audience consisting of close friends and relatives. Think about the transaction, the communication, that occurs between the writer and the reader. The writer knows that the reader is not a critic, is not a judge. The writer knows that the reader is interested in the writer and what the writer has to say. The writer also knows that he or she shares much background with the reader. For our students such readers are real readers, authentic readers (Edelsky, 1986; Edelsky & Smith, 1984), unlike some of their teachers who seem to be more interested in correctness than communication.

Now think about topics included in those personal letters. Very few people, including language teachers, write about "school topics" in personal letters. When most people choose topics to include in personal letters, they write about matters that are familiar and interesting to themselves and to their readers. This concept of knowing and caring about topics for writing is not new; Quintilian (ca. 88 A.D./1922) made much of it in *Institutio Oratoria,* and Plato (ca. 370 B.C./1956) commented on the importance of it in *Phaedrus.* Early in *Phaedrus* there is a scene in which Socrates listens to the young Phaedrus recite a speech on love—a speech delivered earlier by the orator Lysias. As Phaedrus finishes the speech, Socrates says: ". . . it seemed that the author was saying the same thing two or three times, as though he weren't capable of saying a great deal on a single topic—or perhaps he wasn't especially interested in the matter" (p. 13). More recently and specifically addressing ESL teachers, Taylor (1981) and Zamel (1982) have argued for topics that engage writers.

Elsewhere, in *Alice's Adventures in Wonderland* (Carroll, 1865/1971), Alice, in one scene, is trying her best to conduct a communicative transaction with the Caterpillar. Alice explains to the Caterpillar how difficult it is for her to discuss the change in size she has experienced—something she doesn't understand very well.

The Caterpillar, who seems to possess some language teacher characteristics, says:

> "Explain yourself."
> "I ca'n't explain *myself,* I'm afraid, Sir," said Alice, "because I'm not myself, you see."
> "I don't see," said the Caterpillar.

"I'm afraid I ca'n't put it more clearly," Alice replied very politely, "for I ca'n't understand it myself, . . ."

When Alice, in frustration, turns to leave, the Caterpillar yells,

"Come back! I've something important to say!" (pp. 35–36)

We, like the Caterpillar, can have something important to say. We will only have an opportunity to say it, though, if we do not treat students the way the Caterpillar treated Alice when he insisted that she talk about something that she did not understand.

Now consider the purposes of most personal letters. How many people write such letters for the sole purpose of avoiding errors? Few. When people write such discourse, they have authentic, real purposes to accompany the authentic, real audiences and topics. They write to inform: "I just bought a new car, Annie. It's the neatest little Ford Mustang. You'll have to take a ride in it when you're in town." They write to reassure: "I'm okay, Lindsay. I'll be out of the hospital in a day or so." They write to entertain: "Say, Abby, do you know what little Ryan did when we had guests over yesterday? He burped all over my employer's new sport coat." They write to persuade: "Nicholas, I think that you should come to visit me in January. The average daily high temperature in Tucson is in the 60s." They write to renew or mend personal relationships: "I'm sorry I let you down, Linda. Will you give me a second chance? I know that I was wrong." In general, they write to communicate something important to someone important.

I am not saying that students in our courses should be spending all or even most of their time writing personal letters. There is evidence, though, that personal letter writing has been a valued craft in the history of America (Heath, 1981), that it can serve as the foundation of a college composition course (Frye, 1983), and that it can give people practice in many useful composing tasks (Keillor, 1987). If nothing else, personal letter writing is an appropriate beginning place if students are eventually to learn to write other forms of discourse effectively. For many of our students, it is simply a matter of providing assignments that have some of the features of personal letters. That is, early assignments need to encourage students to write to familiar audiences, audiences with whom they share common experiences. A familiar audience is easier to write to because shared experiences mean that writers need not work so hard at figuring out what readers do and do not know (Flower, 1979; Moffett, 1968; Vygotsky, 1934/1962).

For those who doubt that it is easier to write to a familiar audience, I ask you to consider the following grocery list I might write to myself or to my wife: *bread, coffee, milk, cereal.* If I take this list to the store, I know what I will bring home. If I give the list to my wife, Maureen, I know that she will bring home the identical items. My question to the reader is, "What would you bring home for me?" See the footnote for the correct answers.[2]

For inexperienced writers, it is not enough for audiences to be familiar, however. Those audiences should be people who expect writing to constitute a communicative transaction. Our writing assignments also need to allow students to write about topics with which they are familiar and in which they have some interest. Above all, our writing assignments must not have as a primary goal the avoidance of errors.

Let me share with you some assignments I have seen in the many classrooms that I have visited in Arizona. The teachers who created the following assignments made efforts to encourage students to address real audiences, on real topics, for real purposes.

Several years ago my son Nicholas was a student in a classroom for four-year-old children at Academic Preschool and Kindergarten in Tucson. One afternoon when I arrived at the school to take him home for the day, I noticed that the children had used wooden blocks to construct a castle in the middle of the room. When I asked my son about the castle, he excitedly told me about the construction project. Then he told me, with the same excitement, about a story that his classmates and he had written. The story, which the teacher had transcribed on the blackboard, told of a prince, a princess, their marriage, and their life in the castle.

In Marana, Arizona, teachers at Butterfield Elementary School ask sixth graders to write to fifth graders to tell them what fifth graders need to do to be ready for sixth grade. In the school, fifth graders write to fourth graders; fourth graders write to third graders; and so on. Those students are willing writers because they are writing to an interested audience about a familiar and interesting topic for the purpose of sharing important and real information.

At Ganado Elementary School in Ganado, Arizona, 93% of the students are Navajo. In that school I have seen classrooms filled with life-sized figures of Superman, Spiderman, Wonder Woman, Batman, and other superheroes. Children in those classrooms write letters to their favorite heroes. Their teachers, in turn, take on the personae of those superheroes (a feat that is easy for teachers) and write letters back to those students. For the students in Ganado, writing has empowered them to

---

[2] The correct answers are: (1) three frozen loaves of whole wheat or honey wheat bread dough, which I will bake myself; (2) one pound of Colombian coffee that you ground very finely at the store; (3) a half gallon of 2% milk in paper, not plastic containers; and (4) Post Raisin Bran. If you missed one or more answers, you flunked this test.

carry on communicative transactions with their heroes; it has given them power to do something very important.

Also at Ganado Elementary School, children are asked to write complaints about problems in the school: problems with bullies, broken water fountains, and the like. Sig Boloz, the principal, holds a conference with the author of every one of those complaints, Every written complaint results in some sort of resolution to a problem. Writing has empowered these youngsters to solve real problems.

There are two very helpful books published jointly by the National Council of Teachers of English and the United States Postal Service. One, titled *All About Letters* (United States Postal Service & National Council of Teachers of English, 1979), is designed for grades six through twelve. The other, *P.S. Write Soon* (United States Postal Service & National Council of Teachers of English, 1982), is designed for grades four through eight. The two books provide students with information about writing letters of all types. The best part about the books, though, is that they provide addresses of organizations that will forward letters to famous political leaders, to pen pals in foreign countries, to film and television stars, to famous musicians, and even to Dear Abby.

In the fall of 1983, in freshman composition 101, the first batch of papers I had assigned in the course included three that stood out. The first explicated the conflicting Soviet and American accounts of the downing of the South Korean jetliner. The student who wrote this paper chose a more-or-less "school topic," but not because I had directed her to do so. She had become interested in the current event before I asked the class to compare and/or contrast two phenomena. What she did do in writing about this topic was to follow my advice to "write about something that you know and care about." Her paper interested me because it had first interested her.

The second paper, written by a cross-country runner, considered the relative qualities of Nike Eagle and Nike Elite running shoes. The paper went through some major revisions (which I will describe later) before becoming an excellent one, but the student's commitment to the topic was a crucial factor in its evolution.

The third paper (which I will refer to again) first contrasted the *Star Wars* character Han Solo with Beowulf. The early versions of that paper did not work very well because the student had little commitment to or knowledge about Beowulf. In later drafts of the paper, however, the student greatly strengthened the discourse by replacing Beowulf with a character about whom he knew and cared much more: the *Happy Days* character The Fonz. For this student, too, interest in his topic strengthened his purpose and his desire to communicate effectively with his audience.

COMPOSING PROCESSES: SOLVING RHETORICAL PROBLEMS

Concepts of process are far from being new. Indeed, process is a direct descendant of ancient Greek and Roman rhetoric (Bizzell & Herzberg, 1987; Murphy, 1982, 1983). In their work with oral discourse, the Greeks and Romans practiced five operations: invention, arrangement, style, memory, and delivery; these were first discussed in detail in an anonymous (ca. 86 B.C./1954) work titled *Rhetorica ad Herennium*. The last two stages are not part of modern written discourse production, but the first three correspond to (a) prewriting, (b) drafting, (c) revising and editing.

Process approaches to composing allow writers—especially inexperienced writers—to focus on individual parts of rhetorical problems (Flower & Hayes, 1980). Process approaches allow student writers to think about such global rhetorical problems as audience, topic, development, logic, and even local-level rhetorical problems such as spelling, punctuation, sentence structure, and word choice in some systematic fashion. Such approaches help students realize that writing well is not a matter of luck.

To counter a luck-of-the-draw view of composing, language teachers at any level can help students by following Murray's (1985) advice to "take our students backstage to watch the pigeons being tucked up the magician's sleeve" (p. 4). Murray's metaphor suggests that we lead students through composing, that we model all sorts of composing strategies for them, whether they be elementary or university students, L1 or L2 students. In leading students through composing, though, we should not lead them to believe that there is only one way to compose or that composing is linear. There is plenty of scholarship (Berkenkotter & Murray, 1983; Flower & Hayes, 1980; Flower, Hayes, Carey, Schriver, & Stratman, 1986; Selzer, 1984; Sommers, 1980) indicating that skilled writers use quite a variety of strategies. Much scholarship (Emig, 1964; Flower & Hayes, 1981; Raimes, 1985; Sommers, 1980; Spack, 1984,) also indicates that composing is best represented as recursive rather than linear—that "what linear models do produce is a parody of writing" (Sommers, 1980, p. 379). But if we treat our students' composing as somewhat linear, make processes explicit, and explain that processes can be recursive, we are showing the pigeons going up the sleeve. Once they better understand the processes in which effective writers engage, they will be better able to engage in them, recursively, on their own. By asking our students to proceed though four mental operations, commonly called prewriting, drafting, revising, and editing, we essentially help our inexperienced writers marshal and allocate their cognitive resources (Beaugrande, 1984). To do so is important, for, as many (Bereiter, 1980; Flower, 1979; Raimes,

1985; Sommers, 1982; Spack, 1984; Zamel, 1985a) have suggested, inexperienced writers have too many other cognitive demands competing for resources, especially early in the writing process. Unlike their more experienced counterparts, inexperienced writers are less adept at defining the rhetorical problems that face them (Flower & Hayes, 1980; Raimes, 1985).

Early on, students need to focus on generating and developing ideas without concern for the "table manners" (Pirsig, 1974, p. 162) of writing. Doing so will prevent "cognitive overload," a short circuit in thinking that comes with trying to attend to too many problem-solving operations (Newell, 1980; Newell & Simon, 1972) or planning operations (Miller, Galanter, & Pribram, 1960) at once. After students have devoted time and effort to unfettered invention—a concept that we can trace back to Aristotle (ca. 333 B.C./1954)—they can turn their cognitive resources to other concerns, such as organizing all the material they have generated and developed. This sort of controlled allocation of cognitive resources is crucial not only in composing but in all sorts of activities. Until we learn an activity well enough for some of its components to become automatic, we are unable to simultaneously attend to any other activity (Bransford, 1979, pp. 24–27).

Once inexperienced writers have generated, developed, and organized ideas and packaged those ideas in some sort of draft, then they may once again devote adequate attention to revising their ideas. The words *revising* and *ideas* are important here. At this point in the process inexperienced writers, unlike experienced writers, still cannot devote many of their cognitive resources to their table manners (spelling, punctuation, sentence structure, word choice). They still must focus their resources on ideas.

Last come the table manners, those niceties that are pleasing to the eye and the ear. As Hairston (1982) has noted in one of the most frequently cited essays in composition of this decade, these table manners were considered the most important features of writing under the old current-traditional paradigm. Whereas editing may be more than mere table manners for some ESL students because their linguistic errors may interfere with communication, too much emphasis on correct language has led too many ESL students to believe that writing, as well as speaking, is simply a matter of getting things right. With so much emphasis on rights and wrongs, communication gets lost (Díaz, 1986; Jones, 1985; Raimes, 1983, 1986), and "students come to believe that what counts is not the thought they give to a topic but how correctly that thought is conveyed. The results? Clean but empty papers" (Rose, 1983, p. 115). For inexperienced writers, premature concern—too often a preoccupation—with editing means that from the moment composing begins, so many cognitive resources are devoted to table manners that there are no resources left over for getting any ideas on the page (Perl, 1979). As Wyche-Smith (1987) puts it: ". . . students' concern for error interferes with their composing processes, inhibits their ability to think, and in some cases leads to 'writer's block' " (p. 470). Cognitive overload was (and still is in some cases) all too common in current-traditional classrooms. Perhaps Pirsig (1974) has best characterized the effects of such preoccupation: "This was the old slap-on-the-fingers-if-your-modifiers-were-caught-dangling stuff. *Correct* spelling, *correct* punctuation, *correct* grammar. Hundreds of itsy-bitsy rules for itsy-bitsy people. No one could remember all that stuff and concentrate on what he was trying to write about" (p. 162).

To leave you with a thought about errors, I will mention Williams' (1981) frequently read article about our love affair with error hunting. At the end of the article, Williams noted that he had inserted approximately 100 errors into his article. But because readers were reading this respected author's article in a respected journal, few readers—at least among the few dozen I have surveyed—noticed any of those errors. Lees (1987) has argued that we do not find errors in an essay such as Williams' but do in students' because as writing teachers we have developed a propensity to find errors in students' papers.

APPROPRIATE FEEDBACK AND EVALUATION

For writing assignments that work, the third feature, which is related to defining rhetorical problems and attending to process, is that students must receive the right kind of feedback at the right time. Early on, it must be like Wonder Bread; that is, it must help build compositions twelve ways; it must be formative. That feedback must also be detailed enough to help students understand how they can go about the task of writing. It must also deal with communication.

Earlier I noted that Linda Flower and John Hayes have outlined the difficulties facing novice writers attempting to define rhetorical problems. Even after successfully defining those problems, however, many novice writers freeze at the thought of developing solutions because they believe they must attend to various parts of the problem (audience, purpose, content, persona, meaning, surface features) at once. What results is cognitive overload. Writing then becomes an unmanageable feat for these students, and their initial panic soon evolves into despair.

To alleviate or eliminate cognitive overload in our novice student writers, our feedback must help them focus separately on individual parts of rhetorical problems. They should understand that they do not need to generate and organize and develop and refine ideas while simultaneously editing for perfect spelling, punctuation, and sentence structure. That is, our feedback must help them understand that there is a rational and humane reason for refraining from editing until there are enough well-organized and well-developed ideas to warrant editing.

To treat the role of evaluation more concretely, I now return to two of the student papers I mentioned earlier. When I first read the paper about Nike Elite and Nike Eagle running shoes, I noticed the student's commitment to the topic. I also noticed, however, a variety of rhetorical problems to be solved. The major weakness of the paper was that it was written for other cross-country runners, people who know shoes and who understand injuries. The student had sprinkled throughout the paper terms regarding running shoes and injuries, but he had not defined or illustrated any of them. In the conference I held with the student, I asked him to explain some of the terms to me. Each time he provided an explanation that I understood, I said, "Maybe you should include that in your paper to help people like me, who have some interest in running but little knowledge about it. You need to help those of us who have not benefited from the coaching and training that you've received."

The paper also suffered from a lack of purpose, mainly because the student had not thought about one. When I asked him the simple question, "Why would anyone want or need to read a paper like this?" he knew immediately that he needed to view his paper as a buying guide for novice runners. Once he recognized that, he was able to use that purpose to reshape his ideas. The result was a pretty good piece of writing—one that appeared in the next year's edition of the University of Arizona's *A Student's Guide to Freshman Composition* (Diogenes, Johnson, and Moneyhun, 1984) as an example of a well-revised essay.

The other paper, the one dealing with Han Solo and Beowulf, also had a major weakness. While the student was interested in and knowledgeable about Han Solo, his commitment to Beowulf resembled the commitment that young Phaedrus exhibited when he recited the speech by Lysias. When I asked the student why he had contrasted these two particular characters, it became obvious that Han Solo was one of his favorite characters; his eyes almost sparkled as he talked about the space hero. The student went on to admit, though, that he had chosen the second character, Beowulf, because I, an English professor, might like that.

With that, I asked the writer about some of his other favorite characters. Among those he listed was The Fonz from *Happy Days*. We talked about The Fonz for a while, and the student began to notice that The Fonz and Han Solo share a number of characteristics—enough to allow an adequate treatment of the two. The student's interest in the two heroes allowed a fairly good treatment. I enjoyed the resulting revised paper.

Notice that in both student conferences I did not attend to editorial matters; they came much later. The conference discussions focused on the development of ideas. Once the two students had adequately developed their ideas (not mine), they were able to attend to other matters, such as organization, and eventually to spelling, punctuation, and syntax.

As we consider the feedback or evaluation that we offer our students, we need to keep in mind what a special education teacher told me once when I asked how she measured her success with special education students. She told me that she was satisfied each time a student became more independent, less dependent on her, in solving problems that most people solve regularly. Our students must also eventually become independent thinkers and writers, and also readers of their own writing. To begin this process of making students independent as writers, we must as soon as possible train students to carry on the types of conversations I had with the young man who wrote about Han Solo and The Fonz.

Lest you think that working toward this independence is akin to climbing Mount Everest, let me share with you some more war stories that I have seen and heard as I have visited Arizona's schools. These examples come from elementary schools.

Mary M. Kitagawa, a teacher at Richey Elementary School in Tucson, demonstrates the importance of using peer feedback to guide revision. Her fourth and fifth graders, 80 percent of whom are native speakers of Spanish, draw pictures which they subsequently describe in writing. Each student exchanges the description with a peer, who is then asked to recreate the original drawing from the written description. The two students compare versions of the drawing. Where discrepancies exist the writer and the reader discuss reasons for those differences. When they agree that a particular discrepancy is due to an inaccurate or inadequate portion of the written description, it's back to the drawing board; the writer goes back to the writing to revise and/or edit. Kitagawa's students become very aware of the usefulness of revising.

Jackie Cohen, a fourth-grade teacher at Tucson Country Day School, uses a similar strategy in her science units to encourage students to observe, write, and revise carefully. In her exercise, she places five or six rocks (or leaves, pine cones, moths, etc.) on a table and asks each student to describe each of the rocks thoroughly enough so that another student in the class can match each description with a particular rock. When another student cannot make the matches, the writer must revise, again using feedback from a peer.

CONCLUSION

I have discussed three features of writing assignments that research and practice have shown to be effective in improving the writing of students at all levels. First, when teachers strive to engage students in topics that interest them, in real purposes with real and interested audiences, students' writing can improve. Second, explicitly leading students through the various processes that effective writers can use harnesses those processes for students' own, independent use. Third, providing feedback that focuses first on ideas and only later on surface features helps students to solve rhetorical problems with greater confidence. Attention to the three features of writing assignments that I have considered here will not guarantee that all students will write well in our classes—or out of them. A lack of attention to these features, however, will almost guarantee that many students will not write well.

REFERENCES

Anonymous. (1954). *Rhetorica ad herennium* (H. Caplan, Trans.). Cambridge, MA: Harvard University Press. (Original work written circa 86 B.C.)

Aristotle. (1954). *The rhetoric and poetics of Aristotle* (W. R. Roberts, Trans.). New York: Random House. (Original work written circa 333 B.C.)

Beaugrande, R. de (1984). *Text production: Toward a science of composition.* Norwood, NJ: Longman.

Bereiter, C. (1980). Development in writing. In L. W. Gregg & E. R. Steinberg (Eds.), *Cognitive processes in writing* (pp. 73–93). Hillsdale, NJ: Lawrence Erlbaum.

Berkenkotter, C., & Murray, D. (1983). Decisions and revisions: The planning strategies of a publishing writer, and response of a laboratory rat—or, being protocoled. *College Composition and Communication, 34,* 156–172.

Bizzell, P., & Herzberg, B. (1987). *The Bedford bibliography for teachers of writing* (1987 ed.). Boston: St. Martin's Press.

Bransford, J. D. (1979). *Human cognition: Learning, understanding, and remembering.* Belmont, CA: Wadsworth.

Carroll, L. (1971). *Alice's Adventures in Wonderland.* In D. J. Gray (Ed.), *Alice in Wonderland.* New York: W. W. Norton. (Original work published 1865.)

Díaz, D. M. (1986). The writing process and the ESL writer: Reinforcement from second language research. *The Writing Instructor, 5,* 167–175.

Diogenes, M., Johnson, L., & Moneyhun, C. (1984). *A student's guide to freshman composition* (5th ed.). Minneapolis: Burgess Publishing Company.

Edelsky, C. (1986). *Writing in a bilingual program: Había una vez.* Norwood, NJ: Ablex.

Edelsky, C., & Smith, K. (1984). Is that writing—or are those marks just a figment of your curriculum? *Language Arts, 61,* 24–32.

Emig, J. (1964). The uses of the unconscious in composing. *College Composition and Communication, 15,* 6–11.

Flower, L. (1979). Writer-based prose: A cognitive basis for problems in writing. *College English, 41,* 19–37.

Flower, L., & Hayes, J. R. (1980). The cognition of discovery: Defining a rhetorical problem. *College Composition and Communication, 31,* 21–32.

Flower, L., & Hayes, J. R. (1981). A cognitive process theory of writing. *College Composition and Communication, 32,* 365–387.

Flower, L., & Hayes, J. R., Carey, L., Schriver, K., & Stratman, J. (1986). Detection, diagnosis, and the strategies of revision. *College Composition and Communication, 37,* 16–55.

Frye, B. J. (1983). A habit of being: Some uses of personal letters in freshman composition. *Rhetoric Review, 1,* 89–119.

Hairston, M. (1982). The winds of change: Thomas Kuhn and the revolution in the teaching of writing. *College Composition and Communication, 33,* 76–88.

Heath, S. B. (1981). Toward an ethnohistory of writing in American education. In M. F. Whiteman (Ed.), *Writing: The nature, development, and teaching of written communication: Vol. 1. Variation in writing: Functional and linguistic-cultural differences* (pp. 25–45). Hillsdale, NJ: Lawrence Erlbaum.

Jones, S. (1985). Problems with monitor use in second language composing. In M. Rose (Ed.), *When a Writer Can't Write* (pp. 96–118). New York: Guilford Press.

Keillor, G. (1987, September). How to write a personal letter. *Newsweek On Campus,* pp. 28–29.

Lees, E. O. (1987). Proofreading as reading, errors as embarrassments. In T. Enos (Ed.), *A sourcebook for basic writing teachers* (pp. 216–230). New York: Random House.

Miller, G., Galanter, E., & Pribram, K. (1960). *Plans and the structure of behavior.* New York: Holt Rinehart & Winston.

Moffett, J. (1968). *Teaching the universe of discourse.* Boston: Houghton Mifflin.

Murphy, J. J. (Ed.). (1982). *The rhetorical tradition and modern writing.* New York: Modern Language Association.

Murphy, J. J. (Ed.). (1983). *A synoptic history of classical rhetoric.* Davis, CA: Hermagoras Press.

Murray, D. M. (1968). *A writer teaches writing* (1st ed.). Boston: Houghton Mifflin.

Murray, D. M. (1985). *A writer teaches writing* (2nd ed.). Boston: Houghton Mifflin.

Newell, A. (1980). Reasoning, problem solving, and decision processes: The problemspace as a fundamental category. In R. S. Nickerson (Ed.), *Attention and performance VIII.* Hillsdale, NJ: Lawrence Erlbaum.

Newell, A., & Simon, H. (1972). *Human problem solving.* Englewood Cliffs, NJ: Prentice-Hall.

Perl, S. (1979). The composing processes of unskilled college writers. *Research in the Teaching of English, 13,* 317–336.

Pirsig, R. M. (1974). *Zen and the art of motorcycle maintenance.* New York: Bantam.

Plato. (1956). *Phaedrus* (W. C. Helmhold & W. G. Rabinowitz, Trans.). Indianapolis: The Bobbs-Merrill Company, Inc. (Original work written circa 370 B.C.)

Quintilian. (1922). *Institutio Oratoria* (H. E. Butler, Trans.). Cambridge, MA: Harvard University Press. (Original work written circa 88 A.D.)

Raimes, A. (1983). Tradition and revolution in ESL teaching. *TESOL Quarterly, 17,* 535–552.

Raimes, A. (1985). What unskilled ESL students do as they write: A classroom study of composing. *TESOL Quarterly, 19,* 229–258.

Raimes, A. (1986). Teaching ESL writing: Fitting what we do to what we know. *The Writing Instructor, 5,* 153–166.

Rose, M. (1983). Remedial writing courses: A critique and a proposal. *College English, 45,* 109–128.

Selzer, J. (1984). Exploring options in composing. *College Composition and Communication, 35,* 276–284.

Sommers, N. (1980). Revision strategies of student writers and experienced adult writers. *College Composition and Communication, 31,* 378–388.

Sommers, N. (1982). Responding to student writing. *College Composition and Communication, 33,* 148–156.

Spack, R. (1984). Invention strategies and the ESL college composition student. *TESOL Quarterly, 18,* 649–670.

Taylor, B. P. (1981). Content and written form: A two-way street. *TESOL Quarterly, 15,* 5–13.

United States Postal Service & National Council of Teachers of English. (1979). *All About Letters.* Urbana, IL: National Council of Teachers of English.

United States Postal Service & National Council of Teachers of English. (1982). *P.S. Write Soon.* Urbana, IL: National Council of Teachers of English.

Vygotsky, L. S. (1962). *Thought and language* (E. Hanfmann & G. Vakar, Trans.). Cambridge, MA: MIT Press. (Original work published 1934.)

Williams, J. M. (1981). The phenomenology or error. *College English, 32,* 152–168.

Wyche-Smith, S. (1987). Teaching invention to basic writers. In T. Enos (Ed.), *A sourcebook for basic writing teachers* (pp. 470–479). New York: Random House.

Young, R. (1978). Paradigms and problems: Needed research in rhetorical invention. In C. Cooper & L. Odell (Eds.), *Research on composing: Points of departure* (pp. 29–47). Urbana, IL: National Council of Teachers of English.

Zamel, V. (1982). Writing: The process of discovering meaning. *TESOL Quarterly, 16,* 195–209.

Zamel, V. (1985a). Responding to student writing. *TESOL Quarterly, 19,* 79–101.

Zamel, V. (1985b). What unskilled ESL students do as they write: A classroom study of composing. *TESOL Quarterly, 19,* 229–258.

CHAPTER 13

The Peer Review Process: Harnessing Students' Communicative Power

Robert Mittan
University of Arizona

I'm a skeptic. I admit it. I never buy on the first day—always wait at least 24 hours. So when I first heard the phrase *empowering students,* I put it in the category with "new and improved" and "fully revised": sounds good; lacks meaning. But as I began to reconsider the notion of empowerment, I realized that, indeed, empowerment applies to everything I try to do as a college composition teacher. For me it doesn't mean giving students power they don't already possess, imbuing their pens with The Force. Instead, it means highlighting and nurturing the strengths students already have.

But why does that sound new? Why do we suddenly need a name for it? I think it's because much of our time as writing teachers is spent finding out—and pointing out—what students *don't* do well. Faced with a stack of student compositions, which is easier: spotting the surface feature flaws, or finding the greater rhetorical successes? Students, too, have joined this crusade, some demanding that we not rest until every mistake has been daubed with ink, the composition teacher's iodine. They want to know what's wrong, and we want to tell them.

How, then, can we return some of the power to them, power they have so willingly conceded? One way is to search for assignments and activities like those suggested by Johnson (1981), Raimes (1983), Roen (this volume), and Freeman and Freeman (this volume) that encourage students to write about what they know and that give them opportunities to demonstrate their expertise, not their inadequacies. We can likewise shift the focus of our comments on student papers to what *is* working so they can revise what *isn't* successful. Our intention, of course, is to help students succeed in their writing by helping them harness their communicative power.

207

I have found the peer review process a useful method to focus on students' existing communicative powers and to show them how to extend those abilities in their writing. In this chapter, I explore some of the theory which supports the peer review process and then present some practical suggestions for using the process in second language (L2) composition classrooms. Although the examples and suggestions are drawn from my own experience with English as a second language (ESL) composition at the university level, other teachers have successfully used similar procedures with all levels, from elementary (Urzua, 1987) to graduate students (Johnson, 1988).

First, let me explain what I mean by the peer review process. I am referring to the following integrated activities that I use to guide students in responding to each others' writing.

1. In the first activity, students read their peers' writing and write a response to it using a peer review sheet, which is a questionnaire that focuses the reviewer's attention on specific areas of the author's writing. This activity is done either in class or as an outside assignment.
2. Next, often during the following class period, students exchange oral comments on their writing, referring to and further elaborating on their written peer reviews.
3. As a third step, I read and respond not only to each student's writing but also to his or her written comments to a peer on the peer review sheet.

After this three-part sequence has been repeated for several writing assignments during the term, I add another activity.

4. Students complete a self-review sheet based on a first draft of their own writing, and I comment on these.

Although each component of the peer review process is important on its own, I have discovered that the true success of the process depends primarily upon the careful integration of each part. This combination of writing, reading, speaking, listening, and thinking activities assures that students use and practice all their communicative powers. Using "real language in real situations," they gain the "ability to work in the context of the whole" (Morrow, 1981, p. 61).

RATIONALE FOR THE PEER REVIEW PROCESS

The rationale behind this peer review process is both theoretical and practical. The theoretical basis lies in the social nature of language, language use, language learning, and learning in general. Believing that "learning is, above all, a social process," that "knowledge is transmitted in social contexts," and that "the words that are exchanged in these contexts get their meaning from activities in which they are embedded" (Halliday & Hasan, 1985, p. 5), many sociolinguists, like Halliday, have turned attention to the relationship between language and the social context in which it is used and learned. Furthermore, within the social context, as Moffett (1968) points out, "learning to use language . . . requires the particular feedback of human response, because it is to other people" that language is directed (p. 191). But it might be argued that the traditional approach to writing instruction of student-as-writer to teacher-as-reader does constitute a social process in a social context. "Certainly," teachers would argue, "our feedback is human response."

The difference, however, is that involving peers in the process, as Bruffee (1984) argues, "harnesse[s] the powerful educative force of peer influence that ha[s] been—and largely still is—ignored and hence wasted by traditional forms of education" (p. 638). Moreover, collaborative learning, to use Bruffee's term, changes the social context to "a community of status equals: peers," the kind of community that both "fosters the kind of conversation college teachers value most" and "approximates the one most students must eventually write for in everyday life, in business, government, and the professions" (p. 642). In short, the social context created by peer interaction is more realistic, and therefore the feedback more powerful.

In addition to these assumptions about the nature of language and peer interaction, the peer review process I use is founded on several other practical and theoretical considerations. Gathering from published discussions of the use of peer interaction in both L1 and L2 composition and from my own experience, I have compiled the following core list of benefits for both the student and the teacher.

First, peer reviews provide student writers with reactions, questions, and responses from authentic readers who provide a stronger motivation for revision (Beaven, 1977; Chaudron, 1983; James, 1981; Koch, 1982; Moore, 1986). Although teachers try hard to make our comments approximate "real" readers' responses, we are still teachers, numbed by the experience of reading stacks of papers, constantly calculating the pedagogical effects of our responses. Indeed, as highly practiced active readers we sometimes make bold assumptions where most readers would stop and say "Huh?" Students, on the other hand, react honestly. As Samy, a student of mine from Brazil, commented to his partner from Indonesia, Maria, concerning the first draft of her critical analysis of a novel: "You also seem to be describing the story on the second part of your essay. We already know the story so you should explain, criticize and proof your examples in a specific way."[1]

A second and corollary benefit from peer interaction is that student writers receive more feedback from multiple and mutually reinforcing perspectives (Chaudron, 1983; James, 1981; Lamberg, 1980). While Samy's comment honestly pointed out the major flaw in Maria's writing, my teacher response suggested how she might use some of her material as she moved away from plot summary and toward a critical analysis. The process can work the other way as well with peer reviews: When students simply compliment their partner's strengths, the teacher's response can zero in on the weaknesses and suggest improvements. Although I seldom find an extreme "good cop/bad cop" dichotomy between peer reactions and my own, I do find that the combination of responses assures that student writers hear a balance of what Peter Elbow (1983) calls supporting "coach" comments and critical "gatekeeping" evaluations.

Third, because they reciprocate in the role of audience for their peers, students gain a clearer understanding of meeting the reader's needs. At the same time, by responding critically to their colleagues' writing, students exercise the critical thinking they must apply to their own work (James, 1981; Kock, 1982; Lamberg, 1980; Moore, 1986; Witbeck, 1976). Clearly, peer reviews put into practice what we preach about audience awareness. If students are to understand the influence their own writing has on others, they need to experience and examine closely the impact of others' writing on them. The peer review process requires them to do that.

Fourth, there is an affective element to peer interaction: students see that their peers also have difficulty writing and may gain confidence in, or at least feel less apprehension about, their own abilities (Chaudron, 1983; Hafernik, 1983; Witbeck, 1976). Sometimes their support for each other is explicit. One of my students began a peer review of his partner's first draft, written in a fifty-minute class period, by noting, "I think the most important problem for us during the in-class writing is the lack of time. So, I think you can improve [your draft] by yourself." Although the reviewer went on to give details of specific areas that needed work, his preliminary judgment that given more time "you can improve it by yourself," is honest encouragement. Teacher comments, no matter how positive and encouraging, are still judgments rendered by The One Who Knows.

---

[1] All student comments come from peer review letters and are quoted verbatim except where indicated with brackets.

Finally, other practitioners have claimed that one advantage for the teacher is time saved because of a decreased reading load (Beaven, 1977; Chaudron, 1983; James, 1981; Moore, 1986). Frankly, I have found that I save time per paper, but not overall work. If anything, responding to students' written peer reviews has increased the reading load. But I have reduced the amount of time I spend with each piece of student writing because I am no longer the only audience, solely responsible for comments. So although reading and responding are still necessary, I can spend less time on each paper.

In using and developing the peer review process in my own classroom, I have discovered some additional, unexpected benefits. Before I began to use peer reviews I thought of myself primarily as a writing teacher, focusing only on students' composing. But using peer reviews has made me more aware of students' needs in all the modes of language— reading, writing, listening, speaking, and thinking. By observing students' peer discussions and reading their responses on review sheets, I can sometimes trace the source of writing difficulties to one of these other areas.

One example of this is Hadi, an Afghan student, who consistently complained that he could not read his partner's handwriting, even when I paired him with one of the better writers whose handwriting was quite legible. Hadi's written comments further revealed that he only vaguely understood what his partner's writing was about. During a conference in my office, I asked Hadi to read silently a paragraph from an essay in the course reader. I watched his eyes move very slowly along each line of print; after he finished, I asked what the paragraph was about. He couldn't answer beyond the general topic. He could, however, identify the parts of speech of most words in each sentence, and he knew that every word was spelled correctly. Suddenly I realized why Hadi's own writing, although rife with good ideas in fairly well formed sentences, often lacked any sense of cohesion: As a reader he focused on the form of each sentence, not how they linked to form a whole.

I worker individually with Hadi on his reading process, showing him how to first read a passage quickly for its main idea and then to examine it more closely to see how each sentence is connected to that central focus. When I asked him to apply these reading techniques to his own writing, Hadi began to realize that his sentences, each one painstakingly composed and corrected to the best of his ability, didn't "hang together." The rest of the term I focused my comments on this aspect of his writing, and Hadi worked hard to improve. Thus, a seemingly unrelated complaint about his peer's handwriting lead me to investigate Hadi's reading process, which ultimately helped him improve his writing.

The most important benefit I think students gain from the peer review process is the opportunity for what Britton, Burgess, Martin, McLeod, and Rosen (1975) have called the "expressive function" of writing. In their study of the development of writing abilities in children, Britton et al. explain that expressive writing "must surely be the most accessible form in which to write" because it is closely related to and modeled on speech, an area in which writers already have considerable experience. They further hypothesize that "in developmental terms, the expressive is a kind of matrix from which differentiated forms of mature writing are developed" (pp. 82–83). But the value of expressive writing does not decrease once writers "mature." It provides all writers with a comfortable means for discovering their thoughts and feelings. (For further discussion of the important interrelationships between writing and speaking in L2 composition, see Mangelsdorf, this volume.)

Until I asked students to write peer reviews, I seldom saw them flex their expressive muscles. Even the journal writing of many of my students often has the ring of textbook talk. But writing a peer review letter encourages students to "think aloud on paper," to exercise their thinking, feeling voices. Bridget, a Nigerian student, begins her letter to K. K., from Hong Kong, "I like how you started your essay, but I think the introduction is too long. I suggest that you start by stating briefly what you are going to talk about in the essay." Like most expressive writing, isolated from their context these comments seem self-contradictory. But as I look at K. K.'s draft along with Bridget's comments, it's easy for me to follow Bridget's thinking on paper: You're doing the right thing here in the introduction, K. K.; you just do too much of it. Identifying and explaining what she likes about her partner's writing, Bridget reveals—to herself and to her peer—her own thinking, her idea of what makes a good introduction.

I think Bridget's example also illustrates the ultimate benefit of the peer review process for the teacher. Regardless of how I judge the quality of her finished essays, her peer review can show me some of her knowledge about good writing. I can praise her insights and encourage her to apply that knowledge to her own writing. So the peer review process allows my students and me to concentrate on what they know as well as what they can do. Indeed, I have found that students whose writing is consistently average or even poor very often write the most thoughtful and helpful peer reviews. This is true empowerment: encouraging students to demonstrate and use their knowledge and expertise instead of punishing them for their as-yet unpolished performance.

So far, I have concentrated on the reasons for using the peer review process. But the benefits I have listed are not gained by simply telling students to exchange their papers and comment on them. It's not that easy. The following guidelines suggest ways to make the peer review process a successful and empowering part of L2 composition classrooms.

SUGGESTIONS FOR USING THE PEER REVIEW PROCESS

Integrate the Peer Review Process into the Course

As students begin their first writing assignment, they should be aware that their peers as well as the teacher will read and comment on all their writing in the course: journal writing, rough drafts or prewriting, more polished drafts, and final versions. Often ESL students have not shared their writing with peers before, and they may be apprehensive about doing so. To reassure them, I tell students that I will show them how to review a piece of writing. Then, using a "safe" writing sample—a published essay from the course reader, student writing from a previous semester, or a piece of my own writing—we do a practice review as a class. This large-group activity allows students to try out their review voices and enables me to guide them toward useful responses. In subsequent classes I continue to practice peer reviews on every available writing sample so that by the time students have a first draft to exchange they are "experienced" reviewers and they know that peer reviews are an integral part of the course.

Begin with a Few Simple Tasks and Build throughout the Term

For the practice reviews mentioned above, I use an approach adapted from Koch (1982) which takes students through four tasks: (1) offer a positive response to the writing, (2) identify the purpose of the writing, (3) ask questions directed toward the writer, and (4) offer suggestions to the writer (p. 468). In later reviews, I continue to use these core ways of responding; however, each time I raise the ante slightly, asking students to detail why they find a particular passage effective or to explain how a suggested revision will improve the writing. Moore (1986), who suggests using the same evaluation sheet throughout the term, notes that "as the semester goes along . . . not only are [students] able to criticize both positively and negatively, but also they become increasingly adept at pinpointing a problem and even suggesting how to improve something" (p. 23). I find that students discover even more insights if the peer review task continues to challenge their development as active readers and writers. Ultimately, I assign the most difficult task, a self-review, on the last writing assignment during the term. By this time, students are experienced enough to respond to their own writing objectively and critically.

Choose the Most Effective Peer Group Size and Arrange Groups According to Students' Writing Strengths

Hafernik (1983) suggests using groups of three, arranged by the teacher so that each group contains students of varying language backgrounds and with different writing strengths and weaknesses. Moore (1986) allows students to arrange themselves in groups of four. Grimm (1986) proposes groups of four to five students each for L1 composition at the college level.

Any of these arrangements can and does work. But after trying various sizes and methods of grouping, I always return to pairs of ESL writers, using one triad to round off classes with an odd number of students. For me, the loss of one or two additional reader responses is outweighed by the increased opportunity to engage in one-to-one speaking and listening. Early in the term I allow students to choose their own partners, but I always encourage them to choose someone they haven't worked with or don't already know. Later, after I have seen enough of their writing to know their strengths and weaknesses, I assign the pairs, putting a high-ability with a medium-ability, low with medium, or high with high. Pairings of low-low and low-high generally are not effective. But pairing students across language backgrounds, although a consideration, is never a priority for me. In fact, on occasion students from the same L1 have gained insights about their own problems by seeing them mirrored in their partner's writing.

Allow Plenty of Time for Both Written Responses and Oral Discussion of Reviews

Even with dyads I allow at least 20 minutes for reading and responding to short writing samples (about 500 words). Students then need 10 minutes to exchange oral comments. As the semester progresses and the cognitive demands of the peer review sheet increase, I ask students to exchange photocopies of their writing and complete the written peer review sheets as homework. Then each pair spends 20 minutes during the next class period on oral comments. There are two advantages to this format. First, students in general take their responsibilities as peer reviewers quite seriously; they want and need the time outside class to formulate and write their comments. Second, the time lapse between written and oral comments tends to focus students' attention on major problems and suggestions for revision so that discussion time is more fruitful.

Elbow (1973, 1981) points out several advantages of having writers read their writing aloud to peers, and many practitioners view this as essential to the peer review process. But with ESL students I have found these advantages minimized because both reader and listener tend to focus on the act of reading rather than the message. Since students gain valuable listening and speaking practice from the realistic give-and-take of oral discussion, I suggest to students that they read their own writing aloud to themselves at home.

Comment On and Grade Peer Review Sheets

In addition to motivating students, grades and comments communicate the value of the peer reviews. I use a 10-point system (seldom giving lower than 5 points) and make general comments about specificity and helpfulness of the student's suggestions. I also constantly stress that the *primary* audience for the review is the peer, not the teacher, to head off comments written in the third person: "I think he should make his introduction clearer. . . ."

There are two logistical problems in grading peer review sheets: If the peer is the primary audience, when does the teacher grade the papers, and how does the reviewer receive his/her comments from the teacher? One solution to both problems is to ask students to photocopy their peer review sheets; the original goes to the peer during oral comments, the photocopy goes to the teacher for a grade. This system works well with college level students. Another solution is to have students turn in peer review sheets with the final version of their writing, after they have used the sheets during revision. Then reviews can be graded and returned to the reviewer. In either case, students need feedback on peer reviews just as on any other writing assignment.

Design a Peer Review Sheet Specifically for Each Peer Review Session

When my colleagues complain that a peer review session flopped, my first question is always, "Did you write the peer review sheet yesterday, or last semester?" Although I follow the same format each time, every peer review sheet is different; the questions I ask depend on students' responses on the previous sheet and the purpose of the writing task. In fact, when I teach more than one section of the same course, I sometimes write a different peer review sheet for each group. The extra effort invariably pays off in more productive student responses.

I developed and used a peer review sheet (see Figure 13.1) for a high-intermediate level ESL composition course. For this writing assignment,

Figure 13.1. Peer Review

Draft written by: _____

Review written by: _____

Your purpose in answering these questions is to provide an honest and helpful response to your partner's draft and to suggest ways to make his/her writing better. Before beginning your review, be sure to read the writing carefully. After you have done that, respond to each of the following questions. *Be as specific as possible;* refer directly to your partner's paper by paragraph number.

1. What do you like most about your partner's writing? Choose the most interesting idea and EXPLAIN WHY it captured your attention.
2. In your own words, state what you think your partner's focus is. What aspects of paralingual communication is your partner trying to explain to readers?
3. How helpful and informative will this paper be for readers who want to visit your partner's culture? Which parts need to be developed with more detail so that the readers can understand these kinds of communication?
4. Choose the response that you agree with:
   _____ Each of your paragraphs discusses only one idea and everything in it is related to that topic.
   _____ Some of your paragraphs are confusing because they seem to be about more than one idea. I marked them with an X.
   _____ Your writing seems to be all in one paragraph. I can't tell where you start discussing a new idea. Please help!
5. On the back of this page, write a short letter to your partner explaining how his or her writing can be improved. BE VERY SPECIFIC and explain *why* you think these changes will be helpful to the reader. Be sure to sign your letter.

which came approximately two-thirds of the way through a 16-week semester, students were asked to describe and explain different types of paralingual communication from their culture so that their reader, someone from a different culture planning to visit their country, would know when and how these forms of nonverbal communication are used, and what meaning they have to the culture. This typical peer review sheet, used after students had written a first full draft for the assignment, illustrates the format I have discovered, through much trial and effort, is most effective.

First, the review sheet begins with clear and explicit instructions which remind students of the purpose, the audience, and the method for completing the peer review. Because I treat peer review sheets as writing assignments in themselves, I think it's important to provide students with these cues.

Second, the review sheet is limited to a single page. More questions do not yield more response; in fact, students seem to write less overall on longer forms. Also, the amount of white space I provide after each question allows students to gauge the length of their responses.

Third, the questions roughly follow the system I use to introduce students to the peer review process at the beginning of the term: give a positive response, identify the purpose or main idea, offer questions and suggestions. This system is also similar to the way I organize my own comments when responding to their writing. Thus, it is a familiar and integral part of the course.

Fourth, although each question requires students to analyze or judge some aspect of their partner's writing, I vary the question types and tasks. Question two, for example, requires students to reformulate or "translate" an idea, a task more cognitively demanding than this alternative: "What is the thesis of the draft? Find it and copy it here." Question four is also more complex than it may appear. To respond, students must analyze not only their peer's writing but also the range of possible responses in order to judge which is the most applicable. Yes/no questions are the least cognitively demanding. Yet, like multiple choice questions, they are particularly useful for revealing negative responses. A student who would not tell a peer "I think your main idea is really obvious and dull" often feels comfortable checking "No" when asked "Is the main idea unusual or thoughtful enough to hold your interest?"

The final question, the only one I repeat on every peer review sheet, presents students with a form for open-ended, expressive writing. In a small pilot study (Mittan, 1987) I discovered that, when using peer review sheets containing both probing questions and open-ended letters, students tended not to merely repeat their responses to earlier questions; instead their letters focused on one or two major problem areas, with suggestions for improvement. Those who responded only through peer review letters, without first answering specific questions, wrote more general, less helpfully detailed responses.

Even more important, I think, is the form of these responses. Asking students to "write a short letter to your partner" stipulates a particular genre and indicates the roles of the participants, both of which are familiar and informal. Students are thereby free to concentrate on the message. I find that regardless of their writing skills, L2 students often do their best writing in their peer review letters. Mini-essays in themselves, these letters clearly demonstrate the communicative power students possess.

In her plenary address at TESOL '85 in New York, Courtney B. Cazden argued that reductionism, "fractionating complex tasks into component parts that, no matter how well practiced, can never reconstitute the complex whole," is one of the barriers that teachers, as "language advocates," must help language learners overcome (1986, p. 11). Certainly composing in a second language is one of the most complex tasks learners encounter. In addition to all of the requirements of L1 writers—knowledge of the subject, a suitable format in which to present it, and considerations of audience—L2 writers must also manage a language with which many are still becoming familiar.

The peer review process I have described is antireductionist. It does not reduce writing to individual components, though it may focus readers' and writers' attention on them. Instead, it brings students' existing strengths in writing, reading, speaking, listening, and thinking to bear on the complex task of composing. And from this convergence of strengths, the combination rather than separation of skills, L2 writers will gain new power.

REFERENCES

Beaven, M. H. (1977). Individualized goal setting, self-evaluation, and peer evaluation. In C. R. Cooper & L. Odell (Eds.), *Evaluating writing: Describing, measuring, judging* (pp. 135–156). Urbana, IL: National Council of Teachers of English.

Britton, J., Burgess, T., Martin, N., McLeod, A., & Rosen, H. (1975). *The development of writing abilities (11–18)*. London: Macmillan Education.

Bruffee, K. A. (1984). Collaborative learning and the "conversation of mankind." *College English, 46,* 635–652.

Cazden, C. B. (1986). ESL teachers as language advocates for children. In P. Rigg & D. S. Enright (Eds.), *Children and ESL: Integrating perspectives* (pp. 7–21). Washington, DC: Teachers of English To Speakers of Other Languages.

Chaudron, C. (1983). *Evaluating writing: Effects of feedback on revision.* Paper presented at the 17th Annual meeting of Teachers of English to Speakers of Other Languages, Toronto. (ERIC Document Reproduction Service No. ED 227 706)

Elbow, P. (1973). *Writing without teachers.* New York: Oxford University Press.

Elbow, P. (1981). *Writing with power.* New York: Oxford University Press.

Elbow, P. (1983). Embracing contraries in the teaching process. *College English, 45,* 327–339.

Grimm, N. (1986). Improving students' responses to their peers' essays. *College Composition and Communication, 37,* 91–94.

Hafernik, J. J. (1983) *The how and why of peer editing in the ESL writing class.* Paper presented at the State Meeting of the California Association of Teachers of English to Speakers of Other Languages, Los Angeles (ERIC Document Reproduction Service No. ED 253 064)

Halliday, M. A. K., & Hasan, R. (1985). *Language, context, and text: Aspects of language in a social-semiotic perspective.* Victoria, Australia: Deakin University.

James, D. R. (1981). Peer teaching in the writing classroom. *English Journal, 70*(7), 48–50.

Johnson, D. M. (1988, March). Social context and language use in peer reviews. Paper presented at the 22nd Annual meeting of Teachers of English to Speakers of Other Languages, Chicago.

Johnson, K. (1981). Writing. In K. Johnson & K. Morrow (Eds.), *Communication in the classroom: Applications and methods for a communicative approach* (pp. 93–107). Essex, England: Longman Group, Ltd.

Koch, R. (1982). Syllogisms and superstitions: The current state of responding to writing. *Language Arts, 59,* 464–471.

Lamberg, W. (1980). Self-provided and peer-provided feedback. *College Composition and Communication, 31,* 63–69.

Mittan, R. (1987). *Asking the right questions: A study of peer reviews in ESL composition.* Unpublished manuscript.

Moore, L. K. (1986). Teaching students how to evaluate writing. *TESOL Newsletter, 20*(5), 23–24.

Moffett, J. (1968). *Teaching the universe of discourse.* Boston: Houghton Mifflin.

Morrow, K. (1981). Principles of communicative methodology. In K. Johnson & K. Morrow (Eds.), *Communication in the classroom: Applications and methods for a communicative approach* (pp. 59–66). Essex, England: Longman Group, Ltd.

Raimes, A. (1983). *Techniques in teaching writing.* New York: Oxford University Press.

Urzua, C. (1987). "You stopped too soon": Second language children composing and revising. *TESOL Quarterly, 21,* 279–304.

Witbeck, M. C. (1976). Peer correction procedures for intermediate and advanced ESL composition lessons. *TESOL Quarterly, 10,* 321–326.

CHAPTER 14

English as Second Language Composition in Higher Education: The Expectations of the Academic Audience

Joy M. Reid
Colorado State University

INTRODUCTION

For students in higher education, there are essentially two considerations in most writing assignments: purpose and audience. In academic writing, the *purpose* of a writing assignment is usually designed, assigned, and evaluated by the *audience* (the professor), so the two are closely connected. As Donald Murray (1987) states, ". . . in the abnormal situation of school, the [writer] is rarely an authority. . . . Usually the student writes on a subject and in a voice and form of the reader's choosing" (p. 25). Many native speakers (NS) of English, particularly those who are experienced, successful writers, have learned about the close relationship that exists between the purpose and the audience in academic writing. Unfortunately, many nonnative speakers of (NNS) of English, particularly students from other cultures, do not have the necessary cultural background information and experience (schema) that would allow them to complete academic writing tasks in U.S. universities successfully (Blanton, 1987; Carrell, 1986, 1987; Johns, 1986). The result, a breakdown in communication, is one of the most serious problems faced by English as a second language (ESL) writers.

Finding solutions to the problem of the different schema of NNS of English is the responsibility of their composition teachers. Although many NS have become familiar with the general purposes, conventions, and audiences of academic writing, many NNS, even those at an advanced level of general language proficiency, are not (Horowitz, 1986; Johns,

1987; Liebman-Kleine, 1987). In order to write successful academic prose, ESL writers must understand these essentials as they proceed through the processes of what are commonly called prewriting strategies: brainstorming, generating ideas, discovering meaning, and so forth. This chapter therefore focuses on explicit classroom activities that should be an integral part of the prewriting process. Through these activities for advanced ESL writers, students will acquire necessary background knowlege and experience. The result: The students will discover not only the content of their academic writing tasks but also the cultural constraints of U.S. academic writing assignments.

THE PROBLEM

The problem of poor, unsuccessful communication is not, fundamentally, a question of language proficiency, although frustrated university professors may—for want of a more precise way of articulating their frustrations—lay the blame for unsuccessful written communication on what is most immediately obvious: "I can't understand what this student is doing; I think he needs work in grammar." For an ESL student with very limited language proficiency, this assessment may be true, but most students admitted to higher education programs must first meet rigorous standards of language proficiency. Even with adequate language skills, these students will still have some L2 errors in written work, but those errors are generally little more than extraneous noise that academic readers get through, not a major cause of inadequate communication. In other words, professors will overlook L2 errors or consider them less important if the writing fulfills their expectations in terms of content and general form (Carlson & Bridgeman, 1983; Carlson, Bridgeman, Camps, & Waanders, 1985; Lindstrom, 1981; Vann, Meyer, & Lorenz, 1984).

More often, the problem of communicating successfully originates from the ESL student's limited or skewed perception of what is expected. Typically, in the United States NNS from other cultures operate with a somewhat different set of cultural assumptions; they are therefore likely to resort to coping skills that have worked in their native languages and cultures but that are inappropriate for the expectations of the U.S. academic audience. Examples: the freshman composition essay that is highly philosophical and generalized instead of being highly specific and personalized as the professor expected; the political science paper that has elaborate language and irrelevant materials that do not address "the point"; the research paper that has been copied from one or two sources. When an academic audience evaluates these assignments, misunderstandings abound: the professor decides that the student does not understand the content because the writer cannot successfully respond to a (seemingly) transparent task; the student, who does understand the content and expected a more positive evaluation is mystified, frustrated, and insecure. In this case, the student clearly is penalized because he or she is not familiar with the culturally accepted conventions of academic prose.

EXPLAINING THE PROBLEM TO STUDENTS

For composition teachers preparing NNS for academic work, the solution to this problem is both complex and simple. The most difficult—and culturally knotty—part is persuading the students that (a) the U.S. academic audience expects specific strategies and formats, and (b) the teachers do not intend to change the ways their students from other cultures think. Indeed, students must understand that adjusting to a specific writing style will not make them North Americans and should not compromise their cultures or their personalities. However, the students need to understand the realities of academic writing and the choices they have to make. The fact is that the U.S. academic audience does have expectations about the content and the form of written material. Once students have discovered these expectations, they must decide whether to fulfill them.

If students choose to adjust their writing to meet the expectations of their academic audience, they need to understand two consequences. First, a similar readjustment will be necessary when they resume writing in their native languages. Just as their styles and presentations of written material change to fulfill the expectations of the U.S. audience, they will have to reexamine their planning and producing strategies when they write academic papers in their native languages. There is the (perhaps apochryphal) story about the Korean student who received honors on his U.S. doctoral dissertation after having struggled for many years to achieve the necessary mindset to produce acceptable English academic prose. When he returned to Korea and sought to publish a research article based on his dissertation, the article was panned; the editors of the Korean journal said that the article was poorly written and "not good Korean."

Second, students need to know that adjusting writing styles is not easy. Teachers might tell their students of Jean Zukowski/Faust's attempts to learn to write Turkish prose while she was teaching English in Turkey.[1] Her tutor kept returning Zukowski Faust's essays, asking her to revise them because, although the grammar was error-free, the writing was not

---

[1] My thanks to Jean Zukowski/Faust (Northern Arizona University) for permission to use her story.

Turkish, it was "cold, like a fish." During the same time, while marking her Turkish students' papers, Zukowski/Faust "discovered contrastive rhetoric" as she found herself writing comments such as "Get to the point" and "Why say this when it's not relevant?" Students who hear these stories should not, of course, despair. Rather, the stories underscore the importance of teachers explaining to their students what is "not English" and what is. And the students should understand that making adjustments in their writing will probably be hard work that will involve raising their awareness about prose styles and practicing appropriate forms and structures.

USING CONTRASTIVE RHETORIC

One way to begin raising students' awareness of U.S. academic prose is a frank discussion among teachers and students about rhetorical differences between English academic prose and the rhetoric—the presentation of written material—in the students' native languages (cf. Connor & Kaplan, 1987; Doushaq, 1986; Hinds, 1983; Kaplan, 1983; Matalene, 1985). A discussion about contrastive rhetoric, in which the teacher describes characteristics of languages and asks for feedback from students who speak that language, is a good stimulus for structuring discussions about coping strategies. Skeletal summaries of such discussions might begin as follows:

1. Although I don't speak Arabic, students in classes like this one and research I have read have indicated that Arabic is a traditional, poetic language, that the skill of writing is considered extremely difficult, a skill that only the gifted possess, and that the presentation of written material in Arabic relies on philosophical (abstract) statements—the audience "reads between the lines," drawing conclusions and extending the information. However, U.S. academic prose requires competent (simple, not beautiful) writing that consists of paragraphs containing a single main idea supported by facts, examples, or description. U.S. students learn to "prove it or cut it!"

2. Although I don't speak French (Spanish, etc.), for writers of Romance languages like French or Spanish, elaboration, using the language beautifully, is essential to the successful presentation of written material. If you look at a resume prepared by a Spanish speaker, for example, you will see that the document is many, many pages of extended prose. However, U.S. academic English,

especially scientific and technical writing, requires a kind of stripped down prose. Even in elementary school, U.S. students are taught: "Tell 'em what you're gonna tell 'em, tell 'em, and tell 'em what you told 'em."

3. Although I don't speak Janpanese (Chinese, Korean, etc.), there are actually two different levels of writing by which writers present written material in these languages. In other words, writing for a youthful audience relies on simple sentences, direct and directive information, and use of specific detail. If the audience is mature, however, written material is presented more subtly, and readers are expected to draw their own conclusions. In U.S. academic prose, however, the audience expects written material to be direct and specific. The use of detail is prized as clear evidence that the writer's ideas are valid.

4. Although I do not speak Thai, a paragraph of academic material in Thai usually begins with an anecdote, has some specific detail, and occasionally finishes with a statement of overall intent in the last sentence. In U.S. academic English, the general paragraph is reversed: the overall idea is stated first; then specific detail is given to explain, clarify, and support that main idea.

USING AUTHENTIC WRITING TASKS

Once the students trust their teachers, the rest is relatively straightforward. First, students should study authentic, commonly assigned writing tasks such as the critique, the short answer or essay test, and the research paper to determine the purpose(s) of each assignment and the expectations of the academic audience. Teachers must act as informants, as builders of schema, for their students (Carrell, 1986; Chimombo, 1987; Johns, 1987). Initially, they must gather academic assignments from across the curriculum, assess the purposes and expectations, and present them to the class. The students should study these authentic, cross-curricular writing tasks, (a) learning to identify the purpose of each, (b) investigating the specific demands of each, and (c) analyzing the rhetorical conventions expected by the academic audience. In the examples that follow, key words and phrases that are central to the task are italicized. Each could serve as a springboard for discussion; if student writing samples that successfully fulfilled each assignment were also available for study, students could gain additional confidence in their abilities to address each task.

Writing Assignments

Economics short answer test (undergraduate):

Define 4 of the following terms in *1 or 2 sentences:*

A. Fixed input
B. Pure profit
C. Elasticity of supply
D. Variable cost
E. Marginal product

Freshman composition placement examination (1 hour critique):
Read the following passage. In an organized and detailed *essay, summarize* its main ideas. Then *explain why* you agree or disagree with what the article says. *Support* your agreement/disagreement with specific *examples* from your experience or outside reading.

Biology test for undergraduate majors (1 hour):
You are the only doctor in a small, rural town. People of all ages begin coming into your clinic with the following symptoms:

Headache
Fever of 102° F.
Aches in joints
Swelling in the abdomen

The people in the village are not familiar with the germ theory of disease, and they are very frightened. Write an *explanation* of the *disease process* for these people.

Second, the students should have ample opportunity to identify and practice procedures that will assist them in collecting and evaluating materials for writing assignments. Again, the teacher must act as the informant by providing oral communication activities that will allow students to practice acceptable ways of gathering information for their academic writing tasks. For example, what questions would a professor consider legitimate about an assignment, and how and when can students ask those questions? Possible examples for discussion or role playing:

1. About a writing assignment (to the professor):

NOT "I don't understand what you want."
BUT "This is the first paper/review/report I have written at a U.S. university.

May I make an appointment to talk with you during your office hours?"
2. In the library (to the librarian):

NOT "I have to write a paper, and it's due tomorrow. What should I do?"
NOT "Find these books for me."
BUT "I've found three books about the topic of cellular cofferdams, but I can't find *this* one. Could you please help me?"

Teachers might also help their students learn how to consult with other students, including NS, who are working on the same assignments. The most significant barrier for NNS is summoning the courage to initiate communication with classmates. Teachers can prepare students for such encounters by supplying appropriate conventions and oral language, with role playing, or with "What's wrong with this dialog?" discussions.

NOT "Tell me what the teacher said."
BUT "Hi. I'm [NAME] in your [x] class. Do you have the assignment for tomorrow's class?"
NOT "What means this?"
BUT "Do you understand what the professor said about [x]?"

Finally, students need to learn about ways to use their experiences as they analyze and execute writing assignments; that is, they should discover how to use their cultural backgrounds to advantage in approaching academic writing tasks. Possible scenarios for discussion.

1. For a freshman composition assignment about dating or dormitory life, students could use comparison/contrast about what they have observed in the U.S. (with clear qualifications about their limited experiences) with what they know occurs in their countries. Interviews with native speakers in their composition classes could add to the U.S. experiences, and specific detail about their home country experiences will certainly be of interest to their U.S. audience.

2. For a major field writing task pertaining, for example, to irrigation techniques, students should use the information they have learned in that irrigation class (and, if the assignment requires, read articles outside of class to increase their information base); in addition, they can relate the discussion (analysis/report) to the problems and/or solutions of similar situations in their countries. Again, the home country information will be of interest to the audience, and the students will be applying what they are learning—the essence of relevance in international education.

USING RHETORICAL AND
SYNTACTIC CONVENTIONS

Next, teachers should present another group of strategies, this time rhetorical and syntactic (cf. Brodkey, 1983; Hall, Hawkey, Kenny, & Storer, 1986; Jenkins & Hinds, 1987; Martin, 1983; Smith & Reid, 1983). For example, students must learn basic and alternative formats that are expected in academic assignments; possibilities include:

1. The basic format of the summary with its necessary balance and objectivity (cf. Johns, 1987).
2. The formats for English composition: the five-paragraph expository theme, the argumentative essay, and the response to written material (cf. Reid, 1988).
3. The basic organization of the experimental research paper (introduction, literature review, methods and material, data, results, and conclusion) and alternative organizational forms of nonexperimental research papers (cf. Swales, 1987).

In addition to these rhetorical strategies, students should also begin to look closely at syntactic forms that are commonly used in U.S. academic prose. Some questions and exercises to stimulate awareness and discussion:

1. Underline the verbs in this abstract. How many are passive voice? Why is passive voice used so extensively?
2. Are there personal pronouns in this journal article? Why or why not?
3. Look at the introduction to these three articles. What verb tense(s) is/are used in each introduction? Is there a pattern?

In order to give students necessary practice in rhetorical and syntactic strategies, teachers can design initial assignments that parallel the elements of academic assignments but that are easier to produce. For example, using relatively simple reading material—a short controversial article that is not culture bound or field specific—for all students to critique will allow students to concentrate on communicating with the audience. The assignment below is representative of such tasks; because all of the students begin with the same information and the same directions, they do not have to develop additional information to construct their responses. Instead, they can focus, either individually or in group work, on the strategies and writing techniques that will result in acceptable critiques.

Assignment

Directions: A recent magazine article discussed a new trend among young adults in the United States, their tendency to return to their parents' home to live after graduating from university. The following is a brief excerpt from the article:

> Until now, American parents have exhorted their young to . . . go to college, go to work—in short, to get out. But inflation, recession, and rising divorce rates are now persuading young people to . . . move home.

Below are two letters which responded to the article. Read the letters. Then choose the letter you *disagree* with. Write an essay that states your reasons for disagreement, and support those reasons with specific detail from your reading or personal experience.

Dear Sir:

    Children who return home to live with their parents after they graduate from the university are acting in a way that is seriously detrimental to their personal growth and development. Even when live-at-home young adults are contributing money and labor to the household, the fact is that parents provide psychological protection; consequently, the child will not take as many risks, make as many errors, or become as independent. All of these are essential components of learning about life and about oneself.

    Furthermore, parents who allow children to return home after they are adults may be using their

Dear Sir:

    During the past generation in America, the family has deteriorated; children left home at the earliest possible age and became independent in every way. Now they are returning to that sacred institution. The giving, the sharing, the love and the loyalty of that foundation of society have not been lost after all! Both parents and children are finally realizing their mutual need: the parents to care for the children, and, later, the children to care for their parents.

    In fact, often the returning child is a helpful adult who can provide companionship and sometimes additional financial own loneliness to divert attention from their own problems. Therefore, living at home after graduating from college or getting a job is a process of returning to childhood that ultimately is bad for both parent and child.

Sincerely

Dr. Paul King
Chicago, IL

support for the parents. Moreover, the selfishness of the 1970s may now fade; family ties will most certainly be made stronger. More importantly, family solidarity may eventually be reflected in the rest of American society. After all, in order to get along with the rest of the world, you have to start someplace—getting along with your parent may be the starting point.

Anne Hughes
Denver, CO

Similar practice in writing a research paper also requires the teacher to be an informant. To ease the information overload and give the students a change to concentrate on form rather than content, the teacher can provide the students with common data, then demonstrate techniques of integration and referencing, and have students practice those techniques, perhaps in pairs or small groups. Horowitz (1986) offers the following exercises on the reintegration of material, the "encoding of data into academic English":

1. Students are presented with a number of very similar short essays written in such a way that although they are all based on the same data, they are in fact responses to different questions. The students' task is either to match each answer to the correct question or to select the most appropriate answer to one question. The main value of such an exercise would come in the discussion of why one answer was thought to be more appropriate than another. This would focus attention directly on different ways the same data can be arranged and the reasons for arranging them in different ways.

2. A variation of the above makes use of short student essays, all written from the same data in response to the same issue. Students are required to use all the data provided, so the resulting essays vary mainly in how the data are integrated. Students then read their classmates' responses and discuss the strong and the weak points of each essay. To ensure that attention is paid to information structuring rather than to grammar, teachers might want to provide sentence-level corrections before the essays are examined in the class.

3. Since reorganizing data is at least partly a matter of changing the order in which they are presented, students can be given a numbered

list of facts and a question. Their task is to choose the order in which to present the facts in response to the question. Here again, because there is no correct answer, the value of the exercise would be in the discussion of why a given order of presentation was chosen. (pp. 458–489)

Finally, to gain experience in using the rhetorical strategies appropriate for technical writing, students might work individually on a detailed assignment that is content based (Celce-Murcia, 1987) such as the one that follows (Kroll, 1987).

Assignment

Directions: Think of two contrasting terms related to your major field of study. Write a three-part essay based on explaining what one term means in contrast/comparison to the other closely related or quite opposite terms. Your audience might be students new in the field who don't know very much about your subject. Or the audience might be professional peers for whom you are presenting a prelude to a larger discussion. Your essay structure should resemble the following:

Part 1. Introduce the topic briefly and identify the key terms you want to discuss.

Part 2. Focus on explanation of the following sort: "X is not like Y in that. . . . A student must bear in mind that X is really Z and Y is really Q. . . ." Your aim is to contrast the focus term with another term that is easily confused or is not truly related.

Part 3. Concentrate on explaining how your focus can be seen as somehow connected to the contrasting term. You might begin your paragraph with a statement such as, "On the other hand, X and Y have certain . . . in common." Some suggested terms:

Chemistry: organic chemistry vs. inorganic chemistry

Biology: botany vs. zoology

Economics: microeconomics vs. macroeconomics

Engineering: electronics vs. electrical engineering

Philosophy: metaphysics vs. empiricism

Computer Science: hardware vs. software

EVALUATION

Finally, teachers must be prepared to evaluate student writing in light of the anticipated audience. More than simply marking errors and commenting on content, teachers must play the role of the academic readers their students will encounter. In order to do this, they must thoroughly understand what is expected in a variety of academic assignments; just as important, they must be able to identify unacceptable or inappropriate prose from the perspective of the academic reader. Most composition teachers are experienced in evaluating both the rhetorical and the syntactic aspects of student prose. But the next important step is to be able to prioritize the errors as they relate to successful communication; for example, since the expected form is important to the academic audience, both global and discrete questions about form need to be asked—and answered.

1. Is the student following an expected and acceptable format?
2. If not, where does he or she deviate? For what reasons?
3. Is the deviation successful? That is, what is the resulting impact on the academic reader?
4. If the deviation is not acceptable to the academic audience, exactly what should the student do to repair the break in communication?

In terms of syntax errors, prioritizing is even more important. Because L2 errors are almost always going to occur in ESL writing, students must know which of their errors are critical to successful communication and which are not. Recent survey research concerning error gravity—that is, which second language errors interfere with communication and/or irritate the U.S. academic reader—indicates that it is possible to prioritize syntax errors (cf. Green & Hecht, 1985; Khalil, 1985; Kroll, 1982; Lindstrom, 1981). In particular, Vann et al.'s survey of academic readers across the curriculum (1984) reveals that

> . . . respondents tended to be more accepting of those errors commonly made by native speakers of English (e.g., spelling, comma splices, or pronoun agreement) as well as those errors in English which linguists often term the most "idiosyncratic" (e.g., articles and prepositions). On the other hand, respondents judged as least acceptable those errors which, for the most part, are global and/or are relatively rare violations for native speakers (e.g., word order, *it* deletion, tense, relative clause errors, and word choice). (p. 432)

Following the teacher's identification and prioritizing of student writing problems, the next logical step for the teacher is to communicate that knowledge of appropriate responses and acceptable prose to the students, to explain the problems, and to suggest changes that will result in more successful communication. Besides discussion, one excellent way of having the students discover differences in the quality of completed writing tasks is to train *them* to become the academic audience and to have them evaluate writing samples. Perhaps the easiest and quickest form of evaluation training is to teach students to score papers holistically. There are several ways to organize such a training session:

1. The TOEFL Test of Written English has a fully developed scoring guide and "benchmark" papers. These benchmarks are student samples of the thirty-minute writing task at each of the scoring ranges, 1 to 6. Students can see and articulate the differences between a 1 and 6 paper easily; training at the 3 to 4 level takes a little more time.[2]
2. Teachers may have already developed their own scoring guides for placement or exit exam writing samples. Students using these guides with benchmark papers will gain insight into the expectations of their teachers as well as learn more about the expectations of future U.S. academic audiences.
3. Students can design their own scoring guides. By reading through sample student papers (probably written by students not in the present class), the students can, with assistance from their teachers, develop criteria for a scoring guide. This process takes more time than the other two, but the benefits, in terms of awareness and understanding of expectations, are great.

CONCLUSION

In short, writing teachers of NNS must be pragmatists. They must discover what will be expected in the academic contexts their students will encounter, and they must provide their students with the writing skills and the cultural information that will allow the students to perform successfully. They should guide their students explicitly, not just in the prewriting, writing, and revising protocols that have proven worthwhile strategies for NS, but also in the prewriting processes of discovering the purposes of academic writing assignments (i.e., the intentions of the professors assigning the tasks), and of developing strategies to meet the expectations of the academic audience in terms of content, of form, and of language. Demystifying the writing process and its resulting product can offer a variety of opportunities to put these new schema to work: the

---

[2] The TOEFL Writing Examination Evaluation Guide, as well as sample benchmark papers, are available upon request from the TOEFL Program, Educational Testing Service, Princeton, New Jersey 08541.

students will consequently become better able to identify, collect, and articulate acceptable written material. For NNS, this cross-cultural and cross-curricular knowledge will enable them to understand "what the professor wants" and feel secure about being able to fulfill those expectations.

REFERENCES

Blanton, L. L. (1987). Reshaping ESL students' perspectives of writing. *ELT Journal, 41,* 112–118.

Brodkey, D. (1983). An expectancy exercise in cohesion. *TESL Reporter, 16*(3), 43–45.

Carrell, P. L. (1986). Text as interaction: Some implications of text analysis and reading research for ESL composition. In U. Connor & R. B. Kaplan (Eds.), *Writing across languages: Analysis of L2 text* (pp. 55–72). Reading, MA: Addison-Wesley.

Carrell, P. L. (1987, March). *Readability in ESL: A schemaperspective.* Paper presented at the 21st Annual TESOL Convention, Miami.

Carlson, S., & Bridgeman, B. (1983). *Survey of academic writing tasks required for graduate and undergraduate foreign students (TOEFL Research Report #15).* Princeton, N.J.: Educational Testing Service.

Carlson, S., Bridgeman, B., Camp, R., & Waanders, J. (1985). *Relationship of admission test scores to writing performance of native and nonnative speakers of English (TOEFL Research Report #19).* Princeton, NJ: Educational Testing Service.

Celce-Murcia, M. (1987, June). *New concerns in English as a foreign language.* ATESL Plenary speech at the 39th Annual NAFSA Convention, Long Beach, CA.

Chimombo, M. (1987). Towards reality in the classroom. *ELT Journal, 41,* 204–210.

Connor, U., & Kaplan, R. B. (1987). *Writing across languages: Analysis of L2 text.* Reading, MA: Addison-Wesley.

Doushaq, M. H. (1986). An investigation into stylistic errors of Arab students learning English for academic purposes. *ESP Journal, 5*(1), 27–39.

Green, P. S., & Hecht, K. (1985). Native and nonnative evaluation of learner's errors in written discourse. *System, 13*(2), 77–97.

Hall, D., Hawkey, R., Kenny, B., & Storer, G. (1986). Patterns of thought in scientific writing: A course in information structuring for engineering students. *ESP Journal, 5*(2), 147–160.

Hinds, J. (1983). Contrastive rhetoric: Japanese and English. *Text, 3,* 183–195.

Horowitz, D. (1986). What professors actually require: Academic tasks for the ESL classroom. *TESOL Quarterly, 20,* 445–462.

Jenkins, S., & Hinds, J. (1987). Business letter-writing: English, French, and Japanese. *TESOL Quarterly, 21,* 327–349.

Johns, A. (1986). The ESL student and the revision process: Some insights from schema theory. *Journal of Basic Writing, 5*(2), 70–80.

Johns, A. (1987). On assigning summaries: Some suggestions and cautions. *TEC-FORS, 10*(2), 1–5.

Kaplan, R. B. (Gen. Ed.). (1983). *Annual Review of Applied Linguistics, 3*. Rowley, MA: Newbury House.

Khalil, A. (1985). Communicative error evaluation: Native speakers' evaluation and interpretation of written errors of Arab EFL learners. *TESOL Quarterly, 19,* 335–351.

Kroll, B. (1982). *Levels of error in ESL composition*. Unpublished doctoral dissertation, University of Southern California, Los Angeles.

Kroll, B. (1987, March). *Graduate students in ESL writing classes*. Paper presented at the meeting of the Conference on College Composition and Communication, Atlanta.

Liebman-Kleine, J. (1987). Teaching and researching invention: Using ethnography in ESL writing classes. *ELT Journal, 41*(2), 104–111.

Lindstrom, M. (1981). *Native speaker reaction to second language errors in academic prose*. Unpublished master's thesis, Colorado State University, Fort Collins.

Martin, A. (1983, March). *ESL students' perceptions of L1-L2 differences in organizing ideas*. Paper presented at the 17th Annual TESOL Convention, Toronto.

Matalene, C. (1985). Contrastive rhetoric: An American writing teacher in China. *College English, 47,* 789–808.

Murray, D. (1987). *Instructor's manual for write to learn,* (2nd ed.). New York: Holt Rinehart & Winston.

Reid, J. (1988). *The process of composition* (2nd ed.). Englewood Cliffs, NJ: Prentice-Hall.

Smith, V., & Reid, J. (1983). Audience expectation exercises for ESL writing classes. *Curriculum Clearing House Newsletter, 3*(2), 18.

Swales, J. (1987). Utilizing the literatures in teaching the research paper. *TESOL Quarterly, 21,* 41–68.

Vann, R., Meyer, D., & Lorenz, F. (1984). Error gravity: A study of faculty opinions of ESL errors. *TESOL Quarterly, 18,* 427–440.

CHAPTER 15

Writing Apprehension and Second Language Writers

Bruce W. Gungle and Victoria Taylor
University of Arizona

The current-traditional paradigm is a ghost still hovering in English as a second language (ESL) writing classes. Many instructors believe writers should know what they are going to say before they write; that the composing process is linear; that teaching grammar, then the sentence, then the paragraph, and finally the essay—the building block approach—is an effective method of writing instruction.

But grammatically perfect sentences have little power if they do not clearly and forcefully express intelligent ideas. The history of research into the effects of L1 grammar instruction on writing quality has shown that:

> [there is] no reason to expect the study of grammar or mechanics to have any substantial effect on the writing process or on writing ability as reflected in the quality of written products. Experimental studies have shown that they have little or none. These findings have been consistent for many years. (Hillocks, 1986, p. 227)

And surely even novice writing instructors can intuit, as Robert Pirsig does in *Zen and the Art of Motorcycle Maintenance,* that:

> the old slap-on-the-fingers-if-your-modifiers-were-caught-dangling stuff. . . . *Correct* spelling, *correct* punctuation, *correct* grammar. . . . [The] hundreds of itsy-bitsy rules. . . . No one [can] remember all that stuff and concentrate on what he [is] trying to write about. (1974, p. 162)

Apparently not, for the paradigmatic debate still rages all around us. And now we have yet another bit of mud to sling at the old paradigm: that a focus on form—on grammar, punctuation, and generally prescriptive writing—most likely raises the level of ESL students' writing apprehension. This in turn can lead to cognitive overload and prevent ideas from getting on paper (Roen, Taylor, & Mangelsdorf, 1987).

WRITING APPREHENSION IN THE FIRST LANGUAGE

"Writing apprehension" (WA) was first used by Daly and Miller (1975b) to describe the phenomenon certain individuals experience when confronted by a task that requires writing. Based on the communication apprehension research available at the time (see Daly & Miller, 1975b), Daly and Miller posited that there are individuals who have a high degree of writing apprehension (HWAs) and others who have a low degree of writing apprehension (LWAs). HWAs avoid writing when possible, and when forced to write do so with great anxiety. They not only expect to fail at writing but generally do fail, in large part because they get so little practice at it. Daly and Miller suspected that in classroom situations HWAs fail to turn compositions in, fail to attend class when writing will be required, and seldom voluntarily enroll in classes where writing will be demanded. HWAs also seek occupations which they feel involve little writing. Daly and Miller then went on to develop the Daly-Miller Writing Apprehension Test (DM-WAT).

The DM-WAT is a 26-item self-report instrument. The statements were selected from an initial pool of 63 modeled after those incorporated in instruments already in use in the measurement of communication-related apprehension (see Daly & Miller, 1975b). The 63-item instrument was administered to 164 undergraduates at West Virginia University, and through a set of careful statistical procedures, 26 items were selected to constitute the DM-WAT. Examinees respond to each statement on a 5-point Likert-type scale ranging from strongly agree (1) to strongly disagree (5) (Daly & Miller, 1975b).

Subsequent first language (L1) research utilizing the DM-WAT found HWAs approach writing much differently and complete writing tasks less successfully than LWAs (Daly & Miller, 1975a; Selfe, 1984). They exhibit a weaker working knowledge of writing skills beyond the grammatical level (Daly, 1978), produce essays significantly shorter and less syntactically complex than LWAs, do not develop their ideas as well, put less information into each communicative unit, and use a more restrictive repertoire of syntactic constructions than LWAs (Faigley, Daly, & Witte, 1981).

Daly and Miller (1975c) found negative correlations between level of WA and willingness to take an advanced course in writing, and WA and students' success expectations, and a positive correlation between WA and tendency to be placed in a remedial class. WA also correlates with gender; males are significantly more apprehensive than females. Of interest, each of the four dependent variables mentioned shows a significantly higher correlation with WAT scores than with Scholastic Aptitude Test verbal scores. Daly and Shamo also found that HWA undergraduates find desirable those occupations (1976) and college majors (1978) that are perceived as low in writing demand, and concluded that WA is a factor in career and academic decision making.

Thus, the available research points to the restrictions WA can place upon an individual. In essence, highly apprehensive writers perceive that they have fewer career and academic options open to them (Daly & Shamo, 1976, 1978) than do moderate or low apprehensive writers. These findings indicate the instructor's need to utilize pedagogical strategies that will reduce the fears of highly apprehensive individuals. As Daly and Miller note, if a student has a negative predisposition toward writing, it matters little how skilled he or she is at it (1975c). In order for such students to approach their potential as writers, instructors must first recognize that apprehension toward writing can be a serious impediment to learning and advancement inside and outside the classroom, and then take steps to make writing a positive, low-stress experience.

THE L2 RECORD

While there is a body of literature on affective factors in second language (L2) acquisition (see Brown, 1987, for one review), L2 research into WA is much scantier, and it is not yet clear what measurement of WA can tell us here. Taylor, Johnson, and Gungle (1987) examined writing apprehension in an L2 setting. In a pilot study, using a version of the Daly-Miller WAT tailored for ESL students (see Figure 15.1), they found a significant negative correlation ($r = .74$, $p < .01$) between ESL WA and an expressed desire to enroll in an advanced writing class. This finding corroborated those of Daly and Shamo (1978), and Daly and Miller (1975c). However, no significant relationships were found between ESL WA and perceived writing demand in the students' majors, nor between ESL WA and concern with *how* one writes (attention to form) as opposed to *what* one writes.

Zamel (1982) notes that inordinate attention to form leads to continual disruptions of the writer's discovery process, which often leads to writer's block and, finally, HWA. According to Rose (1980, 1984), one behavior

Figure 15.1. The English as a Second Language Writing Apprehension Test (Adapted from the Daly-Miller Writing Apprehension Test, Daly & Miller, 1975b.) Matric. #:_____

DIRECTIONS: Below is a series of statements about writing. Please indicate the degree to which each statement applies to you by circling whether you (1) strongly agree, (2) agree, (3) agree somewhat, (4) disagree somewhat, (5) disagree, (6) strongly disagree with the statement. Some of these statements may seem repetitious; just take your time and try to be as honest as possible. Thank you for your cooperation in this matter.

1. I avoid writing in English.   1 2 3 4 5 6
2. I have no fear of my English writing being evaluated.   1 2 3 4 5 6
3. I look forward to writing down my ideas in English.   1 2 3 4 5 6
4. I am afraid of writing essays in English when I know they will be evaluated.   1 2 3 4 5 6
5. Taking an English composition class is a very frightening experience.   1 2 3 4 5 6
6. Handing in a composition written in English makes me feel good.   1 2 3 4 5 6
7. My mind seems to go blank when I start to work on a composition in English.   1 2 3 4 5 6
8. Expressing ideas through writing in English seems to be a waste of time.   1 2 3 4 5 6
9. I would enjoy sending my English writing to magazines to be evaluated and published.   1 2 3 4 5 6
10. I like to write my ideas down in English.   1 2 3 4 5 6
11. I feel confident in my ability to clearly express my ideas when writing in English.   1 2 3 4 5 6
12. I like to have my friends read what I have written in English.   1 2 3 4 5 6
13. I'm nervous about writing in English.   1 2 3 4 5 6
14. People seem to enjoy what I write in English.   1 2 3 4 5 6
15. I enjoy writing in English.   1 2 3 4 5 6
16. I never seem to be able to clearly write down my ideas in English.   1 2 3 4 5 6
17. Writing in English is a lot of fun.   1 2 3 4 5 6
18. I expect to do poorly in English composition classes even before I enter them.   1 2 3 4 5 6
19. I like seeing my thoughts on paper in English.   1 2 3 4 5 6
20. Discussing my English writing with others is an enjoyable experience.   1 2 3 4 5 6
21. I have a terrible time organizing my ideas in an English composition course.   1 2 3 4 5 6
22. When I hand in an English composition I know I'm going to do poorly.   1 2 3 4 5 6
23. It's easy for me to write good compositions in English.   1 2 3 4 5 6
24. I don't think I write as well in English as most people.   1 2 3 4 5 6
25. I don't like my English compositions to be evaluated.   1 2 3 4 5 6
26. I'm no good at writing in English.   1 2 3 4 5 6

associated with blocking is anxiety, which can lead to confusion, frustration, or anger. Some blockers can produce only a few sentences; others may produce more, but only through repeated false starts, repetitions, or fragments. Students finally come to distrust their writing abilities and develop an aversion to the composing process in general (Rose, 1980) or, in our terms, become highly apprehensive writers.

Raimes (1984) believes that "we have trapped our students within . . . the prison of the word and the sentence" (p. 83) and that we must now "emphasize composing and not just ESL. When we do, much of the necessary work on grammar, sentence structure, and rhetoric begins to take care of itself" (p. 91). Adamson (in press), in a discussion of language variation, suggests that excessive monitoring for grammatical accuracy can be detrimental, especially if students are trying to apply complex rules which are not yet part of their basic L2 competence.

Interviews with ESL writers generally confirm these views. Zamel (1983) found that one student (the least skilled of six she interviewed) was anxious about writing in English because she was overly concerned about grammar and "getting it correct because [ESL writing] teachers care about that" (1983, p. 178). Taylor, Johnson, and Gungle (1987) interviewed four ESL-HWAs as part of their pilot study. Three of the four felt that teachers are more concerned with students' grammar and "being correct" than they are with content. They were concerned that they can't "say what they think," and that the teacher will "point out mistakes."

Before the students in the Taylor, Johnson, and Gungle study attended the University of Arizona, most of their English writing experience was limited to summaries and short, descriptive essays written in English classes at schools or language institutes in their native countries. According to the students, the major emphasis in these schools and institutes is on grammar, vocabulary, and reading. There is very little written or oral communication. HWA for these students may come from a lack of experience with English communication as much as from a classroom emphasis on prescriptive forms and mechanics. Of course, a classroom focused primarily on prescriptive forms at the very least supplants opportunities for students to gain English communication experience.

A benefit of content-focused writing instruction is that it provides added opportunities for positive teacher response. Selfe (1984) found that HWAs attribute their anxiety to a lack of confidence in their writing skills and a fear of their writing receiving a negative evaluation from a teacher. Daly (1985) has observed that females have significantly lower levels of writing apprehension than males because "females receive more positive teacher reactions to their writing than do males" (p. 47). So it may follow that ESL writing instruction that offers more opportunities for positive teacher response can result in lower levels of WA. A content-centered approach can do just that—almost anyone given a little prodding can come up with an idea that deserves congratulating—while a focus on grammar and form, with their labyrinths of rules and irregularities, offers instructors just the opposite; the opportunity to get out the red pen and bury the student's self-esteem with negative feedback.

To summarize, then, scholars in the field agree that an overemphasis on grammar, sentence structure, and prescribed forms at the expense of content-based communication is detrimental to ESL acquisition. Upon closer examination, their work also indicates that such a focus can lead to higher levels of WA. Positive teacher response, on the other hand, appears to lead to lower levels of WA. Thus our primary research hypotheses are:

1. A positive correlation exists between ESL WA and attention to form.
2. A negative correlation exists between ESL WA and attention to content.

We proposed two additional hypotheses to determine whether relationships confirmed through research with L1 populations would hold for an ESL population:

3. A negative correlation exists between ESL WA and the perceived writing requirements of ESL students' majors. (That is, students with high levels of ESL WA perceive the writing requirements of their majors as low, while students with low levels of ESL WA perceive the writing requirements of their majors as high.)
4. A negative correlation exists between ESL WA and ESL students' interest in advanced writing classes. (That is, students with high levels of ESL WA express less desire to enroll in an advanced English class, while students with low levels of ESL WA express greater desire to enroll in an advanced English class.)

It also seemed reasonable to assume that differences in cultural and/or language backgrounds would lead native users of one written code to have greater ESL WA than native users of a different code. Hence, our final hypothesis was:

5. A significant difference in ESL WA exists between native users of different written codes.

THE STUDIES

We carried out two studies, one in spring 1986 and one in summer 1987. The two studies are presented separately below.

STUDY 1: SPRING 1986

Method

Subjects. Subjects were 210 international students enrolled in ESL composition courses at the University of Arizona who were willing to participate in our study and whose instructors made class time available to us for testing. No students refused to participate in the study. Ten students did not complete the ESL-WAT sufficiently for data analysis.

Undergraduate ESL students enrolled at the University of Arizona must take and pass a minimum of two semesters of freshman composition for international students (English 107 and 108). Students whose skill level does not meet the minimum requirement for entrance into English 107 must first pass English 106, a preparatory course. Our population for this test included 41 students who were enrolled in English 106; 78 enrolled in 107; and 81 enrolled in 108. Of the 200 students, 70 identified their L1 as Arabic, 22 as Chinese, 35 as Malay, 27 as Spanish, and 46 as a variety of other languages, of which there were no more than 5 of any one language.

Materials. We constructed an ESL version of the DM-WAT (see Figure 15.1). Based on the assumption that the 26 statements of the DM-WAT would be as relevant for an L2 population as they have proved to be for L1 populations, we simply modified the DM-WAT in two ways. First, in order to communicate the notion that all statements referred only to a student's use of English, we revised each of the 26 items to include a reference to writing in English:

DM-WAT Version:
- I feel confident in my ability to clearly express my ideas in writing.

ESL-WAT Version:
- I feel confident in my ability to clearly express my ideas when writing in English.

Second, we provided students with a 6-point scale rather than the 5-point scale in order to avoid noncommittal responses.

In order to test hypotheses 1, 2, 3, and 4, we created a second, 3-item instrument:

1. The English writing requirements of my major are great (tests H-3).
2. I would be interested in enrolling in an advanced writing class in English (tests H-4).
3. When I write in English, I am more concerned with *how* I say something than with *what* I say (tests H-1 and H-2).

Students responded to these 3 statements on an 8-point scale. A 1 indicated very strong agreement; an 8 indicated very strong disagreement.

To test hypothesis 5, all students were asked to provide their native language on the answer sheet.

Procedure

We tested 210 students and obtained exactly 200 complete sets of data. In addition, 4 students identified as HWAs were later interviewed by questionnaire.

All testing took place at the beginning of class periods. The ESL-WAT was administered by one of the authors or the class instructor, depending upon instructor preference. In all instances administrators followed detailed, formal instructions. Appropriate mode of response was explained to each class in detail on the chalkboard before the test began. Finally, each statement was also read aloud by the administrator. Administration of the ESL-WAT took approximately thirty minutes. Testing the various class sections took three weeks.

Results

A series of Pearson Product-Moment Correlations were run on the data. As predicted, significant negative correlations were obtained between ESL-WAT and responses to statements 1 ("The English writing requirements of my major are great") and 2 ("I would be interested in enrolling in an advanced writing class in English"). That is, students with relatively high apprehension perceived low writing requirements for their majors, and they indicated unwillingness to enroll in advanced writing classes. However, while there was a small negative correlation between ESL-WAT and statement 3 ("When I write in English, I am more concerned with *how* I say something than with *what* I say"), that correlation was not significant. (See Table 15.1.)

Two separate one-way analysis of variance tests revealed no significant differences in level of ESL WA across languages nor across level of writing course (106, 107, 108).

Discussion

The significant correlations between statement 1 and ESL-WAT scores and statement 2 and ESL-WAT scores is consistent with the findings from research on L1 populations: Students whose scores showed high apprehension tended to indicate that they avoid situations that will require writing in English.

The nonsignificant negative correlation between statement 3 and level of ESL WA does not confirm our expectation that apprehension and overattention to form are related, nor does it support the observations and interview results reported above. We suspected that confounding variables may have played a part in the mixed results; students may not have understood statement 3 or simply not read carefully and marked off the same end of the scale as they had for statements 1 and 2. Therefore we revised the 3-item instrument and 15 months later tested a second set of students.

STUDY 2: SUMMER 1987

Method

Subjects. In the second study, subjects were 74 students enrolled in ESL composition courses at the University of Arizona in the summer of 1987.

TABLE 15.1. PEARSON PRODUCT-MOMENT CORRELATIONS: STUDY 1, SPRING 1986

Statement:	Major Writing Requirements 1	Willingness to Take Courses 2	Focus on Form 3
ESL-WAT	$r = .21$ $n = 200$ $*p < .01$	$r = .30$ $n = 200$ $*p < .01$	$r = -.08$ $n = 200$ $p = .13$
Major writing requirements		$r = .23$ $n = 200$ $*p < .01*$	$r = .18$ $n = 200$ $p < .01$
Willingness to take courses			$r = .23$ $n = 200$ $*p < .01$

*Denotes significance at the .01 level.

These were all the students enrolled in ESL courses at that time who attended class during the testing period. Of these, 25 students were enrolled in English 106; 12 in 107; 15 in 108; and 22 in English 407a, a required course for graduate international students who have TOEFL scores below 500. Students receive a grade in English 407a, but it is not used in calculating the student's cumulative grade-point average. Seven students identified their L1 as Arabic, 33 as Chinese, 5 as Portuguese, and 25 as other languages, with no more than 4 of any one language. Three students indicated two native languages (none English), and one did not indicate an L1.

Materials. We used the same 26-item ESL-WAT described for Study 1. To test hypotheses 3 and 4, however, we revised our 3-item instrument from Study 1 to a 4-item instrument for Study 2:

1. The English writing requirements of my major are great.
2. When writing in English I am most concerned with grammar and form.
3. I would be interested in enrolling in an advanced writing class in English.
4. When writing in English I am most concerned with content and ideas.

Again, an 8-point scale was used for responses, with 1 indicating strong agreement, and 8 indicating strong disagreement. A line at the bottom of the 4-item instrument requested students to provide their native language in order to test hypothesis 5.

Procedure. Of the 74 students tested, we received complete sets of data from 73. All testing was done by individual class instructors who included one of the authors. Hand-scored instruments were used this time. Statements were not read aloud to the students. Completion of the revised ESL-WAT took approximately 20 minutes. Testing the four classes took one week.

Results

Pearson Product-Moment Correlations were run on the data. Statement 4 ("When writing in English I am most concerned with content and ideas") was significantly, positively correlated with statement 1 ("The English writing requirements of my major are great"), with statement 2 ("When writing in English I am most concerned with grammar and form"), and with statement 3 ("I would be interested in enrolling in an advanced writing class in English"). Statement 4, however, to a significant degree was negatively correlated with WA: students concerned with content and ideas had low apprehension. While ESL-WAT did not significantly correlate with any other variable, there was a significant correlation between statements 1 ("The English writing requirements of my major are great") and 3 ("I would be interested in enrolling in an advanced writing class in English") (See Table 15.2.)

Two separate one-way analysis of variance tests revealed no significant differences in level of ESL WA, either across languages or across writing courses.

Discussion

Again, the results were mixed. While writing apprehension does show a negative correlation with "concern with content and ideas" when writing (statement 4), it does not show a significant positive correlation with "concern with grammar and form" (statement 2). Furthermore, statements 2 and 4 show a significant positive correlation; students who indicated they are "most

TABLE 15.2. PEARSON PRODUCT-MOMENT CORRELATIONS: STUDY 2, SUMMER 1987

	Major Writing Requirements	Focus on Form	Willingness to Take Courses	Focus on Content
Statement:	1	2	3	4
ESL-WAT	$r = .0830$	$r = -.0974$	$r = .1035$	$r = .2632$
	$n = 73$	$n = 74$	$n = 73$	$n = 73$
	$p = .243$	$p = .205$	$p = .192$	$*p = .012$
Major writing requirements		$r = .1012$	$r = .2151$	$r = .3199$
		$n = 73$	$n = 73$	$n = 73$
		$p = .197$	$*p = .034$	$**p < .01$
Focus on form			$r = .1758$	$r = .3281$
			$n = 73$	$n = 73$
			$p = .068$	$**p < .01$
Willingness to take advanced courses				$p = .2217$
				$n = 73$
				$*p = .030$

*Denotes significance at the .05 level.
**Denotes significance at the .01 level.

concerned with content and ideas" when they write, indicated that they are also "most concerned with grammar and form." It appears that some students did not fully understand the connotative differences between *most* and *very*, and thus did not recognize the mutual exclusiveness of these statements. A fifth significant correlation was found between statements 1 and 3. In general, the results indicate that students who are interested in one aspect of writing tend to be interested in all aspects of writing.

On the other hand, ESL-WAT scores did not significantly correlate with the perceived writing requirements of students' majors (statement 1) nor with students' willingness to enroll in an advanced writing class (statement 3). Because of the lack of a strong association, it appears likely that the ESL-WAT may not prove useful for detecting relationships with small samples, such as a typical class.

GENERAL DISCUSSION

Further research is needed to examine the ways in which an ESL composition class focused on form (mechanics, grammar instruction, and prescriptive essay techniques) relates to the writing apprehension of ESL students. The results of Study 2 provide some evidence of important relationships among several relevant variables. First, a significant negative correlation exists between ESL WA and a focus on content and ideas while writing. Second, a significant positive correlation exists between a focus on content and ideas and willingness to take an advanced English writing class. Third, a significant positive correlation exists between a focus on content and ideas and students' perceptions that the writing requirements of their majors are great. In other words, students who do not mind writing in English, who apparently have had some degree of success writing in English (e.g., they have enough confidence in their English writing skills to enroll in an advanced class and to take on a major that requires much writing), also tend to focus on content and ideas when they write. Students who like to write and who succeed with their writing, pay more attention to shaping their ideas than to shaping the superficial form their ideas take.

Why were we unable to obtain stronger evidence linking HWA to attention to form in the face of consistent and relatively strong interview data? Perhaps the difficulty is the ESL-WAT itself. The concerns ESL students have about writing in English may be substantially different from those of native language users, different enough that even a modified DM-WAT may not be capable of accurately testing their level of ESL WA. And, as we discovered in Study 2, some of the finer distinctions between English vocabulary items (e.g., *most* and *very*) may not be entirely clear to ESL students. The next step in ESL WA research should be the careful development of a completely new ESL-WAT following careful item development procedures. In addition, writing apprehension should be defined for particular composing situations.

Despite the mixed nature of our findings, the observations of scholars in the field (Raimes 1984; Rose 1980, 1984; Taylor, Johnson, & Gungle, 1987; Zamel, 1982, 1983) and our own experience indicate that WA is a real problem among ESL writers. We should begin to think about what we can do in our classrooms today to reduce students' apprehension about writing. In particular, students must have a more positive, lower-stress atmosphere in which to work than most do at present. An approach in which the message receives primary consideration and students learn how to strengthen and polish their essays gradually over a series of revisions (e.g., Calderonello & Edwards, 1986; Elbow, 1973, 1981; Murray, 1984) would achieve both goals: to reduce student stress and to offer instructors more opportunities to give positive feedback.

A workshop atmosphere in the classroom can also achieve these goals by promoting peer involvement throughout the process. Sharing drafts with peer groups and employing peer review and peer editing procedures (e.g., Elbow, 1981; Mittan, this volume) can promote open dialogue about the writing process in general and about individual successes or difficulties in particular. A workshop approach involves students in a constructive process of peer revision which tends to lessen the mystery about what is involved in creating an effective piece of writing, and in turn gives students confidence in their writing abilities.

Fox (1980) conducted a study to determine whether student-centered methods of teaching composition measurably reduced WA more than conventional, teacher-centered methods. Using groups of L1 writers, he concluded that not only was there a notable reduction in WA with the experimental, student-centered group, but this group also produced writing at least as high in overall quality as the writing produced by conventional composition instruction. Peer group work has the added benefit of engaging students in oral communicative activities that enhance second language acquisition (Ellis, 1984; Long & Porter, 1985; Pica & Doughty, 1985). They gain confidence using the L2, which lowers their affective filters and minimizes overmonitoring. These conditions are believed to promote L2 acquisition (Krashen, 1982).

When commenting on the student essay, the instructor should ask questions about the text as a reader would. In this way, the student can be led to address purpose and audience expectations. If we only point out errors or write negative comments we are doing nothing more than damaging the student's self-esteem while raising apprehension levels. On the other hand, asking questions for clarification or focus, either in the text itself or during student-teacher conferences, gives the student the message that the content of the paper is more important than "being correct."

When evaluating the final product, instructors should include positive comments as well as constructive criticisms and suggestions for future writing. Offer comments judiciously with the purposes of helping students to recognize weaknesses in their writing and offering options for improvement. Focus first and foremost on content, and be encouraging. As best as we can tell, such an approach will reduce the English WA of our L2 writers, and ultimately offer them a broader range of academic and career choices as well as greater success as writers.

REFERENCES

Adamson, H. D. (in press). *Variation theory in second language acquisition.* Washington, DC: Georgetown University Press.

Brown, H. D. (1987). *Principles of language learning and teaching* (2nd ed.). Englewood Cliffs, NJ: Prentice-Hall.

Calderonello, A. H., & Edwards, B. L. (1986). *Roughdrafts: The process of writing.* Dallas: Houghton-Mifflin.

Daly, J. A. (1978). Writing apprehension and writing competency. *Journal of Educational Research, 72,* 10–14.

Daly, J. A. (1985). Writing apprehension. In M. Rose (Ed.), *When a writer can't write* (pp. 43–82). New York: Guilford Press.

Daly, J. A., & Miller, M. D. (1975a). Apprehension of writing as a predictor of message intensity. *Journal of Psychology, 89,* 175–177.

Daly, J. A., & Miller, M. D. (1975b). The empirical development of an instrument to measure writing apprehension. *Research in the Teaching of English, 9,* 242–249.

Daly, J. A., & Miller, M. D. (1975c). Further studies on writing apprehension: SAT scores, success expectations, willingness to take advanced courses, and sex differences. *Research in the Teaching of English, 9,* 250–256.

Daly, J. A., & Shamo, W. G. (1976). Writing apprehension and occupational choice. *Journal of Occupational Psychology, 49,* 55–56.

Daly, J. A., & Shamo, W. G. (1978). Academic decisions as a function of writing apprehension. *Research in the Teaching of English, 12,* 119–126.

Elbow, P. (1973). *Writing without teachers.* New York: Oxford University Press.

Elbow, P. (1981). *Writing with power.* New York: Oxford University Press.

Ellis, R. (1984). *Classroom second language development.* Oxford: Pergamon Press.

Faigley, L., Daly, J. A., & Witte, S. P. (1981). The role of writing apprehension in writing performance and competence. *Journal of Educational Research, 75,* 16–20.

Fox, R. F. (1980). Treatment of writing apprehension and its effects on composition. *Research in the Teaching of English, 14,* 39–49.

Hillocks, G., Jr. (1986). *Research in written composition: New directions for teaching.* Urbana, IL: National Council of Teachers of English.

Krashen, S. (1982). *Principles and practice in second language acquisition.* Oxford: Pergamon Press.

Long, M., & Porter, P. A. (1985). Group work, interlanguage talk, and second language acquisition. *TESOL Quarterly, 19,* 207–228.

Murray, D. M. (1984). *Write to Learn.* New York: Holt Rinehart & Winston.

Pica, T., & Doughty, C. (1985). The role of group work in classroom second language acquisition. *Studies in Second Language Acquisition, 1,* 233–248.

Pirsig, R. M. (1974). *Zen and the art of motorcycle maintenance.* New York: Bantam.

Raimes, A. (1984). Anguish as a second language? Remedies for composition teachers. In S. McKay (Ed.), *Composing in a second language* (pp. 81–96). Rowley, MA: Newbury House.

Roen, D. H., Taylor, V., & Mangelsdorf, K. (1987). *ESL writers at work: Process and product.* Manuscript submitted for publication.

Rose, M. (1980). Rigid rules, inflexible plans, and the stifling of language: A cognitive analysis of writer's block. *College Composition and Communication, 31,* 389–401.

Rose, M. (1984). *Writer's block: The cognitive dimension.* Carbondale, IL: Southern Illinois University Press.

Selfe, C. L. (1984). The pre-drafting processes of four high- and four low-apprehensive writers. *Research in the Teaching of English, 18,* 45–64.

Taylor, V., Johnson, D. M., & Gungle, B. (1987). *Affective factors in L2 composing.* Manuscript submitted for publication.

Zamel, V. (1982). Writing: The process of discovering meaning. *TESOL Quarterly, 16,* 195–209.

Zamel, V. (1983). The composing processes of advanced ESL students: Six case studies. *TESOL Quarterly, 7,* 165–187.

PART III

Culture, Second Language Writing, and Creativity

Learning to compose in an additional language means learning to compose in an additional culture. Learning to write native-like, fluent, coherent texts that are effective in a discourse community in an L2 cultural setting involves much more than controlling sentence-level grammar and vocabulary. It involves the use of various kinds of knowledge at the discourse level as well as an understanding of cultural assumptions about how texts function in relation to readers and writers and how communication among people occurs through texts. One of the most interesting areas of recent work in second language (L2) writing is the examination of the way cultural experience is related to aspects of written language use and learning. The authors of the three chapters in this section address ways that cultural factors relate the students' writing processes, the texts they produce, and their perceptions of the writing of others.

Sandra Lee McKay discusses cultural differences in topic development in EFL students' compositions. She argues that topic development is an important, but largely overlooked, aspect of the notion of written discourse accent, which she defines as a lack of native proficiency in areas such as syntax, word choice, cohesion, rhetorical organization, or topic development. McKay examines themes in the personal narrative essays of a group of students in two locations in China, and compares them to themes in the compositions of a culturally and linguistically heterogeneous group of foreign students in the U.S. who wrote on the same topic. By analyzing the way students in each group develop the assigned topic, McKay illustrates that the information they deal with is based on their cultural assumptions and experiences. Cultural differences between life in San Francisco and life in China were evident in the students' writing. A predictable feature in the Chinese students' essays, for example, was a moral lesson, while a predictable feature in the writing of the foreign students in the United States was a concern for time pressure. McKay stresses the importance of allowing students to write on topics about which they have background knowledge and she suggests ways that instructors, as readers, can become sensitive to their own cultural expectations about topic development.

The chapter by William Grabe and Robert B. Kaplan provides an update on contrastive rhetoric—the notion that writing varies across languages, that different languages have different rhetorical preferences in textual organization, and that writers composing in different languages will produce rhetorically distinct texts. For the mature, academically oriented L2 writer, these issues increase the complexities involved in rhetorical problem solving, and contribute to shaping L2 writing.

The authors trace the history of contrastive rhetoric, pointing out some of the difficulties in conducting such research and providing supportive evidence of similar phenomena from work in interactional sociolinguistics, conversational analysis, and text linguistics. They present empirical evidence for the notion from work in many languages.

In discussing how notions of contrastive rhetoric relate to composition theory, Grabe and Kaplan point out that writing in some languages (such as Arabic) tends to be more oriented to "the actual forms and sounds of the language itself," that is, the language aesthetics of text, rather than to idea content and the structure of propositions (as in English). They suggest that such differences reflect enduring cultural values and have important implications for composing processes involved in producing "institution-based rhetoric" within different cultures. They also point out that the amount and type of shared knowledge assumed between writers and readers as well as the responsibilities the writer assumes are important areas of contrast among cultures.

Grabe and Kaplan state that contrastive rhetoric is a notion, a field of inquiry that, through the study of texts, provides a body of knowledge about one set of constraints L2 writers must deal with. Contrastive rhetoric does not, however, impose any teaching method or any curriculum. The authors provide twelve pedagogical objectives for teachers and students and suggest some specific teaching techniques to address the kinds of difficulties in composing that can be identified through contrastive rhetoric.

Robert E. Land Jr., and Catherine Whitley write from the perspective of university composition teachers addressing the challenge of demographic changes in regular (non-ESL) college composition classes. They suggest that instructors of regular composition courses need to rethink the standards of evaluation they use for the ESL students' essays. They argue that standards of evaluation that may be useful and fair when applied to papers written by native English speaking students can lead to erroneous conclusions about ESL students' work. They use their research and that of others to demonstrate the differences in patterns of cohesion between essays written by ESL students and native speakers. When ESL writers' patterns of cohesion are not recognized by readers, they may label the essays "disorganized." ESL students who are good writers, however, may be "skillfully manipulating patterns of organization that we don't recognize." Based on their research, Land and Whitley propose that bilingual and multilingual readers, because of their wider and more varied sets of rhetorical expectations, are more able to adapt to and value writing that employs varying rhetorical organizations. The authors propose that instructors need to recognize these varying rhetorical patterns as alternative and potentially valuable ways in which discourse can be used to discover and explain knowledge. They provide specific suggestions for responding to essays. Although the authors recognize some of the political and practical problems of developing and implementing pluralistic evaluative criteria, they argue that a model of evaluation that can lead to assimilation of new rhetorics, rather than to their exclusion or elimination, not only would empower ESL students, but would enrich our own discourse tradition as well.

CHAPTER 16

Topic Development and Written Discourse Accent

Sandra Lee McKay
San Francisco State University

The field of English as a second language (ESL) has long recognized the concept of a spoken discourse accent that is caused by a nonnative speaker's lack of proficiency in one or more of the following areas of English: phonology, morphology, syntax, lexical choice, or sociolinguistic knowledge. It seems reasonable that a similar phenomenon occurs in written discourse. Again the accent may be due to a lack of native fluency in one or more areas of proficiency which, in the case of writing, includes grammar, word choice, cohesion, rhetorical organization, and topic development. This chapter explores the area of written discourse accent in terms of topic development. I examine two groups of essays: one written by a group of Chinese students studying English in the People's Republic of China and the other written by a group of students of various ethnic backgrounds studying English in the United States. My purpose is to share my findings regarding the predictability of how the two groups of students develop the identical topic in different ways based on their cultural and social experiences.

PREVIOUS RESEARCH ON WRITTEN
DISCOURSE ACCENTS

Two levels of written discourse accent that have received recent attention in the ESL literature are unnative-like use of cohesive devices and culturally determined rhetorical organization (see Land and Whitley, this volume). In investigating the area of cohesive devices, Hu, Brown, and

Brown (1982) found no significant differences in the overall distribution of cohesive devices in the English writing of Chinese and native English speaking Australian students. However, the investigators did find a preference for conjunctions among the Chinese students and for lexical cohesion by the Australian students, which the authors attribute to the more expansive English vocabulary of the native speakers (NSs). Johns (1984), in studying essays written at the Shanghai Foreign Language Institute, confirmed Hu, Brown, and Brown's findings. She discovered the overuse of conjuncts (especially additives) by the Chinese writers in comparison to NSs of English.

A second area of written discourse accent that has received a good deal of attention is that of culturally determined rhetorical patterns. The most well-known proponent of this theory is Kaplan (1966, 1968, 1976; also see Grabe & Kaplan, this volume) who argues that students from specific cultures demonstrate typical patterns of organization. Based on a small sample of essays, Kaplan (1966) hypothesized that English speakers, for example, favor linearity in their written discourse, Arabic speakers, parallelism, and Oriental speakers, indirection. Mohan and Lo (1985) and Wong (1985) criticize Kaplan's theory, particularly as it relates to Chinese writers of English. Mohan and Lo (1985) maintain that if researchers do find indirectness in the papers of Chinese writers, the reasons may be several, among them the students' lack of familiarity with conventions of expository writing in their native language or with the assigned topic. Wong (1985) notes that such matters as digression, lack of paragraph unity, and indirectness are not the monopoly of foreign learners of English but also exist in the papers of basic writers who are unfamiliar with the conventions of written English.

The extent to which topic development may contribute to a discourse accent has not been widely investigated. Two previous studies that have addressed topic development as a factor of discourse accent are those by Scarcella (1983) and Hu, Brown, and Brown (1982). Scarcella, in examining the informal spoken conversation of bilingual NSs of Spanish and English, found that when Spanish speakers talked with other Spanish speakers they discussed topics of a far more personal nature than did English speakers. While all of the Spanish conversations included discussions of family relationships, such talk was virtually absent in the English conversations. In other words, cultural background appeared to strongly affect which topics were acceptable for an informal conversation. Whereas Scarcella's work focused on a spoken discourse accent, Hu, Brown, and Brown (1982) investigated topic predictability in written discourse. In their study, thirty-nine Chinese students who were majoring in English in China and sixty-two Australian students at the University of New South Wales were asked to give short written answers in English to several questions. One of the questions was:

> Pretend that you have a brother who does not work hard at school. What would you say to persuade him to work hard?

In responding to this question, both the Chinese and Australian students mentioned the importance of education to the individual. However, while the Chinese students frequently emphasized the importance of education for the nation as a whole, Australian students rarely mentioned this idea. Furthermore, in developing the essay, the Chinese students wrote the response as if they were directly addressing their brother, using imperatives such as, "Try to make sense of your life and study hard at school." The Australian students, on the other hand, treated the brother as a third party and used tentative suggestions such as, "If he works hard, he may one day be as brainy as his big brother." In short, the Chinese and Australian students approached the topic with a different set of cultural assumptions and role expectations. Hu, Brown, and Brown (1982) conclude that language use is essentially rooted in the reality of the culture, and they call for "close cooperation between native speaking and Chinese teachers of English to work out an approach which allows students in China to express their own experiences and knowledge in acceptable English" (p. 40).

PRESENT RESEARCH ON TOPIC PREDICTABILITY

My own research supports Hu, Brown, and Brown's conclusions that the way students address a writing topic is highly influenced by their cultural background. The basis for my study is a group of 113 essays written by students from the Beijing Institute of International Relations and the Xi'an Foreign Language Institute (located in central China), as well as a group of 27 essays written by foreign students studying in the United States. The essays were written in response to the following suggestion:

> You were standing in a long queue at a bus stop one evening. First, describe the scene, and then go on to say what happened when it rained heavily.

The topic was chosen by a graduate student of mine who was studying at the Chinese University of Hong Kong while I was there on a Fulbright teaching assignment. The student, a teacher at the Beijing Foreign Language Institute, gathered the 113 essays written by the Chinese speakers to use in her dissertation on teachers' responses to student errors. She indicated to me that a narrative topic, such as this one, was typically used in China. Although the topic was assigned by professors at both institutes,

I feel that its open-ended nature allows students, if they so desire, to be inventive in their approach. Any number of scenarios could conceivably take place at the bus stop. However, in initially reading the papers of the students at both institutes, I was struck by the commonality of the topic development. Thus I decided to investigate the predictability of topic development in the papers of the Chinese speakers by first looking for common themes in the essays and then noting the extent to which these themes appeared in the students' essays.

To begin, most students described the reason for their bus trip. Forty-one students indicated that they were going to visit a relative or friend, often because the individual was sick. Thirty-one students mentioned they were going to or returning from work; 15 students indicated that they were going to a party for a film. Undoubtedly most students cited these particular purposes because these are the main reasons Chinese students take the bus. In this case, then, the social purposes for bus travel have most likely restricted the topic development.

Next, many students wrote about the beginning of the rainfall. Fifty-five of the students wrote that the rain began suddenly, even though the topic did not state that this was the case. Perhaps the students described a sudden rainfall because rain and high humidity are common phenomena in the summer throughout the PRC (Kaplan & deKeijzer, 1984, p. 93). Often the students included a metaphor in their descriptions, such as:

> Suddenly a water spot fell down my hand, then two, then three. It is as big as a soybean.

> It was a cloudy day. There were clouds flying in the sky. And suddenly the sky clouded over. . . . Just then there was a rain of bullets.

Perhaps this common reference to the *sudden* rainfall is due to actual weather conditions in the areas of China where the students lived. The use of metaphorical language, however, is something that occurs throughout the essays.

Many students also described the sky. The explicit focus on the natural setting may reflect a cultural appreciation of the natural surroundings, but once again, there was a frequent use of metaphorical language, such as in the following examples:

> An unseen giant was pulling down the big curtain swiftly from behind the sky.

> The sky grew dark. The dark cloud was pushing down. There were no stars and moon, only that street lamp giving a dimlight, just like the eyes of a sleeply man.

Clouds rolled above the roofs and they were seemed as ghosts. I knew it was going to rain.

Next, the students often described the crowd. Fifty-five essays included a specific reference to women with children or old people in the crowd. Many described the crowd as anxious, angry, or cursing. The following are some typical descriptions of the crowd:

There stood a young woman beside me, with a baby in her arms. She looked very worried.

In this queue there were old persons and women who had babies in their arms. Most of the people were anxious.

Everyone was impatient, particularly those women standing before me with babies in their arms.

Finally, 52 students ended their papers with descriptions of the behavior of the crowd. These descriptions frequently mentioned that the crowd rushed to the door of the bus. Indeed, as Kaplan and deKeijzer (1984) point out in their guidebook to China, since buses are very crowded in China, "a deceptively peaceful queue is often found waiting at the stop, but once the bus arrives, the line often degenerates into a chaotic rush toward the door" (p. 113). In many papers someone was in need of help, which other members of the crowd did or did not provide. After relating this incident, 47 students then drew a moral lesson from it. Typical examples of these incidents and morals are:

Almost everybody rushed to the bus. Some people who stood in the front shouted hard: "Don't push! Don't push!" But nobody obey them. I also pushed hard. Because I'm strong, at last I pushed to the bus. . . . I don't think my behavior was good that night. I'm very sorry for that. But, on the other hand, I also think I was right that evening. Because nobody obeyed the public rules at that time. If I had obeyed the rules, I wouldn't have seen my uncle. So I think under the especial circumstance, people needn't do what they should do. Under the especial circumstance, people may behave especially.

As soon as the doors of the bus were opened, many people rushed into the bus. . . . Many many young people rushed in the bus. Just this moment the doors of the bus was shutted and the bus ran away. The other one still stayed here. The rest of the people were almost all children and women. . . . The children were crying. . . .
This thing have passed a few months ago, but I still remember it. I think if there is a special thing, we should have a special treatment. No

matter what we do, we all should not be dogmatist. I also think people should not always think something for themselves anywhere. We should pay more attention to the polite. We should care about children, women and old man. We should get the fine habit of thinking about other people.

There were several old persons, they must have been ill because of the heavy rain. I hesitated for a moment, but I didn't move. "Why shall I give up my seat and the others don't do?" Just then, the young people all came out and gave up their seats. They asked the old to stand in their places. After these, they stood in front of the old to prevent the rain.

All the waiting persons were moved by their deeds. The old person's hearts were very warm though they only could say "Thank you. Thanks very much." My face became red and I felt very shy. So I gave up my seat to a pale middle-aged woman.

The thing happened in 1984. Does everyone only take care of himself? Is everyone selfish? The answer is "No". In today's society, people know it's important to warm each other.

Providing a moral lesson to the story may be due to what Yu (1984) describes as the government policy in education. He maintains that a basic policy in education

put forward by the late chairman is "Education must serve proletarian politics," which still remains one of the guiding principles at present. Another belief related to this policy is that people should be educated in the spirit of socialist morality, which is characterized by collectivism in contrast to individualism and selfishness, mutual help in contrast to personal competition, serving the people and others in contrast to putting personal interest above anything else, and so forth. (p. 34)

To determine how culture specific the approach to this topic by the Chinese students might be, I gave the same writing topic to a group of 27 nonnative writers of various ethnic backgrounds who had been studying in the United States from one to six years. The essays written by these students reflected many themes not present in the papers of the Chinese learners. First, many of the students discussed the rainfall in terms of a weather prediction with statements such as:

Somebody in the line said, "Rain, that is impossible. I heard weather report this afternoon. Tonight will be fine."

Rain was predicted for that evening, but I had forgotten my umbrella, so I was anxious to go home.

None of the Chinese students mentioned the idea of a weather prediction in their papers; this most likely is due to their unfamiliarity with such an occurrence.

Many of the foreign students in the United States also provided some excuse for why they took the bus rather than driving with statements such as:

> I didn't drive my car that night because of serious shortage of parking spaces around the school area.

> Not all of us have cars because not all of us can afford the expenses of a car. . . . Those people depend on other transportations like bus, metro or BART.

> Instead of taking a ride from a friend, I decided to take a bus for a change.

Since for the Chinese students the possibility of having or using a car is almost nonexistent, there were no references to cars.

Another difference in the papers written by the two groups of students was in the descriptions of the crowd. The descriptions by the foreign students were more varied in terms of the kinds of people in the crowd and what they were doing. The following are some representative examples:

> Some of them were wearing suits and carrying a suitcase. Those are the people that work during the daytime and go to school in the evening. From their facial expressions, they are tired from the long day.

> Some people were reading newspaper, books or smoking quietly while some high school students were talking enthusiastically about the last day television program.

> The presence of some high school students couldn't go unnoticed. I think they got there a little while before me because they were still jubilating and discussing the victory of their basketball team in the game they just finished watching. These students made the environment noisy, but lively while on the other hand most of the grown ups looked dull and quiet, except for a few that were conversing near me. I presumed most of them are tired from the days work.

One common theme of the foreign students' essays that did not appear in the Chinese learners' papers was a concern about time pressure, such as those described in the excerpts:

> I was almost the last person in line and I had an exam at 7:00. I was very nervous that I couldn't make it.

> However, it was a Monday and I had to be home by six o'clock to watch the Monday night football game.

Another common theme in the papers of the foreign students was a concern about the opinions of others. Again, this was nonexistent in the papers of the Chinese learners. Two representative examples are:

> Then I missed the bus and tried to pick up all my groceries. What an embarrassing moment! I did not dare to look at the people waiting at the bus stop since I knew they were laughing at me at that very moment.

> I tried to organize my notes, but the wind was very strong, and I was afraid that the wind might blow some of the papers away. I would look ridiculous trying to catch my scattered notes in the street and in the air.

In short, the foreign students' papers contained several topics that were not present in the papers of the Chinese students, such as references to weather predictions and automobiles, as well as a concern for time pressures and public opinion. Furthermore, there were no instances in the papers written by foreign students of a moral lesson drawn from the incident. The different manner in which the two groups of students addressed the topic has important ramifications for composition classes.

PEDAGOGICAL IMPLICATIONS

If, as these essays suggest, topic development is largely a factor of cultural experience as well as social and educational policy, then composition teachers need to consider several important factors in the teaching of writing. First, we need to give careful consideration to the selection of writing topics (see Roen, this volume). As Raimes (1984) puts it, "choosing topics should be the teachers' most responsible activity" (p. 87). We must be certain that the topics we assign do not require students to relate experiences they do not have. Several of my foreign students, for example, told me that they found it difficult to write on the topic of the bus stop because they so infrequently traveled on a bus; therefore, they were not certain how to develop the topic. Thus, in some cases a topic that is highly appropriate for students studying English outside the U.S. will not be relevant to students here in the States because of the realm of their social experience. In the same way, a topic that is motivating for most American students may pose difficulties for foreign students studying English here in the United States. For example, at one junior college where I taught newly arrived foreign students, the department chose the following topic for the students' exit proficiency essay:

> Karl Marx has written that "religion is the opiate of the people." In a short essay either agree or disagree with this statement and give your reasons for your opinion.

One of my Japanese foreign students told me after the test that she was not familiar with Marx's writings, nor did she feel it was appropriate to write a personal essay on matters of religion. Needless to say, she did not write a well-developed essay. Her paper was one of marked indirection which I believe largely reflected her lack of familiarity with the topic.

To write an effective essay, students must have available the relevant schema. Anderson's observation (1977) that "every act of comprehension involves one's knowledge of the world as well" (p. 369) applies equally to the writing process in that every act of writing demands that the writer possess the background knowledge called for by the topic.

A second factor that we need to address is the placement of students in classes. To make sure that students do have the necessary experiential knowledge to write on a topic, we may need to avoid placing recent immigrants to the United States in classes with NNSs of English who have been in the United States for a considerable length of time. Obviously, an individual who has lived here for six years is much more likely to have something to write on an issue like medical care or aging in this country than will an individual who has been here only a few months. To ask recently arrived immigrants to write on topics specific to the United States is not fair to foreign students, yet it is often just such topics that will be motivating for long-term U.S. residents.

Finally, in reading compositions, we need to determine which aspects of the essays are not in keeping with our own social and cultural experiences and thus contribute to a written discourse accent. An essay written by a NNS is likely to lack proficiency in several areas—grammatical accuracy, lexical selection, cohesive patterns, rhetorical organization, and topic development. Hence it may be difficult to determine to what extent the manner in which the topic is developed is contributing to a written discourse accent. One way to become sensitive to our reader expectations about topic development is to write on the topic ourselves before we assign it and then use our essays to reflect on our topic expectations. By doing this we may be able to determine how much of what we perceive as a written discourse accent is a result of differences in topic development. When we do find areas of topic development that violate our expectations, we need to address these areas in student conferences. For example, had I been able to discuss their essays with the Chinese students, I would have discussed why some students included a moral. In this way I would have had a clearer idea of why so many students included a moral lesson and, at the same time, I could have related how drawing a moral lesson is not typical in personal narrative essays in English.

The question of just what part social and cultural experiences play in a writer's development of a topic is an area that needs further research. However, as this chapter demonstrates, what students write is clearly influenced by their cultural, social, and educational experiences. For composition teachers this means we need to place students with similar life experiences in the same writing classes, select topics that are within the realm of those students' experiences, and then strive to become aware of our own cultural expectations about the development of the topics we assign. If we approach our lessons in this way, not only will we help our students have something to write about but we will also have an opportunity to further explore how social and cultural differences affect the manner in which a writer approaches a specific topic.

REFERENCES

Anderson, R. C. (1977). The notion of schemata and the education enterprise: General discussion of the conference. In R. C. Anderson, R. J. Spiro, & W. E. Montague (Eds.), *Schooling and the acquisition of knowledge* (pp. 415–431). Hillsdale, NJ: Lawrence Erlbaum Assoc.

Hu, A., Brown, D. F., & Brown, L. B. (1982). Some linguistic differences in the written English of Chinese and Australian students. *Language Learning and Communication, 1,* 39–40.

Johns, A. (1984). Textual cohesion and the Chinese speaker of English. *Language Learning and Communication, 3,* 69–74.

Kaplan, F., & deKaijzer, A. (1984). *The China guidebook.* Boston: Houghton Mifflin.

Kaplan, R. B. (1966). Cultural thought patterns in intercultural education. *Language Learning, 16,* 1–20.

Kaplan, R. B. (1968). Contrastive grammar: Teaching composition to the Chinese student. *Journal of ESL, 3*(1), 1–13.

Kaplan, R. B. (1976). A further note on contrastive rhetoric. *Communication Quarterly, 24*(2), 12–19.

Mohan, B., & Lo, W. A. (1985). Academic writing and Chinese students: Transfer and developmental factors. *TESOL Quarterly, 19,* 515–534.

Raimes, A. (1984). Anguish as a second language? Remedies for composition teachers. In S. L. McKay (Ed.), *Composing in a second language* (pp. 81–96). Rowley, MA: Newbury House.

Scarcella, R. C. (1983). Discourse accent in second language performance. In S. Gass & L. Selinker (Eds.), *Language transfer in language learning* (pp. 306–326). Rowley, MA: Newbury House.

Wong, S. C. (1985). *What we do and don't know about Chinese learners of English: A critical review of selected literature with suggestions for needed research.* Unpublished manuscript.

Yu, C. (1984). Cultural principles underlying English teaching in China. *Language Learning and Communication, 3,* 29–40.

CHAPTER 17

Writing in a Second Language: Contrastive Rhetoric

William Grabe
Northern Arizona University

Robert B. Kaplan
University of Southern California

INTRODUCTION

The ability to write a fluent, coherent text implies more than the ability to control vocabulary, syntax, and mechanics. In the past decade, virtually all researchers have come to recognize that textual organization, information retrieval, goal planning, and attention to such influencing contextual factors as topic, definition of audience, and selection of discourse genre all represent necessary, but not sufficient, criteria for successful writing. In response to these perceptions, researchers have turned increasingly to experimental research and protocol analyses of the writing process, descriptive case studies and ethnographic research, rhetorical analyses of discourse variation according to genre, topic, and audience, and text linguistic approaches to the analysis of the written product.

The effort to understand how writing in a second language (L2) is also influenced by the cultural and linguistic conventions of the writer's first language (L1) is now recognized as an important element which must be accounted for in any approach to L2 writing research and instruction. These influences of L1 cultural and discourse norms, perhaps most clearly perceived as coherence conventions, have long provided the impetus for contrastive rhetoric.

CONTRASTIVE RHETORIC: A HYPOTHESIS

In simplest terms, scholars have argued that different languages implicate different organizational expectations in written text and demand different types of inferences. Different languages have different rhetorical preferences in textual organization—preferences reflected in syntactic and other textual differences, particularly among those features considered to be discourse sensitive or to influence the structural organization of the text. The structure of text across languages may also be influenced strongly by different understandings of audience (cf., Cooley, 1979; Hinds, 1987). In research terms, contrastive rhetoric predicts that writers composing in different languages will produce rhetorically distinct texts, independent of other causal factors such as differences in processing, in age, in relative proficiency, in education, in topic, in task complexity, or in audience.

This conceptualization of writing variation across languages, while it may have been initially overstated, is readily applicable to writing research and L2 writing instruction. This set of notions does not implicate the deterministic view that speakers of other languages think differently or have differing cognitive frameworks. Rather, these notions assume that literacy skills (both reading and writing) are learned; that they are culturally (and perhaps linguistically) shaped; that they are, at least in part, transmitted through the formal educational system; and that learners are, in principle, capable of learning writing conventions and strategies of various types.

To master such conventions and strategies, learners need to be able to manage both the "executive control" demands of an expert processing model of the sort outlined by Bereiter and Scardamalia (1987) and the organizational (or rhetorical) logic of coherent text as it operates in an L2, including (but not limited to) notions of what constitutes informational writing, of the conventional systems for organizing information (e.g., into argument), and of how the flow of information is regulated. It is improbable that control of expert processing or rhetorical logic may be achieved merely through pleasure reading, or merely through basic syntactic instruction, or merely through unsupervised writing experience (see also Bereiter & Scardamalia, 1987).

In fact, very little research on processing exists which could be taken as evidence for or against the contrastive rhetoric notion. Given the rapidly developing research on the cognitive processing of writers, the increased complexities created by L2 demands, and the recency of explanatory processing models, it is reasonable that the strongest existing evidence supporting contrastive rhetoric is of a text-orientation. The label *product* would not be entirely appropriate in this context, being more an artifact of polemical overreaction among researchers not fully aware of the power of converging research approaches (cf. Bereiter & Scardamalia, 1987; Gere, 1985; Hamp-Lyons, 1987; Horowitz, 1986a, 1986b; Liebman-Keline, 1987; Witte & Cherry, 1986 for different dicussions of this issue). In fact, text-oriented research and its implications has little if anything to do with product-oriented writing instruction—the current-traditional rhetorical approaches to writing instruction as discussed in Berlin, 1984.

Contrastive rhetoric approaches seem entirely appropriate within such emerging cognitive processing models as the one proposed by Bereiter and Scardamalia (1987). In discussing writing development, they distinguish between the demands of narrative and experiential writing on the one hand and the more complex demands of informational and argumentative writing on the other; they suggest that instruction that neglects these differences and the more complex demands of "academic" writing is not likely to develop mature writers. As part of their more complex writing model, they propose a processing component they label "rhetorical problem space." This component subsumes the writer's need to be simultaneously aware of audience, general writing plans, subgoals and subplans, and various sorts of discourse relations.

It is not appropriate to summarize Bereiter and Scardamalia's model in full; the point of raising it is to suggest that, for L2 writers, contrastive rhetoric concerns fall within the "rhetorical problem space," including all of the rhetorical constraints imposed by the target language. For L2 writers, interference created by L1 rhetorical knowledge increases the complexity in the rhetorical problem space. (It is important to note that the incorporation of L1 rhetorical knowledge into L2 writing processes does not account for all of the issues raised by contrastive rhetoric, but only for that fraction which deals directly with L2 writing instruction; that knowledge does not account for more general research comparing text type variation of edited texts across two or more languages, or of texts produced by a single writer composing in two or more languages.)

Research on the composing process and case study/ethnographic research of beginning writers also play some role in contrastive rhetoric research, though primarily in terms of cultural and low-level linguistic influences. Since most beginning (emerging literacy level) writers do not usually become involved with the problems of rhetorical organization in nonnarrative and nonexperiential writing, nor with problems of complex audience differentiation (in either language), they do not provide the most interesting population for contrastive rhetoric research. Contrastive rhetoric is not generally involved with research on children in earlier stages of maturational development because it involves research on issues that become significant only among a population of writers faced with the control of complex rhetorical constraints—constraints that tend to occur in higher educational contexts (e.g., grades eight and above; cf. Newkirk & Atwell, 1985).

Similarly, contrastive rhetoric is not concerned with research on students at beginning stages of L2 acquisition because these students are more centrally concerned with the acquisition of basic syntactic structures, of vocabulary, of writing mechanics, with recording oral descriptions/processes, and (perhaps) with composing strategies involved in retelling oral stories (cf. Lawrence, 1975 for an elementary-level L2 expository textbook).

Because of the specific emphasis of contrastive rhetoric in the differing rhetorical conventions exhibited in the construction of complex texts in two different languages, it has been primarily concerned with the nature of coherence and with the nature of text construction itself, and it has been concerned with the development of writing beyond the initial stages; on an instructional level, it has been concerned with overcoming L1 rhetorical interferences in writing. It must be recognized, however, that contrastive rhetoric is not concerned with differentiating between "good" and "bad" writing. Rather, contrastive rhetoric adds explanatory power to such theoretical models as that offered by Bereiter and Scardamalia (1987) as they apply to L2 writing; in that sense, it complicates the rhetorical issues by focusing on problems that arise for L2 writers but not necessarily for L1 writers.

More might be said about contrastive rhetoric and its relationship to processing models, to text linguistics, to discourse analysis, and to rhetorical theory; the preceding discussion will suffice for purposes of this introductory essay. In summary, then, contrastive rhetoric is the study of L1 rhetorical influences on the organization of text in an L2, on audience considerations, on goal definition; it seeks to define L1 influences on text coherence, on perceived audience awareness, and on rhetorical context features (i.e., topic constraints, amount of subject matter knowledge needed to accomplish a given task, assignment constraints, writer maturity, educational demands, time available for composing, time available for feedback and revision, formal conventions of the writing task, etc.). Accordingly, contrastive rhetoric research must seek to understand and employ some theory of coherence, some theory of audience awareness, and some theory of the rhetorical context.

BACKGROUND OF CONTRASTIVE RHETORIC

Modern contrastive rhetoric had its origin in the research of Kaplan (1966, 1967, 1972). Recognizing that nonnative university students were experiencing difficulty in writing academic English, Kaplan set about to examine a large corpus of nonnative student compositions. Similarities in the writing of individuals from the same L1 background led him to propose the notion of contrastive rhetoric. In the more than twenty years since the initial articulation of contrastive rhetoric, a number of researchers have explored the concept from a variety of perspectives. While a number of arguments in Kaplan's early work have proven contentious, the basic outlines of contrastive rhetoric—the contrasting of culturally based rhetorical systems—appear to be receiving increasing support, granted not always in the manner originally proposed (cf. Kaplan, 1987a).

Over the last two decades, converging evidence from research approaches quite distinct from Kaplan's have provided further support for the notion. Sociolinguists have come to recognize similar constraints on patterns of discourse when speakers from two different language groups interact. Major supporting research has come from the notion of scripts and frames guiding interactional expectations (Gumperz, 1982a, 1982b; Tannen, 1979, 1984, 1986). When these overall patterns of expectations conflict, the distinct discourse (or rhetorical) patterns emerge clearly as sources of the conflict. Similarly, text linguistic research, beginning with the European linguistic schools, has contributed to the notion of contrastive rhetoric by providing useful tools for the analysis of written discourse, and particularly providing a workable theory of coherence in written texts (e.g., deBeaugrande & Dressler, 1981; van Dijk, 1977). The impact of these text linguistic contributions can be readily observed in second language research (cf. Carrell, 1984; Connor, 1984, 1987; Johns, 1986).

One reason contrastive rhetoric has generated controversy over so long a time and has yet to receive full support is the difficulty of examining the notion. Some critics have argued that the approach to contrastive rhetoric through one language (e.g., through ESL compositions) allows only an opaque reflection of the issues to be examined. Others have pointed out that there is no good way to match different texts from two different languages for comparability. Some criticism has come from researchers who assume a universality of text types; this criticism tends to rule out contrastive rhetoric entirely. Other criticism derives from the complexity of the methods of analysis—that is, will two differing language systems permit comparisons of functions (e.g., Chinese lacks tense marking while English lacks zero subject pronoun)? Finally, criticism has been leveled at the general methodology of text analysis; for example, how can researchers say what holistic ratings actually reveal across languages, or how can researchers discuss subordination, linguistic complexity, paragraph structure, expository prose, or logical relations when linguistic research generally lacks adequate definitions of these concepts (Mohan, 1986; Ricento, 1986).

These legitimate criticisms have moved researchers to find the controls and methods necessary for more careful analyses that might provide more persuasive arguments responsive to the criticisms. In all fairness, contrastive rhetoric research is not a simple matter, and there are many obstacles to be overcome before incontrovertible evidence can be amassed. The fact is that contrastive rhetoric evokes a primary discontinuity found in all social science research—the issue of epistemically acceptable definitions of the subject of research and of the nature of objectivity. Be that as it may, in the more conventional North American tradition, there has been over at least the past ten years an impressive accumulation of empirical evidence supporting the notion.

RECENT RESEARCH SUPPORTING
CONTRASTIVE RHETORIC

Work on English composition has provided evidence that rhetorically distinct patterns appear to exist in the English writing of Japanese (Connor & McCagg, 1987; Namba & Chick, 1987), Persian (Dehghanpisheh, 1973; Houghton, 1980), Chinese (Kaplan, 1972, 1987b), Arabic (Ostler, 1987), Spanish (Santana-Seda, 1974/1975; Santiago, 1968), and Native American languages (Bartelt, 1981, 1983; Chessin & Auerbach, 1982; Cook, 1982; Leap, 1983). Direct comparisons of texts in two languages have demonstrated similar sorts of distinctions for Japanese (Hinds, 1979, 1983a, 1983b, 1987; Ricento, 1987), Chinese (Tsao, 1983), Marathi (Pandharipande, 1983), Hindi (Kachru, 1983), German (Clyne, 1981, 1983, 1985, 1987), Portuguese (Dantas, 1987), and Australian Aboriginal languages (Eggington, 1987).

Hinds (1983b), for example, argues that a common expository form of writing in Japanese involves an organizational framework termed *ki-shoo-ten-ketsu*. The point is that the third element in the development, *ten*, represents the development of a subtheme in a manner that would be considered off-topic in English. As Hinds (p. 188) notes, "It is the intrusion of the unexpected element into an otherwise normal progression of ideas." The final element, *ketsu*, represents the conclusion, but that label is misleading in terms of English writing expectations. In this Japanese writing format, the conclusions may only ask a question, indicate a doubt, or reach an indecisive endpoint. By English standards, such a conclusion appears almost incoherent.

Further support for contrastive rhetoric derives from sociolinguistic research, particularly Chafe (1980), Gumperz (1982a, 1982b, 1986), and Tannen (1984, 1986). In the cited sources, as in other research, patterns of interaction between speakers from two different language backgrounds indicate major variation in conversational styles, suggesting distinct patterns of preference in the organization of oral discourse; it is reasonable to assume that similar preferential choices would occur in written text. Such contrasts have been observed for Arabic, Chinese, French, Greek, Hindi, Malagasy, Native American languages, and Samoan, among others.

It seems reasonable to claim, then, that contrastive rhetoric captures an important truth about distinct patterns of rhetorical organization in different languages, regardless of the way in which particular researchers may characterize such distinctions. The fact that theoretical explanations have yet to converge on a single, acceptable general theory does not mean that some group of contrastive rhetoric constraints do not regularly occur. From the available evidence, it may be more accurate to suggest that contrastive rhetoric influences constitute one among a number of factors that shape second language writing. Although the attendant problems have yet to be solved, the evidence to date indicates that contrastive rhetoric notions cannot be ignored. It remains necessary to determine, then, where and to what extent contrastive rhetoric factors appear in second language writing.

CONTRASTIVE RHETORIC AND COMPOSITION THEORY

Contrastive rhetoric provides a way of studying language—albeit with greater attention to products rather than processes—based on the assumption that analyses of text products can lead to a better understanding of how language works. Contrastive rhetoric is not a methodology for teaching, though some of its findings can be (and indeed have been) applied to teaching. While contrastive rhetoric focuses on a product (whether it is termed final or somehow less than final), it does not—cannot—ignore composing processes. Given that academic writing instruction at the secondary and tertiary levels is generally directed at "institution-based rhetoric" (Perelman, 1986), and given that most second language programs at those levels have as an objective the development of skill in "institution-based rhetoric," the question remains whether it is reasonable for significant numbers of individuals at any level to produce "writing through composing" (Kaplan, 1983), where the act of composing is only expressive writing (e.g., Elbow, 1973, 1981; Murray, 1984, 1985). This question is appropriate both because such writing is relatively rare in virtually all cultures and because such writing may not exist at all as a mode of choice in some cultures (Applebee, 1981; Bizzell, 1982, 1986; Matalene, 1985; Perelman, 1986; Reither, 1985). Ostler (1987) points out, for example, some Arabic speakers' text structures exhibit a strong preference for Koranic style—that is, text structure that assumes the text represents, in some important way, *the truth* and that, as a consequence, text cannot be developed heuristically since text has the primary function of producing an elaborate sense of harmony and balance in and through the language. In other words, the primary focus of writing lies in the *language* of the text rather than in its propositional content. English writing instruction stresses idea content, especially in terms of recently developed instructional approaches (i.e., Elbow, 1973, 1981; Graves, 1983, 1984; Murray 1978, 1984). Other languages (e.g., Arabic) tend to be more oriented to the actual forms and sounds of the language itself. This difference is an important one, having serious implications for academic, and particularly scientific, writing.

In English, writing processes subsume a way of dealing with propositional content—of representing a "logic" (not an absolute mathematical logic, but a culturally defined logic), and permits the management of coherence and cohesion systems through which such logic may be reflected in text. This mode of logical representation is culturally constrained. Wilkerson (1986) points out that the development of writing education in the United States reflects two traditions: Aristotelian (syllogistic) and Galilean (taxonomic). Traditional school rhetorics, from the middle of the eighteenth century well into the twentieth, "in keeping with the prevalent materialistic philosophy and its associated essentially technological world view . . ." (Berlin, 1984, p. 9), placed great importance on clarity and precision in the framework of a rigorously logical system (cf. the school rhetorics after George Campbell and Hugh Blair; see Berlin, 1984). Thus, in the United States, in contrast to the situation described above for Arabic speakers, the focus of writing has been on the structure of propositions; it has attended much less to the language aesthetics of text. Wilkerson notes a very different tradition in Japanese, with emphasis on form rather than on understanding (cf. Jenkins & Hinds, 1987 for Japanese; Tsao, 1983 for Chinese). It is possible, in a reductionist sense, to place the responsibility for such differences exclusively on the educational system (as Mohan & Lo, 1985 have done), assuming that educational systems are solely responsible for the maintenance and dissemination of preferred rhetorical types. Such a view reduces contrastive rhetoric to a concern with school curricula and with instructional models. Because educational systems are not generally on the cutting edge of cultural change but serve and reflect enduring cultural values, such a view would constitute a dangerous oversimplification.

The issues just outlined do not constitute the sole area of rhetorical (or process) conflict between cultures. As Widdowson notes: "the responsibility for structuring [written] discourse rests with only one participant (the writer) who will . . . tend to place greater reliance on an assumed shared knowledge" (1984, p. 50). This comment raises two interesting points of contrast: how much responsibility does the writer in fact assume, and what sort of shared knowledge can in fact be assumed to exist in a situation in which a writer is composing in a language not his or her own? Hinds (1987; Jenkins & Hinds, 1987) proposes a typology of language based on relative reader/writer responsibility. He classifies English as a writer-responsible language, French as a reader-responsible language, Chinese as a language in transition from reader-responsible to writer-responsible status, and Japanese as having a nonperson orientation—that is, a reader-responsible language but one in which social relational control is more important than relative reader responsibility. This taxonomy, though still exploratory, provides useful insights into different notions of coherence and rhetorical preferences for the languages referred to.

This question of relative responsibility impacts the propositional structure of text. Readers in a reader-responsible system expect to supply some significant portion of the propositional structure, while readers in a writer-responsible system expect to have most of the propositional structure supplied to them. The BBC world news—a scripted oral text— provides an example of writer-responsible text: The news is introduced with a clearly identified outline of the main points for that particular segment; that introduction is followed by a detailed exposition of each of the outlined main points, in the same order as the outline; and the news ends with a summary of the main points, again in the same order. In this structure, the writer assumes heavy responsibility; such a structure is required when it is assumed that shared knowledge is severely constrained. Japanese texts are very differently organized, placing heavy responsibility on the reader to understand what is being suggested and assuming a very great quantity of shared knowledge (the entire ambient cultural system of Japan).

CONTRASTIVE RHETORIC AND WRITING INSTRUCTION

The above examples illustrate the kinds of evidence collected through contrastive rhetoric. The practical objective in searching for such evidence is to facilitate instruction in second language writing. The intent is not to provide pedagogic method, but to provide a body of knowledge underlying various types of writing for different audiences in different culturally bound settings. In sum, contrastive rhetoric has focused attention on seven types of knowledge in the teaching of writing (and reading).

- Knowledge of rhetorical patterns of arrangement and the relative frequency of various patterns (eg., exposition/argument: classification, etc.).

- Knowledge of composing conventions or strategies needed to generate text (e.g., prewriting, data-collection, revision, etc.).
- Knowledge of the morphosyntax of the target language, particularly as it applies at the intersentential level.
- Knowledge of the coherence-creating mechanisms of the target language.
- Knowledge of the writing conventions of the target language in the sense of both frequency and distribution of types and text appearance (e.g., letter, essay, report, etc.).
- Knowledge of audience characteristics and expectations in the target culture.
- Knowledge of the subject to be discussed, including both "what everybody knows" in the target culture and specialist knowledge.

Clearly, this list is primarily concerned with product, but it should in no way be seen as an endorsement of "current-traditional" writing instruction. While the emphasis is on the composition rather than on the mental processes through which the composition is generated, those processes have not been, and cannot be, ignored. Criticisms that claim contrastive rhetoric gives attention exclusively to product issues result from a number of basic misunderstandings. In fact, a number of the issues from the list, discussed below, may be understood more usefully from a process orientation.

Rhetorical patterns of arrangement provide a good case in point. In and of themselves, rhetorical patterns may transcend the constraints of language systems, but may serve a different purpose in one language as opposed to another (Coe, 1987; Matalene, 1985). Description, for example, may be a universal type, but what can be described, when description is permitted, and how it relates to surrounding types may vary from one system to another. By the same token, if the frequency and distribution of types can vary across systems, it follows that composing strategies may co-vary (Heath, 1986; Hillocks, 1986; Matsuhashi, 1981). Recalling Bereiter and Scardamalia's (1987) processing model, this prediction would place distinct processing constraints on the "rhetorical problem space." Such an assumption forms the core of Kinneavy's *Theory of Discourse* (1971) as well, where the different uses of discourse within English alone are said to entail different thinking processes. Again, it is important to note that the decisions involved in rhetorical organization belong to process considerations, though they become manifested in the product.

A second area where process concerns come to the fore is in the learning and use of composing conventions or strategies needed to generate texts. Students need to learn basic invention strategies, and in particular, contrastive rhetoric would argue for the importance of topoi as essential to the academic writing needs of second language students. In addition, students need to recognize the importance of revising as an expected part of all good writing. Exactly how revising is taught effectively is an interesting and complex issue, one made even more so by second language contexts (cf. Bereiter & Scardamalia, 1987; Faigley & Witte, 1984; Freedman, 1985; Witte, 1985).

Contrastive rhetoric also has implications for the teaching of morphosyntactic knowledge. Teachers frequently assume that morphosyntactic knowledge can be taught in a vacuum; the result of such an assumption is not a writing class but a grammar class. While there may be nothing inherently wrong with a grammar class, it is a fallacy to confuse the teaching of grammar with the teaching of writing. Accumulated research evidence suggests that grammatical knowledge is necessary but not sufficient to the process of writing. Indeed, morphosyntactic knowledge is prerequisite to composing in a second language; learners who write syntactic mazes cannot give sufficient attention to text features. Native speakers have in their repertoire a large inventory of clause-moving and clause-embedding strategies (even if those strategies derive from spoken language and may be at least partially inappropriate to writing). Morphosyntactic instruction, however taught, certainly can inculcate a selected subset of such strategies, but it cannot at present select those strategies having the highest frequency, widest distribution, or greatest productivity, nor can morphosyntactic instruction in isolation inculcate the sociolinguistic information that governs choices among alternatives in relation to situation, audience, and so forth. The point, however, is that students who do not have control of basic morphosyntactic structure—clause-generating strategies—are not prepared to deal with clause-movement strategies, and are certainly not prepared to deal with the sociolinguistic appropriateness constraints on those strategies; thus, morphosyntactic control is prerequisite to learning to write. (How exactly one goes about teaching morphosyntactic knowledge is an open question and one which is not likely to be resolved in the near future.)

The judging of a text as coherent is not entirely a matter of linguistic knowledge, as Brown and Yule (1983) have pointed out. However, there are linguistic principles and systems of text organization that contribute to the coherence of text. Both Grabe (1985) and Johns (1986), summarizing much of the text linguistics literature, have suggested that coherence in text is created by three interacting systems: the macrostructure, or what might be called the underlying thesis; the logical relations among the sentences of a text; and the way information—given, inferred, and new—is arranged. Such a perspective on coherence receives considerable support from cognitive psychology, rhetoric, text linguistics, composition theory, and broader applied linguistics. That nonnative students cannot master these interacting systems is not a surprise, since researchers themselves have only recently come to recognize the complexity of text structure.

Writing conventions involving both more than and other than syntactic accuracy and spelling constitute an important part of the lay conception of literacy. Writing conventions are often dismissed by writing teachers as too obvious to need attention or as beneath the notice of teachers of serious composition. Yet in the cross-lingual situation, there is no reason to assume that the nonnative speaker will know this set of conventions in the target language or that the learner will be able to intuit these conventions for him or herself simply by reading.

Audience awareness is also critical for writing success since it defines the possible extent of shared knowledge and the extent to which the writer can overcome the absence of a rich feedback loop present in most conversational environments. Inexperienced writers tend to choose themselves as audience—a strategy that avoids the problem of extent of shared knowledge, since writer and assumed reader become one and the same in terms of shared knowledge. This is often discussed as writer-based prose (Flower, 1979; Flower & Hayes, 1981), or egocentric writing (Calkins, 1985; Graves, 1983, 1984; Kroll, 1978; Lunsford, 1980; Moffett, 1968), and closely related to the larger notion that complex writing abilities emerge out of more natural oral language abilities (Bereiter & Scardamalia, 1987). It is difficult for inexperienced writers to project themselves into another persona. The artificiality of the classroom environment only complicates the situation by interposing a "real" reader between the writer and any assumed audience—the teacher. The matter of audience lies in the process domain, since decisions about shared knowledge must occur in the composing process before any product exists.

Subject matter knowledge lies outside the domain of the writing teacher (cf. Shih, 1986); the learner brings subject knowledge—both world knowledge and specialist knowledge—with him or her (except perhaps in situations in which the writing class engages in a collective research project, such as ethnographic research on language use or on the classroom culture; cf. Heath, 1985; Heath & Branscombe, 1985; Johns, 1987). The matter of subject knowledge also lies in the process domain, since choices about which segments of the universe of knowledge will be used in relation to particular audiences and particular writing objectives must be made before any product becomes well defined (Reither, 1985; Thomas, 1986).

Contrastive rhetoric, then, works backwards, trying to understand composing processes in certain second language contexts by looking at products both in the target language (by trying to comprehend the strategies and presuppositions used in that language to achieve certain rhetorical ends) and in the learner's other languages (by trying to comprehend what strategies and presuppositions the learner brings with him or her, by searching for strategies that co-occur, and by recognizing strategies that may create tensions with the second language). The particular educational concerns that contrastive rhetoric addresses: the writing of mature, academically oriented second language students, suggests the utility of such text linguistic approaches. It is certainly arguable (if argument is necessary), from research by deBeaugrande (1984), Bereiter and Scardamalia (1987), Coe (1987), Cooper (1983), Cooper and Matsuhashi (1983), Dillon (1981), Faigley and Witte (1984), Heath (1985), Heath and Branscombe (1985), Hillocks (1986), and Tamor and Bond (1983) that many processes involved in composing are discernible through study of the product. A more reasoned perspective is, in fact, emerging gradually out of the product-process dialectic; it proposes that both product- and process-oriented research offer important insights into the highly complex cognitive ability that writing surely represents. This evolution of research in writing will allow for a convergence of many types of evidence and data, and should offer insights into the nature of writing far beyond what is possible within any one "dominant" research perspective (e.g., Hairston, 1982 and Faigley's, 1986 comment on Hairston). As Witte (1987) notes,

> A field that presumes the efficacy of a particular research methodology, a particular enquiry paradigm, will collapse inward upon itself. If it is ever to develop a comprehensive theory capable of explaining acts of writing or of guiding the teaching of writing and if its findings are ever to contribute significantly to educational policy, research in written composition must be able to use, and use well, a multitude of research tools or methodologies. The field of written composition is large enough and vital enough to make good use of both qualitative and quantitative methodologies and to embrace both the logic of discovery and the logic of validation. . . . What the field needs is not more unproductive and even counterproductive bickering about methodologies, but greater recognition of the strengths and limitations of all research methodologies (and there is no perfect research methdology) in providing answers to important questions. (p. 207)

It should be clear from this discussion that insights from contrastive rhetoric are applicable to composing models and suggest pedagogical objectives applicable to academically oriented L2 writers. How these insights are actually translated into classroom instruction is another matter, and one that needs to be touched on briefly. Contrastive rhetoric does not impose any teaching methodology. For our part, we believe that writing instruction which stresses invention strategies and prewriting activities, which teaches planning, writing, and revising strategies as nonlinear and cyclic processes, which employs collaboration and peer-group feedback, which includes conferencing and individual feedback, and which encourages multiple drafting is consistent with all that contrastive rhetoric implies. If it also implies that academically oriented students be made aware, in one manner or another, of preferred English rhetorical patterns and of English coherence structure, we do not find the implication contradictory with the above general instructional methodology.

The pedagogical objectives may be summarized in twelve points:

I. To make the teacher of composition aware:
1. That different composing conventions exist in different cultures and that these differences need to be addressed in teaching composition; the fact that a learner is able to compose in one language does not mean that the learner can compose in *any* language.
2. That certain grammatical features function at the level of discourse; the fact that a learner has control of sentential syntax does not mean that the learner can generate text.
3. That systems of coherence can be examined in texts (at least three such systems are observable and teachable); the fact that a learner may be aware of the interacting structure in his or her first language does not mean that the learner perceives the nature of the interaction in the target language.
4. That there is a relative distribution of reader/writer responsibility in different cultural systems and that the distribution influences assumptions about audience and shared knowledge; the fact that a learner understands the assignment of responsibility in the first language does not mean that the learner understands it in the target language.
5. That a "composition" is a product arrived at through a process; the fact that a learner may succeed in generating one successful text does not mean that the learner understands the process or can replicate it.
6. That some level of morphosyntactic competence is prerequisite to writing; the fact that a learner can control sentential syntax and demonstrate that control through discrete-item tests does not mean that the learner can deal with the structure of coherence in text.

II. To make the learner of composition aware:
1. That audience must be defined before composing can be undertaken; the assumption of writer-as-audience can not be made.
2. That there are a number of different writing acts; the fact that a learner writes successfully in one language does not mean that the learner understands the frequency and distribution of types/tasks in the target language.
3. That there are strategies for text organization that conform to

coherence systems in the target language; learners must grasp the uses of a thesis statement, logical relationships among parts of a text, and available options for selecting and arranging information, and understand that these are likely to vary from the L1.
4. That there are certain writing conventions in the target language; the fact that the learner may be aware of the conventions in the first language does not mean that the learner understands those of the target language.
5. That, to compose anything, the learner must possess and be able to bring to bear on the composing task a universe of knowledge (including world and specialist knowledge); the fact that a learner holds opinions on any given topic does not mean that the learner knows the topic well enough to write about it.
6. That, finally, writing is a social phenomenon—a technique for negotiating meaning with some other (identifiable set of) individuals—requiring more than minimal syntactic and lexical control of the target language.

TEACHING SUGGESTIONS DERIVING FROM THESE IMPLICATIONS

It becomes possible to outline a number of techniques that can follow from these major pedagogical objectives; for example, developing a thesis may be enhanced by:

- Providing topic statements in slots in bloc structures.
- Reorganizing sentences in scrambled blocs.
- Identifying topic structures in real texts.
- Sorting supporting detail from the generalization it supports.
- Matching topics with some organizational type.
- Limiting topics to match world knowledge.
- Brainstorming a thesis (peer collaboration).
- Use of topoi and invention.
- Conferencing.

As this list suggests, any number of techniques can be rationalized as part of an effort to overcome difficulties identified through contrastive rhetoric. Further suggestions for teaching can be found in Arapoff Cramer (1985), deBeaugrande (1985), Hillocks (1981), Hillocks, Khan, and Johannessen (1983), Johns (1986), Kaplan and Shaw (1984), Raimes (1983, 1987), and other sources. It is important to recognize that contrastive rhetoric does not offer a curriculum. The configuration of instructional techniques in an effective curriculum must also depend on more variables than can be offered in a single notion of contrastive rhetoric—a notion which only attempts to highlight one set of constraints among the many that academically oriented second language learners encounter. It would, however, be an error to ignore contrastive rhetoric problems or to assume that they will disappear through the "transfer" of "universal writing strategies," if indeed these strategies exist and are transferred. Whatever its contributions to research and theory building, contrastive rhetoric has influenced L2 teaching, we hope for the better. The accrued evidence suggests that the notion remains promising and that it will continue to make a significant contribution to L2 curricular decisions and writing instruction.

REFERENCES

Applebee, A. (1981). *Writing in the secondary school.* Urbana, IL: National Council of Teachers of English.

Arapoff Cramer, N. (1985). *The writing process.* Rowley, MA: Newbury House.

Bartelt, G. (1981). Some observations on Navajo English. *Papers in Linguistics, 14,* 377–385.

Bartelt, G. (1983). Transfer and variability of rhetorical redundancy in Apachean English. In S. Gass & L. Selinker (Eds.), *Language transfer in language learning* (pp. 297–305). Rowley, MA: Newbury House.

deBeaugrande, R. (1984). *Toward a science of composing.* Norwood, NJ: Ablex.

deBeaugrande, R. (1985). *Writing step by step.* New York: Harcourt.

deBeaugrande, R., & Dressler, W. (1981). *Introduction to text linguistics.* New York: Longman.

Bereiter, C., & Scardamalia, M. (1987). *The psychology of written composition.* Hillsdale, NJ: Lawrence Erlbaum.

Berlin, J. (1984). *Writing instruction in nineteenth century American colleges.* Carbondale, IL: Southern Illinois University Press.

Bizzell, P. (1982). College composition: Initiation into the academic discourse community. *Curriculum Inquiry, 12,* 191–207.

Bizzell, P. (1986). What happens when basic writers come to college? *College Composition and Communication, 37,* 294–310.

Blair, H. (1965). *Lectures on rhetoric and belles lettres.* (H. Harding, Ed.). Carbondale, IL: Southern Illinois University Press. (Original work published 1783).

Brown, G., & Yule, G. (1983). *Discourse analysis.* New York: Cambridge University Press.

Calkins, L. (1985). *The art of teaching writing.* Exter, NH: Heinemann.

Campbell, G. (1963). *The philosophy of rhetoric.* (L. Bitzer, Ed.). Carbondale, IL: Southern Illinois University Press. (Original work published 1776)

Carrell, P. (1984). The effects of rhetorical organization in ESL readers. *TESOL Quarterly, 18,* 441–469.

Chafe, W. (1980). *The pear stories.* Norwood, NJ: Ablex.

Chessin, L., & Auerbach, E. (1982). Teaching composition to Northwest American Indians. In G. Bartelt, S. Penfield-Jasper, & B. Hoffer (Eds.), *Essays in Native American English* (pp. 173–186). San Antonio: Trinity University Press.

Clyne, M. (1981). Culture and discourse structure. *Journal of Pragmatics, 5,* 61–66.

Clyne, M. (1983). Linguistics and written discourse in particular languages: Contrastive studies: English and German. In R. B. Kaplan (Ed.), *Annual Review of Applied Linguistics (Vol. 3)* (pp. 38–49). Rowley, MA: Newbury House.

Clyne, M. (1985). *Language and society in the German-speaking countries.* New York: Cambridge University Press.

Clyne, M. (1987). Cultural differences in the organization of academic texts: English and German. *Journal of Pragmatics, 11,* 211–247.

Coe, R. (1987). An apology for form; or, who took the form out of the process. *College English, 49,* 13–28.

Connor, U. (1984). Recall of text: Differences between first and second language readers. *TESOL Quarterly, 18,* 239–255.

Connor, U. (1987). Argumentative patterns in student essays: Cross-cultural differences. In U. Connor & R. B. Kapan (Eds.), *Writing across languages: Analysis of L2 texts* (pp. 57–71). Reading, MA: Addison-Wesley.

Connor, U., & McCagg, P. (1987). A contrastive study of English expository prose paraphrases. In U. Connor & R. B. Kaplan (Eds.), *Writing across languages: Analysis of L2 texts* (pp. 73–86). Reading, MA: Addison-Wesley.

Cook, M. J. (1982). Problems of southwestern Indian speakers in learning English. In P. Turner (Ed.), *Bilingualism in the Southwest* (pp. 235–243). Tucson: University of Arizona Press.

Cooley, R. (1979). Spokes in a wheel: A linguistic and rhetorical analysis of Native American public discourse. *Proceedings of the 5th Annual Meeting of the Berkeley Linguistic Society* (pp. 552–557). Berkeley, CA: University of California Press.

Cooper, C. (1983). Procedures for describing written texts. In P. Mosenthal, L. Tamor, & S. Walmsley (Eds.), *Research in writing: Principles and methods* (pp. 287–313). New York: Longman.

Cooper, C., & Matsuhashi, A. (1983). A theory of the writing process. In M. Martlew (Ed.), *The psychology of written language: A developmental approach* (pp. 3–38). New York: Wiley.

Dantas, M. (1987). *Contrasts in English and Portuguese editorial prose.* Unpublished manuscript. Flagstaff: Northern Arizona University.

Dehghanpisheh, E. (1973). Contrastive analysis of Persian and English paragraphs. *Proceedings of the Second Annual Seminar of the Association of Professors of English in Iran.* Tehran: Association of Professors of English in Iran.

Dijk, T., van (1977). *Text and context.* New York: Longman.

Dillon, G. (1981). *Constructing texts.* Bloomington: Indiana University Press.

Eggington, W. (1987, August). A contrastive rhetoric of Aboriginal English prose. Paper presented at the 8th World Congress of AILA, Sydney, Australia.

Elbow, P. (1973). *Writing without teachers.* New York: Oxford University Press.

Elbow, P. (1981). *Writing with power.* New York: Oxford University Press.

Faigley, L. (1986). Competing theories of process: A critique and a proposal. *College English, 48,* 527–542.

Faigley, L., & Witte, S. (1984). Measuring the effects of revision on text structure. In R. Beach & L. Bridwell (Eds.), *New directions in composition research* (pp. 95–108). New York: Guilford Press.

Flower, L. (1979). Writer-based prose: A cognitive basis for problems in writing. *College English, 41,* 19–37.

Flower, L., & Hayes, J. (1981). Plans that guide the composing process. In C. Frederiksen & J. Dominic (Eds.), *Writing: The nature, development, and teaching of written communication* (Vol. 2, pp. 39–58). Hillsdale, NJ: Lawrence Erlbaum.

Freedman, S. W. (Ed.). (1985). *The acquisition of written language.* Norwood, NJ: Ablex.

Gere, A. (1985). Empirical research in composition. In B. McClelland & T. Donovan (Eds.), *Perspectives on research and scholarship in composition* (pp. 101–124). New York: Modern Language Association.

Grabe, W. (1985). Written discourse analysis. In R. B. Kaplan (Ed.), *Annual Review of Applied Linguistics (Vol. 5)* (pp. 101–123). New York: Cambridge University Press.

Graves, D. (1983). *Writing: Teachers and children at work.* Exeter, NH: Heinemann.

Graves, D. (1984). *A researcher learns to write.* Exeter, NH: Heinemann.

Gumperz, J. (1982a). *Discourse strategies.* New York: Cambridge University Press.

Gumperz, J. (Ed.). (1982b). *Language and social identity.* New York: Cambridge University Press.

Gumperz, J. (1986). Interactional sociolinguistics in the study of schooling. In J. Cook-Gumperz (Ed.), *The social construction of literacy* (pp. 45–68). New York: Cambridge University Press.

Hairston, M. (1982). The winds of change: Thomas Kuhn and the revolution in the teaching of writing. *College Composition and Communication, 33,* 76–88.

Hamp-Lyons, L. (1987). No new lamps for old yet, please. *TESOL Quarterly, 20,* 790–796.

Heath, S. B. (1985). Literacy or literate skills? Considerations for ESL/EFL learners. In P. Larson, E. Judd, & D. Messerschmitt (Eds.), *On TESOL 84: A brave new world for TESOL* (pp. 15–28). Washington, DC: Teachers of English to Speakers of Other Languages.

Heath, S. B. (1986). The sociocultural contexts of language development. In Bilingual Education Office (Ed.), *Beyond language: Social and cultural factors in schooling language minority children* (pp. 143–186). Los Angeles: Evaluation, Dissemination, and Assessment Center, CSULA.

Heath, S. B., & Branscombe, A. (1985). "Intelligent writing" in an audience community: Teachers, students, and researcher. In S. W. Freedman (Ed.), *The acquisition of written language* (pp. 3–32). Norwood, NJ: Ablex.

Hillocks, G. (1981). The responses of college freshmen to three modes of instruction. *American Journal of Education, 89,* 373–395.

Hillocks, G. (1986). *Research on written composition.* Urbana, IL: National Council of Teachers of English.

Hillocks, G., Khan, E., & Johannessen, L. (1983). Teaching definite strategies as a mode of inquiry: Some effects on student writing. *Research in the Teaching of English, 17* 275–284.

Hinds, J. (1979). Organizational patterns in discourse. In T. Givon (Ed.), *Syntax and semantics 12: Discourse and syntax* (pp. 135–157). New York: Academic Press.

Hinds, J. (1983a). Linguistics and written discourse in particular languages: Contrastive studies: English and Japanese. In R. B. Kaplan et al. (Eds.), *Annaul Review of Applied Linguistics (Vol. 3)* (pp. 78–84). Rowley, MA: Newbury House.

Hinds, J. (1983b). Contrastive rhetoric: Japanese and English. *TEXT, 3,* 183–195.

Hinds, J. (1987). Reader versus writer responsibility: A new typology. In U. Connor & R. B. Kaplan (Eds.), *Writing across languages: Analysis of L2 texts* (pp 141–152). Reading, MA: Addison-Wesley.

Horowitz, D. (1986a). Process, not product: Less than meets the eye. *TESOL Quarterly, 20,* 141–144.

Horowitz, D. (1986b). The author responds. *TESOL Quarterly, 20,* 788–790, 796–797.

Houghton, D. (1980). The writing problems of Iranian students. *ELT Documents 109: Study modes and academic development of overseas students* (pp. 79–90). London: The British Council.

Jenkins, S., & Hinds, J. (1987). Business letter writing: English, French, and Japanese. *TESOL Quarterly, 21,* 327–349.

Johns, A. (1986). Coherence and academic writing: Some definitions and suggestions for teaching. *TESOL Quarterly, 20,* 247–265.

Johns, A. (1987). Our students, ethnography and university culture. *English for Foreign Students in English-Speaking Countries Newsletter, 5*(1), 1–2.

Kachru, Y. (1983). Linguistics and written discourse in particular languages: Contrastive studies: English and Hindi. In R. B. Kaplan et al. (Eds.), *Annual Review of Applied Linguistics (Vol. 3)* (pp. 50–77). Rowley, MA: Newbury House.

Kaplan, R. B. (1966). Cultural thought patterns in intercultural education. *Language Learning, 16,* 1–20.

Kaplan, R. B. (1967). Contrastive rhetoric and the teaching of composition. *TESOL Quarterly, 1*(4), 10–16.

Kaplan, R. B. (1972). *The anatomy of rhetoric: Prolegomena to a functional theory of rhetoric.* Philadelphia: Center for Curriculum Development.

Kaplan, R. B. (1983). Reading and writing, technology and planning: To do what and with what and to whom? In J. Alatis, H. Stern, & P. Strevens (Eds.), *Applied linguistics and the preparation of second language teachers: Toward a rationale* (pp. 242–254). Washington, DC: Georgetown University Press.

Kaplan, R. B. (1987a). Cultural thought patterns revisited. In U. Connor & R. B. Kaplan (Eds.), *Writing across languages: Analysis of L2 text* (pp. 9–21). Reading, MA: Addison-Wesley.

Kaplan, R. B. (1987b, April). *Fact and counter-fact: An exploration in Chinese writing.* Paper presented at the 21st Annual TESOL Convention, Miami, FL.

Kaplan, R. B., & Shaw P. (1983). *Exploring academic English.* Rowley, MA: Newbury House.

Kinneavy, J. (1971). *A theory of discourse*. New York: W. W. Norton.

Kroll, B. (1978). Cognitive egocentrism and the problem of audience awareness in written discourse. *Research in the Teaching of English, 12,* 269–281.

Lawrence, M. (1975). *Reading, Writing and Thinking*. Ann Arbor: University of Michigan Press.

Leap, W. (1983). Linguistics and written discourse in particular languages: Contrastive studies: English and American Indian Languages. In R. B. Kaplan (Ed.), *Annual Review of Applied Linguistics (Vol. 3)* (pp. 24–37). Rowley, MA: Newbury House.

Liebman-Kleine, J. (1987). In defense of teaching process in ESL composition. *TESOL Quarterly, 20,* 783–788.

Lunsford, A. (1980). The content of basic writers' essays. *College Composition and Communication, 31,* 278–290.

Matalene, C. (1985). Contrastive rhetoric: An American writing teacher in China. *College English, 47,* 789–808.

Matsuhashi, A. (1981). Pausing and planning: The tempo of written discourse. *Research in the Teaching of English, 15,* 113–134.

Moffett, J. (1968). *Teaching the universe of discourse*. Boston: Houghton Mifflin.

Mohan, B. (1986). On hypotheses in cross-cultural rhetoric research. *TESOL Quarterly, 20,* 569–573.

Mohan, B., & Lo, W. (1985). Academic writing and Chinese students: Transfer and developmental factors. *TESOL Quarterly, 19,* 515–533.

Murray, D. M. (1978). Internal revision: A process of discovery. In C. R. Cooper & L. Odell (Eds.), *Research on composing: Points of departure* (pp. 85–103). Urbana, IL: National Council of Teachers of English.

Murray, D. (1984). *Write to learn*. New York: Holt Rinehart & Winston.

Murray, D. (1985). *A writer teaches writing* (2nd ed.). Boston: Houghton Mifflin.

Namba, T., & Chick, J. (1987). *Discourse bloc and Bundan in Japanese: A comparative study with English*. Unpublished manuscript. Hyogo, Japan: Hyogo University of Teacher Education.

Newkirk, T., & Atwell, N. (1985). The competence of young writers. In B. McClelland & T. Donovan (Eds.), *Perspectives on research and scholarship in composition* (pp. 185–202). New York: Modern Language Association.

Ostler, S. (1987). English in parallels: A comparison of English and Arabic prose. In U. Connor & R. B. Kaplan (Eds.), *Writing across languages: Analysis of L2 text* (pp. 169–185). Reading, MA: Addison-Wesley.

Pandharipande, R. (1983). Linguistics and written discourse in particular languages: Contrastive studies: English and Marathi. In R. B. Kaplan (Ed.), *Annual Review of Applied Linguistics (Vol. 3)* (pp. 118–136). Rowley, MA: Newbury House.

Perelman, L. (1986). The context of classroom writing. *College English, 48,* 471–479.

Raimes, A. (1983). *Techniques in teaching writing*. New York: Oxford University Press.

Raimes, A. (1987). *Exploring through writing*. New York: St. Martin's Press.

Reither, J. (1985). Writing and knowing: Toward redefining the writing process. *College English, 47,* 620–628.

Ricento, T. (1986). Comments on Bernard Mohan and Winnie Au-Yeung Lo's "Academic writing and Chinese students: Transfer and developmental factors." *TESOL Quarterly, 20,* 595–568.

Ricento, T. (1987). *Aspects of coherence in English and Japanese expository prose.* Unpublished doctoral dissertation, University of California at Los Angeles.

Santana-Seda, O., Sr. (1975). A contrastive study in rhetoric: An analysis of the organization of English and Spanish paragraphs written by native speakers of each language (Doctoral dissertation, New York University, 1974). *Dissertation Abstracts International, 35,* 8562A.

Santiago, R. (1968). *A contrastive analysis of some rhetorical aspects of writing in Spanish and English of Spanish-speaking college students in Puerto Rico.* Unpublished doctoral dissertation, New York University.

Shih, M. (1986). Content-based approaches to teaching academic writing. *TESOL Quarterly, 20,* 617–648.

Tamor, L., & Bond, J. (1983). Text analysis: Inferring process from product. In J. Mosenthal, L. Tamor, & S. Walmsley (Eds.), *Research on writing* (pp. 99–138). New York: Longman.

Tannen, D. (1979). What's in a frame? Surface evidence for underlying expectations. In R. Freedle (Ed.), *New directions in discourse processing* (pp. 137–181). Norwood, NJ: Ablex.

Tannen, D. (Ed.). (1984). *Conversational style: Analyzing talk among friends.* Norwood, NJ: Ablex.

Tannen, D. (Ed.). (1986). Discourse in cross-cultural communication [Special issue]. *Text, 6.*

Thomas, G. (1986). Mutual knowledge: A theoretical basis for analyzing audience. *College English, 48,* 580–594.

Tsao, F. (1983). Linguistics and written discourse in particular languages: Contrastive studies: English and Chinese. In R. B. Kaplan et al. (Eds.), *Annual Review of Applied Linguistics (Vol. 3)* (pp. 99–117). Rowley, MA: Newbury House.

Widdowson, H. (1984). *Issues in Applied Linguistics, II.* New York: Oxford University Press.

Wilkerson, B. (1986). *On the principles of coherence in English academic expository discourse.* Unpublished manuscript, Meiji University, Tokyo.

Witte, S. (1985). Revising, composing theory, and research design. In S. W. Freedman (Ed.), *The acquisition of written language* (pp. 249–283). Norwood, NJ: Ablex.

Witte, S. (1987). [Review of *Research on written composition: New directions for teaching*]. *College Composition and Communication, 38,* 202–207.

Witte, S., & Cherry, R. (1986). Writing processes and written product in composition research. In C. R. Cooper & S. Greenbaum (Eds.), *Studying writing: Linguistic approaches* (pp. 112–153). Beverly Hills: Sage.

CHAPTER 18

Evaluating Second Language Essays in Regular Composition Classes: Toward a Pluralistic U.S. Rhetoric

Robert E. Land, Jr., and Catherine Whitley
University of California at Irvine

How we go about empowering English as a second language (ESL) students when they enter regular college composition classes in the United States is determined by our response to two questions: What do we wish them to be empowered to do, and for whom are they being empowered? Our first response to these questions (a traditional, nominal one) is that we wish ESL students to acquire enough facility with standard written English (SWE) to succeed in school and in the workplace for their own benefit and, second, especially in the case of the large numbers of ESL students who are immigrants to this country, for the benefit of our society. To achieve these goals, we need to emphasize grammatical and syntactic correctness and, certainly at the college level where students are called upon to use written communication in a variety of disciplines and for a variety of purposes, we need to emphasize the larger rhetorical conventions of academic writing. Although, as Raimes (1986) notes, we have problems of implementation even in separate ESL classes, we have at hand the means of establishing programs to meet these goals.

Our nominal goal of helping students avoid linguistic disenfranchisement seems, at first glance, both pragmatic and responsible. However, the prevalent methods of evaluating writing—especially in classes where ESL students compete directly with native speakers (NSs) and where instructors have little or no training in teaching second language (L2) learners—suggest that we don't wish ESL students to attain only a "facility" with written English; instead, we expect them to become entirely fluent in English, a goal different in nature and implication from our purported one. The discrepancy between our purported and apparent goals for instructing

ESL students emerges in our standards of evaluation as a hidden agenda—that is, an agenda that is rarely made known to the students whose writing is being evaluated and one that is seldom clear to the evaluator (see Sommers, 1982; Zamel, 1985). Thus, even when an ESL writer produces an error-free composition in English, a hidden agenda leads the evaluator to find fault with other formal features. Our research (Land and Whitley, 1986) suggests that the text features influencing English NS readers most negatively are the ESL students' patterns of organization, patterns established in what Purves (1986) calls "rhetorical communities" where ESL students learned their native language. At present, our understanding of the cultural determination of rhetorical patterns is limited, although investigations like those by Purves (1986), Hinds (1983), and Kaplan (1983) are extending these limits. We probably know too little about the mechanisms of our own preferred rhetorical patterns, let alone about those that ESL students bring with them, to establish programs aimed at reifying "ours" by isolating and eliminating "theirs" from their written English. But even if such knowledge were available, our efforts at making ESL students entirely fluent would almost certainly fail.

To be truly "fluent," our ESL students would have to be able to produce essays in English that were not only grammatically and syntactically, but also rhetorically indistinguishable from those written by their NS peers. But, as Haugen (1986) points out, even writers who are isolated for years from their first language (L1) culture produce texts in their L2 which carry noticeable L1 features; and most of our ESL students maintain strong associations with members of their L1 rhetorical communities. The distinct world views of these communities influence members' thoughts, actions, and, consequently, their patterns of communication for many generations (see, e.g., Giordano, 1976; Havighurst, 1978; McGoldrick, 1982). "English only" movements and literacy crises notwithstanding, we can neither legislate nor educate away culturally determined rhetorical differences in writing.

To enable ESL students to write English with "facility," we should, of course, pay special attention to teaching the linguistic conventions of SWE. We may also be able to teach them how to use some of SWE's rhetorical conventions. But such instruction may not be an end in itself. In the United States, SWE rhetorical conventions generally emphasize strong sentence-to-sentence connections, resulting in "linear" prose (see Kaplan, 1966), and a deductive logical arrangement that satisfies what Lakoff and Johnson (1980) call our "objectivist myth." But there are many patterns of cohesion, other logics, other myths through which views of the world may be constructed (see Knoblauch and Brannon, 1984). In teaching SWE rhetorical conventions, we are teaching students to reproduce in a mechanical fashion our preferred vehicle of understanding.

As MacCannell and MacCannell (1982) note, "culture that reproduces itself as a series of endless mirrorings, yet adds nothing to either the original 'natural culture' or the original 'image' of it, is literally the death of culture" (p. 28). Elsewhere they stress that "the heart of cultural evolution . . . begins with a production and proceeds to a reproduction that is not a simple doubling but a reflection at a higher power" (p. 26). In this view, we are encouraging our ESL students to contribute to the death of our culture: Their textual productions are simply to mirror, in their use of our rhetorical tradition, an experience that might be entirely foreign to them. We are not asking ESL writers to add to our culture from their own storehouses of experience; the sense is that our culture has reached the end of its evolution: There's nothing more to add. Trying to teach ESL students to reproduce SWE rhetoric may be not only likely to fail, but even if it were to be successful, it would be a pyrrhic victory.

Thus, we must change the way we read, respond to, and evaluate ESL writers' work at all stages of its development. If we fail to do so, our composition courses will be as retributive as they are instructive. If we wish to admit rhetorical concerns openly to our system of evaluation (thus unmasking the hidden agenda), if we believe that concerns of "correctness," content, and rhetoric are inseparable, then we must learn to recognize, value, and foster the alternative rhetorics that the ESL student brings to our language. In this chapter, we argue for such an approach, one that will not only empower students to succeed in school and at work, but will also free them to incorporate their own forms of logic into their writing, to the potential benefit of our language and culture.

RHETORICAL DIFFERENCES

No one who has ever read through a stack of compositions written by native and nonnative speakers needs to consult research to confirm that there are differences. Differences in the number of surface errors made by ESL students are obvious to teachers and have been well documented by researchers (Ahrens, 1984; Fein, 1980; Kroll, 1983). But error is not the only difference between texts written by ESL students and their NS peers. Even with error removed from all essays, researchers (McGirt, 1984; Whitley, 1984) have found that NS readers give higher scores to papers of NSs than to those written by ESL students. Clearly, other important differences exist.

Most of the research designed to find these important differences has focused on patterns of organization. Some of this research, following the work of Halliday and Hasan (1976), has focused on contrasting cohesive ties and drawing conclusions about textual cohesion from analysis of the ties, or from global measures of cohesion, or both (Connor, 1984; Land &

Whitley, 1986; Lindsay, 1984; Scarcella, 1984). Along with more general investigations of differences (Hinds, 1983; Kaplan, 1966; Purves, 1986), these studies taken as a whole demonstrate fairly clearly that ESL writers connect their ideas differently than do NS writers. They demonstrate as well that these differences in organization are, at least in part, the result of ESL students' membership in distinct rhetorical communities and not necessarily the result of inadequate mastery of U.S. English. Finally, they demonstrate that these organizational differences are partly responsible for ESL students' essays being judged by NS readers as inferior to native speakers' essays.

One of the questions we have asked in our research (Land & Whitley, 1986) is whether or not the L1 status of readers would affect their perceptions of batches of student essays sampled from freshman composition classes where about half the students were nonnative speakers of English. We found, predictably, that U.S.-born NS readers rated the papers of ESL writers lower than the papers of NS students. But we also found that readers whose L1 was not English (our sample included native speakers of German, Spanish, and Japanese) rated essays from both ESL and NS students as being of about equal quality. Data from analytic rating scales revealed that the differences in perceptions of quality were probably the result of differences in perceptions of organization: The U.S.-born NS readers marked down ESL essays for what they perceived as problems of organization; readers whose L1 was not English did not mark down ESL texts for organization. In this respect our results mirror the language-specific research of Hinds (1983), who found that native English speaking readers rated the organization of English translations of Japanese newspaper articles lower than Japanese speaking readers rated the originals.

From our results we concluded that either our English NNS readers have lax standards and can't tell a poorly organized essay from a well organized one or they can accommodate to more kinds of rhetorical patterns than can NS readers. Because both groups of readers agreed on the ratings of NS essays, and because both groups were sampled from our pool of experienced teachers of freshman writing, we opted for the second conclusion. We believe that our bilingual and multilingual readers' experience with different kinds of texts used in different cultures allow them to adopt to and value writing that employs varying rhetorical organizations.

READERS READING

Any reader confronting any text faces it with a preconceived set of expectations; as Iser (1976/1978) and Carrell (1982) note, the reader comes to a text armed with the sum of previous reading experiences. The reader and the text interact in the process of reading. The wandering viewpoint is a means of describing the way in which the reader is present in the text. This presence is at a point where memory and expectation converge, and the resultant dialectic movement brings about a continual modification of memory and an increasing complexity of expectation. These processes depend on the reciprocal spotlighting of the perspectives, which provide interrelated backgrounds for one another. The interaction between these backgrounds provokes the reader into synthesizing activity (Iser, 1976/1978). The expectations of a teacher of writing in the United States would be based upon the grammatical, syntactic, and rhetorical conventions of SWE, expectations which the student essay should trigger and bring into play, thus beginning the dialectic movement. For instance, the presence of an identifiable, analytic thesis sentence signals a certain rhetorical pattern and allows the reader to begin building a set of expectations specific to that particular text. The reader remembers the thesis, moves on, and expects to find its promise fulfilled.

Because ESL readers seem to find organization in ESL texts–texts that NS readers judge to be poorly organized—perhaps they have a wider and more varied set of expectations when they come to a text, expectations resulting from a wider and more varied reading experience. As Purves (1986) has shown, "good" student writers from different countries (students selected by their own instructors as being exemplary), when asked to write an essay on the same topic, write those essays in different rhetorical modes that vary in stance, descriptive quality, and levels of abstraction and concreteness. He notes that "the fact that the compositions come from 'good' students suggests that these students have learned and are applying the norms of their rhetorical community" (Purves, 1986, p. 43); these students have learned to conform to the expectations of the community in which they find themselves. Likewise, the ESL readers have negotiated between the norms of their native communities and the one in which they find themselves; these readers recognized the SWE patterns of organization in the NS essays.

If every time we face a student paper we do so with the expectations of SWE firmly in mind, and we expect to find a linear, deductive argument, our experience of reading ESL students' essays will be different from our experience of reading NS students'. Most ESL students, even those in "regular" (i.e., linguistically heterogeneous) college writing classes, have not learned to use the organizational patterns of U.S. academic prose. This does not mean they are "bad" writers or that their essays are "badly organized"; it could mean that they are very skillfully manipulating patterns of organization that we don't recognize. A reader with expectations shaped by SWE will not interact successfully (in Iser's terms) with such essays; ESL writers' essays will not trigger dialectic movements because they do not fulfill the reader's expectations.

If the "wandering viewpoint" is a way to describe the way in which the reader is present in the text, then a reader with SWE expectations continues to wander rather aimlessly in a text by an ESL writer because the reader cannot recognize the signposts left by the writer. (For instance, we have found that ESL writers tend to use a few distantly separated cohesive ties as a way of establishing coherence, something very uncommon in their NS peers' work.) Readers should allow themselves to be lost for a while, for readers who suspend judgment and thus become accustomed to recognizing a wider variety of rhetorical modes, will begin to alter their expectations, to widen them, a process which will ultimately permit them to interact with more types of texts, thereby enriching their reading processes.

In contrast, readers who rigidly insist on finding a set of distinct expectations met in every encounter with student writing squelch in themselves responses to different approaches to presenting and receiving ideas; in effect, they suppress new information. SWE, as a set of conventions, is itself a rigid and rather artificial stratum of English if, as Bakhtin (1975/1981) describes, all national languages are stratified into social dialects, characteristic group behavior, a professional jargon, generic languages, languages of generations and age groups, tendentious languages, languages of authorities, of various circles, and of passing fashions, languages that serve the specific sociopolitical purpose of the day (pp. 262–263). In this view, SWE is just a particular stratification of English, the one privileged by and identified with academia, a sublanguage which, by its nature, is sociopolitical.

In demanding that ESL students write SWE and use a deductive, linear argument, we are asking them to situate themselves within a particular sociopolitical context, and we respond to and judge their writing according to how accurately they are able to do so. If students are not natives of this culture they will be less likely to signal satisfactorily to us, the readers, their understanding of their position within the English language as a sociopolitical construct; even if their writing is in more or less error-free English, they will still be writing according to the norms of their native communities. By asking these students to use our signals according to our expectations, we are not taking language to be "a system of abstract grammatical categories"; instead, we are at least implicitly understanding "language conceived as ideologically saturated, language as world view" (Bakhtin, 1975/1981, p. 271). We require our ESL students to share and reproduce in their writing our world view, one to which they are, of course, alien. Such instruction is composition as colonization.

CHANGING THE WAY WE READ, RESPOND, AND EVALUATE

In general we would argue that all teachers should become more like the ESL readers in our study; that they acquire the ability to suspend judgment, to allow the piece of writing at hand to develop slowly, like a photographic print, shading in the details. But what does this mean in practice? It may mean that teachers with ESL students should become familiar with rhetorical traditions their students bring with them (see Reid, this volume). It certainly means that we need to consciously suppress our desire to label ESL writers' work as "out of focus" or "lacking in organization."

In our regular freshman writing classes, for example, assignments written by writing program directors are given to the teachers to be distributed. These assignments often require the ESL students in these classes, many of whom are U.S. residents who have spoken English for five or fewer years, to use conventional SWE structures such as thesis paragraphs. The ESL students comply, at least superficially, with these conventions. Eventually, however, usually in the second or third paragraph, ESL students return to the organizational conventions of their native rhetorics. This return does not go unnoticed; based on our examination of hundreds of marked essays, when ESL students stop consciously attending to the formal concerns of SWE patterns and begin focusing on what they have to say, teachers begin to note "problems" of clarity, focus, and organization. We would argue that it is here, at this point of departure from SWE expectations, that readers should suspend judgment and read on for meaning. After reading the entire text, a teacher might suggest that the introductory thesis paragraph is superfluous, instead of noting that the rest of the essay doesn't live up to the promise of the introduction. Or the teacher might suggest alternatives to seemingly disembodied topic sentences, alternatives that would meet the obligation of teaching the student how to produce passable prose that would not be dismissed, out of hand, by less open readers. In some cases, the teacher might not know how to respond to the text except by asking lots of questions about what the student was trying to say. In some situations we have known exactly where to help our ESL students; in others we have had only very vague ideas.

Perhaps the most common specific deviation from SWE expectations that we find in ESL students' papers is what seems like redundancy. Sometimes students seem to repeat themselves pointlessly or they seem to argue the same point in slightly different ways, paragraph after paragraph, each paragraph a modest addition or alteration of given information. We have chosen a similar structure for this chapter; we have argued for the same point, "that teachers should change the way they evaluate

ESL writers' papers," in several ways. We hope our readers will be generous and recognize that we do so by trying to appeal separately to logic, the "facts" of research, the "authority" of theory and, finally, to our own personal experience—all of which are fairly standard "artistic" and "inartistic" proofs of Western classical rhetoric, although it might have been more traditional for us to have outlined our plan earlier in the text. More generosity is often needed when we read our students' texts.

One helpful strategy for reading seemingly redundant essays is to use a form of "topical structure" analysis like the one Connor and Farmer (1985) suggest as a revision strategy for writers. In its simple form, one circles, during the second reading, all of the grammatical subjects of all the independent clauses. Rereading the list of subjects can lead readers to revisions of their initial understanding of the essay as patterns of meaning that were not at first evident are revealed. Often the subjects seem to operate as higher-order cohesive devices. For example, one student (whose essay we used in our research) used thunder, or a variant thereof, as the subject of three very distantly removed sentences in his essay on the possibility of afterlife. Of course this bit of imagery stood out and it was fairly easy to recognize that the repetition seemed to operate as a device connecting distinct parts of his essay, but this was an essay that NS readers scored low because of its poor organization and that ESL readers scored high and found to be acceptably organized. Now, when we receive a paper like that one, we usually recognize its structure; we no longer make comments about its organization.

CONCLUSION

Research suggests that evaluative focus on sentence-level mechanics may be a waste of the teacher's time (Robb, Ross, & Shortreed, 1986) and confusing and even harmful to students (Land & Evans, 1987; Zamel, 1985). Thus, against all the forces that seem to keep our attention riveted on surface concerns, good pedagogy demands that we respond to larger features of our students' texts. As we learn to rid ourselves of surface-level tunnel vision, we will have to struggle against the forces that can lead us to rigid, oversimplified notions of how essays should be structured: rhetoric-level myopia.

Assuming that our responses to students' essays are intended to inform them in specific ways about how to make those pieces of writing (or the next ones) better, we can ask students to add to, delete from, or alter the paper; or we can let students know that they should keep up the good work. We have argued that teachers of ESL students should broaden their concept of what constitutes "good work" and that they should not automatically request additions of SWE features and deletions and modifications of everything else. In the end, because ESL texts customarily contain a lot of the "everything else," such practices should cut down on the amount of marking teachers feel they must do. At first (and even much later, especially when faced with high stacks of papers in the wee hours), reading "interactively" is hard work. It would be easy, in the midst of trying to figure out a particularly puzzling text, to dismiss the whole project as idealistic, impractical, or stupid and to return to the more comfortable, familiar mode of reading with narrow SWE rhetorical expectations.

To do so would be to ignore what is happening to our culture and our language: they are becoming more pluralistic, not coincidentally with the rise of English as the world language. If we are indeed part of a culture which admits change, this change will obviously appear at the linguistic level because one's epistemology underlies one's language. When our language changes, it is a sign that our way of thinking has changed. Unless we want to institute a structure like the Academie Française or the British Royal Academy, we have no choice but to recognize and examine the changes that are happening daily everywhere in order to see what we think now.

REFERENCES

Ahrens, C. D. (1984). *Comparing composition skills of native and non-native born students at the junior high school level.* Unpublished master's thesis, University of California at Los Angeles.

Bakhtin, M. M. (1981). *The dialogic imagination* (C. Emerson & M. Holquist, Trans.; M. Holquist, Ed.). Austin: University of Texas Press. (Original work published 1975.)

Carrell, P. (1982). Cohesion is not coherence. *TESOL Quarterly, 16,* 479–488.

Connor, U. (1984). A study of cohesion and coherence in ESL students' writing. *Papers in Linguistics: International Journal of Human Communication, 17,* 301–316.

Connor, U., & Farmer, M. (1985, April). *The teaching of topical structure analysis as a revision strategy: An exploratory study.* Paper presented at the annual meeting of the American Educational Research Association, Chicago.

Fein, D. (1980). *A comparison of English and ESL compositions.* Unpublished master's thesis, University of California at Los Angeles.

Giordano, J. (1976). Community mental health in a pluralistic society. *International Journal of Mental Health, 5,* 5–15.

Halliday, M. A. K., & Hasan, R. (1976). *Cohesion in English.* London: Longman Group, Ltd.

Haugen, E. (1986). Bilinguals have more fun! *Journal of English Linguistics, 19,* 106–120.

Havighurst, R. J. (1978). Structural aspects of education and cultural pluralism. *Educational Research Quarterly, 2,* 5–19.

Hinds, J. (1983). Contrastive rhetoric: Japanese and English. *Text, 3,* 183–195.

Iser, W. (1978). *The act of reading: A theory of aesthetic response.* Baltimore: Johns Hopkins University Press. (Original work published 1976)

Kaplan, R. B. (1966). Cultural thought patterns in intercultural education. *Language Learning, 16,* 1–20.

Kaplan, R. B. (1983). Contrastive rhetoric: Some implications for the writing process. In A. Freedman, I. Pringle & J. Yalden (Eds.). *Learning to write: First language/second language* (pp. 138–161). New York: Longman.

Knoblauch, C. H., & Brannon, L. (1984). *Rhetorical traditions and the teaching of writing.* Upper Montclair, NJ: Boynton/Cook.

Kroll, B. (1983). Levels of error in ESL composition (Doctoral dissertation, University of California at Los Angeles, 1982). *Dissertation Abstracts International, 43,* 3307A-3308A. (University of Southern California Micrographics No. 2898A)

Lakoff, G., & Johnson, M. (1980). *Metaphors we live by.* Chicago: University of Chicago Press.

Land, R. E., & Evans, S. (1987). What our students taught us about paper making. *English Journal, 76*(2), 113–116.

Land, R. E., & Whitley, C. (1986, April). *Influences of second-language factors on the performance of freshman writers.* Paper presented at the annual meeting of the American Educational Research Association, San Francisco.

Lindsay, D. B. (1984). *Cohesion in the compositions of ESL and English students.* Unpublished master's thesis, University of California at Los Angeles.

MacCannell, D., & MacCannell, J. F. (1982). *The time of the sign: A semiotic interpretation of modern culture.* Bloomington: Indiana University Press.

McGirt, J. D. (1984). *The effect of morphological and syntactic errors on the holistic scores of native and non-native compositions.* Unpublished master's thesis, University of California at Los Angeles.

McGoldrick, M. (1982). Ethnicity and family therapy: An overview. In M. McGoldrick, J. K. Pearce, & J. Giardano (Eds.), *Ethnicity and family therapy* (pp. 3–30). New York: Guilford.

Purves, A. C. (1986). Rhetorical communities, the international student, and basic writing. *Journal of Basic Writing, 5,* 38–51.

Raimes, A. (1986). Teaching ESL writing: Fitting what we do to what we know. *The Writing Instructor, 5,* 153–166.

Robb, T., Ross, S., & Shortreed, I. (1986). Salience of feedback on error and its effect on EFL writing quality. *TESOL Quarterly, 20,* 83–93.

Scarcella, R. (1984). How writers orient their readers in expository essays: A comparative study of native and nonnative English writers. *TESOL Quarterly, 17,* 165–187.

Sommers, N. (1982). Responding to student writing. *College Composition and Communication, 33,* 148–156.

Whitley, C. (1984). *Error, content, and grading: ESL vs NES.* Unpublished manuscript, University of California at Irvine.

Zamel, V. (1985). Responding to student writing. *TESOL Quarterly, 19,* 79–101.

Index